A QUALIDADE DO CRESCIMENTO

Vinod Thomas
Mansoor Dailami
Ashok Dhareshwar
Daniel Kaufmann
Nalin Kishor
Ramón López
Yan Wang

Tradução:
Élcio Fernandes

OS ACHADOS, INTERPRETAÇÕES E CONCLUSÕES EXPRESSOS NESTE ESTUDO SÃO DE RESPONSABILIDADE DE SEUS AUTORES E DE NENHUM MODO DEVERIAM SER ATRIBUÍDOS AO BANCO MUNDIAL, A SUAS ORGANIZAÇÕES AFILIADAS, AOS MEMBROS DE SUA DIRETORIA EXECUTIVA OU AOS PAÍSES QUE ELES REPRESENTAM. OS LIMITES, DENOMINAÇÕES E OUTRAS INFORMAÇÕES MOSTRADAS EM QUALQUER MAPA DESTE VOLUME NÃO IMPLICAM, DA PARTE DO WORLD BANK GROUP, NENHUM JULGAMENTO SOBRE O STATUS LEGAL DE QUALQUER TERRITÓRIO OU A ACEITAÇÃO DE TAIS LIMITES.

© 2000 The International Bank for Reconstruction
and Development / The World Bank

This Work was originally published by the World Bank in English as *The Quality of Growth in 2000*. This Portuguese language edition is not an official World Bank translation. Editora UNESP is responsible for the accuracy of the translation.

Esta obra foi originalmente publicada em inglês pelo Banco Mundial, como *The Quality of Growth in 2000*. A edição em língua portuguesa não é uma tradução oficial do Banco Mundial. A Editora UNESP é responsável pela exatidão da tradução.

Título original em inglês: *The Quality of Growth*.

© 2001 da tradução brasileira:
Fundação Editora da UNESP (FEU)

Praça da Sé, 108
01001-900 – São Paulo – SP
Tel.: (0xx11) 3242-7171
Fax: (0xx11) 3242-7172
Home page: www.editora.unesp.br
E-mail: feu@editora.unesp.br

Dados Internacionais de Catalogação na Publicação (CIP)
(Câmara Brasileira do Livro, SP, Brasil)

A Qualidade do crescimento / Vinod Thomas... [et al.]; tradução Élcio Fernandes. — São Paulo: Editora UNESP, 2002.

Título original: The quality of growth
Vários autores.
Bibliografia.
ISBN 85-7139-441-5

1. Bem-estar econômico 2. Desenvolvimento econômico 3. Desenvolvimento sustentável 4. Política econômica I. Thomas, Vinod.

02-6467   CDD-338.9

Índice para catálogo sistemático:

1. Crescimento econômico: Economia política 338.9

Editora afiliada:

Asociación de Editoriales Universitarias de América Latina y el Caribe   Associação Brasileira de Editoras Universitárias

SUMÁRIO

Preâmbulo XIII

Prefácio XVII

A Equipe do Relato XXI

Visão Geral XXIII
   Resultados de Desenvolvimento e Processos de Crescimento XXIII
   Princípios de Desenvolvimento XXV
   Ações Negligenciadas no Processo de Crescimento XXIX
   Substituir Prioridades XXXII

1. O Registro de um Desenvolvimento Confuso 1
   Avaliar Desenvolvimento 2
   O Registro do Desenvolvimento 6
   Crescimento e Bem-Estar 16
   Questão de Fatores Externos 16
   Políticas Internas Fazem uma Diferença Fundamental 19
   Questões Cruciais para a Ação 23

2. Valores, Crescimento e Bem-Estar 29
   Uma Estrutura.. 31
   Evidência Empírica 39
   Conclusões 47

3. Melhorando a Distribuição de Oportunidades 51
   Benefícios Potenciais da Educação 52
   Quantidade Não É o Bastante – Qualidade É o Que Importa 53
   Realizar uma Educação Eqüitativa e a Inclusão Social 59
   Melhorar a Eficácia do Gasto Público 69

SUMÁRIO

	Tornar a Educação Mais Produtiva	76
	Conclusões	84

4. Sustentar o Capital Natural ... 87
- Perdas Extensivas ... 88
- Benefícios Significativos da Ação Ambiental ... 92
- O Nexo do Crescimento do Capital Natural e do Bem-Estar ... 93
- Incorporar a Sustentabilidade Ambiental a Políticas de Crescimento ... 102
- Repensar o Papel do Estado ... 106
- Questões Ambientais Globais Devem Ser Confrontadas ... 112
- Conclusões ... 114

5. Tratar com Riscos Financeiros Globais ... 119
- Expansão dos Mercados de Capital e Volatilidade dos Fluxos de Capital ... 120
- Causas e Conseqüências da Volatilidade do Fluxo de Capital ... 122
- Gerenciamento do Risco Passado e Presente ... 128
- Uma Ampla Estrutura do Gerenciamento do Risco ... 131
- Conclusões ... 138

6. Governo e Anticorrupção ... 141
- O Governo Afeta a Qualidade do Crescimento ... 142
- A Corrupção Solapa o Crescimento e o Desenvolvimento ... 151
- Causas da Corrupção ... 157
- Uma Estratégia Anticorrupção Multifacetada ... 159
- Conclusões ... 173

7. Agarrar as Oportunidades de Mudança ... 177
- A Estrutura e os Temas ... 178
- Ações para Garantir a Qualidade ... 181
- Onde as Políticas para Qualidade Funcionam – Ou Não? ... 182
- Economia Política de Quantidade *versus* Qualidade ... 185
- Seguir em Frente ... 186

Bibliografia e Referências ... 243

Anexos

1. Objetivos Amplos e os Instrumentos ... 189
- Metas e Medidas Políticas ... 189
- Índices Compósitos do Desenvolvimento Humano e do Desenvolvimento Sustentável ... 193

SUMÁRIO

2. Estrutura e Evidência 195
    Uma Função de Bem-Estar 195
    A Otimização do Setor Privado 196
    Especificação Econométrica Utilizada para Avaliar
    Funções de Crescimento 206

3. Distribuição da Educação, Abertura e Crescimento 215
    A Função de Produção Ampliada com a Distribuição
    da Educação 216
    Análise Empírica em Retornos de Investimento na Educação 219
    Estudos Selecionados Sobre Distribuição de Recuros
    e Crescimento 222

4. Aferindo o Capital Natural 225

5. Abertura Financeira 227
    Nota Sobre a Vulnerabilidade do País e Medidas de Volatilidade 230
    Nota Sobre as Brechas no Produto Interno Bruto 230
    Nota Sobre um Modelo Binomial de Logit 230
    Estatísticas Sumárias para Variáveis Utilizadas no Capítulo 5 232

6. Índices de Governo e Corrupção: Métodos de Agregação,
    Medidas Empíricas Novas e Desafios Econométricos 235
    Definir e Desvelar o Governo 235
    Aferir e Desvelar a Corrupção 238

Quadros

1	Acumulação de Bens, Crescimento e Bem-Estar	XXVII
2.1	Capital Social	36
2.2	Abordagens Alternativas para a Sustentação do Crescimento: Brasil, Chile e Coréia	40
3.1	Brechas de Saúde Entre Ricos e Pobres Também São Grandes	64
3.2	Sustentar a Educação Feminina em Bangladesh	67
3.3	População e Desenvolvimento	74
4.1	Degradação Ambiental na Índia	90
4.2	Esforços pelo Mundo Afora para Ação Ambiental	94
4.3	População, Pobreza e Meio Ambiente	98
4.4	O Desenvolvimento e o Meio Ambiente	107
4.5	Lucro Privado a Expensas do Gasto Público: Corrupção no Setor Florestal	111
4.6	Cooperação Internacional para Mitigar a Mudança Climática Global	112

SUMÁRIO

5.1	Abertura para Fluxos de Capital Internacional	124
5.2	Chile: Abertura, Controles de Capital e Proteção Social	137
6.1	Governo e Instrumentos para Estudos Diagnósticos: O Poder dos Empíricos	168
6.2	A "Voz" Como um Mecanismo para Fazer Valer a Transparência e a Responsabilidade	169
6.3	Milhões de "Auditores" Fazem Valer a Transparência e o Governo nos Cálculos Orçamentários e Além	172
7.1	Ações para a Qualidade	181

Figuras

1	Uma Estrutura	XXVII
1.1	Crescimento do PIB e Mudanças na Qualidade de Vida, nas Décadas de 1960 e 1990	5
1.2	Mudança no Desenvolvimento Humano e Crescimento de Renda, 1981-1998	6
1.3	Taxas de Pobreza e Número de Pobres, em Anos Seletos	7
1.4	Incidência de Pobreza em Economias de Transição Seletas, 1987-1988 e 1993-1995	8
1.5	Mudanças Ambientais *versus* Crescimento de Renda, 1981-1998	9
1.6	Total de Partículas Suspensas, Cidades Selecionadas, no Início da Década de 1990	10
1.7	Adquirindo Paridade do Poder Aquisitivo do Produto Interno Bruto (PIB) *per capita*, 1975-1998	11
1.8	Crescimento do PIB *per capita*, Economias Seletas, 1975-1998	12
1.9	Desigualdade de Renda Dentro dos Países, nas Décadas de 1980 e 1990	14
1.10	Volatilidade das Taxas de Crescimento do PIB, por Década	15
1.11	Gastos Públicos com Educação por Região, em Anos Seletos	20
1.12	Barreiras Comerciais, Regiões Selecionadas, 1984-1993	22
1.13	Premium do Mercado Paralelo, nas Décadas de 1970 a 1990	23
3.1	Relacionamento Entre Gasto Público *per capita* e Conclusão Educacional, em Anos Variados	54
3.2	Taxas de Conclusão da Escola Secundária para a Faixa Etária de 20-25 por Nível de Renda Familiar, Anos e Países Seletos da América Latina	58
3.3	Os Coeficientes Gini de Educação, Países Seletos, 1960-1990	61

3.4	As Curvas Educacionais de Lorenz para Índia e Coréia, 1990	61
3.5	Os Coeficientes Gini de Educação para 85 Países, 1990	63
3.6	Mortalidade de Crianças de Dois Anos e Mais Jovens, pela Riqueza, Brasil, 1996	64
3.7	Conclusão de Grau Médio para Jovens entre 15-19 Anos de Famílias Ricas e Pobres, Países e Anos Seletos	65
3.8	Anos de Escolaridade para Jovens na Faixa Etária de 25 Anos em Famílias Ricas e Pobres na América Latina	66
3.9	Brechas de Gênero e Desigualdade de Educação, 1970 e 1990	68
3.10	As Tendências das Taxas de Redução da Pobreza e Saídas Não Agrícolas do Crescimento Econômico na Índia, 1960-1994	70
3.11a	Pobreza e Posse da Terra, Bangladesh, 1988-1989	77
3.11b	Divisão de Renda na Década de 1980 e Coeficiente Gini para a Terra, na Década de 1960	77
3.12	Educação, Abertura e Taxas Econômicas de Retorno em 1.265 Projetos do Banco Mundial	83
4.1	Caminhos do Crescimento e Qualidade Ambiental	101
5.1	O Tamanho do Mercado Financeiro Global e o Comércio Mundial, 1980-1996	121
5.2	Ascensão e Queda de Fluxos de Capital Internacional, 1990-1999	123
5.3	Relacionamento Entre Variabilidade do Crescimento Econômico e Volatilidade nos Fluxos de Capital Privado Externo, 1975-1996	127
5.4	Relacionamentos Entre Abertura Financeira e Democrática, Mobilidade de Capital e Gastos Sociais do Governo	135
5.5	Relacionamento entre Abertura Financeira e Gastos Sociais	135
5.6	Classificação por País: Direitos Políticos e Abertura Financeira	136
6.1	Qualidade do Indicador da Regra de Direito: A Abordagem Apresentacional dos "Sinais de Tráfego"	146
6.2	Controle de Corrupção: A Abordagem Apresentativa dos "Sinais de Tráfego"	148
6.3	O Dividendo Desenvolvimentista do Bom Governo	150
6.4	A Corrupção É Regressiva: Resultados dos Estudos Diagnósticos	154
6.5	Corrupção e Ausência de Meritocracia nas Repartições Públicas Desigualam os Acessos aos Serviços para os Pobres: Estudos Diagnósticos dos Resultados dos Funcionários Públicos	155

SUMÁRIO

6.6	"Pequenas Propinas" *versus* Captação Estatal: Será que Comprometer-se com a Corrupção Beneficia a Empresa?	157
6.7	Corrupção e Direitos Civis	158
6.8	A Meritocracia Pode Reduzir a Corrupção: Evidência para Cada Departamento com Base em Estudos dos Funcionários Públicos em Três Países	160
6.9	Estratégias Multidentadas para Combater a Corrupção e Melhorar o Governo – Reconhecer a Economia Política	162
6.10	Alta Variação na Qualidade dos Tribunais em Economias Seletas	165
6.11	Captação Legal e Judiciária pelo Setor Corporativo em Algumas Economias de Transição Seletas	166
A1.1	Objetivos Desenvolvimentistas e Instrumentos Políticos	191
A2.1	Retornos Constantes à Escala e Nenhuma Expansão Tecnológica	203
A2.2	Subsistência, Crescimento e Armadilhas da Pobreza Entre os Pobres: O Caso de Retornos Constantes à Escala e Nenhuma Expansão	206
A5.1	Correlações da Abertura Financeira com Direitos Políticos e Liberdades Civis	234

Tabelas

1.1	Correlações de Medidas de Desenvolvimento, 1981-1998	4
1.2	Resultados Desenvolvimentistas por Classe de Crescimento, nas Décadas de 1980 e 1990	17
1.3	Questão de Fatores Externos para Resultados Internos, Exemplos de 1977-1999	17
1.4	Desempenho Político por Classe de Crescimento, nas Décadas de 1980 e 1990	24
2.1	Variáveis Seletas para Brasil, Chile e Coréia	41
2.2	Revisão dos Indicadores de Desenvolvimento para Sessenta Reformadores e Não Reformadores, em Anos Seletos	42
3.1	Repetência de Escola Primária e Taxas de Evasão, em Anos Seletos	56
3.2	Gasto Público por Níveis de Educação, Coréia, em Anos Seletos	71
3.3	Gasto Público por Estudante, por Nível, 1960-1990	72
3.4	Gastos Públicos Atuais por Estudante, Índia e Coréia, em Anos Seletos	73
4.1	Custos Anuais de Saúde Associados com a Poluição do Ar	89
4.2	Custos Anuais da Saúde Associados com Doenças Provindas da Água e da Poluição	89

4.3	Comércio, Crescimento, Pobreza e Degradação do Meio Ambiente, em Anos Seletos	96
4.4	Classificação de Países Seletos pela Trajetória do Crescimento Ambiental	102
4.5	Serviços Ambientais das Florestas Costa-Riquenhas e seus Beneficiários	103
5.1	Crescimento dos Mercados Derivados, 1991-1997	122
5.2	Países Agrupados pela Abertura Financeira	134
5.3	Resultados Estimados do Modelo Lógico Binomial Sobre a Probabilidade dos Países Pertencerem a Altas Categorias de Abertura Financeira	134
6.1	Uma Matriz-Síntese: Corrupção e Pobreza	153
6.2	Impacto das Liberdades Civis Sobre o Projeto de Taxas de Retorno Socioeconômicas	171
A1.1	Relacionamentos Entre Objetivos do Desenvolvimento em Instrumentos Políticos, 1981-1998	190
A2.1	A Equação do Crescimento Sob Várias Especificações	209
A2.2	Taxas do Crescimento do PIB Regressadas nos Estoques por Operário, Utilizando Todos os Países com Dados Disponíveis de 1965 a 1990	210
A2.3	Elasticidades para os Estoques por Operário, nas Taxas de Crescimento do PIB *per capita*	211
A2.4	Estudos Empíricos Seletos Sobre o Impacto e a Extensão dos Subsídios de Capital	212
A3.1	Os Coeficientes Gini de Educação para Países Seletos, em Anos Seletos	217
A3.2	Função de Produção: Estimativa Linear	218
A3.3	Função de Produção: Estimativa Não-Linear	219
A3.4	Educação, Abertura e Desempenho do Projeto de Empréstimo	221
A3.5	Estudos Empíricos Seletivos Sobre a Distribuição de Recursos, Crescimento e Pobreza	223
A5.1	Transações Internacionais	228
A5.2	Índice de Abertura Financeira, Países Seletos, 1997	229
A5.3	Países em Desenvolvimento Classificados por Graus de Volatilidade para Fluxos de Capital Estrangeiro	231
A5.4	Estatísticas Sumárias para Países Industrializados Seletos e Países em Desenvolvimento	233
A5.5	Os Relacionamentos Entre Abertura Financeira, Democracia e Gastos Sociais	234
A6.1	Porcentagem de Empresas Afetadas pelas Diferentes Formas de Captação do Estado e Índice de Captação Geral do Estado, Países Seletos, 1999	241

PREÂMBULO

Temos muito a comemorar ao iniciarmos o novo milênio. Uma criança nascida hoje, no mundo em desenvolvimento, pode esperar viver 25 anos a mais e ter melhor saúde, melhor educação e ser mais produtiva que uma criança nascida há cinqüenta anos. A expansão da democracia trouxe novas liberdades e oportunidades inimagináveis para muita gente em todo o mundo. E a revolução das comunicações assumiu a promessa do acesso universal ao conhecimento.

Mas, se observarmos mais de perto, veremos algo mais – algo alarmante. Atualmente, nos países em desenvolvimento, excluindo a China, há pelo menos mais cem milhões de pessoas do que há uma década vivendo em miséria. E a distância entre ricos e pobres torna-se cada vez mais evidente. Em muitos países, o golpe da Aids tem diminuído de maneira cruel a expectativa de vida – em alguns países africanos, há mais de dez anos. Cerca de um bilhão de pessoas não têm acesso à água tratada, e a cada ano 2,4 milhões de crianças morrem de doenças provenientes de água contaminada. Igualmente, cerca de um bilhão de pessoas adentraram no século XXI sem saber ler ou escrever. Apenas nas áreas rurais, aproximadamente 1,8 milhão de pessoas morrem a cada ano em conseqüência da poluição do ar. Florestas têm sido destruídas a uma média de um acre por segundo, com uma perda inimaginável de biodiversidade.

Apontamos algumas medidas de nossas deficiências: apesar da prosperidade de uma minoria, a qualidade de vida permaneceu sombria para muitos. A despeito de quase duas décadas de crescimento econômico rápido em determinados países, outros não se beneficiaram de tal progresso. Em muitas políticas levadas a efeito, favoreceu-se o capital investido da elite, em detrimento de investimentos adequados nos capitais humano e natural, essenciais para o crescimento de base ampla. A qualidade dos fatores convergentes para o crescimento requer uma atenção fundamental se se deseja reduzir a pobreza e atingir uma melhor qualidade de vida para todos. Este é o tema central deste livro.

PREÂMBULO

Uma melhor qualidade de vida para os pobres demanda melhores salários, o que, por sua vez, requer políticas econômicas e instituições sólidas que contribuam para o crescimento sustentado. Ao atingir salários mais altos e uma melhor qualidade de vida, requer-se também muito mais – melhores, maiores e iguais oportunidades para educação, emprego, maior qualidade na saúde e nutrição, um meio ambiente mais limpo e mais sustentável, um sistema legal e judicial imparcial, maiores liberdades civis e políticas, instituições confiáveis e transparentes e livre acesso a uma vida cultural rica e diversificada. O livro publicado recentemente pelo Banco Mundial, *Voices of the Poor: Can Anyone Hear Us?* (Vozes dos pobres: alguém pode nos ouvir?), reforça esta mensagem. Homens e mulheres pobres do mundo todo perceberam enfaticamente a importância da dignidade, do respeito, da segurança, das questões de gênero,* de um meio ambiente limpo, da saúde, além da inclusão ao bem-estar material.

Enquanto a renda *per capita* cresce, vários aspectos da qualidade de vida também melhoram, mas não todos, nem na mesma proporção, e não inevitavelmente. Em diferentes países, o mesmo passo de crescimento econômico tem sido associado com graus muito diferentes de melhoria sobre o tempo de educação, saúde, liberdades civis, participação dos cidadãos nas decisões afetas às suas vidas, libertação da corrupção, qualidade ambiental e sustentabilidade. Este livro demonstra como o crescimento é gerado e se ele é matéria sustentada crucialmente para a qualidade de vida de todos.

A estratégia do Banco Mundial é projetar e avaliar suas atividades por meio das lentes da redução da pobreza, a visão que informa a Estrutura do Desenvolvimento Abrangente que abraçamos nos países com os quais trabalhamos. Essa estrutura encoraja os países a buscarem uma abordagem equilibrada do desenvolvimento, tentando simultaneamente aumentar as dimensões humana, social, natural e física. Somente assim os frutos do desenvolvimento podem ser amplamente compartilhados e sustentados.

Arrolando essas dimensões complementares, essa estrutura integrada também tenta juntar os atores-chave do desenvolvimento. Isto coloca instituições, governo e responsabilidade corporativa, em questões de inclusão, voz, liberdades e participação, aliados a interesses econômicos convencionais e atuação política. Levantando estas questões relacionadas simultaneamente, a estrutura enfatiza a necessidade para a liderança do país, igualmente para uma sociedade entre o governo, o setor privado, a sociedade civil e a comunidade internacional, ao dirigir a agenda do desenvolvimento. Estamos comprometidos a auxiliar essa estrutura não apenas com financiamento, mas cada vez mais também com os programas do conhecimento do estado de arte e da aprendizagem com utilização de novos dados, instrumentos e metodologias, e sustentada pelas tecnologias, informação e comunicação mais recentes.

---

* Diferenças de tratamento para homens e mulheres, tendendo a discriminar o sexo feminino. (N. E.)

PREÂMBULO

De fato, viajando por todos os continentes, tenho sido constantemente lembrado pelo povo – em aldeias rurais, assim como em centros urbanos superpopulosos – que a qualidade de vida para eles transcende a contribuição de tão-somente financiar. Aquela qualidade diz respeito ao acesso de garotos e garotas à educação e a empregos, quando se graduam. Diz respeito ao acesso do pobre rural à medicina básica, quando se dirigem às suas clínicas da aldeia. Diz respeito à limpeza do ar e das águas e sobre a proteção da preciosa biodiversidade. Diz respeito à dignidade que os pobres devem desfrutar e à segurança de suas vidas. Diz respeito à participação do povo, juntamente com os reformistas no governo, na implementação de um programa de combate à corrupção. Diz respeito ao combate do capital investido de uma elite econômica que influencia indebitamente, até mesmo compra, as políticas, as regulamentações e leis do Estado.

Este livro abre um debate, por focalizar essas dimensões institucionais e políticas, e por fazê-lo com propriedade e parceria do país entre participantes do processo de desenvolvimento. Investir no povo, sustentando recursos naturais, administrando riscos e melhorando o governo, evidentemente são dimensões que suprem o crescimento qualitativo. É mais deste crescimento que pode promover maior redução da pobreza, desenvolvimento sustentável ambiental e social, e uma melhor qualidade de vida compartilhada por todos.

James D. Wolfensohn
Presidente
do World Bank Group

PREFÁCIO

A década de 1990 – no fim de um século e de um milênio – foi um período de inventário sobre o desenvolvimento. Os estudos reexaminaram e estabeleceram alguns dos pontos de vista centrais do desenvolvimento. O crescimento econômico sustentado surgiu sem dano como sendo fundamental para a redução da pobreza. E o registro do desenvolvimento confirmou a eficácia de algumas reformas para o crescimento sustentado, tanto em países em desenvolvimento como nos industrializados: investindo mais – e de modo mais eficiente – na educação e na saúde, reduzindo as barreiras ao comércio e ao investimento, desmantelando controle de preços domésticos na agricultura e na indústria e reduzindo déficits fiscais. Nem as altas nem as baixas econômicas da década de 1990 questionaram estes relacionamentos.

As taxas também deixaram a descoberto algumas brechas cruciais. Carente de ação política do país, assim como do conselho, das condições e do financiamento de entidades externas, tem havido falta de atenção adequada à qualidade de sustentabilidade do crescimento. Sem isso, o potencial real das reformas não pode ser realizado.

E as taxas realçaram algumas mudanças profundas no desenvolvimento, repensando os últimos cinqüenta anos, assim como nosso entendimento dos processos de desenvolvimento amadureceu, delineado pela experiência. Não que as interpretações tivessem sido inteiramente uniformes. Por exemplo, alguns entenderam o "Washington Consensus" somente como uma prescrição política para a liberalização dos mercados. Outros aceitaram a conhecida interpretação da abordagem das boas condições de mercado do *World Development Report 1991* como um mercado a vista, ambos envolvendo liberalização e um papel positivo e forte para o Estado e outros investidores.

Deixando de lado as diferentes interpretações, as taxas mostram um consenso emergente em algumas lições-chave sobre complementaridade e equilíbrio entre políticas e instituições. Mercados atuantes e liberalização

XVII

PREFÁCIO

são cruciais. Mas isto é reconhecer os limites do mercado e um papel essencial para os governos e outros investidores no processo de reforma.

Algumas vezes expectativas baseadas na experiência têm surgido, e outras não. Discussões anteriores previram o sucesso de países com tais riquezas naturais, como Myanmar, Filipinas e outros na África, e a falência de economias pobres em recursos naturais, como a República da Coréia ou Cingapura. As expectativas de desenvolvimento rápido por meio da liberalização do mercado nas economias de transição falharam em materializar-se. E, na década de 1980, a redução da produtividade nas economias industriais norte-americana e européia, contrastando com o sucesso evidente do Japão, solicita rápidas mudanças no paradigma de crescimento.

Às vezes a realidade não corresponde às expectativas, porque as mudanças nas circunstâncias globais locais neutralizaram o impacto das ações e forçaram os governos a rever as prioridades. "As indústrias pesadas primeiro" parecia o melhor caminho para avançar na virada do século XIX; a informação tecnológica parece ser a chave do sucesso na virada do século XX. E enquanto os mercados eram liberalizados nas décadas recentes, algumas vezes os resultados frustrantes mostraram a importância da edificação institucional para fazer esses mercados funcionarem.

Apresentamos este livro com o espírito de investigação contínua e realimentação na estruturação do pensamento desenvolvimentista. Ele dirige-se aos políticos, aos profissionais e outros, tanto nos países em desenvolvimento como nos industrializados. Isto reafirma a contribuição crucial de política para as boas condições de mercado. Assim como salienta a carência de ingredientes-chave e nova evidência. O livro apresenta não uma revisão completa do desenvolvimento, mas o exame de questões vitais que são freqüentemente descuidadas como uma base para a ação: distribuição de oportunidades, especialmente a educação; sustentabilidade ambiental; gerenciamento de riscos; governo e combate à corrupção. Ele não levanta alguns fatores importantes como a economia política da mudança, a influência da instabilidade social, a conseqüência de doenças transmissíveis como HIV/Aids, ou o impacto de questões globais e alfandegárias – pressões populares, migração trabalhista, aquecimento global, tecnologia da informação e arquitetura global financeira e de negócios. Sua conclusão é de que o crescimento é crucial, assim como a qualidade do crescimento.

O trabalho para a elaboração deste livro contou com a participação de uma equipe do Instituto do Banco Mundial e com a dotação de pesquisa do Banco Mundial. Tratou-se de uma contribuição para o material de ensino para um curso sobre desenvolvimento, e de fundamento para o *World Development Report 1999/2000: Entering the 21st Century* e o *World Development Report 2000/2001: Attacking Poverty*. Foi inspirado por uma diretriz jornalística e discussão por Stanley Fischer na Annual World Bank Conference on Development Economics de 1998. A equipe beneficiou-se de comentários de muitas pessoas, dentro e fora do Banco Mundial. Agradecimentos especiais

PREFÁCIO

são devidos àqueles que ofereceram sugestões para o desenvolvimento do livro. Isto inclui Nancy Birdsall, Paul Collier, Eduardo Doryan, Ravi Kanbur, Mats Karlsson, Gautam Kaji, Rung Kaewdang, Vijay Kelkar, Mohsin Khan, Aart Kray, Nora Lustig, Rakesh Mohan, Mohamed Muhsin, Robert Picciotto, Jan Piercy, Jo Ritzen, Lyn Squire, T. N. Srinivasan, Nicholas Stern, Thomas Sterner, Joseph Stiglitz, Anand Swamy, Shahid Yusuf, Shengman Zhang, e a equipe do *World Development Report 2000/2001*.

A equipe agradece aos que se seguem por suas entradas para o volume: Montek Ahluwahlia, Jane Armitage, Kaushik Basu, Surjit Bhalla, Jan Bojo, Deepak Bhattasali, Gerard Caprio, Shaohua Chen, Kevin Cleaver, Maureen Cropper, Monica Dasgupta, Shanta Devarajan, Ishac Diwan, David Dollar, William Easterly, Gershon Feder, Andrew Feltenstein, Deon Filmer, Pablo Guerrero, Cielito Habito, Kirk Hamilton, Jeffrey Hammer, Joseph Ingram, Farrukh Iqbal, Ramachandra Jammi, Emmanuel Jimenez, Mary Judd, Philip E. Keefer, Homi Kharas, Elizabeth M. King, Kathie Krumm, Ashok Lahiri, Kyung Tae Lee, Andres Liebenthal, Magda Lovei, Muthukumara Mani, Michele de Nevers, David Nepomuceno, Jostein Nygard, Michael Pomerleano, Tanaporn Poshyananda, Lant Pritchett, Martin Ravallion, David Reed, Neil Roger, William Shaw, Mary Shirley, Ammar Siamwalla, Hadi Soesastro, T. G. Srinivasan, Tara Vishwanath, Christina Wood, Michael Woolcock, Roberto Zagha, além de discutidores e participantes nos seminários no Fundo Monetário Internacional/Encontros Anuais do Banco Mundial, Conselho Nacional de Pesquisa de Economia Aplicada (Índia), Fórum de Desenvolvimento Asiático (Cingapura), Instituto de Pesquisa de Desenvolvimento da Tailândia, assim como uma apresentação numa conferência sobre reformas do Fundo Monetário Internacional. Várias unidades do Banco Mundial revisaram o manuscrito.

A EQUIPE DO RELATO

Esta obra foi elaborada por uma equipe do Instituto do Banco Mundial liderada por Vinod Thomas e incluindo Mansoor Dailami (Capítulo 5), Ashok Dhareshwar (Capítulo 1), Daniel Kaufmann (Capítulo 6), Nalin Kishor (Capítulo 4), Ramón E. López (Capítulo 2), e Yan Wang (Capítulo 3 e gerente de tarefa). A equipe foi auxiliada em sua pesquisa por Cary Anne Cadman, Xibo Fan e John Van Dyck. Ofereceram apoio: Taji Anderson, Alice Faria e Jae Shin Yang.

Bruce Ross-Larson e Meta de Coquereaumont, do Comunications Development Incorporated and International Communications, Inc. (ICI) de Sterling, Virgínia, editaram o manuscrito em diferentes estágios. A ICI também providenciou a digitação e a leitura das provas. Desenvolvimento do produto, projeto, edição, produção e disseminação foram dirigidos e administrados pelo escritório do editor do Banco Mundial.

VISÃO GERAL

A última década do século XX conheceu grandes progressos em algumas partes do mundo. Mas conheceu também estagnação e reveses, até mesmo nos países que haviam alcançado anteriormente as mais rápidas taxas de crescimento econômico. Essas diferenças intervalares e inversões agudas ensinam-nos muito sobre o que contribui para o desenvolvimento. No centro situa-se o crescimento econômico, não apenas seu andamento, mas – tão importante – também sua qualidade. Tanto as fontes como os padrões da forma de crescimento delineiam os resultados do desenvolvimento.

Será que aqueles padrões foram adequados para reduzir rapidamente a pobreza ou melhorar a qualidade de vida das pessoas? Por que tão poucos países mantiveram grandes taxas de crescimento durante períodos prolongados? Por que algumas dimensões cruciais – igualdade de renda, proteção ambiental – se deterioraram em tantas economias, ambas crescendo rápida e lentamente? Como o governo sustenta o processo de crescimento? Como respostas, oferecemos três princípios de desenvolvimento em um conjunto de ações, para acentuar a qualidade dos processos de crescimento.

Resultados de Desenvolvimento e Processos de Crescimento

O desenvolvimento está prestes a melhorar a qualidade de vida das pessoas, expandindo sua capacidade de delinear seus próprios futuros. Isto geralmente requer uma maior renda *per capita*, mas, ao mesmo tempo, coloca em jogo muito mais. Põe em jogo educação mais eqüitativa e oportunidades de emprego. Maior igualdade de gênero. Melhor saúde e nutrição. Um meio ambiente mais limpo, mais sustentável. Um sistema judicial e legal imparcial. Liberdades civis e políticas mais amplas. Uma vida cultural mais rica. Enquanto a renda *per capita* de alguns cresceu, muitos destes aspectos

melhoram em diferentes graus – mas outros não. Como os processos de crescimento podem ser influenciados de maneira que as dimensões qualitativas de desenvolvimento resultem também em melhoria? Este livro explora essas questões de crescimento mais rápido e melhor.

Um estudo recente, *Voices of the Poor: Can Anyone Hear Us?* (Narayan et al., 2000), indica que os resultados crescentes são uma parte da redução da pobreza. Maior segurança na vida e um meio ambiente mais sustentável são outros. A experiência das décadas passadas e as vozes dos pobres fornecem razões obrigatórias para enfatizar esses fatores qualitativos.

De fato, da Bolívia, Egito e Uganda para Romênia, Sri Lanka e Tailândia, a comunidade de desenvolvimento está ampliando a definição tradicional de pobreza e bem-estar. Além de uma renda contada de forma individual ou familiar, o bem-estar inclui oportunidade, enquanto taxada pelo funcionamento do mercado e dos investimentos e melhorias na saúde e educação. Inclui segurança, como refletida por reduzida vulnerabilidade econômica e choques físicos. Inclui permissão, como avaliada pela inclusão social e a voz dos indivíduos. E inclui sustentabilidade, como representada pela proteção do meio ambiente, recursos naturais e biodiversidade.

O crescimento econômico tem sido associado positivamente com a redução da pobreza. As taxas antecipadas projetaram uma taxa de crescimento para o mundo em desenvolvimento, para a década de 1990, de um pouco acima de 5%, ou quase 3,2% *per capita*. Projetaram uma redução no número de pobres de mais ou menos trezentos milhões, ou uma taxa anual de declínio de quase 4%. Mas o crescimento real durante 1991-1998 foi de quase metade desse percentual, ou seja, de 1,6% *per capita*. Se os países da Europa oriental e da Ásia central forem excluídos dessas estimativas (como nas projeções posteriormente mencionadas), o crescimento *per capita* real está mais perto do crescimento projetado, de 3,5% – com o número dos pobres inalterado e a incidência de pobreza abaixo de 2% ao ano (World Bank, 2000a).

A redução da pobreza associada ao crescimento tem variado amplamente, assim como variaram o progresso social e as melhorias de bem-estar, tanto na educação, na saúde, como em voz ou participação (Capítulo 1). Onde o crescimento estagnou ou declinou, as dimensões sociais e de bem-estar deterioraram-se. A medida amplamente diferenciadora na qual o crescimento contribui para melhorias no bem-estar significa que deve haver uma relação direta para avanços sustentáveis no bem-estar. Significa, também, que o modo pelo qual o crescimento é gerado é muito importante. A qualidade do processo de crescimento, não apenas seu andamento, afeta os resultados do desenvolvimento – tanto quanto a qualidade da dieta do povo, não apenas a quantidade de comida, influencia a saúde e a expectativa de vida; por isso, é essencial explorar as complexas interações dos fatores que delineiam o crescimento.

O andamento do crescimento tem sido mais sustentável nos países em desenvolvimento e industrializados, que se preocupam com os atributos

qualitativos do processo de crescimento. De fato, há um relacionamento de mão dupla entre o crescimento econômico e as melhorias nas dimensões sociais e ambientais. A atenção à sustentabilidade do meio ambiente, por exemplo, ajuda a alcançar um crescimento mais sustentado, especialmente onde as taxas de crescimento são altamente variáveis e os impactos negativos são particularmente acentuados para o pobre. Isto sugere um prêmio para taxas de crescimento firmes, acima do crescimento intermitente, mesmo que a iniciativa inclua pequenos períodos de crescimento rápido. Quando os países esgotam as possibilidades de aumento de crescimento mediante reformas de mercado, os fatores qualitativos que sustentam o crescimento a longo prazo tornam-se muito mais importantes.

As dimensões do processo de crescimento interagem freqüente e positivamente em um círculo vicioso. Mas pode haver também alguns intercâmbios difíceis entre quantidade e qualidade. Rapidamente, o crescimento temporário, apoiando-se em políticas tão distorcidas como subsídios ao capital, desprezo às externalidades ambientais e gastos públicos oblíquos, pode realmente diminuir prospectos para um crescimento mais sustentado. Ainda mais difíceis de corrigir são as situações nas quais o crescimento conflita com sustentabilidade ambiental e social, já que ambas contribuem diretamente para o desenvolvimento. Gerenciar esses aspectos qualitativos torna-se essencial para atingir melhorias sustentáveis de bem-estar.

Então, o que é a qualidade de crescimento? Complementar o andamento do crescimento refere se a aspectos-chave que delineiam o processo de crescimento. As experiências do país revelam a importância de vários destes aspectos: a distribuição das oportunidades, a sustentabilidade do meio ambiente, o gerenciamento dos riscos globais e o governo. Estes aspectos não apenas contribuem diretamente para os resultados desenvolvimentistas. Eles também acrescem ao impacto que o crescimento tem sobre estes resultados, e dirigem os conflitos que o crescimento pode colocar à sustentabilidade ambiental ou social. É a mistura dessas políticas e instituições que delineia o processo de crescimento, o principal foco deste estudo.

Princípios de Desenvolvimento

Observando os lados quantitativo e qualitativo do processo de crescimento conjuntamente, coloca-se o foco em três princípios-chave para os países em desenvolvimento e industrializados:

- foco sobre todos os valores: capitais físico, humano e natural;
- atender aos aspectos distributivos no decorrer do tempo;
- enfatizar a estrutura institucional para o bom governo.

VISÃO GERAL

Os Principais Valores

De modo geral, os valores que importam para o desenvolvimento são capital físico, capital humano e capital natural. O progresso tecnológico afeto ao uso desses valores é igualmente importante. Para taxas aceleradas de crescimento, tem-se dado tradicionalmente grande atenção à acumulação de capital físico. Mas outros valores-chave merecem atenção – tanto ao capital humano (e social) quanto ao capital natural (ambiental) (Quadro 1). Esses valores são igualmente cruciais para os pobres, e sua acumulação, progresso tecnológico e produtividade, juntamente com capital físico, determinam o impacto a longo prazo sobre a pobreza.

Focalizando predominantemente o capital físico, os países industriais e em desenvolvimento podem ser tentados a implementar políticas que o subsidiem a um custo (Capítulo 2), o que pode criar uma situação que beneficie interesses de capital – sendo difícil conseguir reverter tal situação. Enquanto isso, do ponto de vista social, há subinvestimento na educação e na saúde (Capítulo 3) e superexploração do capital natural, freqüentemente em decorrência de sua depreciação ou fracos direitos de propriedade (Capítulo 4). Num nível agregado (bruto), subsídios para agricultura, energia, transporte rodoviário e aquático, somados a uma estimativa de US$ 700 bilhões para US$ 900 bilhões no início da década de 1990, sendo quase dois terços nos países industrializados e um terço nos países em desenvolvimento (De Moor & Calamai, 1997).

Sustentar uma relativa dependência da acumulação do capital físico poderia requerer distorções contínuas. Enquanto o capital físico se aprofunda mantendo sua taxa de retorno, poderia requerer amplos subsídios públicos, por exemplo, para atrair capital estrangeiro. Além disso, o crescimento acelerado mediante políticas que conduzem à superexploração de florestas e de outros bens naturais esgota o capital natural e fere a sustentabilidade ambiental. Em 1997, a poupança bruta interna era mais ou menos 25% do Produto Interno Bruto (PIB) entre os países em desenvolvimento. Contudo, corrigidas pelo esgotamento do capital ambiental, as poupanças domésticas familiares genuínas eram apenas uma estimativa de 14% do PIB. Isso inclui o caso da Nigéria, com poupanças familiares brutas de 22% mas poupanças genuínas negativas de 12%, e a Federação Russa, com taxas 25% e negativa de 1,6% (World Bank, 1999d).

Uma abordagem menos distorcida (mais neutra ou equilibrada) para a acumulação dos três tipos de bens é preferível. As políticas podem contribuir para a acumulação destes bens. Investimentos na educação em todos os níveis, enquanto ajudam a gerar crescimento, também contribuem para a acumulação de capital humano e bem-estar. Investir no capital natural é essencial para a saúde humana e, para a grande quantidade de pessoas pobres, que dependem dos recursos naturais para sua sobrevivência, para a segurança econômica (Capítulo 4). Tão importante quanto a acumulação

Quadro 1 – Acumulação de Bens, Crescimento e Bem-Estar

A Figura 1 desenha um simples esquema de como o capital humano (H), o capital natural (R) e o capital físico (K) contribuem para o crescimento econômico e o bem-estar. O capital físico contribui para o bem-estar por meio do crescimento econômico. O capital humano (e social) e natural (e ambiental) fazem-no de modo similar, e são igualmente componentes diretos do bem-estar.

O capital humano e o natural também contribuem para a acumulação de capital físico ao aumentar seus retornos. O capital físico aumenta os retornos do capital humano e do capital natural e, se os mercados os refletirem, sua acumulação. Acrescentando a tudo isso investimentos em capital físico, humano e natural, juntamente com muitas políticas reformadoras, contribuem para o progresso tecnológico e o crescimento do fator total de produtividade, aumentando, desse modo, o crescimento (Capítulo 2).

Mas distorções políticas, corrupção, mau governo, falências de mercado e externalidades podem colocar os países em um caminho de acumulação de bens distorcido e desequilibrado. Esta situação pode assegurar um crescimento de renda e melhorias de bem-estar abaixo de seu potencial. Mais especificamente, pode conduzir a um fator total de produtividade inferior e subinvestimentos em:

- Capital físico produtivo, reduzindo o aproveitamento do investimento por meio de propinas e burocracia ou distorcendo a alocação de investimentos físicos – ou seja, rumo a determinados contratos lucrativos.
- Capital humano, promovendo tais áreas favorecidas como a militar e ampla infra-estrutura e mediante a relação regressiva de gastos públicos.
- Capital natural, solapando taxas, *royalties* e regulações que poderiam sustentar os recursos naturais.

Distorções, falências de mercado, implícitas garantias governamentais e regulação inadequada podem provocar:

- Superinvestimento ou investimento devastador no capital físico, pelo aumento do aproveitamento de determinados bens físicos mediante garantias – que influenciam a aceitação de comportamento de risco pelos bancos, corporações e investidores –, e baixando o valor de determinados recursos naturais.
- Subinvestimento nos recursos humanos e naturais, depreciando estes bens e reduzindo os recursos devotados a eles.

Os efeitos dessas políticas distorcidas na acumulação do capital humano e natural, relativo ao capital físico, podem reduzir o crescimento e o bem-estar. Ao contrário, se a corrupção for controlada e o governo for adequado, políticas não distorcidas poderiam elevar a acumulação de bens, contribuindo para o crescimento de maneira mais rápida (Capítulo 6). Assim, ao remover distorções políticas, fomentando bom governo e edificando falências de mercado e externalidades, os países podem realizar investimentos de bens menos distorcidos, mais equilibrados. E isto pode conduzir a um crescimento mais estável e sustentado e a amplos aumentos em bem-estar.

Figura 1 – Uma Estrutura

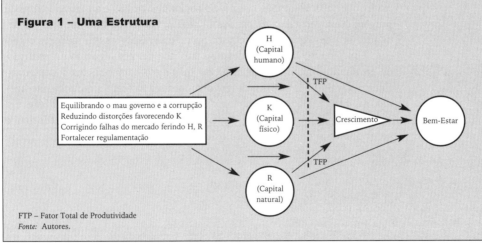

FTP – Fator Total de Produtividade
Fonte: Autores.

destes bens é seu uso de forma eficiente. Para isso – e para um fator de produtividade maior desses valores –, bom governo, mitigação da influência indevida dos interesses da elite e ações de combate à corrupção são vitais.

Aspectos Distributivos

Este foco sobre a qualidade traz à luz a importância dos aspectos distributivos para o processo de crescimento. Uma distribuição mais eqüitativa do capital humano, da terra e de outros bens produtivos implica uma distribuição mais eqüitativa de remuneração, acentuando a capacidade de pessoas tirarem proveito das tecnologias e gerarem resultados. É por isso que uma determinada taxa de crescimento está provavelmente para ser associada com melhores resultados da pobreza, nos cenários onde as oportunidades educacionais são distribuídas mais eqüitativamente (Capítulo 3).

É provável que a estabilidade nos resultados de crescimento ao longo do tempo seja igualmente importante. Os resultados dos pobres podem ser muito sensíveis a ciclos e crises, especialmente porque os pobres são carentes de bens – terra, habilidades e poupanças financeiras – para aliviar seu consumo em maus tempos. Vivendo pouco acima da linha de pobreza, milhões de quase-pobres foram lançados de volta à pobreza em decorrência de choques externos. Assim, para o crescimento reduzir a pobreza, ele precisa não apenas ser, de forma habitual, relativamente estável, como seus benefícios serem amplamente distribuídos.

O que dizer, então, dos ganhos de renda esperados da globalização na década de 1990? Estes começaram a materializar-se, mas não em todos os lugares. Uma das razões para isso é a inadequação de estruturas reguladoras e supervisoras, ambas nos níveis nacional e global, e a carência geral de preparo para participar da economia global. Outra razão refere-se à volatilidade, às vezes relacionada ao risco moral e às respostas de jogadores externos. Um terceiro motivo se deve ao fato de que, por algumas estimativas, os resultados na última década, ou quase, tornaram-se mais desiguais. Então, objetivos da política desenvolvimentista incluem a redução não apenas da desigualdade de oportunidades, mas também a desigualdade e a volatilidade de resultados de crescimento. Nisso, é importante acentuar o gerenciamento do risco financeiro e reduzir a sensibilidade do povo pobre para mudar fortunas econômicas (Capítulo 5).

A Estrutura de Governo

As estruturas institucionais de bom governo escoram tudo o que foi

feito para aumentar o crescimento. O funcionamento efetivo das burocracias, estruturas reguladoras, liberdades civis e instituições responsáveis e transparentes, para assegurar a regra do direito e as questões de participação para crescimento e desenvolvimento. Os efeitos do governo pobre, os entraves burocráticos e a corrupção são regressivos e danosos para o crescimento sustentado. A captação de políticas estatais, leis e recursos pelos interesses da elite freqüentemente desvia incentivos e gastos públicos em direção a bens socialmente menos produtivos, erodindo os benefícios que iriam para a sociedade, e, conseqüentemente, reduzindo o impacto sobre o bem-estar. Estimativas do "dividendo desenvolvimentista" na forma de rendas maiores ou melhores resultados sociais são dramáticas, partindo de baixos níveis de regra de direito ou altos níveis de corrupção para até mesmo níveis médios (uma diferença nos níveis de corrupção de apenas um desvio-padrão pode ser associada a enormes diferenças no impacto desenvolvimentista). Logo, investir na capacidade para um melhor governo é a principal prioridade para uma melhor *performance* econômica (Capítulo 6).

Uma sociedade civil vibrante – autorizada pelas ferramentas de computação da Internet, diagnostica técnicas de estudo e a última informação sobre o governo – é indispensável na luta contra a corrupção e outras formas de mau governo. As liberdades civis não são ligadas apenas positivamente ao governo melhorado, corrupção reduzida e produtividade aumentada dos investimentos públicos, mas também contribuem diretamente para o bem-estar. De fato, a atenção deveria ir além de obter o lado direito governamental da equação. Também é necessário acentuar os direitos civis e dar maior voz a grupos diferentes, promover empresas competitivas e complementar de cima a baixo as reformas políticas governamentais com uma formulação de baixo para cima e implementação de estratégias de desenvolvimento.

Ações Negligenciadas no Processo de Crescimento

Agora que vemos o processo de desenvolvimento com maior amplitude, há freqüentemente atenção inadequada, especialmente numa crise, a dois ou três valores em que o pobre se baseia: capital humano e capital natural. Esta negligência, por sua vez, parece levar à negligência de algumas ações-chave:

- melhorar a distribuição de oportunidades;
- sustentar o capital natural;
- lidar com riscos financeiros globais;
- melhorar o governo e controlar a corrupção.

Equilibrá-los contribui não apenas para a acumulação de bens, mas igualmente para o progresso tecnológico e maior fator total de produtividade.

Melhorando a Distribuição de Oportunidades

O principal bem dos pobres é seu capital humano. Das 85 economias examinadas, a Polônia e os Estados Unidos (estimados para ter a mais alta média de anos de escolaridade) possuem a distribuição mais eqüitativa de conclusão educacional entre pessoas na força de trabalho. E a República da Coréia registrou uma das mais amplas melhorias na igualdade educacional durante as três últimas décadas. Mas a desigualdade na educação continua vacilante, como acontece na Argélia, na Índia, no Mali, no Paquistão e na Tunísia.

A relação de qualquer taxa de crescimento dada para a redução da pobreza depende dos investimentos no povo. Quanto mais eqüitativos os investimentos, maior o impacto do crescimento para baixar a incidência de pobreza, como observado numa comparação dos efeitos do crescimento sobre a pobreza através dos estados indianos (Ravallion & Datt, 1999). Se as habilidades do povo são normalmente distribuídas entre a população, a tendência de distribuição dos resultados de educação e saúde poderia parecer representar especialmente amplas perdas de bem-estar para a sociedade, enquanto uma significativa proporção de pessoas é desprovida de oportunidades para utilizar novas tecnologias e elevar-se acima da linha de pobreza.

Uma revisão do desperdício educacional em 35 países descobre que ele deve ser francamente relacionado com a conclusão educacional depois do controle para rendas. Na saúde, os Estados Unidos, com o mais alto índice de gasto *per capita* em saúde, estão no 37° lugar entre 191 países, numa medida da *performance* do sistema geral de saúde. A França, com menos de 60% dos gastos *per capita* em saúde, está em primeiro lugar. A Colômbia, que está muito abaixo disto em gasto *per capita* em saúde, está em primeiro lugar na categoria de justiça da contribuição social (WHO, 2000). Assim, gastar nos serviços de educação e saúde não é o bastante. É preciso, também, atenção com a amplitude e profundidade do capital humano – sua qualidade e sua eqüidade, medida pela educação feminina, acesso para os pobres e grau de escolaridade.

Os governos precisam realocar os gastos públicos para a educação básica, para garantir sua distribuição qualitativa e igualitária. Sociedades público-privadas precisam ser encorajadas mediante políticas baseadas no mercado, para aumentar os esforços em promover a educação em todos os níveis, inclusive a educação superior. Precisa-se também de políticas de mercado de trabalho patrocinadas e políticas de proteção social. Além disso, o capital humano dos pobres pode ser mais bem aplicado aprumando a distribuição da terra e perseguindo estratégias de trabalho intensivo num meio ambiente global e aberto (Capítulo 3).

VISÃO GERAL

Sustentando o Capital Natural

A degradação ambiental piorou agudamente, em decorrência, entre outros, do crescimento populacional, das pressões domésticas e globais sobre recursos escassos, das políticas econômicas, como, por exemplo, subsídios que ignoram conseqüências ambientais, e da negligência das propriedades públicas globais e locais. Os custos da poluição ambiental e da superexploração de recursos são enormes; as perdas, em muitos casos, são irreversíveis. Os incêndios nas florestas da Indonésia – resultado da política humana e de fatores naturais – produziram algo em torno de US$ 4 bilhões em perdas diretas em 1997 e novamente em 1998, com dano extensivo às nações vizinhas. E são os pobres, devido à sua relação com o capital natural, como terra, florestas, minerais e biodiversidade, que sofrem desproporcionalmente com a degradação do meio ambiente.

Poucos países enfrentaram adequadamente as causas subjacentes da degradação ambiental e de recursos – as distorções políticas, falências de mercado e falta de conhecimento sobre a totalidade dos benefícios da proteção ambiental e conservação de recursos. Crescimento e rendas mais altas podem criar condições para promover a melhoria ambiental, aumentando a demanda por uma melhor qualidade ambiental e tornando disponíveis os recursos para preencher essa demanda. Entretanto, apenas uma forte combinação de incentivos baseados no mercado doméstico e global, investimentos e instituições pode tornar o crescimento ambientalmente sustentado, uma realidade com os exemplos vindos da China, da Costa Rica, da Indonésia e de muitos outros países europeus (Capítulo 4).

Lidar com Riscos Financeiros Globais

A integração financeira global possui amplos benefícios, mas também torna os países mais vulneráveis a riscos ocultos e a desequilíbrios repentinos no sentimento do investidor. Os fluxos voláteis do capital privado parecem estar associados com taxas de crescimento voláteis, que atingem especialmente o pobre, a quem faltam os bens para suportar uma tempestade econômica. Para lidar melhor com tais riscos, os países precisam manter macropolíticas sólidas. Precisam, igualmente, aprofundar os mercados financeiros domésticos, fortalecer a regulação doméstica e a supervisão financeira, introduzir mecanismos de governos corporativos e prover redes de segurança social.

Para tudo isso precisam de instituições sólidas e capacitações fortes, que levam tempo para ser cultivadas. Desenvolvendo-as, enquanto abrem um mercado de capital do país, podem ajudar a lidar com os riscos para o sistema financeiro e a economia. Nesse ínterim, enquanto os governos abrem suas contas de capital, podem considerar um espectro de ações como na Ar-

XXXI

gentina, no Chile, no México, e assim por diante. Um deve evitar incentivos especiais para fluxos de curto prazo. Outro deve estabelecer reserva de exigência e taxas para fluxos de risco a curto prazo. Ainda outro deve fortalecer a regulamentação e a supervisão prudenciais. A coordenação da política internacional e a atividade de emprestador de últimos recursos podem prover liquidez e assistência financeira de emergência (Capítulo 5).

Melhorar o Governo e Controlar a Corrupção

O governo precisa mover-se para o centro do palco em estratégias de construção institucional. Isso requer melhor análise e medida das dimensões de governo e uma compreensão mais clara do capital investido de grupos poderosos. Onde as estruturas legais e judiciais são fracas e o capital investido ultrapassou a atuação política do Estado e os aparatos de alocação de recursos, o custo social pode ser enorme. Neste caso, a edificação institucional necessária para intervenções desenvolvimentistas efetivas pode ser extensiva, garantindo uma abordagem ativa.

A participação e a voz seriam vitais para aumentar a transparência, fornecer as checagens e os balanços necessários, opondo-se à tomada do Estado pela elite. O comprometimento da sociedade civil no processo participativo e transparente, com reformistas no Executivo, Legislativo e Judiciário e setores privados, pode fazer a diferença entre um Estado bem governado e outro mal governado, entre uma sociedade estagnada e uma próspera. Uma compreensão rigorosa de governo precisaria ser apoiada por novas tecnologias (como na Albânia, na Bolívia, na Geórgia, na Latíbia e em muitos países africanos).

Criar clima para um desenvolvimento bem-sucedido requer, então, uma abordagem integrada, ligando elementos econômicos institucionais legais e participativos: edificar instituições transparentes e efetivas para orçar os programas de investimento público (como na Austrália, na Nova Zelândia e no Reino Unido), como componentes para políticas macroeconômicas; estabelecer uma administração pública baseada no mérito (como na Malásia, em Cingapura e na Tailândia) e em costumes honestos e eficientes e nas agências de licitação, bem como promover as liberdades civis e a participação popular (Capítulo 6).

Substituir Prioridades

Por que focalizar a qualidade quando a marcha do crescimento é lenta em muitas partes do mundo? O crescimento tem sido modesto em muitos países – mais ou menos de 1,6% *per capita* para países de baixa e média rendas desde a década de 1980, e mais baixa ainda quando a China e a Índia

são excluídas. Alguns países também estão passando ou saindo de crises financeiras. Nessas circunstâncias, a questão não é de qualidade ou quantidade. Ambas são essenciais e ambas estão envolvidas numa relação de mão dupla.

A troca relativa nas prioridades poderia acelerar a marcha do crescimento a longo prazo. Investimentos no capital humano – educação, cuidados com a saúde e políticas populacionais – podem melhorar diretamente a qualidade de vida. Podem igualmente melhorar incentivos de investimento mediante o efeito de uma força de produtividade de capital mais saudável e mais educada. Assim, trocando a ênfase mais em direção ao capital humano, poderia promover um crescimento mais rápido a longo prazo. O ponto-chave? Um foco sobre a qualidade de resultados poderia ajudar a sustentar um crescimento mais rápido.

Equilibrar as dimensões qualitativas que contribuem para a marcha do crescimento pode, em troca, acentuar diretamente o bem-estar. Por exemplo, menos poluição da água e do ar, ou menos degradação dos recursos naturais, somados à contribuição para o crescimento, acentuam diretamente o bem-estar, melhorando a saúde ou fornecendo maiores oportunidades de renda e consumo.

Este livro mostra que alguns processos e políticas em países em desenvolvimento ou industrializados geram crescimento econômico com maior igualdade do desenvolvimento humano, sustentabilidade do meio ambiente e transparência das estruturas governamentais – enquanto outros não. Além do mais, provavelmente uma seqüência de ações pode ser efetiva – se liberalizar primeiro e regular depois, privatizar primeiro e assegurar a competição depois, crescer primeiro e limpar mais tarde, ou crescer primeiro e fornecer liberdades civis depois. Para fazer o máximo para o crescimento a longo prazo, a liberalização, por exemplo, precisa andar junto com ações reguladoras, gerenciamento ambiental e medidas de combate à corrupção.

Definir a Troca

As ações que enfocam a qualidade do crescimento precisam ser parte central do pacote político, não adendos a uma agenda já lotada. Isso significa que os investidores terão de aumentar as ações pelos governos, trocando a ênfase para:

- *Acumulação de bens e utilização*, reduzindo distorções políticas, por exemplo, aquelas que subsidiam o capital físico, ao mesmo tempo que complementem mercados ao valorizar recursos naturais e investindo adequadamente nos recursos humanos. A implicação é para assegurar um crescimento sustentável de base ampla, não para crescimento lento.

VISÃO GERAL

- *Estruturas reguladoras*, construindo estruturas reguladoras para a competição e eficiência para acompanhar a liberalização e privatização e dando maior atenção a reformas legais e judiciais, e, ao mesmo tempo, assegurando a estabilidade macroeconômica. A implicação é tomar ações reguladoras de suporte, juntamente com a liberalização, não para a liberalização lenta.
- *Bom governo*, alimentando as liberdades civis, processos participativos e responsabilidade nas instituições públicas, promovendo esforços de combate à corrupção; e envolvendo ativamente o setor privado para reduzir a influência do capital investido, enquanto certifica a capacidade para mudanças políticas. A implicação é aumentar a atenção para o edifício de coalizão na sociedade civil, não para depreciar a política governamental e sua capacidade de construção.

Fazer a Troca – Agora

Como pode ser financiado mais e melhor o investimento no povo e no capital natural? De várias maneiras. Primeiro, melhorar o governo, reduzir a busca por aluguéis e corrupção e encorajar uma responsabilidade corporativa maior pode aumentar as poupanças nacionais. Segundo, aumentar os preços para a utilização dos recursos naturais e taxar tais externalidades, como a poluição, pode disponibilizar recursos para o desenvolvimento. Terceiro, reduzir as distorções que favorecem o capital físico pode ser benéfico – assim como com muitas das experiências na remoção das distorções. Pode permitir uma realocação das poupanças nacionais em prol do desenvolvimento humano. E, quarto, reduzir subsídios dentro dos setores para serviços que são danosos ao meio ambiente pode realocar recursos públicos para beneficiar os pobres ou promover o desenvolvimento sustentável.

Resumindo, este livro apóia a ampliação do foco das ações para abranger uma estrutura desenvolvimentista compreensiva, uma agenda mais cheia e qualitativa envolvendo aspectos estruturais humanos, sociais e ambientais do processo de crescimento. Este foco mais amplo complementa a liberalização com uma elevação dos bens e da capacidade dos pobres. Transfere a atenção de uma confiança exclusiva no governo como agente de mudança para o comprometimento de todas as partes da sociedade. E isso requer uma capacidade muito mais efetiva de construir inteiramente.

Com todos os sócios desenvolvimentistas complementando um ao outro, uma estrutura mais integrada pode ser implementada com maior efetividade. Primeiro, as amplas desigualdades de oportunidade – especialmente na educação –, equilibradas agora, apresentarão maior promessa para os ganhos de bem-estar para a sociedade. Segundo, o dano ambiental e as perdas de biodiversidade de padrões de crescimento atual são assustadores; no entanto, se forem equilibrados agora, o crescimento pode realizar um

meio ambiente natural melhor e reduzir o número de pobres. Terceiro, a globalização apresenta riscos para os pobres, mas se esses riscos fossem aprumados agora, a globalização poderia tornar possível os recursos tecnológicos para a redução da pobreza. Quarto, a corrupção do governo e a falta de liberdades civis e voz ameaçam os ganhos de qualquer ação, mas se estas ameaças fossem equilibradas agora, melhores governos apresentariam uma grande promessa de melhoria do bem-estar.

As oportunidades propiciadas pela abertura aumentada, em conhecimento e tecnologias, nunca foram tão abundantes. Igualmente, os desafios da pobreza, do crescimento populacional, da degradação ambiental, das dificuldades financeiras e do mau governo nunca foram maiores. Precisa-se mais é de um crescimento com foco na qualidade. Isto não é um luxo. É crucial aos países agarrarem as oportunidades de uma vida melhor para suas gerações presentes e futuras.

CAPÍTULO 1

O REGISTRO DE UM DESENVOLVIMENTO CONFUSO

A economia não apenas se relaciona com a geração de renda mas também com o fazer bom uso daquela renda para acentuar nossa vida e nossas liberdades.

— Amartya Sen, *Uma Conversa com Sen*

Na década de 1990, um grupo de economistas na Ásia oriental divulgou algumas das taxas de crescimento mais rápidas e os mais agudos declínios, assim como recuperações, dando às políticas de liberalização do mercado um forte apoio e séria qualificação. De muitas maneiras, a década de 1990 concentrou as experiências de desenvolvimento das décadas anteriores, oferecendo abordagens e precauções para guiar a ação no século XXI.

Observando as décadas anteriores de desenvolvimento, vários estudos de todo o mundo na década de 1990 focalizaram os sucessos na Ásia oriental, os reveses na África subsaariana, e os modestos ganhos em outros lugares. O *World Development Report de 1991* (World Bank, 1991) articulou um consenso emergente sob a rubrica de uma abordagem de boas condições de mercado, requerendo uma revalorização dos papéis do Estado e do mercado. Esta e outras revisões assinalaram os papéis cruciais do Estado e dos mercados na redução da pobreza (World Bank, 1990), na proteção ambiental (Ibidem, 1992), na previsão de infra-estrutura (Ibidem, 1994) e nas estruturas legais de governo e o sistema financeiro (Ibidem, 1997j).

Examinamos aqui a *performance* do desenvolvimento durante a última década. Atualizamos taxas anteriores sobre como os países estão atuan-

do em relação à redução da pobreza, desenvolvimento sustentável e crescimento econômico. E examinamos os fatores globais e as mudanças político-institucionais subjacentes à atuação dos países. Evidências da década de 1990 expandem a história do desenvolvimento, especialmente a relacionada com as exigências institucionais para o sucesso, e fornecem um rico conjunto de hipóteses a ser considerado em relação à política. Primeiro, investimentos no povo precisam estar relacionados com a qualidade e a distribuição daqueles investimentos. Segundo, crescimento rápido, enquanto apóia o desenvolvimento social quando de base ampla, pode ferir a sustentabilidade ambiental na presença das ações adequadas. Terceiro, enquanto a abertura do mercado e a competição continuam a fornecer benefícios, os riscos financeiros devem ser gerenciados com atenção por fatores específicos do país. Quarto, deveria ser dada prioridade ao bom governo e aos fatores institucionais, e não adiados para posteriores estágios de reforma.

Avaliar Desenvolvimento

O desenvolvimento diz respeito ao povo e seu bem-estar, o que envolve a habilidade para delinear suas vidas. De acordo com isso, o desenvolvimento deve ser, inclusive, das gerações futuras e da terra que irão herdar. Deve-se comprometer as pessoas, pois sem a participação delas nenhuma estratégia pode ter sucesso duradouro. Esta noção de desenvolvimento como bem-estar significa que medidas de desenvolvimento devem incluir não apenas taxas de crescimento, mas a dispersão, a composição e a sustentabilidade daquele crescimento.

Praticantes de desenvolvimento utilizaram freqüentemente o crescimento no Produto Interno Bruto (PIB) *per capita* como uma procuração para o desenvolvimento, em parte porque o progresso social está associado com o crescimento do PIB e, parcialmente, devido à conveniência. Contudo, a confiança no PIB como única medida do desenvolvimento é seriamente limitadora. O crescimento do PIB pode ser tanto de alta quanto de pouca qualidade. Alguns processos e políticas geram crescimento do PIB juntamente com o crescimento dos bens humanos e naturais, que afetam diretamente o bem-estar das pessoas além de seus papéis produtivos. Outros geram crescimento de baixa qualidade que não está associado com melhorias dos bens humanos e naturais. Para integrar a qualidade do crescimento em avaliações de desenvolvimento são necessários índices multidimensionais de bem-estar.

A teoria econômica distingue o conceito de crescimento da idéia mais ampla de desenvolvimento. Com que cuidado essa distinção tem sido feita variou ao longo do tempo.[1] O crescimento rápido das décadas de 1950 e 1960 motivou um aumento de interesse por objetivos de desenvolvimentos

mais amplos. No decorrer das décadas seguintes, como se estabeleceu a estagnação, a ênfase mudou para o crescimento econômico. Nos anos 90, um ponto de vista mais amplo ressurgiu, como exemplificado no *United Nations Development Programme* (UNDP) *Human Development Report* (produzido anualmente desde 1990) e em *A Proposal for a Comprehensive Development Framework* do World Bank (Wolfensohn, 1999).

Em uma avaliação ideal do desenvolvimento, o progresso deveria ser medido pelos avanços humanos e ambientais, antes de considerar indicadores intermediários, tal como o PIB. Contudo, faltam bons dados de qualidade para construir fortes indicadores do progresso humano e ambiental e, conseqüentemente, baseia-se pesadamente no PIB. Suplementamos de análises com índices de sustentabilidade de desenvolvimento e ambiental, tendo em mente sérias limitações de dados em algumas variáveis. Falta de dados consistentes na incidência da pobreza, internacionalmente comparáveis e ao longo do tempo, forçou-nos a excluir um componente da redução da pobreza em nosso índice de desenvolvimento humano. Contudo, documentamos, quando possível, o progresso na diminuição da pobreza e o impacto das políticas de crescimento e desenvolvimento sobre a pobreza (ver também Dollar & Kraay, 2000; Ravallion & Chen, 1997; World Bank, 2000i). O trabalho de futuro deveria melhorar o escopo e a base empírica desses índices e expandir a discussão para outras dimensões, inclusive bem-estar cultural.

A Tabela 1.1 mostra as correlações entre os componentes dos três indicadores do progresso desde 1981: desenvolvimento humano, crescimento de renda e sustentabilidade ambiental. Ele mostra que o crescimento do PIB está relacionado:

- Positivamente, com redução da pobreza, desigualdade de renda, mortalidade infantil e aumento na expectativa de vida, com consideráveis diferenças de força.
- Negativamente, com o declínio das emissões de dióxido de carbono, e, positivamente, com o declínio da poluição da água.

Outras associações entre crescimento do PIB e mudanças nos componentes da sustentabilidade do desenvolvimento humano e ambiental não são estatisticamente significativas. Essas correlações preliminares sugerem que o crescimento do PIB é indicador de crescimento crucial, ainda que parcial, como quando é indevidamente associado a certos aspectos do desenvolvimento humano e em tempos que é associado com o aumento de dano ambiental.

Easterly (1999a) aplicou várias técnicas a um amplo conjunto de indicadores de qualidade de vida, incluindo testes de relacionamentos causais. Ele descobriu que menos de 10% dos 81 indicadores examinados melhoraram com o crescimento. Uma fração similar deteriorou com o crescimen-

Um passo rumo a medidas de desenvolvimento melhores e mais amplas

Tabela 1.1 – Correlações de Medidas de Desenvolvimento, 1981-1998

Medida de desenvolvimento	Desenvolvimento humano					Crescimento de renda	Sustentabilidade ambiental		
	Diminuição da pobreza	Aumento da alfabetização	Diminuição da mortalidade infantil	Aumento da expectativa de vida	Diminuição da desigualdade de renda	Crescimento do PIB	Diminuição da emissão de dióxido de carbono	Aumento do reflorestamento	Diminuição da poluição da água
Desenvolvimento Humano									
Diminuição da pobreza	1,00	*-0,40*	0,18	0,14	*0,44*	*0,52*	*-0,45*	-0,23	0,28
		27	28	28	20	27	27	26	22
Aumento da alfabetização		1,00	*0,15*	-0,19	-0,23	0,03	-0,14	0,15	*-0,21*
			115	115	41	89	102	94	72
Diminuição da mortalidade infantil			1,00	*0,54*	*0,28*	*0,20*	*-0,20*	-0,12	-0,13
				146	43	104	121	107	81
Aumento na expectativa de vida				1,00	*0,54*	*0,17*	*-0,16*	-0,15	-0,05
					43	104	121	107	81
Diminuição na desigualdade de renda					1,00	*0,34*	*-0,33*	-0,20	*-0,32*
						39	41	41	37
Crescimento da Renda									
Crescimento do PIB						1,00	*-0,53*	-0,06	*0,33*
							100	81	65
Sustentabilidade Ambiental									
Diminuição das emissões de dióxido de carbono							1,00	*0,27*	*-0,38*
								87	70
Aumento do reflorestamento								1,00	-0,14
									70
Diminuição da poluição da água									1,00

Nota: Os dois valores em cada célula são correlações de coeficiente em numerosos países. Entradas no itálico/negrito são significativas ao nível de 10%, ou melhor.
Fontes: World Bank (2000c); cálculos dos autores.

to, e muitas não mostraram nenhuma associação significativa com o crescimento (Figura 1.1). Essas descobertas fortalecem a hipótese para a ampliação das medidas em desenvolvimento.

É muito importante notar que os relacionamentos discutidos anteriormente estão entre *crescimento* de renda e *mudanças* na sustentabilidade do desenvolvimento humano e ambiental. Nos relacionamentos, na maioria dos casos, são muito mais fortes com *níveis* de renda e indicadores, particularmente para a indicação do desenvolvimento humano (Dasgupta, 1993; Fedderke & Klitgaard, 1998; Kakwani, 1993; Sen, 1994) (World Bank, 2000i). O estudo de Easterly também observa essa discrepância, tornando hipótese que análises de campo dos níveis de renda podem captar tendências de longo prazo que não são discerníveis na análise de períodos mais curtos, e que o crescimento pode levar a melhorias no desenvolvimento humano, com longos e variáveis atrasos. De modo alternativo, fatores nacionais específicos, tais como doações, locação e infra-estrutura social, poderiam ser determinantes dominantes dos níveis tanto da renda como dos indicadores do desenvolvimento humano. Nesse caso, as correlações de campo entre renda e indicadores de qualidade de vida precisariam ser qualificados.

Figura 1.1 – Crescimento do PIB e Mudanças na Qualidade de Vida, nas Décadas de 1960 e 1990

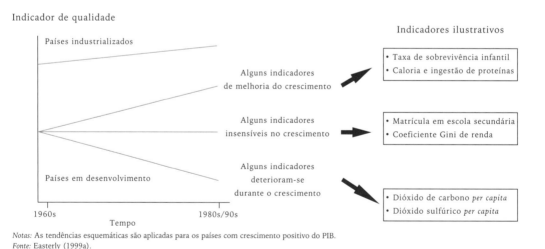

Notas: As tendências esquemáticas são aplicadas para os países com crescimento positivo do PIB.
Fonte: Easterly (1999a).

O Registro do Desenvolvimento

O progresso em algumas áreas do desenvolvimento humano, especialmente em alongar a vida das pessoas e aumentar a alfabetização, tem sido considerável ao longo das décadas de 1960 a 1990, um período sobre o qual alguns dados estão disponíveis. Contudo, muitos outros aspectos de vida qualitativos atrasaram, como, por exemplo, um aumento sustentado e firme nas rendas, na redução da pobreza, ganhos igualitários e qualidade ambiental.

Desenvolvimento Humano

Um crescimento robusto da economia é acompanhado por melhorias nas medidas do desenvolvimento humano, tais como maior alfabetização e expectativa de vida. A associação ampla é vista na Figura 1.2.

Em geral, os ganhos no desenvolvimento humano no decorrer das quatro décadas passadas foram enormes em algumas áreas – em parte refletindo melhorias tecnológicas – e modestas em outras. As taxas de mortalidade infantil e de analfabetismo adulto caíram drasticamente quase no mundo todo.

O progresso no aumento de rendas e a redução da pobreza foram misturados, baseados nos dados e estimativas disponíveis (Figura 1.3). No mundo em desenvolvimento, o índice de incidência de pobreza, definido como a proporção de pessoas com uma renda de menos de US$ 1 por dia, baseada

Figura 1.2 – Mudança no Desenvolvimento Humano e Crescimento de Renda, 1981-1998

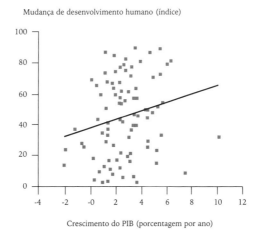

Nota: r = 0,22; p < 0,05; n = 89. Os dados são para 89 países em desenvolvimento. Controle para renda *per capita* em 1981 fornece um padrão mais forte, com coeficiente de correlação de 0,33.
Fontes: World Bank (2000c); cálculos dos autores.

Figura 1.3 – Taxas de Pobreza e Número de Pobres, em Anos Seletos

Índice de incidência de pobreza

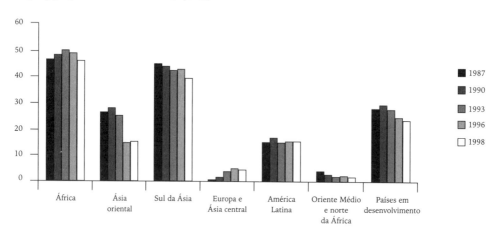

Número de pobres

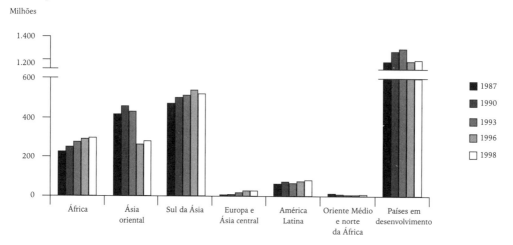

Nota: Baseado nas taxas de valores de paridade em 1993. Os valores de 1998 são estimativos. A pobreza é definida como renda de menos de US$ 1 por dia.
Fonte: World Bank (1999d).

na Paridade do Poder Aquisitivo (PPP) de 1993, decresceu de 28,3% em 1987 para 24% em 1998. A Ásia oriental e a região do Pacífico mostraram a mais ampla melhoria, particularmente a China nos meados da década de 1990. As melhorias foram modestas nas regiões do Oriente Médio, África do Norte e sul da Ásia. As taxas de pobreza permaneceram teimosamente altas

na África subsaariana, na América Latina e no Caribe, e aumentaram de modo notável na Europa e na Ásia central. Geralmente, a diminuição da taxa de pobreza não poderia acompanhar a marcha do crescimento populacional, e o número de pobres no mundo em desenvolvimento fora da China aumentou mais ou menos 106 milhões entre 1987 e 1998 (World Bank, 1999c).

No fim do século XX, a incidência de pobreza aumentou em muitas partes do mundo. Em particular, nos países da Ásia oriental diretamente afetados pelas crises financeiras de 1997 e a conseqüente lentidão dos reveses do crescimento experimentados na redução da pobreza conseguida durante seu período de crescimento rápido (World Bank, 2000f). Ainda maior é o aumento da pobreza nas economias de transição da Europa e Ásia central, onde, recentemente, como em 1987, a pobreza e a renda desiguais foram ambas extremamente baixas. A análise dos dados mostram-nos um enorme aumento no número de pobres como resultado dos declínios sustentados na saída econômica, piorando as distribuições de renda (Milanovic, 1997) (Figura 1.4).

Degradação Ambiental

O impacto no crescimento econômico sobre as condições ambientais tem sido confuso, constituindo um problema sério. Em muitas instâncias,

Figura 1.4 – Incidência de Pobreza em Economias de Transição Seletas, 1987-1988 e 1993-1995

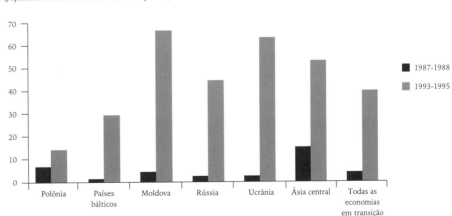

Nota: A linha de pobreza de US$ 4 por dia é consideravelmente mais alta que aquela encontrada em qualquer outra parte.
Fonte: Milanovic (1997).

O REGISTRO DE UM DESENVOLVIMENTO CONFUSO

o crescimento do PIB e rendas mais altas estão associados com melhor saneamento e qualidade da água, tanto quanto os investimentos em tecnologias menos poluentes. Mas o crescimento também está relacionado a aumentos em emissões de partículas de dióxido de carbono.[2] Com pesos iguais para as mudanças nos indicadores de qualidade da água e do ar, e do desmatamento, entre 1981 e 1998 o crescimento de renda foi associado com deterioração ambiental e esgotamento de recursos naturais, como na Figura 1.5.

Entre 1990 e 1995, a *taxa* de desmatamento diminuiu na maioria das regiões em desenvolvimento, mas a cobertura de florestas já estava desaparecendo rapidamente. A camada de florestas aumentou apenas nos países de alta renda e na Europa e na Ásia central. Não é claro o quanto da melhoria no último é o resultado de uma ação ambiental combinada.

Entre 1980 e 1995, as emissões de dióxido de carbono total, assim como *per capita*, aumentou nos grupos de renda e regiões. Apenas a África sub-saariana, provavelmente em decorrência da estagnação econômica geral, não experimentou um aumento da produção de dióxido de carbono. A Ásia oriental teve o mais rápido desmatamento e as mais altas emissões de dióxido de carbono *per capita*, sugerindo um conflito entre crescimento e desenvolvimento sustentável (World Bank, 2000c).

E, em grande parte do mundo em desenvolvimento, a qualidade ambiental está muito pior do que os indicadores retratam. A qualidade do ar piorou, enquanto as rendas aumentaram.[3] A exposição a altos níveis de

Figura 1.5 – Mudanças Ambientais *versus* Crescimento de Renda, 1981-1998

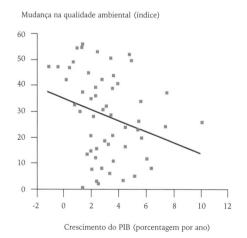

Nota: r = 0,27; p < 0,05; n = 56. Os dados são para 56 países em desenvolvimento. Controle da renda *per capita* de 1981 resulta num modelo parecido e um mesmo valor para o coeficiente de correlação (-0,27).
Fontes: World Bank (2000c); cálculos dos autores.

poluição do ar, ou seja, o total de partículas suspensas, dióxido sulfúrico e dióxido de nitrogênio, representa a maior ameaça à saúde humana. Em Delhi, uma das cidades mais poluídas do mundo, o total de partículas suspensas era quatro vezes maior que o nível identificado como seguro pela Organização Mundial de Saúde (OMS) (World Bank, 1999d). Para os níveis de partículas em cidades escolhidas, ver a Figura 1.6.

O custo humano da deterioração ambiental é vacilante. Escassos suprimentos de água, saneamento inadequado, poluição do ar interno, poluição do ar urbano, malária e resíduos químicos agroindustriais e desperdício contam para uma estimativa de um quinto do total de doenças e morte prematura no mundo em desenvolvimento – baseado em uma medida padronizada de resultados de saúde-incapacidade, regulou anos de vida, ou DALYs. Para a África, escassos suprimentos de água, saneamento inadequado e poluição do ar interno contam para 29,5% da carga de doenças, uma parte maior do que a atribuída à desnutrição, 26% (Lvovsky et al. 1999).

A poluição do ar é alarmantemente alta em muitas cidades dos países em desenvolvimento

Figura 1.6 – Total de Partículas Suspensas, Cidades Selecionadas, no Início da Década de 1990

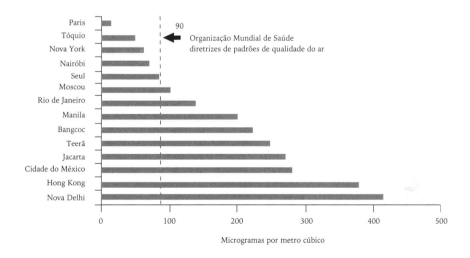

Nota: A maioria dos dados é para 1995. A figura para Nova York refere-se a 1990.
Fonte: World Bank (1997i, 2000c).

Crescimento da Renda, Desigualdade e Volatilidade

O progresso a longo prazo do crescimento da renda no mundo tem sido muito irregular. A Figura 1.7 mostra as tendências na renda *per capita* nas regiões em desenvolvimento e nos países industrializados desde 1975. A Ásia oriental aumentou os padrões de vida de modo significativo, ao passo que a África subsaariana conheceu a tendência oposta. A ampla variação nas taxas de crescimento ao nível das economias individuais pode ser vista na Figura 1.8. Das 15 economias de crescimento mais acelerado, oito situam-se na Ásia oriental. Muitas daquelas no outro espectro são países afetados por guerras civis e outros deslocamentos.

A julgar pelas taxas de crescimento habituais, oprimidas por resultados dos países, 1980 foi uma década perdida para o mundo em desenvolvimento. O quadro parece melhor quando as taxas de crescimento são pesadas pela população, porque as diminuições entre países de renda média, especialmente na América Latina, pesam menos, e os aumentos nos maiores países de baixa renda, China e Índia, pesam mais. Na década de 1990, a

Figura 1.7 – Adquirindo Paridade do Poder Aquisitivo do Produto Interno Bruto (PIB) *per capita*, 1975-1998

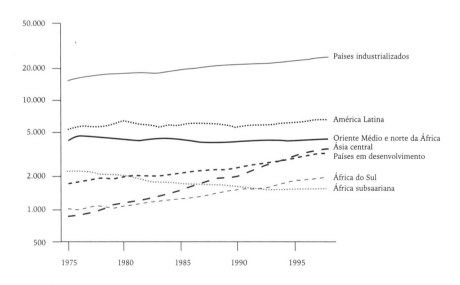

Nota: A Europa e a Ásia central estão excluídas devido à disponibilidade de dados.
Fonte: Dados do World Bank.

Figura 1.8 – Crescimento no PIB *per capita*, Economias Seletas, 1975-1998

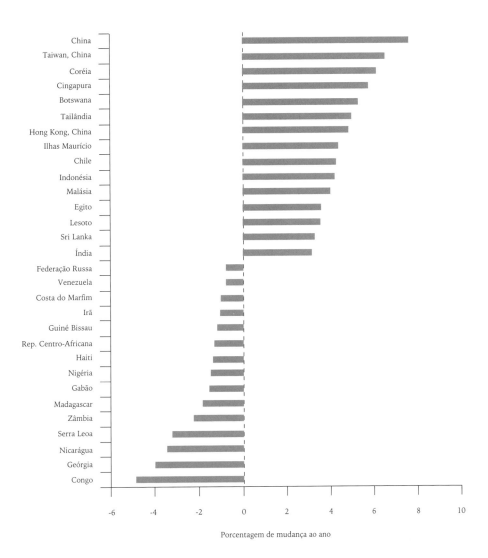

Fontes: World Bank (2000c); cálculos dos autores.

diferença entre renda ponderada e população ponderada agregada à taxa de crescimento para os países em desenvolvimento estreitou-se, ao passo que o crescimento melhorou nos países de renda média na América Latina.

Desigualdade de Renda. Nesse quadro de crescimento geral de renda, também é importante que se considere como a renda estava sendo compartilhada, pela observação das mudanças na desigualdade de renda. Várias dimensões na desigualdade de renda são relevantes neste ponto: entre países, mediante a administração doméstica dentro dos países e dentro das administrações domésticas. Como foi notado no World Bank (2000i), a brecha entre a renda média dos vinte países mais ricos e a média para os vinte mais pobres dobraram nos últimos quarenta anos – para mais de trinta vezes.

As exigências de dados para a estimativa de distribuição da renda *per capita* no mundo são onerosas e os dados disponíveis sofrem de uma fragilidade aguda. Dito isso, Dikhanov & Ward (2000) estimaram tais distribuições para 1988 e 1993 e descobriram que a desigualdade geral da renda *per capita* no mundo aumentou de um coeficiente Gini de 0,63 para 0,67 (ver também Cornia, 1999).

Schultz (1998) observou as tendências de desigualdade de renda entre países. Os resultados diferem consideravelmente quando a China está incluída na análise. A desigualdade de renda entre países aumentou de 1960 a 1968, permaneceu alta durante 1976, e declinou gradualmente depois disso, terminando com uma alta ligeiramente maior em 1989 do que em 1960. Quando a China é excluída, o declínio na desigualdade entre países desde 1976 desaparece. A extensão da análise durante 1994 para um conjunto ligeiramente menor de países confirmou tais tendências.

Utilizando dados comparáveis sobre a renda, os coeficientes Gini para 45 países desde o início dos anos 60 ao começo da década de 1990, Deininger & Squire (1996) não encontraram nenhuma tendência geral na desigualdade dentro do país, que permaneceu aproximadamente a mesma em 29 países, cresceu em oito e caiu em oito. Para uma comparação diferente entre o início da década de 1980 e o início da década de 1990, a desigualdade cresceu em 19 países e diminuiu em 24 (Figura 1.9). Entre os países nos quais a desigualdade cresceu, estão aqueles com grandes populações: Brasil, China e Índia. População ponderada, a desigualdade média para os 43 países da amostragem aumentou mais ou menos 0,52% ao ano na década de 1980 e início da década de 1990.[4]

Volatilidade do Crescimento. As flutuações econômicas parecem afetar os pobres desproporcionalmente, mas é possível que o impacto seja particularmente severo nos países em que as redes de segurança social são, ou sejam, tipicamente menos desenvolvidas (Furman & Stiglitz, 1998). Declínios no crescimento econômico eram diretamente associados com

A QUALIDADE DO CRESCIMENTO

Nenhuma tendência geral na desigualdade interna dos países

Figura 1.9 – Desigualdade de Renda Dentro dos Países, nas Décadas de 1980 e 1990

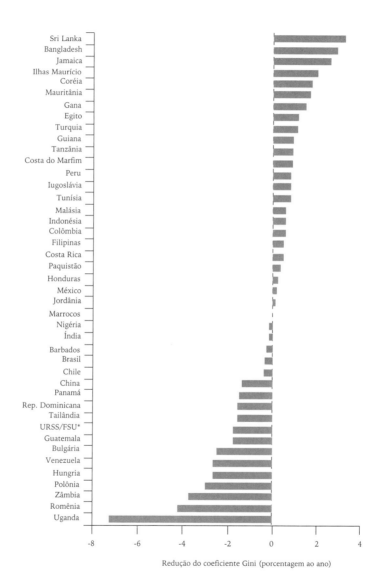

* FSU: Antiga União Soviética.
Nota: A quantidade diagramada é a redução dos coeficientes Gini de renda no início da década de 1990 sobre o início da década de 1980, nos declínios percentuais ano a ano. Valores negativos indicam uma alta na desigualdade.
Fonte: Deininger & Squire (1996).

aumentos abruptos da pobreza na Europa oriental e mais recentemente na Ásia oriental. Baixas econômicas parecem ter efeitos adversos duradouros sobre a economia. Os estudos sugerem que maiores flutuações nas taxas de crescimento estão associadas com média mais baixa de crescimento.[5] A volatilidade do crescimento pareceria importar.

Na média, a volatilidade do crescimento estima-se ter declinado na década de 1980 em decorrência de certas medidas para a maioria dos grupos de países (exceto países de renda média, principalmente devido a crises de débito na América Latina), comparado com a década de 1970, quando os choques petrolíferos ocorreram. O quadro é mais confuso na década de 1990. Estima-se que a volatilidade declinou para a América Latina, o Oriente Médio, a África do Norte e o sul da Ásia, mas aumentou ligeiramente para os países industrializados e para a Ásia oriental (Figura 1.10).

A Europa em desenvolvimento e a Ásia central tiveram especialmente crescimento mais volátil do que as outras regiões na década de 1990, comparada com a de 1980.

Os países em desenvolvimento parecem ter experimentado uma volatilidade mais alta do que os países industrializados. Easterly et al. (1999)

Figura 1.10 – Volatilidade das Taxas de Crescimento do PIB, por Década

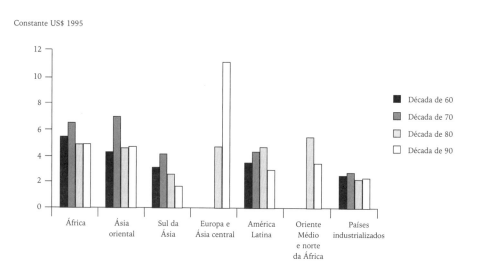

Nota: A volatilidade em uma década foi computada tomando-se um desvio-padrão das taxas de crescimento na década para cada país e a média imponderada através dos países no grupo.
Fontes: World Bank (2000c); cálculos dos autores.

exploraram as determinantes do aumento de volatilidade dos países, descobrindo que:

- a abertura para o mercado e a volatilidade dos fluxos de capital estão associadas com o aumento da volatilidade de crescimento;
- melhorias nos indicadores do desenvolvimento financeiro estão associadas com volatilidade mais baixa;
- restrições na política a partir das limitações institucionais e do setor financeiro revelam insuficiências que contribuem para a variabilidade de resultados;
- flexibilidade de renda não parece ser um fator importante.

Crescimento e Bem-Estar

A Tabela 1.2 divide os países em desenvolvimento em três grupos, com base em suas taxas de crescimento do PIB *per capita*: países de alto crescimento, aqueles com taxas de crescimento moderadas ou melhorando e países de baixo crescimento.[6] Pela definição aqui utilizada, 13 obtiveram crescimento rápido, 53 alcançaram crescimento moderado e 39 tiveram crescimento baixo. Também por esta definição, os países de crescimento moderado alcançaram melhorias mais consistentes no crescimento. Vários dos indicadores do desenvolvimento humano geralmente melhoraram para os três grupos, com os países de alto crescimento demonstrando as melhorias mais acentuadas. Os países de alto crescimento apresentaram as mais altas e crescentes emissões de dióxido de carbono *per capita*.

Questão de Fatores Externos

Na década de 1990, as sublevações sociais e políticas externa e domesticamente dirigidas, juntamente com as guerras, continuaram a descarrilar o progresso em numerosos países (Collier, 1999; Collier & Hoeffler, 1998) (Tabela 1.3). Questões globais e fronteiriças relacionadas com crises financeiras, pressões da população, trabalho de migração e desastres ambientais continuaram a afetar os resultados internos.

Apesar da diminuição positiva do crescimento populacional, aumentos populacionais em muitos países poderiam solapar os esforços para alcançar um desenvolvimento sustentável. O aquecimento global, a degradação ambiental e a perda de biodiversidade continuam a piorar em um planeta cada vez mais populoso, colocando mais pressão sobre os limitados recursos globais (World Bank, 2000b, e várias edições do *Global Economic Prospects* e *Global Development Finance*).

O quarto de século mais ou menos depois da Segunda Guerra Mundial

O REGISTRO DE UM DESENVOLVIMENTO CONFUSO

Tabela 1.2 – Resultados Desenvolvimentistas por Classe de Crescimento, nas Décadas de 1980 e 1990

(médias imponderadas)

Mudança no indicador: comparando os anos 80 e os anos 90	Unidade	Período	Alto crescimento	Crescimento melhorado ou moderado	Baixo crescimento
Pobreza	Porcentagem com menos de US$ 1 por dia	Anos 90	24,1	31,4	36,9
		Anos 80	31,0	32,1	30,2
Mortalidade infantil	Por mil	Anos 90	29,2	54,3	60,7
		Anos 80	41,0	66,6	71,0
Analfabetismo	Por cento	Anos 90	17,2	31,2	31,4
		Anos 80	22,9	37,6	38,8
Expectativa de vida	Anos	Anos 90	70,0	62,9	59,8
		Anos 80	66,8	60,6	58,4
Emissão de dióxido de carbono	Toneladas *per capita*	Anos 90	2,4	2,3	1,7
		Anos 80	1,5	2,3	1,8
Desmatamento	Porcentagem ao ano	1990-95	0,83	1,05	1,11
		1980-90	1,08	0,65	1,15
Poluição da água	Quilogramas por dia por trabalhador	Anos 90	0,16	0,21	0,21
		Anos 80	0,18	0,21	0,21
Crescimento PIB	Porcentagem ao ano	Anos 90	5,3	4,2	0,3
		Anos 80	6,5	2,3	2,1
Número de países			13	53	39

Nota: Para detalhes referentes à classificação dos países, ver o texto. Algumas variáveis não estão presentes para determinados países. Particularmente dados sobre a pobreza estão apenas disponíveis para um pequeno número de países.
Fontes: World Bank (2000c); cálculos dos autores.

Tabela 1.3 – Questão de Fatores Externos para Resultados Internos, Exemplos de 1977-1999

	Crises financeiras	Desastres naturais	Conflitos	Desastres causados pelo homem
Região ou país em crise	Ásia oriental Rússia Brasil	Bangladesh América Central	Albânia Bósnia Congo Iugoslávia Ruanda Serra Leoa	Indonésia (incêndio florestal)
Impacto	Aumento da pobreza a curto prazo	Perda de vidas humanas e capital físico e natural	Destruição do capital humano e social	Aumento da pobreza a longo prazo

Fonte: Compilação dos autores.

marcou um período de crescimento rápido e firme, tanto para os países industrializados como para os em desenvolvimento, e o meio ambiente econômico esteve relativamente livre de maiores choques. O meio ambiente econômico internacional mudou drasticamente em 1973, com o choque do preço do petróleo e o fim do sistema de Bretton Woods de fixação de taxas de câmbio entre os principais países industrializados. As décadas subseqüentes assistiram a um declínio agudo no crescimento da produtividade nos países industrializados, inflação alta e taxas de juros, ciclos de larga amplitude nos preços das mercadorias e taxas de câmbio das principais moedas correntes.

Tem-se discutido que o baixo registro de crescimento da maioria dos países em desenvolvimento (com algumas exceções, principalmente na Ásia oriental) depois de 1973 e na década de 1990 foi decorrência, primariamente, da lentidão do crescimento nos países industrializados (Easterly, 1999b). Enquanto esse constituiu um fator significativo, o registro dos países em desenvolvimento que prosperaram durante esse período, tal como na Ásia oriental, sugere que a política doméstica, o governo e as instituições também influenciam nos resultados. O dano causado por choques e conflitos depende das instituições estabelecidas e sua efetividade no fortalecimento do governo, dos direitos civis, das regras de direito, dos programas sociais e redes de segurança (Collier, 1999; Collier & Hoeffler, 1998; Easterly et al., 1999; Rodrik, 1998 e 1999).

O meio ambiente econômico global sofreu uma nova mudança significativa na década de 1990, tornando-se de maior utilidade para o desenvolvimento em alguns aspectos, e de menor em outros (ver várias edições do *Global Economic Prospects* do World Bank). A demanda de importação pela Organização de Cooperação e Devenvolvimento Econômicos (OECD) foi menos volátil na década de 1990 do que nas anteriores, em parte devido aos ciclos da América do Norte, Europa e Japão já não estarem mais sincronizados, e em parte razão do crescente peso dos países em desenvolvimento, especialmente a Ásia oriental, no comércio mundial. Graças à restrição monetária e ao progresso na consolidação fiscal, o investimento real e as taxas de inflação nos principais países da OECD caíram na década de 1990, e a volatilidade nas taxas de câmbio das principais moedas correntes foi consideravelmente menor em relação ao pronunciado ciclo do dólar da década de 1980.

Particularmente importante foi a relativa afirmação nos países em desenvolvimento nos termos de comércio com os países industriais, especialmente nos preços das mercadorias primárias não energéticas. Os países não exportadores de petróleo conheceram uma grave deterioração nos seus termos de comércio desde a metade da década de 1970 até o início da década de 1990. Contudo, para a grande parte da década de 1990, os preços das mercadorias não petrolíferas permaneceram firmes e o declínio desde 1997 tem sido menos abrupto que nos primeiros ciclos de preço.

Embora os preços de exportação sejam muito mais voláteis para mercadorias do que para produtos manufaturados, os preços das mercadorias foram menos voláteis na década de 1990 do que na década de 1980 por 22 de 30 mercadorias-chave (World Bank, 2000a; várias questões do *Commodities Quarterly*).

O forte crescimento no comércio mundial ultrapassou agudamente o crescimento na produção mundial durante 1998. O comércio internacional do meio ambiente permaneceu liberal em seu conjunto, com o aumento de multilateralidade, não obstante o surgimento de práticas questionáveis como o *antidumping*. E havia um crescimento fenomenal nos fluxos de capital privado para os países em desenvolvimento, embora somente para uns poucos.

A crise financeira da Ásia oriental revelou que, assim como as oportunidades, que cresceram enormemente, o mesmo sucedeu com as demandas nas instituições e os custos dos erros. O sucesso num conjunto altamente globalizado requer mecanismos adequados para gerenciar riscos e políticas bem-sucedidas para abertura e competição precisa de estruturas reguladoras e legais efetivas.

Políticas Internas Fazem uma Diferença Fundamental

Subjacente aos resultados variados do desenvolvimento tem sido a efetividade da política, principalmente nas quatro áreas que se seguem: a qualidade e distribuição dos serviços de educação e saúde, o gerenciamento do meio ambiente, o gerenciamento das oportunidades e dos riscos da globalização e a efetividade do governo. Estes elos são analisados nos capítulos seguintes.

Investir no Povo

Nenhum país conseguiu desenvolvimento sustentado sem investir substancial e eficientemente na educação e na saúde de seu povo. Países em desenvolvimento geralmente vêm investindo mais recursos públicos na educação e muitas regiões ampliaram os gastos na década de 1990 (Figura 1.11). Os gastos públicos com educação declinaram na Ásia oriental, no Oriente Médio e na África do Norte. Há evidência que na Ásia oriental a divisão dos gastos privados está em alta. Dados de campo dos gastos com a saúde estão disponíveis apenas para os anos 90, de modo que tendências a longo prazo não são conhecidas.

O que acontece com a divisão dos gastos sociais em países submetidos a ajustamento e austeridade fiscal? Análises sobre a questão têm sido divididas. O Banco Mundial (1992) concluiu que as divisões permanecem into-

Figura 1.11 – Gastos Públicos com Educação por Região, em Anos Seletos

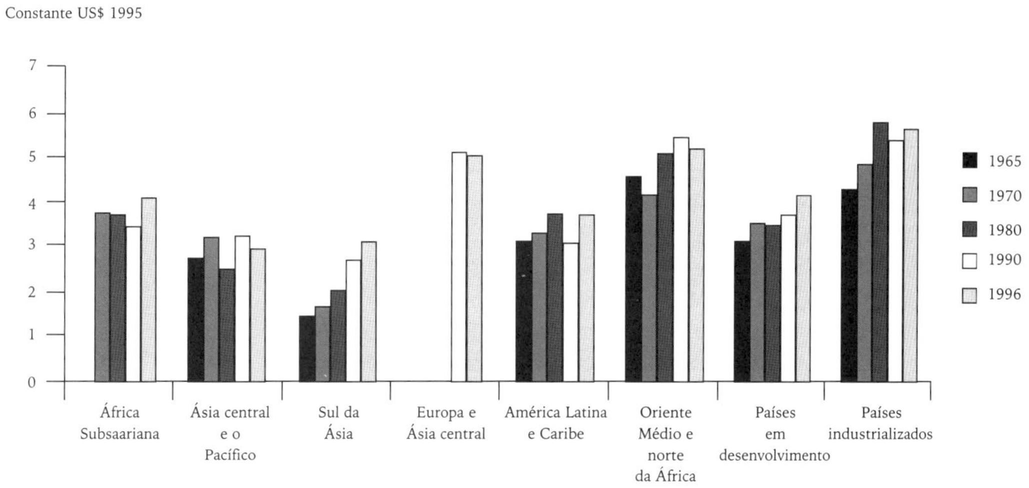

Constante US$ 1995

Fonte: World Bank (2000c).

cadas, ao passo que Corbo et al. (1992) afirmaram que as dotações para a educação declinaram. Estudo recente do Fundo Monetário Internacional (FMI, 1998) dos países de baixa renda submetendo-se a ajuste descobriu que, geralmente, as dotações para a educação e gastos com saúde têm sido protegidos. Gastos privados são também importantes nos fundos de serviços sociais, especialmente na Ásia oriental, onde sua dotação aumentou com o crescimento econômico. Mas o gasto público nem sempre produz bons resultados. Aqueles dependem da distribuição e da qualidade dos gastos públicos e dos incentivos para maior gasto privado. Estas questões são examinadas no Capítulo 3.

Administrando o Meio Ambiente

Sabemos que as políticas governamentais negligenciaram o meio ambiente, mas não temos medidas-padrão para avaliar as políticas ambientais de um país. Um indicador desenvolvido recentemente, *poupanças genuínas*, mensura a taxa de poupança depois do cálculo para investimento no capital humano, depreciação de bens produzidos e esgotamento e degradação do ambiente (World Bank, 1999f, p.175-7). Tais medidas ainda são experimentais e refletem tanto as políticas como os resultados.

Temos observado o progresso em acordos alcançados envolvendo questões ambientais. Contudo, a partir disso, obtemos somente um sentido de

comprometimento dos governos de terem completado um perfil ambiental de um país, formulando estratégias de preservação e biodiversidade e participação nos tratados globais. Tais medidas parecem ser apenas fragilmente relacionadas com os resultados ambientais. Precisamos de meios mais eficazes na captação das políticas nacionais para um desenvolvimento ambiental sustentável.

Criando Políticas de Boas Condições de Mercado

Abertura e Liberalização. A abertura aumentou nos países em desenvolvimento na década de 1990. A razão de comércio para o PIB aumentou em todas as regiões em desenvolvimento. Níveis de proteção comercial declinaram na maioria das regiões, auxiliados por rodadas sucessivas de negociações comerciais multilaterais. As tarifas médias caíram na década de 1990, agudamente em muitos casos (Figura 1.12). Barreiras não tarifárias também foram reduzidas de modo significativo na maioria das regiões, excetuando-se a África subsaariana (Rodrik, 1999; UNCTAD, 1994).

A abertura para o capital também cresceu drasticamente em algumas regiões. Um índice de controles financeiros mostra um acentuado declínio na década de 1990, seguindo-se a um aumento abrupto na década anterior (Capítulo 5). A liberalização também ficou assegurada nos mercados domésticos, já que os governos se tornaram mais desejosos de confiar nos mercados e de aumentar os incentivos para a iniciativa privada mediante a privatização de indústrias e levantaram outras restrições na comercialização e distribuição. Muitos países exportadores de matéria-prima na África estão liberalizando as alfândegas, permitindo muito mais passes livres para os preços das mercadorias internacionais para os produtores (Akiyama, 1995).

Estabilidade Macroeconômica. Dois refletores do gerenciamento econômico freqüentemente utilizados são a taxa prêmio de câmbio no mercado paralelo e déficits governamentais. A Figura 1.13 mostra que, na maioria dos países, os prêmios do mercado paralelo declinaram abruptamente na década de 1990. Depois dos aumentos abruptos na década de 1980, os déficits governamentais declinaram na maioria das regiões, exceto na Europa e na Ásia central. Em parte como um resultado, a inflação baixou na maioria dos países em desenvolvimento.

Resultados de Crescimento e Desempenhos Políticos. A Tabela 1.4 mostra os perfis políticos para três classes de crescimento e para as décadas de 1980 e 1990. Esses perfis não requerem que se estabeleça a direção do elo entre políticas e resultados, mas os padrões e tendências são dignos de nota. Muitos dos trabalhos prévios mostraram o impacto das políticas sobre o crescimento (um sumário bibliográfico de observação está disponível sob

A QUALIDADE DO CRESCIMENTO

Barreiras comerciais declinam na maioria das regiões

Figura 1.12 – Barreiras Comerciais, Regiões Selecionadas, 1984-1993

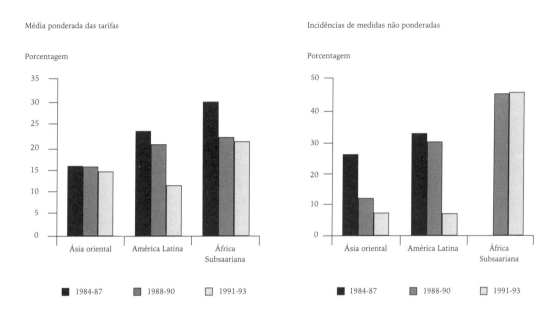

Fonte: Rodrik (1999).

solicitação). Embora algumas políticas de boas condições de mercado permaneçam contenciosas, muitos países em desenvolvimento fizeram significativos esforços para adotá-las na década de 1990. Déficits de orçamento médio foram mais baixos para todos os grupos na década de 1990 – abruptamente para os grupos de crescimento alto e moderado. Todos os três grupos apresentaram tarifas significativamente baixas e um comércio mais alto para a razão PIB na década de 1990 do que na de 1980. Os três grupos estavam mais abertos para transações de cálculo de capital na década de 1990 – o grupo de alto crescimento de forma mais cautelosa. Os sistemas financeiros domésticos também foram geralmente menos reprimidos na década de 1990, em relação à de 1970 – novamente o alto crescimento de modo mais cauteloso em relação ao grupo de crescimento moderado. Os de crescimento mais rápido apresentaram maiores profundidades financeiras, medida pela razão M2-para-PIB, e políticas macroeconômicas mais prudentes, em parte evidente no aumento de reservas. E eles tinham maiores taxas sobre as medidas do governo. Há uma imensa bibliografia empírica sobre os elos dessas políticas de resultado.

Figura 1.13 – Premium do Mercado Paralelo, nas Décadas de 1970 a 1990

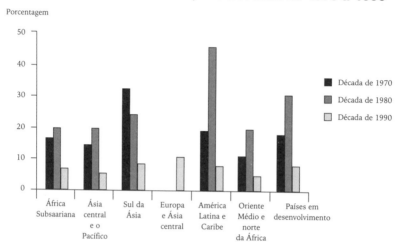

Nota: Os valores traçados são (taxa de mercado paralelo/taxa oficial-1) como uma porcentagem, para uma unidade de moeda corrente estrangeira em unidades de moeda corrente local.
Fontes: Easterly & Yu (2000); World Bank (2000c).

Questões Cruciais para a Ação

O mundo em desenvolvimento continua a ir em frente na década de 1990. O progresso na política foi substancial: reduzindo déficits fiscais, investindo mais na educação, baixando as barreiras de comércio e investimentos e desmantelando os controles de preços domésticos na indústria e na agricultura. O registro foi mais confuso quanto aos resultados do desenvolvimento. Mas tanto o registro da década de 1990 como o registro a longo prazo confirmam que essas ações acompanham a melhoria do crescimento econômico. Eles também corroboram o elo entre crescimento econômico e redução da pobreza. Assim, no conjunto, o mundo em desenvolvimento recuperou-se dos reveses da década de 1980, mas ambas, a profundidade e a abrangência da recuperação, deixaram muito a desejar.

O registro sugere igualmente que as ações, governamentais e outras, para afetar a qualidade e a sustentabilidade do crescimento retardaram. Os acontecimentos na Ásia oriental, Europa, Ásia central e por toda parte sublinham a fragilidade dos avanços para reduzir a pobreza e atingir um desenvolvimento sustentável. Os números de pobres continuam a aumentar e atualmente estima-se que 1,2 bilhão vivem em estado de pobreza absoluta, com menos de US$ 1 por dia. A incidência da pobreza é altamente sensível a mudanças na distribuição de renda e ao crescimento populacional. Assim, políticas que afetam o crescimento amplo e eqüitativo e o crescimento populacional merecem uma atenção considerável.

Tabela 1.4 – Desempenho Político por Classe de Crescimento, nas Décadas de 1980 e 1990

(médias imponderadas)

Mudança no indicador: comparando os anos 80 e 90	Unidade	Período	Alto crescimento	Crescimento melhor ou moderado	Baixo crescimento
Excedente do orçamento	Porcentagem PIB	Anos 90	-1,8	-1,4	3,4
		Anos 80	-4,2	-2,9 -	-4,7
Taxa de tarifa efetiva	por cento	Anos 90	22,7	25,4	18,3
		Anos 80	29,1	31,9	22,7
Comércio/PIB	por cento	Anos 90	92,1	77,0	70,2
		Anos 80	82,0	71,0	59,9
Aberturas das contas de capital	Índice	1996	2,4	3,0	3,1
		1988	1,7	1,9	1,7
Repressão financeira	Índice	1996	3,6	3,2	4,0
		1973	5,9	6,8	4,5
M2/PIB	por cento	Anos 90	55,4	36,9	28,6
		Anos 80	42,8	34,6	28,4
Reservas internacionais	Meses de importação	Anos 90	4,2	3,9	2,9
		Anos 80	3,1	2,8	2,4
Regra do direito	Índice	1997-98	0,2	-0,2	-0,7
Controle da corrupção	Índice	1997-98	-0,1	-0,2	-0,6
Gastos com educação	Porcentagem do PNB	Anos 90	3,7	4,4	4,3
		Anos 80	3,6	4,2	4,4
Ação ambiental	Índice 0-1	Internacional	0,89	0,95	0,88
	Índice 0-1	Nacional	0,89	0,86	0,65
Número de países			13	53	39

Nota: Para detalhes relacionados com a classificação dos países, ver o texto. Faltam algumas variáveis para determinados países. Em particular, as variáveis de taxa de tarifa efetiva e repressão financeira estão disponíveis apenas para um pequeno número de países. As variáveis são descritas no Anexo 1.
Fontes: World Bank (2000c); cálculos dos autores.

Os relacionamentos entre objetivos do desenvolvimento e instrumentos políticos foram analisados com detalhamento considerável na bibliografia do desenvolvimento. O Anexo ao Capítulo 1 inclui um conjunto de coeficientes de correlação para objetivos e políticas, com espírito de prover os dados básicos. Como correlações, nada dizem sobre a direção da causalidade ou dos mecanismos. Contudo, a combinação mostrou-se significativa e digna de investigação posterior como hipótese. Igualmente importante são as combinações plausíveis que não são significativas com o sinal esperado. Muitas das relações hipotéticas são tomadas nos Capítulos 3 a 6, e no Capítulo 2, que elabora uma estrutura básica.

O REGISTRO DE UM DESENVOLVIMENTO CONFUSO

Neste ponto, emolduramos os relacionamentos em forma de questões que motivaram este estudo:

- Será que as melhorias observadas no capital humano são suficientes para sustentar o crescimento em países que experimentaram crescimento acelerado na década de 1990?
- Será que o aumento do capital humano nos países de crescimento lento é suficiente para propalar melhor e mais rápido crescimento em um futuro próximo?
- Será que a deterioração do capital natural reduzirá o potencial para crescimento futuro, especialmente entre os países pobres?
- Será que a degradação do capital natural está se tornando um obstáculo sério para a melhoria do bem-estar da população?
- Poderão os riscos da globalização financeira ser gerenciados de modo a diminuir a volatilidade do crescimento e melhorar sua sustentabilidade?
- Até que ponto é séria a maneira de governar para o processo de crescimento e resultados, e como o progresso pode ser feito no controle da corrupção?

Os capítulos que se seguem fornecem vislumbres para estas questões, se não respostas.

O restante desta publicação está organizado da maneira a seguir. O Capítulo 2 fornece uma estrutura analítica para a interpretação da experiência de desenvolvimento desenhada neste capítulo e tira lições sobre a importância do crescimento não distorcido dos bens humanos, naturais e físicos e a significação do bem-estar nos padrões de crescimento alternativo (ver também o Quadro 1 na Visão Geral). O Capítulo 3 explora como os investimentos no povo – na quantidade, na qualidade e na distribuição – podem aumentar diretamente o bem-estar e também tornar os processos de crescimento mais sustentáveis. O Capítulo 4 faz o mesmo quanto aos recursos ambientais e naturais, nos quais o conflito entre crescimento e bem-estar é aparente e o equilíbrio muito mais difícil. O Capítulo 5 revisita a questão da volatilidade do crescimento e os riscos financeiros, e considera os aspectos qualitativos das reformas que tornariam os processos de crescimento mais sustentáveis no cenário globalizado de hoje. Todos os três lados – humano, natural e financeiro – dependem da qualidade do governo geral, que é fundamental para a qualidade e a sustentabilidade dos processos de crescimento. Instituições de governo formais e informais são discutidas no Capítulo 6, com enfoque especial no combate à corrupção. O Capítulo 7 considera uma agenda para a ação.

Por que haverá falha em adotar políticas que se revelaram concretas? É improvável que a falta de entendimento dos agentes dessas políticas seja a razão principal. Mais provável é a dificuldade política de implementar políti-

cas concretas. Grupos de interesse limitam o âmbito das reformas viáveis e abrem um golfo entre o objetivo político e a implementação. Como melhor contrapor-se a estas forças por meio de acentuadas participações e domínio de um governo mais forte constitui um tópico importante não completamente explorado no registro (exceto por uma breve discussão de aspectos escolhidos no Capítulo 6).

Outro tópico crucial são as circunstâncias especiais em face das antigas economias planejadas centralmente enquanto elas lutam para fazer a transição para economias de mercado. Essas economias estão incluídas nas análises quando os dados permitem, e as ilustrações e casos calcados nas experiências delas são utilizados em alguns dos capítulos, especialmente o que trata do governo e anticorrupção (Capítulo 6). Contudo, uma discussão completa das questões para economia de transição está além do escopo deste livro.[7]

Notas

1. Muitos estudos ergueram o ponto de vista multidimensional dos objetivos do desenvolvimento (Dasgupta, 1993; Hicks & Streeten, 1979; Lewis, 1955; Nordhaus & Tobin, 1972; Sengupta & Fox, 1969; Tinbergen & Theil em Hughes-Hallet, 1989). Muitos estudos utilizados multivariam as análises de um amplo número de variáveis econômicas, sociais e políticas (Adelman & Taft-Morris, 1967; Baster, 1972; Morris, 1979; UNRISD, 1970). Alguns índices construídos de qualidade de vida ou desenvolvimento humano (Dasgupta, 1990a; Diewert, 1986; Drewnowski & Scott, 1966; Griliches, 1971; McGranahan, 1972; Ram, 1982a, b; Slottje, 1991). As estruturas em alguns destes trabalhos são tratadas no Capítulo 2.

2. As emissões de dióxido de carbono não têm muito impacto direto na saúde local, mas são importantes no contexto das emissões no efeito estufa e associadas com o problema de mudança global do clima. Igualmente, as emissões de dióxido de carbono são habitualmente associadas com a emissão de outros poluentes do ar, que possuem impacto sobre a saúde local, mas sobre o qual os dados ainda estão menos amplamente disponíveis.

3. Medidas da qualidade do ar para muitas cidades tornaram-se disponíveis apenas na metade da década de 1990. Um relacionamento em forma de U invertido entre poluição e renda *per capita*, a curva ambiental de Kuznets, tem sido estimado para vários tipos de poluentes (Grossman & Krueger, 1995). Contudo, isso não invalida a necessidade de intervenção ambiental porque os momentos decisivos da renda *per capita* para melhoria dos indicadores ambientais são geralmente bem altos. Esta questão é discutida no Capítulo 4.

4. Os dados sobre a distribuição de renda são escassos para os anos mais recentes. Um estudo do Banco Mundial em 29 países avaliou que cinco deles experimentaram o declínio na desigualdade, enquanto quase cinco vezes mais países (24) conheceram o aumento (Buckley, 1999).

O REGISTRO DE UM DESENVOLVIMENTO CONFUSO

5. Por exemplo, uma regressão das taxas médias de crescimento do PIB para 112 países contra a volatilidade das taxas de crescimento do PIB, medida pelo desvio-padrão das taxas de crescimento, permitiu um significativo coeficiente negativo (ver também Ramey & Ramey, 1995).

6. Países de alto crescimento como definidos aqui são aqueles com crescimento da renda *per capita* de mais de 2,3% ao ano, nas décadas de 1980 e 1990, uma taxa que dobra as rendas em trinta anos. O segundo grupo – de crescimento moderado ou melhorado – inclui países que mantiveram um crescimento positivo da renda *per capita* em ambas as décadas, ou melhoraram o crescimento na década de 1990 por pelo menos dois pontos percentuais. Os restantes são classificados como países de baixo crescimento.

7. Ver World Bank (1996b) para um tratamento complexo das questões de transição. Ver também os trabalhos recentes de Åslund (1999); Commander et al. (1999); Kornai (2000); Qian (1999); Stiglitz (1999); e Wyplosz (1999).

CAPÍTULO 2

VALORES, CRESCIMENTO E BEM-ESTAR

A dificuldade reside não nas novas idéias, mas fugindo delas para antigas que ramificam ... em qualquer de nossas mentes.

— John Maynard Keynes, *Teoria Geral do Emprego, Investimento e Dinheiro*

O crescimento econômico rápido tem sido habitualmente considerado o principal indicador do desenvolvimento. Ainda assim, tem havido insatisfação com a utilização da medida do crescimento pelos cômputos nacionais como o Yardstick (ver, por exemplo, Adelman, 1975; Dasgupta, 1993; Dréze & Sen, 1995; Lewis, 1955; Sen, 1988). Mais significativo é o bem-estar que compreende consumo, desenvolvimento humano e sustentabilidade ambiental, e sua qualidade, distribuição e estabilidade. Freqüentemente, o crescimento da renda *per capita* e as melhorias de bem-estar seguem lado a lado. Mas algumas vezes, não.

Amplas divergências entre crescimento e melhorias de bem-estar podem surgir quando o crescimento é volátil e não sustentado. Será que tais divergências entre crescimento e bem-estar podem mudar e ainda crescer quando o crescimento econômico for sustentado? Ou seja, será que os países podem manter crescimento rápido durante prolongados períodos sem aumentos comensurados no bem-estar? Em caso negativo, o foco deveria voltar-se para as políticas que garantem o crescimento sustentado – porque essas políticas iriam igualmente em geral melhorar o bem-estar. Mas, em caso afirmativo, o foco do crescimento deve ser complementado com um exame dos padrões alternativos de crescimento (sustentado).

Neste ponto, a análise focaliza-se em padrões de investimento em três valores-chave: capital físico associado muito próximo ao capital financeiro,[1] capital humano associado muito próximo aos capitais social e natural e o

29

proximamente associado capital ambiental. A tecnologia que afeta a utilização desses valores também importa muito. A hipótese central, que é taxada empiricamente na seqüência, é que promover investimento adequado em todas as formas de capital constitui uma forma de induzir a maior e melhor crescimento e a melhorias no bem-estar. Mas as políticas freqüentemente introduzem distorções que encorajam tanto supra como infra-investimentos em diferentes formas de capital. Exemplos dessas distorções são taxas de investimento artificialmente baixas, subvalorização dos recursos naturais, ou menosprezo da educação básica na política pública. Com o foco principalmente no acúmulo de capital físico, a relativa negligência dos capitais humano e natural não é nenhuma garantia para sustentar o crescimento. Algumas evidências recentes apresentam pouca correlação entre taxas de investimento e taxas de crescimento a curto prazo (Easterly, 1999c). É provável que esforços especiais para encorajar o acúmulo de capital físico imponham amplos custos.

Algumas mudanças políticas na década de 1980 e começo da de 1990 pareceriam ter elevado especialmente a taxa de retorno para o capital físico refletido por explosões de investimento em muitos países, mas essas reformas por si sós não garantiram automaticamente o crescimento sustentado, na medida em que não houve investimentos complementares nos valores humanos e naturais. Além disso, alguns países não geraram crescimento – parcialmente em decorrência de regulamentação errônea (por exemplo, licenças que reduzem os incentivos de investimento), e regulamentação insuficiente (por exemplo, para os mercados financeiros e para lidar com os monopólios).

De modo alternativo, o crescimento induzido por uma expansão dos capitais humano, físico e natural relativamente não distorcida ou equilibrada pode ser sustentado por períodos prolongados.[2] Equilibrada não significa uma expansão igual dos bens, mas, antes, refere-se à acumulação de bens em resposta a uma estrutura política não distorcida. É mais provável que tal padrão reduza a pobreza e melhore a distribuição de renda, que, por sua vez, cria as condições para um crescimento mais rápido, com a conseqüente melhoria, também com maior rapidez, do bem-estar. Desse modo, prevenir subinvestimento nos capitais natural e humano é um modo de promover crescimento rápido e sustentado.

Iniciamos com uma estrutura que nos permite explorar essas hipóteses e suas implicações: padrões de acúmulos de bens, fator de produtividade e bem-estar social. Em particular, observamos as implicações de crescimento de bens distorcidos para os pobres. A próxima seção fornece evidência empírica a partir de uma variedade de fontes. Juntando-se à revisão histórica de sessenta países, fornecemos evidência econométrica de dois grupos de países nas determinantes do crescimento. Finalmente, transformamos a evidência empírica numa variedade de subsídios (brutos), seguidos por uma avaliação dos impactos dos subsídios de capital.

Uma Estrutura

Melhorando a qualidade dos cálculos nacionais, incluindo capitais humano e natural, a estimativa de preços (não obstante as complexidades em computá-los) é um modo de reconciliar a divergência entre melhorias de crescimento e bem-estar. Mas mesmo o limitado progresso na avaliação desses valores ainda não foi incorporado nos cálculos nacionais, e ainda existem sérios problemas conceituais em relação a incorporá-los (e a ponderá-los). Por essas razões, uma abordagem mais prática (e mais modesta) deve identificar padrões de medida de crescimento e instrumentos políticos, provavelmente para promover maior bem-estar.

Três Padrões de Crescimento

Consideremos estas alternativas:

- *Padrão 1.* Crescimento não sustentado, onde a economia cresce com algumas fases de crescimento rápido, mas a uma taxa reduzida, eventualmente conduzindo a estagnação ou quase.

- *Padrão 2.* Crescimento distorcido, comprado a expensas da deterioração dos recursos naturais, por exemplo, de suas subavaliações: atrasando os investimentos no capital humano, por exemplo, salvaguardas inadequadas referentemente ao trabalho infantil, e subsídios ao capital físico, tais como isenções de impostos, permitindo atrasos nas contas dos impostos, dando garantias financeiras para recompensar determinados investimentos, e fornecendo subsídios de crédito de investimento.

- *Padrão 3.* Crescimento sustentado por meio da acumulação de valores não distorcidos ou equilibrados, com apoio público para desenvolver a educação primária e secundária, melhorando a saúde pública e protegendo o capital natural. Isto previne um declínio nos retornos dos bens privados (especialmente capital físico) e fornece os níveis mínimos de crescimento de capital humano necessários para facilitar as inovações tecnológicas e o crescimento do Fator Total de Produtividade (FTP).

O padrão 1 é habitualmente associado com crescimento lento e altamente instável ou volátil. Previne a redução da pobreza e conduz a recursos inadequados para investir nos capitais humano e natural. Ou seja, o padrão 1 causa estagnação econômica e perdas de bem-estar; ele habitualmente ocorre num contexto de governo pobre e corrupto, mas que gera baixos investimentos e alocação ineficiente de gastos públicos.

Comparado ao padrão 1, o crescimento intermitente do padrão 2 melhora o bem-estar e reduz a pobreza. Mas o crescimento de padrão 2 poderia depender do apoio público ao capital físico, o qual é difícil de sustentar. O padrão 3 é mais apropriado para melhorar o bem-estar e para a redução da pobreza. Contudo, para sustentar uma taxa razoável do crescimento econômico, os principais valores da economia – física e financeira, humana e social, natural e ambiental – precisam crescer em taxas não distorcidas ou bastante equilibradas. A distribuição de bens entre a população, especialmente do capital humano, é também importante. Um crescimento estável sustentado é altamente benéfico para os pobres, que habitualmente sofrem mais nas reversões do crescimento-pare-e-acelere.

Externalidades e Acumulação de Bens

Todas as formas de capital podem pôr em jogo externalidades. Componentes dos capitais humano e natural freqüentemente têm um valor social que vai além dos que provêm dos indivíduos que o usam. Como (parcialmente) bens públicos, eles possuem expansões positivas que não são necessariamente levadas em conta pelas ações de indivíduos ou empresas. É por isso que a política pública e outros mecanismos devem prever o subinvestimento neles. Tem havido alguma ênfase na produção tecnológica positiva e nas externalidades tecnológicas associadas com a acumulação de capital físico (Barro & Sala-I-Martin, 1995; Romer, 1986). Mas as externalidades associadas com capitais humano e natural são muito mais difíceis de levar em conta, e são, provavelmente, mais amplas.[3] Capitais natural e humano são importantes não apenas como fatores de produção, mas, também, como determinantes diretos do bem-estar social.

Os governos podem utilizar instrumentos de mercado para lidar com esses efeitos externos. Mas a questão envolve igualmente a alocação de gastos públicos. Os gastos governamentais computam tipicamente para 25%-30% do PIB, exercendo um efeito direto poderoso (como oposto aos efeitos de políticas e regulamentações) sobre a alocação de recursos e distribuição de renda. Poucos países utilizaram instrumentos de mercado com sucesso para computar o verdadeiro valor social dos capitais humano e natural. Os governos responsáveis pela região amazônica, por exemplo, exacerbaram as externalidades ambientais negativas. Subsídios públicos e taxas de incentivo para grandes criadores de gado e lenhadores foram responsáveis por mais de 50% dos desmatamentos na região amazônica nas décadas de 1970 e 1980 (Binswanger, 1991). Além disso, os investimentos públicos na infra-estrutura no âmbito das áreas fronteiriças amplificaram as externalidades associadas com a falta de direitos de propriedades bem definidos em tais áreas.

Fazendo pouco para prevenir o subinvestimento em bens humanos e naturais, deve, provavelmente, levar a um acúmulo desequilibrado de bens, pelo menos a curto prazo, por focalizar-se sobre o acúmulo de capital físico. Baseando-se principalmente no acúmulo de capital físico em vez de em um crescimento de bens equilibrado, pode aumentar o crescimento do PIB (utilizando métodos de cômputo convencional nacional). Mas o bem-estar pode não aumentar com tanta rapidez – podendo até mesmo diminuir, se, por exemplo, o capital natural fosse declinar drasticamente, ou se a qualidade da educação e a da saúde pública caíssem. As conseqüências distribucionais de crescimento de bens distorcido ou desequilibrado poderiam também ser severas, especialmente se o desequilíbrio torna o crescimento instável, atingindo os pobres de forma desproporcional.

O crescimento rápido do PIB sem algum grau de aumento equilibrado de bens pode igualmente ser difícil de sustentar. A menos que haja expansões tecnológicas ou economias escalonadas, o acúmulo rápido de capital físico, juntamente ao crescimento lento em capital humano e um esgotamento dos bens naturais, levaria a uma produtividade marginal declinante de capital – enquanto os estoques de capital aumentam relativamente a outros bens produtivos (ver Anexo 2).

Crescimento no Fator Total de Produtividade e Acúmulo de Bens

A maior parte da ênfase dada neste capítulo foi a respeito do acúmulo de bens e da estrutura de bens como fonte de crescimento. Um importante conjunto de análises argumenta que a principal fonte de crescimento não é a acumulação de bens, mas, sim, o crescimento do FTP, ou seja, Fator Total de Produtividade (Easterly & Levine, 2000; King & Rebelo, 1993; Klenow & Rodriguez-Clare, 1997a; Romer, 1986 e 1993). Esta conclusão, elaborada com base em modelos teóricos baseados em crescimento endógeno, é sustentada por estudos empíricos anteriores demonstrando que o crescimento no decorrer do tempo, especialmente nos Estados Unidos e em alguns outros países industrializados, é, de fato, em grande parte explicado pelo FTP.

Análises dos países da Ásia oriental, contudo, sugerem que o crescimento FTP pode não ser uma fonte tão importante de crescimento para países em desenvolvimento como tem sido para os Estados Unidos e alguns outros países industrializados. Os países da Ásia oriental são praticamente os únicos em desenvolvimento que experimentaram crescimento rápido e consistente, por longos períodos. Collins & Bosworth (1996), Kim & Lau (1994), Krugman (1996) e Young (1991, 1994 e 1995) mostram que o crescimento rápido da Ásia oriental antes de 1997 baseou-se em grande acumulação de bens. Dois relatórios recentes, contudo, apontam para fatores que qualificam estas análises. Klenow & Rodríguez-Clare (1997b) e

Nelson & Pack (1998) enfatizam melhorias na mensurabilidade dos bens e sutilezas metodológicas que poderiam alterar significativamente as conclusões atingidas por outros autores.

O FTP nos países em desenvolvimento é potencialmente importante para o crescimento. É, também, diretamente ligado à acumulação de bens por duas razões. Primeira, um principal veículo da nova tecnologia está encarnado no capital importado e em novos bens intermediários. Segunda, para beneficiar-se do progresso tecnológico, o nível de educação precisa ser continuamente aumentado, tanto em profundidade como em amplitude. Expandir a educação geral é mais crucial nos países em desenvolvimento do que naqueles industrializados, onde já existe uma base ampla. No entanto, na maioria dos países em desenvolvimento a educação geral é ainda insuficiente para facilitar a difusão tecnológica. Assim, o crescimento FTP apenas pode ser rápido se o capital humano se amplia e se aprofunda rapidamente. É por isso que ele guarda uma ligação muito próxima com a acumulação de bens, e porque pode ser difícil distinguir FTP e crescimento de bens como fontes de crescimento.

Investimentos no Capital Físico

Reformas de mercado – liberalização do comércio e do mercado de capital, privatizações, eliminação do controle de preços, a liberação do mercado de trabalho e outros – têm sido instrumentos vitais para o crescimento ao aumentar as recompensas para todas as formas de capital. Em razão da maior receptividade dos investimentos privados em capital físico em relação aos capitais natural e humano, eles ajudaram alguns países (especialmente aqueles não severamente afetados pela corrupção) a conhecer uma explosão de investimento, acelerando o crescimento. Algumas dessas reformas – por exemplo, liberalização do comércio ou mudanças enviesadas antiagrícolas – também aumentaram as recompensas para o capital humano. Contudo, na ausência de investimentos complementares nestes bens (principalmente capital humano), a expansão do capital físico poderia produzir um retorno declinante e, eventualmente, uma desaceleração do crescimento (ver Anexo 2). Para alguns países esta tendência tem sido computada pelo aprofundamento do processo de reforma, ao passo que outros utilizaram um aumento de recursos públicos para sustentar distorções (embora gerando crescimento padrão 2).

Além disso, enquanto os países em desenvolvimento participam mais dos mercados globais, governos nacionais (e subnacionais) podem comprometer-se na competição para atrair capital mediante a criação artificial de condições favoráveis, como se viu na recente evidência sobre os subsídios, para atrair investimentos estrangeiros nos países industrializados e em desenvolvimento. (Para uma análise dos países como

Argentina, Brasil e os da Europa ocidental, ver Oman, 2000; e também na próxima parte.) Há uma variedade de evidências, de incentivos, de subsídios relacionados com investimentos nas indústrias, tais como a indústria automobilística de várias regiões, ou na superexploração mediante a depreciação dos recursos naturais, como na mineração e no florestamento. Um mecanismo para aumentar o atrativo dos investimentos domésticos e estrangeiros é "dispensar" os recursos humanos e naturais a baixos custos, por exemplo, permitindo o trabalho infantil; não melhorando a saúde e as regras de saneamento no local de trabalho; não regulamentando os bancos e outras instituições financeiras; não melhorando as regulamentações ambientais; e dispensando a mineração, a água e os direitos de exploração da madeira.[4]

Em alguns países, esses subsídios de capital e isenções de impostos podem contrabalançar os custos associados das firmas com o mau governo e a corrupção, que reduzem seus incentivos para investir nas atividades produtivas (ver Capítulo 6). Isto sugere que, ao reduzir a corrupção e o mau governo, torna-se possível, para os países, poupar recursos. Somado ao governo, outro ingrediente que pode desempenhar papel positivo na qualidade do crescimento são as forças das instituições informais de um país, às quais freqüentemente se referem como capital social (Quadro 2.1).

Investimentos nos Capitais Humano e Natural

O outro lado da moeda dos incentivos especiais aos capitais físico e financeiro é a atenção insuficiente dada ao capital humano e a rápida destruição de várias formas no capital natural, mediante a superexploração. Esforços para levantar artificialmente os incentivos para investimentos nos capitais físicos e financeiros poderiam ser ligados a investimentos suficientes nos capitais naturais e humanos.

O setor privado contribui para o acúmulo de capital humano – por meio de treinamento, escolas particulares e serviços de saúde privados. Mas escolaridade privada e serviços de saúde privados vão principalmente para os mais ricos, que têm condições de pagar para sua prosperidade e a de seu capital humano. Muitas pessoas, particularmente aqueles de baixa e média rendas, dependem do apoio público para acumular capital humano. Imperfeições nos mercados de capital proíbem que eles façam empréstimo contra ganhos futuros, tornando esta dependência ainda mais acentuada.

Crescimento em capital físico pode derramar-se no capital humano por meio de investimentos privados na pesquisa e no desenvolvimento, e no treinamento em mais altas tecnologias – ou seja, no crescimento do conhecimento dirigido. Mas para sustentar este crescimento, uma ampla (e crescente) parte da força de trabalho deve ter escolaridade geral suficiente, que

Quadro 2.1 – Capital Social

A noção de capital social recebeu muita atenção dos peritos e profissionais em desenvolvimento nos últimos tempos. O grupo dos fenômenos reunidos sob a rubrica de capital social inclui confiança, normas cooperativas, eleição, participação em referendos e atividades associativas horizontais em diversos grupos.

De que maneira o capital social afeta o desempenho econômico?

- Pouquíssimos recursos precisam ser gastos para proteger-se contra as fraudes, as transações econômicas, que seriam quase um corolário de ambientes de alta confiança.
- Há menos necessidade para os empreendedores monitorarem fornecedores e trabalhadores, liberando mais recursos para a atividade inovadora.
- Confiança interpessoal pode ser substituída por direitos de propriedades formais.
- Um maior grau de confiança na política do governo é bom para o investimento.
- Um maior grau de confiança parece importante para o acúmulo do capital humano. Galor & Zeira (1993) sugerem que maior confiança está associada com maior número de matrículas na educação secundária.
- Confiança e participação cívica são igualmente associadas com o melhor desempenho das instituições governamentais, inclusive aquelas para a educação pública.
- Ação comunitária ou cooperativa por grupos locais podem diminuir "a tragédia do povo", superexploração e submanutenção (Ostrom, 1990).
- Maiores ligações entre os indivíduos facilitam melhores fluxos de informação e uma difusão mais rápida da inovação (Besley & Case, 1994; Foster & Rosenzweig, 1995; Rogers, 1983).
- O capital social pode atuar como seguro informal, mais do que como a diversificação de um portfólio. Riscos divididos por muitos negócios internos e administração podem atuar como uma rede de segurança social e evitar que elas assumam atividades de mais alto risco e de mais alto retorno (Narayan & Pritchett, 1999).

Mas, será que o capital social pode ser medido, e qual é a sua efetividade de contribuição para o cresci-mento? E será que há intervenções políticas que podem contribuir para sua formação? Evidências envolvendo tantos microdados agregados de campo e interior acumulam-se para sugerir o potencial do capital social. Knack & Keefer (1997) utilizam-se de dados do World Values Survey para 29 economias de mercado durante o período de 1980-1994 para provar a importância da confiança e do envolvimento civil. Depois de controlar de início a renda *per capita*, o capital humano e o capital de preços de bens básicos, descobriram que ambos os índices de capital social mostram ligações significativas para o crescimento econômico. Descobriram também que a confiança é ainda mais importante para os países mais pobres com sistemas legais e setores financeiros frágeis. Uma implicação política: estabelecer instituições legais formais e de crédito é especialmente importante em sociedades de baixa confiança.

O conceito de capital social tem gerado discussões e debates. Seus proponentes reclamam que ele seja tão importante quanto – ou abrangendo – capitais humano, físico e natural. Outros consideram este foco excessivo e inapropriado. Alguns dos trabalhos nesta área também são criticados por deixar de fora importantes dimensões sociais Temple & Johnson (1998) sugerem uma perspectiva geral: simplesmente que a sociedade tem importância. Eles analisam os dados sob variáveis socioeconômicas compiladas por Adelman & Taft-Morris (1967) e mostram que muitas variáveis sociais têm um significativo poder explicativo na predição do crescimento econômico a longo prazo. Essas variáveis vão das "variáveis de confiança" tipicamente estudadas por pesquisadores do capital social. Entre tais variáveis, a mais importante delas para capturar diferenças nos arranjos sociais inclui a extensão da comunicação de massa (jornais e rádios), o caráter da organização social básica, a modernização da perspectiva, a extensão da mobilidade social e a importância das classes médias nativas.

Algumas leituras-chave são Dasgupta & Serageldin (1999), Narayan & Pritchett (1999) e Woolcock (1998). Ver também dois conjuntos de artigos que aparecem nas partes especiais do *World Development* (Evans, 1996) e no *Journal of International Development* (Harris, 1997). Incluído no último, encontra-se um artigo crítico de utilização e noção de uso do capital social do World Bank (Fox, 1997).

lhe permita adquirir habilidades e tecnologia e participar da expansão das atividades de pesquisa e desenvolvimento. Assim, a escolaridade geral oferecida publicamente e o conhecimento gerado de maneira privada são complementares. Se a qualidade e a cobertura da escolaridade geral não aumentarem de modo rápido o suficiente, o crescimento de conhecimento dirigido pode ser sufocado, particularmente nos países mais pobres onde a maior parte da força de trabalho não tem educação de nível primário (Capítulo 3).

Crescimento sem políticas ambientais complementares pode ameaçar o ambiente enquanto o acúmulo do capital físico acelera. Isso é especialmente provável nos países com vantagens comparativas em indústrias de recursos naturais intensivos, que também requerem muito capital físico para sua exploração, como a mineração, a economia florestal e a pesca. Prevenir a degradação excessiva dos recursos ambientais e naturais depende igualmente de políticas públicas e de investimentos. Muitos recursos ambientais têm valores sociais – como gastos na produção e no consumo – que estão geralmente bem acima daqueles que o setor privado leva em consideração em suas alocações de recursos. Quando os recursos naturais são abundantes, não é provável que a degradação do capital natural tenha muito efeito sobre a produtividade do capital físico. Mas depois que os recursos naturais caem abaixo de determinados patamares, a degradação posterior pode reduzir a produtividade do capital físico (Capítulo 4).

Enquanto a degradação do capital natural deve, provavelmente, reduzir o bem-estar, seu impacto sobre o crescimento econômico está sujeito a debate (ver a discussão entre Daly, Solon e Stiglitz em Daly, 1997). Esse impacto articula a substituição de outros bens para o capital natural (ver Anexo 2). Algumas evidências recentes implicam que o capital humano, mas não o capital físico, pode ser substituído por capital natural. Assim, as economias que expandem o capital humano podem reduzir a dependência do crescimento de saída em capital natural. Os altos níveis de capital humano permitem que a economia se diversifique em atividades progressivamente menos intensivas no capital natural. Por exemplo, um país com alto nível de capital humano pode especializar-se em atividades de conhecimento intensivas, tornando a exploração do capital natural menos essencial para a sustentação do crescimento de renda.

Mas é provável que a degradação do capital natural seja devastadora para os pobres, que geralmente possuem pouco capital humano e continuam a depender do capital natural (solos, fontes de água natural, pescas) para suas rendas, até mesmo em economias de renda média. Porque os pobres têm poucas possibilidades para substituir outros bens por recursos naturais, a degradação daqueles recursos poderia levar a círculos viciosos irreversíveis de pobreza e destruição ambiental (ver López, 1997, para uma análise dos traços dinâmicos da degradação dos recursos naturais e mudança institucional para os pobres rurais).[5]

Crescimento Distorcido de Bens e os Pobres

Os pobres, em razão de sua carência de bens, teriam maiores dificuldades que os ricos para diminuir seu consumo nos tempos ruins. Próximo aos limites da subsistência, trabalham habitualmente em atividades mais atingidas pelos ciclos econômicos (agricultura, construção). Assim, o crescimento instável geralmente tem efeitos severos para eles, e uma crise econômica pode, então, degradar seus bens humanos e naturais, que podem não estar aptos a beneficiar-se de explosões subseqüentes (ver Anexo 2).

A economia dos pobres é separada freqüentemente de muitos modos da economia moderna, mas a demanda por seus produtos depende, pelo menos em parte, da economia moderna (taxas de câmbio, por exemplo, afetam os preços de seus produtos de exportação). A instabilidade na economia moderna, então, afeta os incentivos para os pobres, e a deterioração desses incentivos atinge os pobres. Mesmo que os retornos dos incentivos voltem aos níveis originais, os pobres podem não estar aptos para se aproveitar deles. Isto implica duas alternativas possíveis de equilíbrio: um equilíbrio de crescimento sustentado e um equilíbrio de subsistência estagnante. Durante os tempos malogrados, os pobres perdem os bens necessários para manter o consumo em níveis de subsistência e de responder a incentivos mais fortes no próximo *boom*.

Alguns países em desenvolvimento, por exemplo, na América Latina, conheceram uma relativa alta na desigualdade de renda, especialmente devido à distribuição incorreta do capital físico, da educação e da terra. Expandir a educação poderia mudá-la. Tornar a educação menos concentrada, digamos, realocando os gastos públicos para a educação básica e secundária, é, provavelmente, não só a redistribuição menos controversa, mas também a mais viável.

A desigualdade de bens afeta o bem-estar social por meio de dois mecanismos. Um efeito é direto: amplos segmentos da população têm poucos bens e consomem pouco, enquanto uma minoria conta com amplas quantidades de bens e consomem muito (ver Anexo 2). O outro efeito é indireto: a desigualdade de bens mostrou-se capaz de reduzir o potencial para o crescimento econômico e a redução da pobreza mediante uma variedade de canais (sobre a desigualdade de bens e crescimento, ver, por exemplo, Alesina & Rodrik, 1994; Deininger & Squire, 1998; Persson & Tabellini, 1994; Ravallion & Sen, 1994; e para uma revisão bibliográfica, Capítulo 3 e Tabela A3.5).

Até mesmo pequenas mudanças na distribuição de renda podem ter amplos efeitos na extensão e na profundidade da pobreza nos países em desenvolvimento (Lundberg & Squire, 1999). Vários estudos tentaram estabelecer uma relação entre distribuição de renda e crescimento. Contudo, como argumentam Lundberg & Squire, crescimento e desigualdade deveriam ser analisados como variáveis endógenas associadas. Como a desigualdade de bens afeta tanto o crescimento como a distribuição de renda, está intimamente

relacionada com o modo em que o nível e a composição dos gastos públicos na educação e na saúde afetam a desigualdade do capital humano.

É improvável que as distribuições incorretas da educação produzam os melhores resultados de crescimento.[6] Se o capital humano for relativamente concentrado, qualquer concentração posterior diminuiria o crescimento, ao passo que esforços para melhorar sua distribuição beneficiariam o crescimento (Capítulo 3). Uma economia com menor número de pessoas altamente educadas e com alto número de analfabetos pode achar difícil sustentar altas taxas de retorno para o capital físico, porque as expansões tecnológicas potenciais associadas com o acúmulo de capital podem não se materializar. Maiores acessos à educação secundária e superior permitiriam maiores expansões tecnológicas.

Evidência Empírica

Nesta parte, fornecemos quatro tipos de evidência:

- *Experiência em sessenta países em desenvolvimento.* A experiência de crescimento tem freqüentemente seguido os padrões 1 e 2, baseando-se principalmente em uma alta de investimento no capital físico, enquanto o investimento no capital humano atrasou-se e o investimento no capital natural tem sido, na maioria das vezes, negativo (ver Quadro 2.2).

- *Evidência econométrica.* É improvável que o crescimento que se baseie principalmente na expansão do capital físico seja sustentável. As possíveis expansões positivas do investimento de capital físico não parecem ser suficientes para manter uma taxa de crescimento estável, na ausência de uma expansão significativa de capital humano e de uma utilização sustentável do capital natural.

- *Evidência nos subsídios.* Países industrializados e em desenvolvimento gastaram recursos públicos nos subsídios. No caso do capital, envolvem uma variedade de mecanismos que incluem isenções de impostos, subsídios de crédito e bolsas. Os subsídios absorvem uma parte abrangente dos lucros governamentais, que nos países em desenvolvimento parecem comparáveis ao que é gasto na educação, saúde e setores sociais.

- *Impacto dos subsídios.* Uma descoberta da bibliografia é que os subsídios de capital não contribuíram para uma produtividade aumentada e tiveram apenas efeitos modestos sobre o crescimento. Além disso, seus efeitos no crescimento parecem ter tido vida curta.

Quadro 2.2 – Abordagens Alternativas para a Sustentação do Crescimento: Brasil, Chile e Coréia

Duas abordagens em busca do crescimento sustentado poderiam ser arroladas:

Abordagem 1. Políticas cada vez mais amplas e distorções de gasto (incentivos e subsídios) em favor do capital (padrão 2 de crescimento).

Abordagem 2. Altos níveis de apoio para o crescimento de outros bens de modo igual, particularmente capital humano (padrão 3 de crescimento).

A abordagem 1 implica que manter uma alta taxa de crescimento requer que o viés pró-capital seja crescente todo o tempo. Afora ser menos efetivo que a abordagem 2 na sustentação do crescimento a longo prazo, esta abordagem significa crescimento estável a curto prazo e crescentes concentrações de renda e riqueza. É provável que a abordagem 2 seja melhor para sustentar uma taxa de crescimento razoável a longo prazo, reduzindo a curto prazo a instabilidade e promovendo a eqüidade.

Favorecer o Capital Físico

A maioria dos países utiliza uma combinação destas duas abordagens com ênfases diferentes. O Brasil, como vários outros, algumas vezes parece ter utilizado a abordagem 1. Revisões de vários países mostram exemplos de alocações públicas para apoiar a lucratividade de capital mediante subsídios de financiamento direto para investidores nacionais e estrangeiros; esforços para construir uma infra-estrutura de serviços com dinheiro público, orientado para a expansão de indústrias particulares, e desenvolver áreas ambientais sensíveis; assim como o crédito, taxas e políticas de preço a favor do capital. Em muitos países, a alocação dos recursos públicos para a educação enfatizou subsídios para a educação de 3° grau e subinvestiu na escola de 1° e 2° graus.

Durante as duas últimas décadas, o desvio-padrão das taxas de crescimento anual tem sido maior do que a taxa de crescimento médio (Tabela 2.1). Tal instabilidade poderia ser devido, em parte, à capacidade variável do setor público em gerar os recursos necessários para continuar a apoiar o capital físico, em termos relativos. Igualmente, o relativamente pequeno apoio aos setores sociais pareceria ter contribuído para a desigualdade social.

Atenção ao Capital Humano

A Coréia também parece ter subsidiado investidores que iniciaram antes da década de 1990. Seus subsídios eram seletivos, focalizando principalmente umas poucas indústrias de uma vez – objetivando o desenvolvimento para umas poucas indústrias dos exportadores em um período razoável. Algumas indústrias favorecidas tornaram-se líderes em provocar expansões de crescimento para outras. Enquanto essa abordagem foi problemática de vários modos, ela implica relativamente menos de um ônus financeiro explícito para o setor público. Somando-se a isso, a alocação de recursos públicos para a educação priorizou a educação básica, o que permitiu ao setor público apoiar a rápida construção do capital humano, juntamente com um rápido declínio do Coeficiente Gini de Educação (Capítulo 3). Isso também equilibrou os incentivos para o crescimento dos bens físicos e humanos, permitiu que a desigualdade de renda permanecesse em níveis aceitáveis e ajudou a pobreza a declinar.

Houve crescimento econômico sustentado durante as décadas de 1980 e 1990 até 1997. O crescimento foi relativamente estável – possivelmente em parte porque o setor público manteve o seu apoio tanto ao capital humano como ao físico ao longo dos anos.

Neutralidade Relativa

Desde o início da década de 1980, o setor público do Chile geralmente absteve-se de favorecer diretamente o capital físico. Nem os setores sociais, particularmente educação e saúde, receberam apoios especiais, senão durante o período 1997-2000. O setor público não assumiu nenhum papel significante em estratégia de orientação de crescimento nestas áreas. Contudo, o Chile teve uma taxação baixa ao utilizar seus recursos naturais, fornecendo fortes incentivos para investidores estrangeiros explorarem a mineração, a economia florestal e a pesca.

Houve um *boom* em 1987-1995, que se beneficiou de uma ampla aceleração de investimento no capital físico, com o capital humano ficando para trás. A falta de dependência do capital dos subsídios diretos pode ter levado a taxas de crescimento estáveis na expansão dos anos 80.

VALORES, CRESCIMENTO E BEM-ESTAR

Quadro 2.2 Continuação

Tabela 2.1 – Variáveis Seletas para Brasil, Chile e Coréia

Variável	Brasil	Chile	Coréia
Crescimento do PIB (porcentagem ao ano)			
Nível médio	2,8	5,9	7,6
Coeficiente de variação[a]	1,4	0,9	0,4
Gastos públicos com educação e saúde (porcentagem do PIB)			
Nível médio	2,9	5,6	3,4
Tendência ao longo do tempo	0,1	-0,1	0,0
Investimento interno bruto (porcentagem do PIB)			
Nível médio	20,5	19,7	32,6
Tendência ao longo do tempo	-0,1	0,6	0,4
Itens memo (último ano disponível)			
Pobreza (porcentagem abaixo de US$ 1 ao dia)	23,6	15,0	–
Coeficiente Gini de Renda	0,60	0,59	0,32
Coeficiente Gini de Educação	0,39	0,31	0,22
Analfabetismo (porcentagem)	16,7	4,8	2,0
Mortalidade infantil (por 1.000)	34,0	11,0	9,0

– Não disponível.
Nota: Os valores são para 1978-1997, exceto para os gastos em educação e saúde que são para 1980-1997 (1980-1994 para o Brasil), e anos específicos para algumas variáveis.
[a] O desvio-padrão de crescimento dividido pela taxa de crescimento.
Fontes: Várias edições do *World Development Indicators* (World Bank), e do *Government Finance Statistics Yearbook,* do Fundo Monetário Internacional.

Reformas e Crescimento Desequilibrado em Sessenta Países

Uma revisão de sessenta países no fim das décadas de 1980 e 1990 mostra que mais ou menos 16 países foram considerados sérios reformadores ao implementar um conjunto de mudanças políticas (Tabela 2.2). Os outros 44 países não implementaram tal conjunto de reformas durante o período. Os reformadores já possuíam taxas de acúmulo de capital físico na década de 1980 maiores do que os não reformadores.[7] Embora uma experimentação controlada revelasse melhor contrafactuais, o contraste é sugestivo. Na década de 1990, as taxas de acúmulo de capital físico aumentaram em torno de 70% para os reformadores, enquanto declinaram para os não reformadores. No entanto, o crescimento do capital humano aparentemente não sofreu um aumento muito grande tanto para uns como para outros. Os gastos com a educação como uma parte do PIB foram mais baixos para os reformadores do que para os não reformadores, aumentando modestamente para ambos os grupos na década de 1990.[8]

Tabela 2.2 – Revisão dos Indicadores de Desenvolvimento para Sessenta Reformadores e Não Reformadores, em Anos Seletos

Indicador de desenvolvimento	Anos	16 reformadores	44 não reformadores
Valor crescimento PIB *per capita* (por cento)	1984-89	2,8	-0,5
	Anos 90	3,5	0,01
Valor crescimento estoque capital físico (por trabalhador/por cento)	1984-89	2,1	0,0
	Anos 90	3,5	-0,5
Taxa de desmatamento (por cento)	1984-89	0,7	1,2
	Anos 90	1,1	1,4
Gasto com educação na porcentagem do PIB	1984-89	3,2	4,6
	Anos 90	3,5	4,7

Nota: Os reformadores nesta tabela são definidos com base no rápido índice de integração (World Bank, 1996a). Os países que implementaram reformas econômicas significativas (reformadores) no fim da década de 1980 ou no início da de 1990 por essa medida são: Argentina, Chile, Bolívia, China, Indonésia, Coréia, Gana, Malásia, Ilhas Maurício, México, Marrocos, Nepal, Peru, Filipinas, Sri Lanka e Tailândia.
Fonte: Cálculos dos autores.

Embora as taxas de desmatamento, uma rude procuração para a degradação dos recursos naturais, tenham sido mais baixas para os reformadores do que para os não reformadores em ambos os períodos, os desmatamentos realizados pelos reformadores quase dobraram na década de 1990, enquanto os não reformadores apresentaram um leve aumento.

Logo, os reformadores tiveram significativo crescimento econômico acelerado durante a década de 1990, o qual parece ter se baseado na acumulação de capital físico, enquanto, em termos relativos, os investimentos no capital humano e capital natural ficaram para trás.

Serão os aumentos de gastos educacionais pelos reformadores o suficiente para sustentar as novas taxas de crescimento? Será que a aceleração da degradação do capital natural atinge seriamente a sustentabilidade do crescimento para os reformadores e os não reformadores? Para responder a estas questões, precisamos saber como os gastos aumentam o capital humano, como aprofundar-se nos capitais humano e físico afeta o crescimento, e como a perda de capital natural também pode afetar o crescimento.

Evidência Econométrica: Vinte Países de Renda Média

A análise de crescimento econométrica na maioria dos vinte países de renda média durante 1970-1992 mostra o seguinte (ver anexo da Tabela A2.1 e López et al., 1998):[9]

- A produtividade marginal de capital, dados outros níveis de bens, diminui com aumentos no capital físico. A economia de escala e as expansões tecnológicas a partir do investimento no capital físico aparentemente menor podem não ser suficientes para contrabalançar o declínio da produtividade marginal de capital físico – o sugere que,

baseado primariamente no acúmulo de capital físico, não pode ser sustentado a longo prazo.

- Capital humano, aqui representado pela educação formal, pareceria ter um efeito positivo poderoso sobre o crescimento econômico em episódios reformadores, mas não na ausência de reformas. Isto implica que a educação não contribuiria muito para a produtividade do capital físico em economias super-reguladas, com pouco espaço para mercados. Mas poderia fazer muito para empurrar a produção marginal do capital físico e crescimento econômico em uma estrutura de boas condições de mercado – o que confirma nossa hipótese apresentada anteriormente, de que o acúmulo de capital humano com rapidez suficiente pode induzir ao crescimento sustentado. Ao mesmo tempo, essa evidência sugere que reformas de mercados-chave são uma condição necessária para o crescimento sustentado a longo prazo.

- Nas economias e episódios não reformadores, as taxas de crescimento econômico não são sustentadas, sem levar em conta as adições ao capital humano, de acordo com esses resultados. Ao contrário, eles encaram a estagnação depois de períodos de crescimento moderado, engatilhado pelos choques exógenos favoráveis que temporariamente estimulam os retornos ao capital físico.

- As boas taxas de crescimento econômico nos episódios de reforma podem ser sustentadas se o capital humano crescer de modo suficientemente rápido para contrabalançar a diminuição marginal, os retornos declinantes de capital marginal provocados pelo acúmulo de capital físico. O crescimento *per capita* de mais ou menos 4% ao ano, de acordo com estas estimativas, pode ser sustentado se o capital humano *per capita* expandir-se a mais ou menos 1,7%-1,8% ao ano.

De modo que o crescimento baseado principalmente no acúmulo de capital físico – desprezando o capital humano – não pareceria ser sustentado. Reformas de mercado podem acelerar o crescimento. Mas se as reformas não forem acompanhadas por investimentos de capital humano, provavelmente o crescimento estará fadado a dar sinais. Ao contrário dos não reformadores, países que implementam reformas de mercado possuem uma chance de crescimento sustentado.

Evidência Econométrica: Setenta Países em Desenvolvimento

Os estudos prévios não consideraram capital natural como um determinante do crescimento, mas poucos dos vinte países analisados anterior-

mente mostram uma dependência forte sobre o capital natural como fonte de renda. Um estudo que relaciona setenta países em desenvolvimento, incluindo tanto países pobres como de renda média e até mesmo várias nações subsaarianas, considera os capitais físico, humano e natural fatores que afetam o crescimento (López et al., 1998; ver também nota 8).[10]

Diferentemente da maioria dos estudos prévios, este utiliza-se de uma forma funcional flexível (flexível às equações de crescimento) que permite efeitos não-lineares das variáveis explicativas e efeitos interativos por meio destas variáveis. Os efeitos interativos são de extrema importância para elucidar a substituição ou complementaridade de interesses no processo de crescimento (ver Tabelas do Anexo A2.2 e A2.3).

- De acordo com essas estimativas, a taxa de crescimento econômico sobre a média declina com o aumento nos estoques de capital físico – para capitais natural e humano constantes –, mas não para todos os países. Países com capital físico muito baixo para razões de trabalho tendem a ter suas taxas de crescimento aumentadas. Assim, em países de capital pobre, a acumulação de capital primeiramente tende a tornar ainda mais rápido o crescimento. Mas, depois de atingir uma certa intensidade de capital, um acúmulo posterior de capital físico – para dados capitais humano e natural – possui um efeito declinante no crescimento econômico.

- O capital humano, na média, poderia parecer aumentar a taxa de crescimento econômico, embora este elo seja menor que no estudo anterior. Enquanto o capital humano cresce, o elo positivo com o crescimento econômico torna-se maior. Em baixos níveis de capital humano, seu elo com o crescimento econômico é negligenciável, mas em níveis elevados de capital humano ele torna-se maior, com o efeito marginal de estoque do capital humano no crescimento sempre em elevação.

- Para sustentar o crescimento econômico, o capital humano, ao contrário do capital físico, pode em alguma extensão ser substituído pelo capital natural. A taxa de crescimento dos países com altos níveis de capital humano, ao contrário dos países pobres, é muito menos sensível à perda de capital natural. Para os países pobres, o capital natural é crucial para a sustentação do crescimento econômico rápido, contudo eles precisam investir em capital humano para reduzir sua dependência do capital natural.

Tais resultados sugerem que o crescimento especialmente baseado no acúmulo de capital físico tende a ser difícil de sustentar. Economias de escala e expansão técnica crescendo a partir do acúmulo de capital físico

existem, mas podem não ser suficientes para sustentar o crescimento. Para permitir o crescimento sustentado, o acúmulo de capital físico precisa ser acompanhado por uma expansão de capital humano.[11] O desinvestimento em capital natural atinge a sustentabilidade do crescimento, especialmente em países pobres em capital humano. Este resultado, que apenas o acúmulo de capital físico pode não sustentar o crescimento, é coerente com estudos empíricos recentes (Barro & Sala-I-Martin, 1996; Jones, 1995; Mankiw et al., 1992; Young, 1994 e 1995).

Evidência nos Subsídios

O acúmulo de evidências durante a década passada indica que os subsídios governamentais para a indústria, a agricultura e a infra-estrutura global são amplos. A Tabela A2.4 no Anexo 2 apresenta alguns exemplos que ilustram tanto o tamanho como o impacto de tais subsídios. Os dados são fragmentados e parciais, tornando difícil colocar-se em perspectiva a verdadeira magnitude desses subsídios em relação ao PIB e em relação aos gastos governamentais. Em acréscimo, os dados disponíveis incluem apenas subsídios diretos envolvendo despesas financeiras diretas (ou lucros e taxas precedentes) para o setor público. A evidência no subsídio indireto como concessão de recursos naturais é, na maioria das vezes, anedótico. As evidências disponíveis, contudo, permitem-nos estabelecer uma estimativa de limite mais baixo dos subsídios financeiros, pelo menos para alguns países.

É importante que se note que esta continua sendo uma estimativa grosseira. Ela não considera a magnitude da rede depois de computar taxas ou outras distorções contrabalançadas. Essa estimativa também não diferencia entre casos em que tais subsídios poderiam ser justificados em campos sociais e em quais não poderiam ser. Juntamente com as taxas, eles influenciam o valor dos impostos, introduzindo elementos de não-transparência, discriminação por meio de diferentes atividades e pressões sobre recursos escassos – tornando-os não fidedignos.

Durante o início da década de 1990, os países industrializados (OECD) gastaram estimativamente US$ 490-615 bilhões por ano em subsídios para a agricultura (US$ 335 bilhões), energia (US$ 70-80 bilhões) e transporte rodoviário (US$ 85-200 bilhões) (De Moor & Calamai, 1997). O montante é de quase 2,5%-3,0% do PIB total dos países da OECD e em torno de 7,6%-9,1% do total dos gastos governamentais. Os países em desenvolvimento gastaram entre US$ 220-270 bilhões ao ano para subsidiar a energia, o transporte rodoviário, a agricultura e a água durante os primeiros anos da década de 1990. Esse montante para mais ou menos 4,3%-5,2% do PIB e 19%-24% dos gastos totais do governo. Essas estimativas de subsídios apontam para possíveis distorções e não sugerem, necessariamente, superinvestimento nesses setores no agregado.

Por um lado, esta é, provavelmente, apenas uma parte da totalidade dos subsídios, assim como os subsídios à manufaturação não estão aqui incluídos. Por outro, alguns destes subsídios (especialmente para a energia) dizem respeito à demanda do consumidor e não à produção corporativa, que é nosso foco principal. Contudo, parte significativa dos subsídios para a energia parece ser captada por entidades corporativas, e as estimativas ora apontadas poderiam ainda estar bem próximas de representar subsídios corporativos.

A partir de uma estimativa diferente, os subsídios corporativos nos Estados Unidos, no ano de 1996, foram de US$ 170-200 bilhões (Collins, 1996), ou 2,3%-2,7% do PIB e 10%-12% dos gastos totais do governo. Os subsídios governamentais para as corporações do Fortune 500, que em 1997 marcaram lucros de US$ 325 bilhões, representavam mais ou menos US$ 75 bilhões – compreendendo bolsas governamentais, seguro a baixo preço, empréstimos e garantias subsidiadas (Moore, 1999).

Fora dos subsídios de energia e agricultura, os países provêem subsídios diretamente para indústrias manufatureiras. A evidência sugere que esses subsídios industriais podem ser mais amplos do que os subsídios para energia e agricultura. Subsídios aos investidores estrangeiros parecem ser significativos em um certo número de casos de países. O tratamento de impostos preferenciais para empresas estrangeiras às vezes pesa no governo em abster-se de lucros de impostos. A competição por investimentos estrangeiros é, em alguns casos, uma razão para estes subsídios, que se dirigiram a investidores na mineração e a várias indústrias que compõem um leque que vai desde o automóvel até o aço (*Aviation Week and Space Technology*, 1999; Castaneda, 1997; *La Nación*, 10 de junho de 1997; Sieh Lee, 1998; Oman, 2000; e igualmente Tabela A2.4 no Anexo 2). Eles são essencialmente discriminatórios na natureza, e levantam as questões da efetividade de favorecer alguns sobre outros.

Estes dados, admitidamente parciais, sugerem o significado dos subsídios corporativistas como uma proporção dos gastos do governo – com implicações para os subsídios de capital, embora não tenhamos sido capazes de desembaraçar completamente o capital e os subsídios corporativistas. Enfatizamos, anteriormente, um padrão de bens de crescimento mais neutro e menos distorcido, que inclui a expansão dos bens naturais e humanos juntamente com o físico. Esses subsídios competem com escassos recursos públicos com usos alternativos. A questão é saber se eles poderiam ou não ser mais bem gastos a partir do ponto de vista social no setor em questão, ou em outras áreas, como edificar o capital humano, e na prevenção da rápida deterioração do capital natural. Também é possível que os subsídios corporativistas contribuam para uma expansão sustentada do investimento no capital físico, aumentando a eficiência econômica e a produtividade e gerando expansões sociais positivas. Se isto fosse verdade, o processo contra os subsídios diminuiria.

O Impacto dos Subsídios

Estudos recentes, baseados nos dados das indústrias ou das microempresas, examinaram como subsídios corporativistas afetam o crescimento econômico e a produtividade a longo prazo. Eles sugerem amplamente que os subsídios governamentais para as indústrias têm um modesto impacto sobre o investimento das empresas e crescimento no primeiro ano, mas, a médio prazo, causam pouco efeito no crescimento. Subsídios de capital também parecem induzir a um efeito negativo no fator total de produtividade das indústrias que recebem subsídios. Beason & Weinstein (1996) para o Japão; Bergström (1998) para a Suécia; Bregman et al. (1999) para Israel; Fakin (1995) para a Polônia; Fournier & Rasmussen (1986) para os Estados Unidos; Harris (1991) para a Irlanda; e Lee (1996) para a Coréia, concluem que os subsídios corporativistas são inapropriados se o aumento da renda nacional e a produtividade forem o objetivo (ver Tabela A2.4 no Anexo 2).

Os documentos de Bregman et al. (1999) e de Bergström (1998) são particularmente importantes, porque se utilizam de um painel de dados de nível de empresas detalhado. Bregman et al. (1999) descobriram que o subsídio de capital induzia a perdas de eficiência, oscilando entre 5% e 15%. Seus estudos mostram também que subsídios foram basicamente incorporados em lucros ou rendas, enquanto as empresas subsidiadas alcançaram taxas mais altas de retorno que aquelas que não foram subsidiadas. De modo semelhante, Bergström (1998) encontrou poucas evidências de que os subsídios afetam a produtividade. Seus efeitos na taxa de crescimento das empresas pareceram temporários. Este achado é coerente com a afirmação neste capítulo, de que subsídios de capital poderiam oferecer um relevo apenas temporário à diminuição das taxas do crescimento econômico, associado com o crescimento distorcido de bens.

Conclusões

Este capítulo apresentou uma estrutura para o aumento dos três valores principais: capitais humano, físico e natural. Sua hipótese principal sustenta que a melhoria do crescimento e do bem-estar requer a expansão eficiente e a utilização dos três valores. Contudo, os países podem ser tentados a subsidiar o capital físico. A evidência é que tal subsídio (isenção de impostos, subsídios diretos, fácil acesso aos recursos naturais, e assim por diante) abrange amplas partes dos gastos governamentais e do PIB. É improvável que tal abordagem produza crescimento sustentado. Ela também despreza os valores humanos e naturais – que contribuem diretamente para o bem-estar. Assim, tal crescimento pode oferecer apenas uma pequena contribuição para o bem-estar.

Ao investir a maior parte das poupanças nacionais na expansão dos valores humanos e sociais – e o uso sustentável dos bens naturais –, poderiam contribuir para mais e melhor crescimento a longo prazo. Esse crescimento sustentado, de acordo com esses três valores, tem mais possibilidade de aumentar o bem-estar. É por isso que uma abordagem relativamente não distorcida ou equilibrada para o acúmulo de todos os bens é, provavelmente, superior para a principal focalização dos capitais físico e financeiro.

Notas

1. O capital financeiro não se refere, aqui, ao desenvolvimento de instituições financeiras e ao aprofundamento de mercados financeiros em uma economia, os quais são desejáveis no apoio ao desenvolvimento (ver Capítulo 5).

2. Como será discutido mais adiante, crescimento equilibrado de bens não implica que todos os bens devam crescer sob o mesmo índice. O foco do crescimento equilibrado, como o termo é usado neste capítulo, é nas composições desses bens, mais do que na composição setorial de saída, que é a convenção comum (Hirschman, 1958; Nurkse, 1953).

3. A falta de equilíbrio no crescimento de bens apresenta-se como a conseqüência das externalidades e falências de mercado. O capital físico talvez seja menos sujeito a externalidades do que os capitais humanos e natural. Imperfeições do mercado de crédito proíbem os pobres de investir na sua educação em níveis desejados, mesmo que só possam obter uma alta taxa de retorno. Externalidades relativas ao capital natural, incluindo o meio ambiente, são extremamente penetrantes. Igualmente, os investimentos nos capitais humano e natural requerem longo tempo para amadurecer relativamente à maioria dos investimentos no capital físico. As imperfeições no mercado de capital, provavelmente, devem afetar mais negativamente o financiamento dos mais antigos do que o financiamento dos mais recentes. Assim, o mercado econômico tende a concentrar mais o acúmulo de capital físico do que dos outros dois valores. Outras razões que poderiam levar a um crescimento de valores desequilibrado enfatizado na bibliografia são as falhas de coordenação. Estas são provocadas por interações de agentes que não são totalmente mediados pelos preços de mercado (ver, por exemplo, Stiglitz (1975) para um modelo recente de equilíbrio múltiplo surgindo da informação imperfeita relativa à habilidade e à educação, e Murphy et al. (1989) e Rodríguez (1993) para falhas de coordenação intersetoriais).

4. Outros exemplos de subsídios para o capital são abundantes. Argentina e México forneceram direitos de monopólio para companhias telefônicas privatizadas durante períodos prolongados. O Brasil concedeu subsídios e isenções de impostos para investimentos em automóveis (*Financial Times*, 21 de julho de 1999). O Chile subsidiou três plantios realizados por poucas e grandes corporações para sustentar a expansão da polpa particular e da indústria do papel. Desde o início dos anos 80, a China forneceu isenção de impostos e redução de impostos a investidores estrangeiros. Na Europa central e oriental, os subsídios governamentais diretos

assumem a forma de impostos atrasados que somam de 5% a 10% do PIB e aumentam mais ou menos 2% do PIB a cada ano (Schaffer, 1995). No Brasil, produtores de borracha receberam amplos subsídios do governo. Oito companhias receberam R$ 5 bilhões (US$ 2 bilhões) (*Gazeta Mercantil*, 21 de maio de 1999). Na Coréia, os dois maiores produtores de aço receberam US$ 6 milhões entre 1993 e1999 em subsídios governamentais, de acordo com as queixas arquivadas junto à Organização Mundial de Comércio (*New Steel*, 1998). Herrera (1992) discutiu detalhadamente o impacto regressivo da falta de regulamentação no sistema telefônico privatizado na Argentina (ver Tabela A2.4, no Anexo 2).

5. É possível que, em razão de equilíbrios múltiplos e processos irreversíveis, haja escopo para as intervenções políticas públicas destinadas a evitar círculos viciosos de pobreza e degradação ambiental.

6. A distribuição da educação é medida pelos coeficientes Gini e desvios-padrão da educação (ver Capítulo 3 para detalhes destas medidas, e López et al. (1998) para uma análise estatística).

7. A taxa de crescimento médio no investimento interno entre os reformadores mais agressivos foi mais alta durante a década de 1990, depois que as reformas foram implementadas, do que nas décadas de 1970 e 1980. Na Argentina, na Bolívia, no Chile e no Peru, quatro dos reformadores mais agressivos na América Latina, o crescimento do investimento bruto durante o período 1990-1997 foi de mais de 9% ao ano, quase três vezes as taxas históricas (IDB, 1998).

8. Na Tabela 2.2 utilizamos gastos na educação como uma porcentagem do PIB em vez de gastos *per capita*, porque é provável que o estoque subjacente de educação seja positivamente relacionado com o PIB. Logo, é provável que uma mudança na divisão com os gastos do PIB com educação esteja mais proximamente relacionada com a taxa de crescimento no capital humano do que com o nível de gastos *per capita*.

9. O estudo baseou-se em um modelo teórico comportamental. Isso é importante porque as equações empíricas estimativas derivadas de um tal modelo sugerem uma especificação que está relativamente livre do viés equacional que afetou alguns estudos anteriores. Particularmente, o modelo empírico consiste em explicar taxas de crescimento anuais por estoques em atrasos de valores, mais do que pelas taxas de mudança de bens como habitualmente é feito. O que reduz consideravelmente a correlação contemporânea com o termo de erro, que habitualmente leva a sérias dificuldades por derivar a causalidade a partir dos resultados. Além do mais, o fato de utilizar efeitos fixados nos países poderia diminuir a possibilidade de viés, em decorrência de relacionamentos causais omitidos. Controles para vieses variáveis omitidos e vieses equacionais simultâneos sugerem que estamos, em larga medida, levantando problemas de causalidade. Finalmente, o estudo utilizou uma análise detalhada das reformas políticas de vários países durante as duas décadas consideradas, de modo que os coeficientes estimativos se permitiram avaliar sistematicamente por meio dos regimes políticos. Isto permitiu que o estudo mostrasse que os frágeis impactos da educação no crescimento relatado pelos outros estudos estavam corretos apenas sob certas economias

fechadas e regimes políticos distorcidos, mas não para os ambientes de boas condições de mercado. Para mais detalhes sobre o procedimento estimativo, ver o Anexo 2.

10. Este estudo utilizou-se de áreas de florestas como uma procuração para o capital natural. Perda de cobertura florestal está habitualmente associada à deterioração das bacias de água, perda de espécies de madeira, esgotamento da água e erosão do solo, todos cruciais para a produção, e é provável que seja uma boa procuração para a degradação do capital natural.

11. Este achado não é necessariamente incoerente com a bibliografia sobre a convergência do crescimento, que geralmente considera lenta a convergência por intermédio dos países. De fato, considera-se que uma taxa de crescimento estável pode ser mantida indefinidamente se os capitais físico e humano crescerem a taxas equilibradas (não iguais). O problema é apenas que a taxa de crescimento econômico declina enquanto os estoques de capital físico aumentam para um dado nível de capital humano, ou o capital humano se expande a uma rapidez abaixo da taxa mínima requerida.

CAPÍTULO 3

MELHORANDO A DISTRIBUIÇÃO DE OPORTUNIDADES

Para nós, riqueza não é meramente material, mas uma oportunidade para realização.

— Tucídides, 460-400 a.C.

O principal bem da maioria dos pobres é seu capital humano. Por isso, investir no capital humano deles é um modo poderoso de aumentar seus bens, corrigir a desigualdade de bens e reduzir a pobreza. Este capítulo examina a qualidade da educação associando a distribuição desta com crescimento e redução da pobreza. Ele também interroga como tornar a educação mais produtiva em todos os níveis. Com certeza, o acesso à boa qualidade da educação é importante na medida em que aumenta a capacidade do povo para gerar renda. Contudo, isto não é o bastante. Para ser mais produtivo, ele precisa estar apto para combinar seu capital humano com outros bens produtivos, tais como terra e igualdade de capital, juntamente com oportunidades de emprego num mercado aberto.

O Capítulo 2 discutiu a importância de um aumento não distorcido ou equilibrado dos bens. Este capítulo focaliza-se nos bens que os pobres possuem, especialmente capital humano, e aqueles nos quais eles se baseiam mais drasticamente, tais como a terra. Para que o crescimento tenha impacto sobre a pobreza, os bens dos pobres, especialmente de seu capital humano, devem ser aumentados e distribuídos com maior eqüidade.[1] Ainda que as desigualdades nos resultados da educação e saúde sejam assustadoramente altas, refletindo as falhas de mercado e de subinvestimento no

capital humano dos pobres. A distribuição de bens representa a distribuição de oportunidades, e é uma pré-condição para a produtividade e renda individuais. Enquanto redistribuir bens e rendas existentes é politicamente difícil, construir novos bens, tal como capital humano, é amplamente aceito.

Para ser sustentado, o desenvolvimento deve ser eqüitativo e inclusivo. Assegurar gastos públicos adequados na educação e nos serviços de saúde é algo importante, mas que por si só não garante o progresso. É necessária uma estratégia multidimensional para habilitar o povo. Ações complementares incluem:

- aumento dos bens dos pobres, assegurando acesso a uma educação de alta qualidade e serviços de saúde;
- aumento da atenção para o efeito distributivo do investimento público e redução de subsídios para os tipos de educação e serviços de saúde que beneficiem os ricos;
- facilidade do uso completo do capital humano para habilitar os pobres com terra, crédito, treinamento e oportunidades de trabalho;
- complemento de todos os investimentos de capital com reformas econômicas e abertura de mercado, o que aumenta a produtividade da educação.

Benefícios Potenciais da Educação

Educação e boa saúde melhoram a capacidade das pessoas para dar forma às suas vidas – fortalecendo seu funcionamento na sociedade e contribuindo diretamente para o seu bem-estar. A educação das mulheres, por exemplo, não apenas aumenta sua capacidade de ganhar renda, mas também melhora sua saúde reprodutiva, reduz a mortalidade infantil e da criança, e beneficia as gerações atuais e futuras. Investir em capital humano é, contudo, crucial para o desenvolvimento econômico, a redução da pobreza e a proteção ambiental. Os benefícios do investimento no capital humano são bem conhecidos, mas algumas das ligações com outras dimensões do desenvolvimento – segurança, justiça social e sustentabilidade – são mais bem entendidas hoje do que o foram há dez anos.[2]

Investir nas pessoas pode contribuir para proteger trabalhadores e melhorar a segurança – um importante aspecto da qualidade de vida. Educação e boa saúde aumentam as habilidades dos pobres para lutar contra as mudanças em seu meio ambiente, permitem-lhes mudar de trabalho e fornecer alguma proteção contra as crises financeiras e reviravoltas econômicas (Capítulo 5).

A exclusão social reduz o incentivo individual para atender a escola e o trabalho (Bourguignon, 1999; Loury, 1999). O investimento no capital humano, se bem distribuído e direcionado para os pobres, pode facilitar a

inclusão social. Melhor educação e melhores serviços de saúde para os vulneráveis – freqüentemente para os grupos excluídos, tais como aqueles que são analfabetos, desabilitados, idosos, doentes crônicos, ou separados por barreiras de língua – podem ajudá-los a transpor os obstáculos sociais e aumentar sua produtividade.

Investir nas pessoas pode ajudar também a proteger o meio ambiente. Mulheres mais bem educadas melhoraram de saúde e, em muitos casos, tiveram menos filhos, reduzindo a pressão demográfica sobre os recursos naturais e o meio ambiente; com mais educação, as pessoas podem assimilar mais informações e empregar investimentos para proteger o meio ambiente e gerenciar melhor os recursos (Capítulo 4).

Investir nas pessoas contribui para melhorar os direitos humanos e a justiça social, o que oferece satisfação direta. A educação básica capacita os pobres para aprender sobre seus direitos civis e políticos, a exercer aqueles direitos pelo voto e a corrida aos cargos públicos, e para ouvir seus interesses, procurar encaminhamentos legais e exercitar visão pública. Isso concorre para a construção de instituições, melhorando o governo e combatendo a corrupção (Capítulo 6).

Esses benefícios estão longe de ser automáticos. Muitos estudos mostram que anos adicionais de educação por pessoa aumentam os rendimentos reais ou taxas de crescimento. Contudo, alguns poucos pesquisadores sugerem que o acúmulo de capital humano tem um impacto insignificante ou negativo sobre a economia e o crescimento da produtividade (Benhabib & Spiegel, 1994; Griliches, 1997; Islam, 1995; Pritchett, 1996). Mais governos gastando com educação, porém, se mal alocados, podem contribuir pouco para a redução da pobreza e, ao contrário, aumentar a desigualdade e o arrendamento. Como Murphy et al. (1991, p.503) denunciam: "O povo do país mais talentoso tipicamente organiza a produção por outros ... Quando eles abrem novas empresas, inovam e crescem com maior rapidez, mas quando se tornam arrendatários, eles apenas redistribuem riqueza e reduzem o crescimento".

Quantidade Não É o Bastante – Qualidade É o Que Importa

Desde 1980, os países em desenvolvimento investiram quantidades substanciais dos recursos públicos em educação (ver Figura 1.11). Na década de 1990, mais de três quartos das crianças em idade escolar dos países em desenvolvimento estavam matriculadas nas escolas, para menos da metade na década de 1960. As taxas de analfabetismo caíram de 39% para 30% entre 1985 e 1995 (World Bank, 1999a). O progresso foi irregular em diferentes regiões. As taxas de matrícula caíram na África subsaariana: a proporção de 6-11 anos de idade matriculadas nas escolas caiu de 59% em

1980 para 51% em 1992 (World Bank, 1999a). Falta de acesso à educação básica continua sendo o principal desafio em muitos países. Aumento de gastos públicos é desejável, mas não suficiente pelas razões que se seguem.

Gastos Públicos são Apenas Fragilmente Relacionados com os Resultados

A análise dos países revela um fraco relacionamento entre a generosidade nos gastos com a educação e os resultados com educação. Utilizando dados dos países, Filmer & Pritchett (1999b) examinaram a correlação entre gastos com educação governamental por estudante e a porcentagem de pessoas na idade de 15-19 anos que completaram o grau cinco. A correlação pareceu positiva e significativa de início, mas, depois de controlar a renda *per capita*, a correlação mostrou-se bastante frágil (Figura 3.1). Uma correlação de fragilidade similar foi encontrada entre gastos governamentais

Gastos públicos com educação são apenas fragilmente relacionados com os resultados educacionais

Figura 3.1 – Relacionamento Entre Gasto Público *per capita* e Conclusão Educacional, em Anos Variados

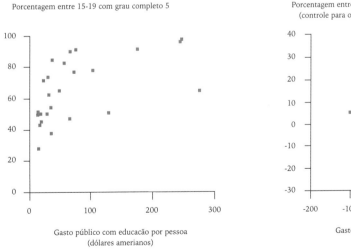
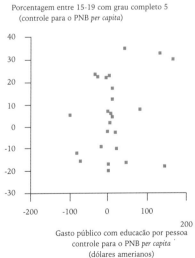

Nota: Os índices referem-se aos gastos públicos apenas com a educação pré-primária, primária e secundária (35 países em desenvolvimento foram incluídos no estudo).
Fontes: Dados sobre os resultados educacionais estão de acordo com Filmer & Pritchett (1999b), combinados com dados sobre gastos do banco de dados das Nações Unidas, Organização Educacional, Social e Cultural (UNESCO).

MELHORANDO A DISTRIBUIÇÃO DE OPORTUNIDADES

com saúde e taxas de mortalidade para crianças com menos de cinco anos de idade (Filmer & Pritchett, 1999c).

Por que será que o gasto público só é frágil quando relacionado aos resultados? O que faz a diferença são a qualidade e a distribuição dos serviços de educação e a produtividade do capital humano. Para os países em desenvolvimento que já alocaram uma parte substancial dos recursos públicos em serviços sociais, gastos posteriores podem não melhorar os resultados para a educação para os pobres. A realocação de gasto público e a melhoria de sua eficácia freqüentemente podem melhorar resultados, especialmente quando os recursos públicos estão subsidiando a educação para os ricos. Estratégias de abrangência econômica e políticas também importam: subsídios para atrair capital estrangeiro podem, sob certos aspectos, tornar oblíqua a taxa de retorno contra o capital humano.[3] Distorções no mercado de trabalho criam desincentivos para investimento na educação. Além disso, para ser produtivo, o povo deve ter acesso a outros bens produtivos, incluindo terra, crédito, igualdade e oportunidades de trabalho em mercados abertos e competitivos.

A Variabilidade na Qualidade Escolar

Apesar do progresso no acesso à educação, a qualidade da escolaridade varia consideravelmente de acordo com o país e a região. Uma extensa bibliografia estuda como melhor definir e mensurar a qualidade da escolaridade: se as entradas, processos ou conclusões estudantis deveriam ser usados em taxas (ver, por exemplo, Berhman & Birdsall, 1983; Card & Krueger, 1992; Greaney & Kellaghan, 1996; Lockheed & Verspoor, 1991). Mensuramos a qualidade como uma combinação de indicadores que refletem entradas, definidas por gastos por estudante e o número e a qualidade dos professores, processos, ou seja, o alcance dos temas escolares e o conteúdo curricular; e resultados mensurados pelas realizações cognitivas, atitudes, resultados de testes e taxas de evasão.

Nos países de alta renda onde estes indicadores são bem desenvolvidos, a conclusão estudantil varia amplamente; mesmo nos países com educação básica universal, as taxas de alfabetização funcional para adultos jovens entre 16-25 anos de idade variam em alguns países industrializados, por exemplo, de 45% nos Estados Unidos para 80% na Suécia, enquanto as taxas de matrícula na rede secundária são acima de 85% (World Bank, 1999a).

Nos países em desenvolvimento, nos quais os indicadores de conclusão são escassos, indicadores menos apurados, tais como taxas de repetência e evasão, foram utilizados para taxar os resultados educacionais. Os dados gerados por essas mensurações imperfeitas mostraram uma variação considerável na qualidade das escolas (Tabela 3.1). As taxas de repetência e evasão para a escola primária são muito mais baixas e os resultados de

As taxas de repetência e de evasão escolar variam enormemente de acordo com o país

Tabela 3.1 – Repetência de Escola Primária e Taxas de Evasão, em Anos Seletos
(por cento)

País	Taxa de repetência da escola primária		Taxa de evasão da escola primária			Gasto público com educação (porcentagem do PNB)		
	Anos 80	Anos 90	1970	1980	1990	Anos 70	Anos 80	Anos 90
Argentina	–	6	36	34	34	1,65	1,79	3,07
Brasil	20	18	78	78	80	2,95	4,04	3,60
Chile	–	6	23	24	23	4,60	4,52	2,84
Colômbia	17	9	43	43	44	2,05	2,75	3,43
México	10	8	11	12	28	2,90	4,06	4,45
Peru	17	15	34	30	30	3,30	3,09	3,40
Venezuela	10	11	41	32	52	4,30	5,09	4,56
Média América Latina	15	10	38	36	42	3,11	3,62	3,62
China	–	3	15	15	15	1,45	2,45	2,20
Indonésia	10	9	20	20	23	2,65	1,38	1,34
Coréia	–	–	5	6	1	2,80	3,89	3,92
Malásia	–	–	1	1	4	5,10	6,61	5,37
Filipinas	2	–	25	25	30	2,40	2,02	2,54
Tailândia	8	–	57	23	13	3,35	3,58	3,88
Média Ásia oriental	7	6	21	15	14	2,96	3,32	3,21

– Não disponível.
Fontes: Banco de dados do World Bank e UNESCO para dados sobre gastos.

notas são mais altos na Ásia oriental que nos países da América Latina, onde as rendas são mais altas. Enquanto os gastos com educação pública cresceram em alguns países latino-americanos na década de 1990, a média das taxas de evasão escolar primária também aumentou.[4] Outros estudos baseados nos dados limitados disponíveis sobre notas de provas igualmente mostraram que um gasto público generoso não garantiu a alta qualidade da educação.

O que explica as amplas variações na qualidade? Os resultados educacionais dependem tanto da demanda como de fatores suplementares e, assim, das políticas e das estruturas de incentivo, que afetam o conjunto da economia. Descobriu-se que a estabilidade macroeconômica representada por termos internacionais de comércio e pela volatilidade do PIB, por exemplo, é a mais importante das determinantes significativas da conclusão educacional na América Latina. Utilizando dados de 18 estudos internos, Behrman et al. (1999) descobriram que as crises do débito da década de 1980 contribuíram para a queda no acúmulo da escolaridade nos países lati-

no-americanos. Kaufmann & Wang (1995) descobriram que políticas microeconômicas afetam o setor social de projetos de investimento. Quando um país abre-se para o comércio e o investimento internacionais, a taxa de retorno para a educação cresce. O povo demanda qualidade mais alta de educação e dispõe-se a pagar mais por isso. Demandas de maior peso, investimentos privados mais elevados, professores mais bem pagos e alunos mais motivados produzem conclusões educacionais mais altas, com diferentes tempos de atraso. Quanto mais alta for a demanda por educação, mais alta será sua qualidade, e vice-versa. Se um país dedica recursos públicos para subsidiar o capital físico em vez da educação básica, ele pode distorcer as taxas de retorno contra o trabalho não especializado e atingir os pobres (ver Tabela A2.4 sobre subsídios de capital).

No nível micro, muitos estudos examinaram as ligações entre a qualidade da escolaridade e o desempenho estudantil. Behrman & Knowles (1999) descobriram uma forte associação positiva entre a qualidade do pessoal docente, a qualidade das entradas atuais e do sucesso infantil na escola. Hanushek & Kim (1995) descobriram que as medidas convencionais de recursos escolares, que são razão professor-aluno e gasto educacional, não afetam o desempenho nos testes estudantis. Em regressões pelo país, as notas de teste foram relacionadas positivamente às taxas de crescimento de um PIB real *per capita*, indicando uma realimentação potencial do crescimento para uma forte demanda e bom desempenho estudantil. Lee & Barro (1997) acharam que a base familiar, comunidades fortes, entradas escolares e amplitude dos termos escolares são positivamente relacionados com o desempenho estudantil; contudo, eles não podem explicar completamente por que os países da Ásia oriental conheceram melhores resultados educacionais do que outros países em desenvolvimento. Isto sugere que outros fatores podem estar em jogo, inclusive aqueles associados com um meio ambiente econômico mais aberto e orientado para a exportação.

Conseqüências da Pobreza de Qualidade

Baixa qualidade de escolaridade atinge os pobres desproporcionalmente e limita suas futuras oportunidades de ganho. Por exemplo, estudantes vietnamitas de famílias de alta renda desfrutam de maior acesso à educação de alta qualidade (Berhman & Knowles, 1999). Na América Latina, a maioria dos estudantes vindos de famílias de baixa renda freqüenta escolas públicas, que oferecem metade das horas de aula e cobrem apenas metade do currículo, comparadas com as escolas particulares. Quanto maior a renda familiar, maior a aversão a escolas públicas (IDB, 1998).

Estimativas baseadas em estudos sobre famílias da América Latina mostram que os alunos vindos das camadas de mais baixa renda receberam uma educação primária inferior. A qualidade medida pelo desempenho dos

estudantes no mercado de trabalho foi 35% mais baixa para estudantes de baixa renda do que para aqueles de mais alta renda (IDB, 1998, p.54). A Figura 3.2 mostra a enorme brecha nas taxas de conclusão da escola secundária para os ricos e para os pobres. Porque a educação particular é viável apenas para os ricos, a baixa qualidade do ensino público reduz severamente o potencial gerador de renda das crianças de famílias pobres.

Qualidade e Quantidade: Um Equilíbrio?

Melhorias na qualidade complementam a expansão do acesso à educação. Se crianças pobres só podem ir para escolas de baixa qualidade, possuem poucas oportunidades de obter trabalhos mais bem pagos e os pais

Figura 3.2 – Taxas de Conclusão da Escola Secundária para a Faixa Etária de 20-25 por Nível de Renda Familiar, Anos e Países Seletos da América Latina

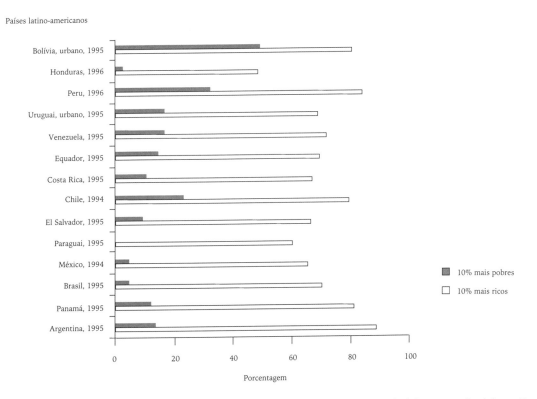

Nota: Números próximos às barras são brechas nas taxas de conclusão (em porcentagem). Os estudos para a Argentina incluem apenas a Grande Buenos Aires.
Fonte: IDB (1998, p.27).

são desestimulados a mandá-las para a escola. Quando a cobertura educacional não é universal, a melhor estratégia é focalizar nas intervenções políticas que aumentam a demanda tanto pela quantidade como pela qualidade da educação. Por exemplo, programas para reduzir o trabalho infantil e manter as crianças na escola – tais como merenda e contribuição em dinheiro – cairiam bem no treinamento docente para melhorar a qualidade.

Contudo, com populações crescentes e orçamentos reduzidos, as sinergias da quantidade e da qualidade podem virar equilíbrio, especialmente se as medidas de qualidade selecionadas não estiverem ligadas a aprendizagem estudantil. Qual a medida de qualidade que deveria ser utilizada para a intervenção? Seriam os incentivos estudantis, ou o aumento dos termos escolares, ou a qualidade do pessoal docente? A evidência mostra que a redução das razões professor-aluno, que é cara, tem pouco impacto sobre o aprendizado estudantil (Mingat & Tan, 1998).[5]

Apesar da relativamente alta razão professor-aluno nas décadas de 1980 e 1990, a média das notas dos estudantes coreanos em testes de Ciência Internacional e Matemática ficaram entre as mais altas. Gastar mais para contratar mais professores poderia implicar um equilíbrio contra cobertura e distribuição mais ampla de educação, que seria ineficiente e desigual, particularmente onde muitas crianças ainda não têm acesso à educação básica (Mingat & Tan, 1998).

Realizar uma Educação Eqüitativa e a Inclusão Social

Acesso igual à educação e aos serviços de saúde está entre os direitos humanos básicos para os quais todos estão autorizados. Como para a terra e o capital físico, uma distribuição igualitária do capital humano é importante para um crescimento de base ampla e redução da pobreza. Além disso, uma distribuição de oportunidade eqüitativa é preferível para a redistribuição dos bens disponíveis, porque investir no povo cria novos bens e melhora o bem-estar social.[6] Garantir o acesso aos pobres pela distribuição de serviços educacionais com maior igualdade é uma política vencedora, que está ganhando apoio tanto nos países industriais como naqueles em desenvolvimento.

Por que colocar o foco na distribuição da educação? Porque assegurar o acesso à educação básica pelos pobres está intimamente relacionado com uma melhor distribuição da educação. Dados os recursos públicos limitados para a educação, concentrar investimento público na educação para os pobres, habitualmente, implica uma realocação dos gastos públicos a partir dos subsídios para os tipos de serviços de educação que beneficiam os ricos. Tais medidas são politicamente impopulares e muitos países foram incapazes de implementá-las. Contudo, como foi mostrado nesta parte, há razões coercitivas para que um governo persiga tais medidas políticas.

Medidas de Dispersão nos Resultados Educacionais

Desde os tempos de Adam Smith, a educação tem sido ligada ao progresso econômico e social eqüitativo. Há uma pequena mas crescente bibliografia sobre a desigualdade de escolaridade ou a distribuição da educação (ver, por exemplo, Lam & Levison, 1991; Londoño, 1990; Maas & Criel, 1982; Ram, 1990). Como os dados ficaram disponíveis para medir a distribuição da educação, as disparidades tornaram-se mais aparentes. Utilizando desvio-padrão de conclusão escolar, Birdsall & Londoño (1997) investigaram o impacto das distribuições de bens iniciais sobre o crescimento e a redução da pobreza e encontraram uma significativa correlação entre desigualdade educacional inicial e crescimento reduzido de renda.

Mais tarde os pesquisadores construíram Coeficientes Gini de Educação, que são similares aos coeficientes Gini amplamente utilizados para medir as distribuições de renda, riqueza e terra. O coeficiente Gini abrange desde 0 (zero), que representa perfeita igualdade, a 1 (um), que representa perfeita desigualdade (ver Anexo 3 para os dois métodos utilizados para calcular o coeficiente Gini). Os coeficientes Gini para a educação podem ser calculados utilizando-se matrícula, financiamento ou dados de conclusão, reconhecendo que diferentes grupos em uma população foram educados em tempos diferentes. López et al. (1998) estimaram coeficientes Gini de conclusão educacional para vinte países e descobriram diferenças significativas na distribuição da escolaridade. A Coréia teve a mais rápida expansão na cobertura educacional e o mais rápido declínio no Coeficiente Gini de Educação; caiu de 0,51 para 0,22 em vinte anos. O coeficiente Gini para a educação na Índia declinou com moderação de 0,80 em 1970 para 0,69 em 1990. Os coeficientes Gini para a educação na Colômbia, Costa Rica, Peru e Venezuela tiveram um aumento lento desde a década de 1980, mostrando que a desigualdade está em alta (Figura 3.3).

Um exame das curvas de Lorenz de educação para a Índia e a Coréia nos anos 90 mostra uma grande amplitude entre os países em desenvolvimento (Figura 3.4). Apesar do progresso na expansão das matrículas primárias e secundárias na Índia, mais de metade da população (na faixa etária dos 15 anos e mais velhos) não recebe nenhuma educação, enquanto 10% da população recebeu quase 40% do total acumulado de anos de escolaridade. Fornecer acesso universal à educação básica continua sendo um enorme desafio para o país.

A Coréia expandiu seu programa de educação básica rapidamente, com uma distribuição eqüitativa muito maior da conclusão educacional, como indicado por uma curva Lorenz mais plana e um coeficiente Gini menor. Mesmo em 1960, quando a renda *per capita* coreana era semelhante à da Índia, a educação coreana pelo coeficiente Gini era de 0,55, muito mais baixa do que a da Índia em 1990. Note-se que a distribuição da educação na

Figura 3.3 – Os Coeficientes Gini de Educação, Países Seletos, 1960-1990

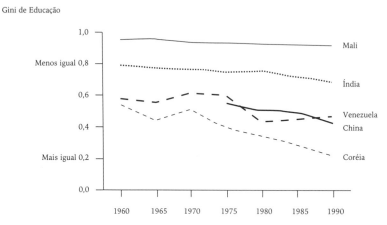

Fonte: López et al. (1998).

A distribuição da educação varia enormemente, desde altamente tendenciosa para mais igual

Figura 3.4 – As Curvas Educacionais de Lorenz para Índia e Coréia, 1990

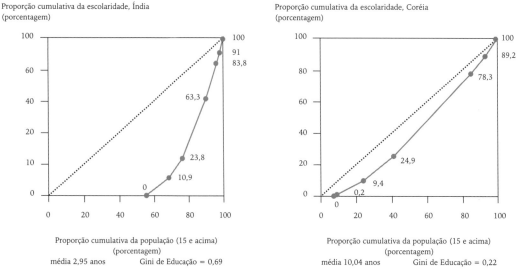

Fonte: Thomas et al. (2000).

Coréia foi mais eqüitativa do que a da renda, mas a distribuição da educação na Índia foi muito mais tendenciosa do que a da renda entre 1970 e 1990.[7]

Uma distribuição da educação tão tendenciosa como a da Índia implica uma enorme perda social pela subutilização do capital humano potencial. Assumir aquela aptidão ou talento é normalmente distribuído pelos grupos populacionais; a produção aumenta até o seu máximo quando a dispersão da educação iguala a distribuição da aptidão humana. Quando a distribuição da educação é tão tendenciosa para igualar a distribuição da aptidão, há uma perda de peso morto para a sociedade do talento subdesenvolvido e subutilizado. Neste caso, as sociedades deveriam estar em melhor situação para expandir maciçamente a educação básica, especialmente melhorando o acesso à educação pelos pobres.

Examinando o padrão através do país de distribuição da educação, descobrimos que os coeficientes Gini para a educação declinam, enquanto a média educacional e níveis de renda aumentam, embora haja claramente outras possibilidades. Será que o coeficiente Gini para a educação precisa piorar antes de melhorar? Como sugerido por Londoño (1990) e Ram (1990), há um "conto kuznetsiano" com a distribuição da educação. Ou seja, enquanto um país se move a partir do nível 0 (zero) para o nível máximo da educação, a variação primeiro aumenta e, então, declina. Contudo, análises dos países sugerem que isso pode não ser o caso, se o coeficiente Gini for utilizado para medir desigualdade. Além do mais, para os países industrializados, Argentina, Chile e Irlanda possuem relativamente baixos Coeficientes Gini de Educação desde a década de 1960 até a década de 1990. O coeficiente Gini para a educação na Coréia e alguns outros países diminuiu drasticamente. Apenas uns poucos países – Colômbia, Costa Rica, Peru e Venezuela – conheceram uma piora significativa do Coeficiente Gini de Educação. Uma piora na distribuição da educação não é inevitável (Figura 3.5). Entre 85 países para os quais os Coeficientes Gini de Educação foram calculados, o Afeganistão e o Mali tiveram as distribuições menos eqüitativas nos anos 90, em aproximadamente 0,90, enquanto a maioria dos países industrializados estava no fim da lista, com os Estados Unidos e a Polônia, tendo a distribuição mais eqüitativa (Thomas et al., 2000). Semelhante às amplas variações na distribuição da educação, outros estudos descobriram amplas variações nos resultados para saúde através de grupos de renda (Quadro 3.1).

Causas da Desigualdade na Educação

As disparidades na educação são um dos muitos aspectos da pobreza, mas também são associadas com a má alocação do investimento público e guerras, por brechas de riqueza e brechas de gênero, exclusão social e crises econômicas. Numerosos estudos descobriram que a educação dos pais e a

Os Gini para a educação declinam enquanto a média do nível educacional cresce

Figura 3.5 – Os Coeficientes Gini de Educação para 85 países, 1990

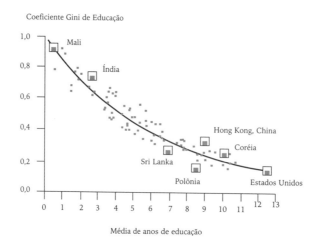

Fonte: Thomas et al. (2000).

renda familiar, tanto quanto a riqueza, afetam as conclusões da educação das crianças.

Brechas de riqueza. Utilizando os dados do *National Family Health Survey* coletados nos estados indianos em 1992 e 1993, Filmer & Pritchett (1999a) descobriram as brechas de riqueza, definidas como a diferença entre o máximo de 20% de um índice de bens e o mínimo de 40%, calculadas para uma ampla proporção de diferenças nas taxas de matrícula. As taxas de matrícula variaram de 4,6% em Kerala para 42,6% em Bihar.

Em alguns países, as diferenças nos resultados educacionais entre o rico e o pobre são vacilantes. Um estudo sobre jovens na faixa etária de 15-19 anos em vinte países mostrou que os 40% dos miseráveis em cinco países tinham uma média de 0 (zero) anos de escolaridade completa; mais da metade deste grupo completou menos que 1 (um) ano de escola (Figura 3.7). A diferença de educação entre os mais ricos e os mais pobres atingiu a altura de dez graus na Índia. Disparidades semelhantes na conclusão da educação são encontradas na América Latina (Figura 3.8).

Uma implicação desta ampla brecha de riqueza é que a demanda pela educação não é independente de outras dotações orçamentárias. Fornecer acesso à educação (suplementar) não é suficiente. Levantar muitas desigualdades estruturais e sociais que influenciem a demanda, tais como bre-

Quadro 3.1 – Brechas de Saúde Entre Ricos e Pobres Também São Grandes

As brechas de saúde entre pobres e ricos são tão grandes quanto as brechas educacionais, o que reflete as dificuldades em alcançar os mais pobres fora da corrente econômica principal. Muitos estudos descobrem que os miseráveis estão em pior estado de saúde (Berhman & Deolalikar, 1998) e são freqüentemente atingidos mais drasticamente pelas guerras, choques externos e convulsões sociais e políticas. As taxas de mortalidade infantil entre os miseráveis são muito mais altas que as entre as pessoas que possuem rendas mais altas. A Figura 3.6 mostra que, no Brasil, as taxas de mortalidade infantil eram altas entre os mais pobres (10% da população), e caíam quando a riqueza crescia. Isso indica que os miseráveis estão em pior estado de saúde que os demais. Eles sofrem muito mais de doenças infecciosas do que os mais ricos, sendo, no entanto, mais dependentes das boas políticas públicas que os ricos (Bonilla-Chacin & Hammer, 1999).

Os pobres são mais doentes que outras pessoas

Figura 3.6 – Mortalidade de Crianças de Dois Anos e Mais Jovens, pela Riqueza, Brasil, 1996

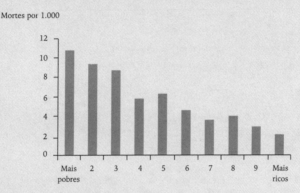

Fonte: Bonilla-Chacin & Hammer (1999).

chas de gênero e distribuição de outros bens produtivos como a terra, discutidos mais adiante, é igualmente importante.

Exclusão Social. É menos provável que as pessoas que são excluídas da corrente principal da sociedade sejam educadas. Loury (1999) mostrou como a exclusão social modifica o comportamento humano e reduz a demanda pela escolaridade em cidades do interior dos Estados Unidos. Uma razão para a evasão dos estudantes da escola é o fato de seus amigos já terem se evadido. Na Bolívia, a incapacidade dos pais para falar espanhol está associada com taxas mais altas de mortalidade abaixo dos dois anos de idade. Na Índia, membros das castas estruturais possuem taxas mais altas de mortalidade que os outros grupos (Bonilla-Chacin & Hammer, 1999).

MELHORANDO A DISTRIBUIÇÃO DE OPORTUNIDADES

Diferenças em conclusão de grau para famílias ricas e pobres são enormes em alguns países

Figura 3.7 – Conclusão de Grau Médio para Jovens entre 15-19 Anos de Famílias Ricas e Pobres, Países e Anos Seletos

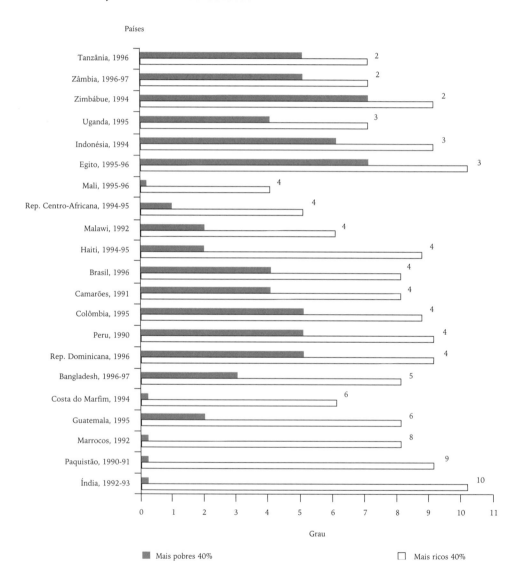

Nota: Os números junto às barras são as brechas em graus entre ricos e pobres.
Fonte: Filmer & Pritchett (1999b).

A QUALIDADE DO CRESCIMENTO

Figura 3.8 – Anos de Escolaridade para Jovens na Faixa Etária de 25 Anos em Famílias Ricas e Pobres na América Latina

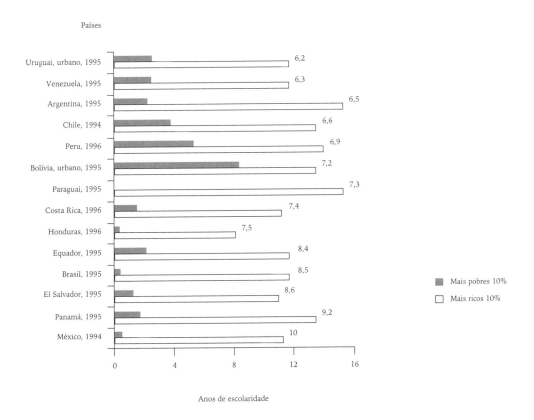

Nota: Os números junto às barras são as brechas em anos de escolaridade entre ricos e pobres. Os estudos para a Argentina incluem apenas a Grande Buenos Aires.
Fonte: IDB (1998, p.27).

Brechas de Gênero. Em alguns países, as brechas de gênero são uma importante causa da desigualdade de educação. Entre muitos estudos aprumando as brechas de gênero na educação, Schultz (1998) descobriu que mais ou menos 65% da desigualdade mundial ocorre entre países, 30% entre famílias dentro de um país e 5% entre desigualdade de gênero. Bouis et al. (1998) descobriram uma significativa diferença em investimentos de capital humano, tais como nutrição, serviços de saúde e conclusão educacional, entre garotos e garotas nas regiões rurais das Filipinas. Em Bangladesh, que possui a maior brecha de gênero entre os países passados em revista, as atitudes das mulheres em relação à educação de suas filhas demoraram muito a mudar (Amin & Pebley, 1994).

Contudo, esforços recentes foram bem-sucedidos ao encorajar o progresso (Quadro 3.2). Knight & Shi (1991) descobriram que as oportunidades educacionais ainda eram desigualmente distribuídas na China, apesar de um progresso considerável. O padrão de conclusão educacional é afetado pelo gênero, assim como por outros fatores, tais como a renda das províncias, as diferenças urbanas e rurais, em renda e base familiar. Embora declinante, a discriminação de gênero persiste nas áreas rurais chinesas (ver Dubey & King, 1996; King & Hill, 1993; e World Bank (2000g) para experiências através dos países).

A correlação é drástica entre desigualdade educacional e brechas de gênero na alfabetização. Utilizando uma amostragem de 85 países para os quais os coeficientes Gini para a educação estão disponíveis, Thomas et al. (2000) descobriram que a correlação dos coeficientes entre brechas de gênero no analfabetismo e o coeficiente Gini para a educação aumentou significativamente de 0,53 na década de 1970 para 0,69 na década de 1990. Enquanto a desigualdade educacional declinava, a desigualdade de gênero contribuiu muito com as disparidades remanescentes para a conclusão educacional (Figura 3.9). Reduzir as brechas de gênero na educação é crucial para corrigir a desigualdade na educação.

Quadro 3.2 – Sustentar a Educação Feminina em Bangladesh

Uma revolução está ocorrendo nas escolas por intermédio de Bangladesh. As tendências para matrícula estão mudando e agora mais garotas que garotos podem ser vistos freqüentemente nas escolas.

A conclusão educacional das mulheres em Bangladesh está entre a mais baixa do mundo e as brechas de gênero estão entre as mais amplas. Em 1997, a diferença entre o analfabetismo masculino e o feminino era tão alta quanto 23 pontos percentuais. De acordo com os dados do senso de 1991, apenas 20% das mulheres sabiam ler e escrever, e apenas um em três estudantes nas escolas secundárias eram garotas.

Em 1994 o governo lançou um programa para aumentar a sustentação para a educação secundária feminina, visando aumentar a taxa de alfabetização feminina de 16% para 25% e criar oportunidades de emprego para as mulheres. Com apoio do Banco Mundial e de outros parceiros desenvolvimentistas, o programa está sendo implementado com sucesso e transformou Bangladesh em pioneiro nesta área do sul da Ásia.

O programa de incentivo para as garotas, incluindo isenções de matrículas e ajuda de custo, gerou um tremendo entusiasmo pela educação feminina, aumentando a matrícula de garotas nas escolas secundárias. A matrícula de garotas nos projetos de distritos está acima de explicações; as matrículas cresceram ano a ano por todas as classes. Um total de 554.077 garotas foram agraciadas com as ajudas de custo em 1996 e o número foi maior em 1997. Na Faculdade Fulbária Mohamed Ali, em Savar, perto de Dhaka, o número de garotas ultrapassa o de garotos em quatro por um; uma situação que era impensável poucos anos atrás.

Fonte: Robby (1999).

Enquanto a desigualdade educacional declina, a desigualdade de gênero significa muito para o que permanece

Figura 3.9 – Brechas de Gênero e Desigualdade de Educação, 1970 e 1990

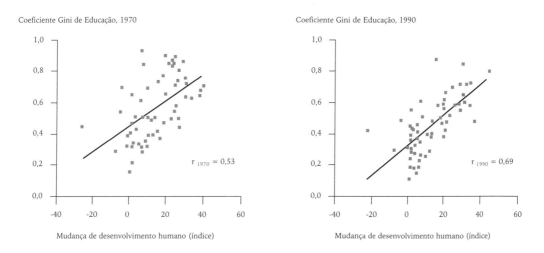

Nota: As figuras incluem dados para 85 países.
Fontes: Coeficientes Gini de Educação de Thomas et al. (2000); brechas de gênero no analfabetismo do World Bank (1999d).

Conseqüências das Amplas Dispersões nos Resultados Educacionais

Uma sociedade preocupa-se com a distribuição desigual da educação porque isto afeta desigualmente o bem-estar humano. A distribuição desigual da educação é tanto uma fonte quanto uma conseqüência da pobreza e da exclusão social. Crianças pobres que se evadem da escola eventualmente formam um centro de cidadãos desfavorecidos que serão deixados fora da corrente principal da vida econômica e social. A menos que as pessoas possam obter um treinamento posterior na vida para encontrar um trabalho significativo, a redução da pobreza e a inclusão social permanecerão fora de nosso alcance.

Uma distribuição da educação altamente desigual tende a ser associada com crescimento reduzido de renda *per capita*, mesmo depois de dirigida para o trabalho e para o capital físico (López et al., 1998). Diferentemente da terra e do capital físico, que são comercializáveis por intermédio de empresas e indivíduos, a educação e as habilidades não são perfeitamente comercializáveis. Conseqüentemente, tanto a distribuição como o nível da educação entram na função produtiva e afetam o nível de crescimento final.

MELHORANDO A DISTRIBUIÇÃO DE OPORTUNIDADES

Utilizando dados do painel de vinte países em desenvolvimento, López et al. (1998) demonstraram a associação negativa entre a distribuição desigual da educação e o crescimento econômico. Quando grande parte da população não é educada, a baixa produtividade das forças de trabalho desencoraja o investimento no capital físico e o crescimento econômico sofre (ver análise de regressão no Quadro 2.1 e Anexo 3).

A distribuição da educação também tem implicações drásticas para o impacto da redução da pobreza, do crescimento. Ravallion & Datt (1999), utilizando-se de dados de 15 estados indianos entre 1960 e 1994, descobriram que a associação do crescimento com a redução da pobreza variava de acordo com as condições iniciais: o crescimento contribuía menos para a redução da pobreza em estados com taxas de alfabetização mais baixas, produtividade agrícola e padrão rural de vida relativo a áreas urbanas. Em Kerala, onde a educação básica é bem distribuída, as taxas de alfabetização são as mais altas; para homens e mulheres, um ponto percentual que aumenta na taxa de crescimento estava mais fortemente associado à redução da pobreza.

Em Assam e Bihar, que possuíam taxas de crescimento de produção agrícola não semelhantes àquelas de Kerala, mas as baixas taxas de alfabetização e a mais alta desigualdade na educação básica, o crescimento contribuiu pouco para a redução da pobreza (Figura 3.10). Por exemplo, em Bihar, com a mais baixa taxa de alfabetização feminina entre os estados estudados, 29% mostraram uma diferença de 32% nas taxas de alfabetização e seis milhões de crianças na faixa etária de 6-10 anos não estavam matriculadas nas escolas entre 1992 e 1993. Outros estados, como Maharashtra e Madhya Pradesh, tiveram taxas de crescimento mais altas, mas taxas de redução da pobreza mais baixas que as de Kerala. Mais que de crescimento rápido, precisa-se de crescimento a favor dos pobres para redução da pobreza. Se todos os estados indianos tivessem uma elasticidade de redução da pobreza como Kerala, a pobreza como medida pelo índice de incidência poderia ter caído a uma taxa de 3,5% em vez de 1,3% ao ano desde 1960.

Melhorar a Eficácia do Gasto Público

Somente os mercados não podem fornecer o acesso eqüitativo à educação básica pelos pobres. Como parcialmente um bem público, a educação fornece expansões positivas que não são totalmente captadas por indivíduos e empresas. Contudo, um mercado falha principalmente no lado mais baixo da distribuição de renda: sem o investimento público na educação dos pobres, o investimento da sociedade na educação seria subótimo. Ainda assim, como vimos, o gasto público é apenas fragilmente associado com os resultados da educação, em parte devido ao viés em direção aos privilegia-

O crescimento tem um poderoso impacto na redução da pobreza nos estados com educação mais eqüitativa como Kerala

Figura 3.10 – As Tendências das Taxas de Redução da Pobreza e Saídas Não Agrícolas do Crescimento Econômico na Índia, 1960-1994

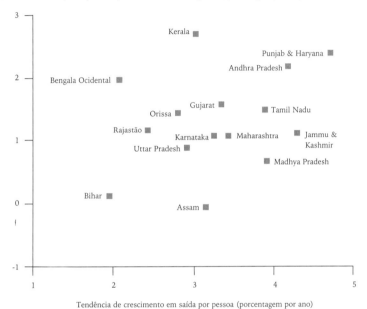

Nota: Tendência das taxas de crescimento estimadas pelos mínimos comuns dos quadrados de regressões dos logaritmos sobre tempo.
Fonte: Ravallion & Datt (1999).

dos. Aumentar o gasto público é desejável, mas não suficiente para lidar com um resultado inadequado do desenvolvimento humano; agora voltamos para melhorar a alocação e a eficácia do gasto.

Alocar Mais Gasto Público para a Educação dos Pobres

A composição dos gastos governamentais com educação e saúde influencia os resultados do desenvolvimento humano. Os gastos públicos precisam concentrar-se em áreas onde a falência do mercado é penetrante e onde expansões positivas são maiores: nas escolas primária e secundária, especialmente para os pobres. Dados os recursos públicos limitados, o equi-

líbrio precisa mudar mais em direção aos investimentos na educação primária e na secundária. Além disso, o setor privado e as parcerias público/privado deveriam ser encorajadas para fornecer educação superior, onde a falência do mercado é mínima.

A Coréia mostrou como uma forte ênfase na educação primária e na secundária poderia eliminar o analfabetismo e reduzir a desigualdade educacional. Esse país alocou dois terços de seus gastos com educação pública para a educação primária nos anos 60 e início de 1970 (Tabela 3.2). Gastos públicos com a educação secundária cresceram de 22% em 1965 para 33% em 1990. Ainda assim, os gastos públicos com educação superior raramente excediam 12% do total dos gastos públicos entre 1965 e 1990; esse nível de ensino foi principalmente financiado pelos investimentos privados. Antes dos anos 90, a Índia despendeu uma parte maior do que gastou a Coréia com educação superior e uma parte menor, mas crescente, com a educação primária na metade da década de 1990. A Índia aumentou seus gastos com as escolas elementares e programas de alfabetização de adultos de 20% a 31% de seu total de gastos públicos com educação, o que permanecia ainda muito abaixo do da Coréia. Para fornecer um acesso mais amplo na educação e reduzir a desigualdade, ainda há muito a ser feito para a melhoria da alocação de investimentos públicos na Índia.

Medidos pelo gasto público por estudante, os subsídios públicos para a educação superior vêm caindo em muitos países, mas não suficientemente rápido para capacitar a realocação dos fundos públicos para a educação básica (Tabela 3.3). A alocação de recursos ainda é enviesada em relação à educação primária e à secundária em muitos países. Nos Estados Unidos, a alocação dos gastos públicos vem sendo equilibrada há mais de trinta anos, com subsídios para a escolaridade primária para mais de 20% do Produto Nacional Bruto (PNB) *per capita*, o mais alto do mundo. Na Coréia, devido ao grande número de estudantes nas escolas primárias, o apoio governamental por estudante não enfatizou de modo suficiente a educação primária na década de 1960, embora mais de 60% do total gasto fosse alocado para a educação primária. Este padrão foi revertido na década de 1980, quando o gasto por estudante de escola primária excedeu o do estu-

Tabela 3.2 – Gasto Público por Níveis de Educação, Coréia, em Anos Seletos

(porcentagem do total de gastos com educação)

Níveis	1965	1970	1975	1980	1985	1990
Primário	64,7	67,4	52,2	47,9	44,5	43,2
Secundário	21,8	20,9	37,1	33,8	37,7	33,1
Superior	13,3	8,2	10,7	11,4	11,5	9,6

Fonte: Banco de dados da UNESCO.

Tabela 3.3 – Gasto Público por Estudante, por Nível, 1960-1990

País	Nível	Gasto público por estudante (porcentagem PNB per capita)				Coeficiente Gini de Educação (Média nacional, todos os níveis)	
		Anos 60	Anos 70	Anos 80	Anos 90	1980	1990
Argentina	Primário	–	3,06	6,49	8,32	0,29	0,27
	Secundário	26,17	10,43	–	–		
	Superior	59,29	23,58	17,45	19,84		
Chile	Primário	6,92	6,08	12,53	9,20	0,32	0,31
	Secundário	–	12,01	12,58	8,80		
	Superior	151,71	67,46	79,69	23,36		
Coréia	Primário	6,21	7,86	12,79	14,86	0,34	0,22
	Secundário	8,64	7,39	10,76	11,88		
	Superior	36,67	28,02	10,49	5,83		
México	Primário	4,34	–	3,97	7,18	0,50	0,38
	Secundário	–	–	8,61	13,93		
	Superior	70,72	–	32,43	35,66		
Estados Unidos	Primário	22,05	28,45	26,28	19,83	0,12	0,15
	Secundário	–	–	18,77	23,86		
	Superior	73,73	58,84	37,85	22,91		
Venezuela	Primário	8,50	7,37	4,80	2,39	0,39	0,42
	Secundário	21,26	17,60	18,34	7,07		
	Superior	121,76	100,0	65,74	37,38		

– Não disponível.

Fontes: Dados sobre gastos públicos do banco de dados da UNESCO; coeficientes Gini de Thomas et al. (2000).

dante universitário. Associada a uma forte ênfase na educação básica, a Coréia foi capaz de reduzir a desigualdade na educação rapidamente. Os Estados Unidos vêm, desde 1965, mantendo o mais baixo Coeficiente Gini de Educação no mundo.

A Venezuela, em contraste, favoreceu a educação superior em relação à educação básica por mais de quatro décadas. Enquanto o gasto público total com educação cresceu de 4,3% do PNB na década de 1970 para 5,1% na de 1980 e 4,6% na de 1990, sua alocação piorou. De fato, os subsídios à educação primária e à secundária foram reduzidos na década de 1990. Essa má alocação dos recursos públicos poderia explicar parcialmente a piora do Coeficiente Gini de Educação na década de 1990.

A Interação entre Demografia e Educação

O gasto público por estudante em idade escolar primária na Coréia cresceu em mais de dez vezes entre 1970 e 1995, ao passo que as taxas de crescimento populacional diminuíram e a economia se expandiu (Ta-

MELHORANDO A DISTRIBUIÇÃO DE OPORTUNIDADES

bela 3.4). O gasto público por estudante secundarista também cresceu. O crescimento econômico rápido, juntamente com o declínio estabilizante e regular da base estudantil, significou que muito mais recursos foram sendo destinados a menos crianças, permitindo drásticas melhorias na qualidade da educação primária.

Na Índia, o rápido crescimento populacional e coerções sobre a dotação pública significaram que quantidade e qualidade equilibradas estavam provavelmente para ocorrer. Em 1995, a Índia despendeu US$ 39 (em dólares constantes de 1995) por aluno nas escolas primárias, ou 10% de seu PIB *per capita*, enquanto a Coréia gastou 17% (Tabela 3.4). Em Tamil Nadu, na Índia, a matrícula nas escolas primárias e médias expandiu-se 35% entre 1977 e 1992 – uma grande realização –, mas a razão professor-aluno cresceu de 36% para 47% e as condições da escola pioraram. Como resultado disso, o aproveitamento do aluno foi sofrível (Duraisamy et al., 1998). Esses relacionamentos apontam para a necessidade de considerar a interação entre política demográfica e educacional e para a necessidade de se implementarem políticas direcionadas para a educação de garotas e mulheres, educação para melhorar a saúde reprodutiva e o planejamento familiar voluntário como parte de uma estratégia de desenvolvimento global, centrada no povo (ver também Quadro 3.3).

Tabela 3.4 – Gastos Públicos Atuais por Estudante, Índia e Coréia, em Anos Seletos

País	Nível	1965	1970	1975	1980	1985	1990	1995
Quantia (1995 US$ por estudante)								
Coréia	Primário	92	207	182	386	701	955	1.890
	Secundário	–	223	134	339	541	786	1.295
	Superior	545	757	622	589	546	460	599
Índia	Primário	8	10	20	23	29	39	39
	Secundário	–	54	35	34	38	–	43
	Superior	–	–	–	189	227	299	260
Porcentagem do PIB per capita								
Coréia	Primário	6,3	9,5	6,3	10,2	13,5	12,0	17,4
	Secundário	–	10,3	4,6	9,0	10,4	9,9	11,9
	Superior	37,2	35,0	21,5	15,6	10,5	5,8	5,5
Índia	Primário	4,3	4,8	9,2	9,7	10,6	11,8	9,9
	Secundário	–	24,9	15,8	14,8	13,9	–	11,0
	Superior	–	–	–	81,8	84,0	90,3	66,4

– Não disponível.

Nota: As quantidades de dólares não são comparáveis em países como o são em PPP dólares, mas são comparáveis no decorrer do tempo.

Fontes: Dados calculados pela UNESCO e pelo World Bank.

Quadro 3.3 – População e Desenvolvimento

A ligação entre crescimento populacional e desenvolvimento econômico é um tema de acalorados debates. As décadas de 1960 e 1970 foram dominadas pelas predições pessimistas e algumas vezes alarmistas de que o crescimento rápido da população levaria à fome, à exaustão dos recursos, a deficiências na poupança, a danos ambientais irreversíveis e ao colapso ecológico (Ehrlich, 1968). A população otimista acreditava que o crescimento rápido da população fosse permitir que os países captassem economias de escalas e promovessem inovação tecnológica e institucional (Simon, 1976). Na década de 1980, os pontos de vista alarmistas foram substituídos pelos moderados, investimentos específicos de tempo e país dos impactos da rede negativa do rápido crescimento populacional que foram considerados menores. Apenas ligações frágeis ou inconclusivas foram descobertas entre mudanças demográficas e desenvolvimento econômico (Bloom & Freeman, 1988; Keley, 1988).

Investigações mais recentes revelaram, de modo muito mais amplo, efeitos negativos do crescimento populacional rápido e os componentes demográficos relativos ao crescimento econômico per capita. Kelley & Schimidt (1999) descobriram que o crescimento populacional rápido exercia um impacto adverso muito forte no andamento do crescimento econômico em 89 países entre 1960 e 1995. Os impactos positivos da densidade, tamanho da população e a entrada da força de trabalho foram dominados pelos custos da criação infantil das crianças e a manutenção ampliada da idade estrutural da dependência juvenil. O declínio da mortalidade e da fertilidade cada um contribuiu com aproximadamente 22% para as mudanças no crescimento resultante entre 1960 e 1992, uma figura que corresponde a aproximadamente 21% da média de resultado do crescimento *per capita* que foi aferida em 1,5% .

Vários componentes da mudança demográfica foram introduzidos com sucesso nos modelos de crescimento. Bloom & Williamson (1998) mostraram que a transição demográfica rápida na Ásia oriental levou a crescimento rápido na população em idade produtiva entre 1965 e 1990, expandiu a capacidade produtiva *per capita* e contribuiu para o milagre econômico da Ásia oriental. Outras políticas econômicas também facilitaram aos asiáticos orientais realização do crescimento potencial da transição demográfica.

Menos evidência estava disponível na ligação entre mudança demográfica e pobreza, até recentemente. Contudo, se o crescimento populacional rápido tem um efeito negativo no crescimento econômico e dos salários, iria igualmente afetar negativamente a pobreza. Eastwood & Lipton (1999) descobriram que a maior fertilidade aumenta a pobreza tanto por retardar o crescimento quanto por fazer tender a distribuição contra os pobres. Além disso, a evidência mostra que os programas do setor público cujo alvo eram os pobres, tais como programas de educação básica e serviços de saúde, contribuíram para reduzir a pobreza. Crescimento populacional rápido diminuirá a intensidade do investimento público e, conseqüentemente dificultará a realização de melhorias na qualidade do serviço.

Fontes: Bloom & Williamson (1998); Eastwood & Lipton (1999); Kelley (1998); Kelley & Schmidt (1999).

Melhorar a Parceria de Gastos Públicos e Privados

A Coréia também realizou uma boa parceria de financiamentos público e privado na educação. Desde a metade da década de 1960, as faculdades privadas e as universidades contabilizaram mais de 70% das matrículas, e as instituições secundárias privadas, para mais de 40%. As famílias assumem uma grande parte dos custos educacionais, entre 30% e 50%, dependendo do nível de educação do aluno. O custo da instrução e as taxas de exame relacionadas respondem por 40% dos gastos escolares para a escola

média, mas aumenta drasticamente para 72%, e mais, para os estudantes secundaristas e universitários.

A maioria das parcerias efetivas públicas/privadas depende da extensão das falências de mercado e de uma variedade de outros fatores. A educação superior é crucial para o progresso tecnológico e o crescimento da produtividade, mas pode ser considerado um bem privado, porque a maior parte dos retornos pode ser interiorizada por indivíduos e empresas. Enquanto a educação primária e a secundária têm uma expansão ampla, os efeitos não são totalmente captados pelos indivíduos e empresas. Assim, enquanto o governo tem o papel direto na educação primária e na secundária, ele precisa encorajar investimentos privados e parcerias públicas/privadas para a educação superior. Os Estados Unidos, por exemplo, desse ponto de vista, oferecem valiosas experiências.

O ambiente político que pode ser definido pelo grau de abertura ao comércio e ao investimento, por exemplo, afeta a demanda por trabalhadores especializados e, conseqüentemente, por pessoas desejosas de pagar pela educação. A qualidade da previsão de serviço para a educação, relacionada com as capacidades institucionais, também afeta o desejo de pagar. De modo semelhante, a parceria público/privado nos serviços de saúde também depende da natureza, dos serviços e do grau de falhas de mercado, em particular nos subsetores (disponível em Filmer, Hammer & Pritchett).

Uma intervenção bem-sucedida é o programa *Quetta Girls Felowship*, no Paquistão. Lançado em 1995, o projeto-piloto visava determinar se o estabelecimento de escolas privadas nas periferias pobres seria um caminho efetivo para a expansão do ensino primário destinado a meninas. O programa encorajou escolas privadas controladas pelas comunidades, garantindo-lhes apoio governamental por três anos. Uma análise avaliativa indica que o programa aumentou as matrículas de meninas em 33% e as matrículas dos meninos cresceram no mesmo nível. Tais programas oferecem promessa para o aumento das taxas de matrículas nas áreas urbanas pobres (Kim et al., 1999).

Descentralizar as Tomadas de Decisão e Encorajar a Participação

A maneira como as decisões são tomadas afeta também a eficácia dos serviços públicos. Onde a capacidade institucional é baixa, os gastos públicos e intervenções planejadas e organizadas de forma centralizada são provavelmente ineficientes. Muitos países estão se movimentando para as tomadas de decisões descentralizadas visando a melhor equiparação de gastos para necessidades locais. A evidência empírica nos benefícios da administração descentralizada da escola era, até recentemente, rara. Uma avaliação do programa EDUCO de El Salvador (programa escolar administrado pela comunidade), realizada há pouco, mostra que o envolvimento acentuado da comu-

nidade e dos pais nas escolas do EDUCO melhorou as habilidades lingüísticas dos estudantes e diminuiu as ausências dos estudantes, as quais podem ter efeitos a longo prazo na conclusão (Jimenez & Sawada, 1999). Outros estudos também mostraram que escolas dirigidas pela comunidade alcançam melhores resultados na Indonésia e nas Filipinas (James et al., 1996; Jimenez & Paqueo, 1996).

Muitos países têm feito experiências com fiadores, que transferem recursos aos pais para ajudar a pagar a matrícula da escola particular. A Colômbia utilizou um programa nacional de fiadores de 1991 a 1997 para descentralizar a administração e expandir a matrícula. O programa pretendia corrigir as deficiências no sistema de educação pública, especialmente a baixa taxa de transição das escolas primárias para as secundárias, pelos pobres. Apenas os pobres eram qualificados para os avais, o que negava que se subsidiassem os ricos, como em programas anteriores de fiadores. Contudo, a participação era o problema: apenas 25% dos municípios colombianos aderiram ao programa, limitando os benefícios. Uma avaliação cuidadosa do programa descobriu que a demanda pela educação secundária e o espaço disponível das escolas privadas foram determinantes-chave da participação municipal (King et al., 1999). Tais programas de fiadores são potencialmente benéficos para os pobres.

Em países com governos predatórios e corruptos, contudo, a descentralização das tomadas de decisões pode não ser a resposta. Funcionários públicos corruptos irão, provavelmente, realocar recursos públicos dos pobres para os grupos de interesse das elites, subsidiando os tipos de serviços sociais que beneficiam os ricos. Habilitar o povo a influenciar a política por meio da democratização e de um papel maior para a sociedade civil, e encorajar maior participação da comunidade e das famílias são passos na direção correta (ver Capítulo 6 sobre o papel da participação da sociedade civil no combate à corrupção e realização de um melhor governo).

Tornar a Educação Mais produtiva

Para melhorar a produtividade da educação dos pobres é preciso mais do que investimentos na educação destes. Para serem mais produtivos, os pobres devem estar capacitados para combinar seu capital humano ou outros bens produtivos, como a terra e a eqüidade de capital, e oportunidades de trabalho em mercados abertos e competitivos.

Distribuir a Terra com Mais Eqüidade

Os pobres não são apenas pobres de renda; também carecem de bens. Nas economias agrárias, as famílias são, habitualmente, sem-terra, ou dispõem de terras pobres. No sul da Ásia, na África do Sul e grande parte da

América Latina, a pobreza está altamente relacionada com os sem-terra (Figura 3.11a). A desigualdade de renda também parece estar associada com a desigualdade da posse da terra (Figura 3.11b), embora os dados sobre a posse da terra sejam frágeis.

Figura 3.11a – Pobreza e Posse da Terra, Bangladesh, 1988-1989

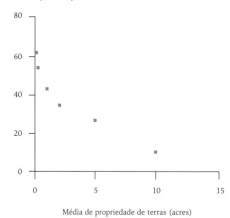

Fonte: Ravallion & Sen (1994).

Figura 3.11b – Divisão de Renda na Década de 1980 e Coeficiente Gini para a Terra, na Década de 1960

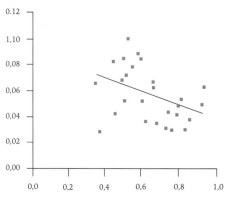

Nota: Os dados são específicos aos países em média por décadas. N = 27.r = -0,40.
Fonte: Deininger & Squire (1996).

A reforma agrária tem muitos benefícios para o crescimento e para a redução da pobreza, como sugerido por estudos empíricos discutidos mais adiante. Nas sociedades em que um amplo segmento da população não possui acesso aos recursos produtivos da economia, uma forte demanda para a redistribuição dá oportunidade a perturbações civis. Os estudos sugerem que a desigualdade na posse da terra e da renda está relacionada com um subseqüente crescimento econômico mais baixo (Alesina & Rodrik, 1944); o desvio-padrão e o aumento em igualdade estão associados com os aumentos no crescimento de 0,5 para 1 ponto percentual (Persson & Tabellini, 1994). Outros estudos mostraram que a desigualdade inicial de bens, medida pela distribuição de terra, é mais significativa do que a desigualdade de renda no que se refere a afetar o crescimento subseqüente (Deininger & Squire, 1998; Li et al., 1998; Lundberg & Squire, 1999). Outros, ainda, descobriram a desigualdade inicial de terra, juntamente com uma desigualdade inicial de educação, para ter fortes elos negativos com o crescimento da economia e com o crescimento da renda dos pobres (Birdsall & Londoño, 1998). Ademais, para ser negativamente relacionada com o crescimento, a desigualdade de terra aparece também para reduzir o efeito positivo do capital humano sobre o crescimento, mediante a interação de efeitos (Deininger & Olinto, 1999).

A reforma distributiva da terra possibilitou a existência de produtores mais eficientes e reduziu as imperfeições no mercado de crédito, levando a decisões de investimentos melhoradas pelos pobres. Maior riqueza, como medida pela posse da terra, oferece uma rede de segurança para os pobres contra choques externos e aumenta sua capacidade para participar dos processos políticos (Binswanger & Deininger, 1997; Binswanger et al., 1995). Ravallion & Sen (1994) notaram que a redistribuição de terra rica para famílias de terra pobre reduziria a pobreza agregada na Bangladesh rural. Também descobriram que transferências do orçamento teriam um enorme impacto sobre a pobreza se concentradas em fazendeiros sem terras e marginais (ver Tabela do Anexo 3.5 para uma revisão de bibliografia).

A difusão da posse da terra melhora não apenas a igualdade, mas também a produtividade (Berry & Cline, 1979) e a eficiência (Banerjee, 1999). Melhores direitos sobre a terra facilitaram o investimento em Gana (Besley, 1995), e as escrituras de posse legal da terra na Tailândia impactaram significativamente os desempenhos dos agricultores (Feder, 1987 e 1993). Muitas economias da Ásia oriental expandiram posses da terra como um resultado da propriedade tradicional ou reforma agrária. Na Coréia, as terras confiscadas no fim da Segunda Guerra Mundial foram primeiramente distribuídas aos agricultores. Na década de 1950, o governo distribuiu escrituras de propriedade da terra com compensação nominal para novecentos mil locatários, eliminando efetivamente a locação. Em Taiwan, na China, o governo obtive terra dos latifundiários no início da década de 1950, compensando os proprietários com ações nas empresas estatais e, então, vendeu a terra para os lavradores em termos favoráveis.

Na China, a responsabilidade do sistema de família introduzido em 1979 distribuiu coletivamente a posse da terra para as famílias por até 15 anos. O sistema, renovado para outros trinta anos em 1998, criou recompensas mais intimamente aos esforços dos agricultores. Juntamente com o preço e outras reformas, a iniciativa resultou em 5,7% de aumento anual na média de rendimentos de grãos de 1978 a 1984 e 1,8% depois disso. Quase metade do resultado total aumentado no período pode ser atribuída ao sistema de responsabilidade familiar (Lin, 1992). Um estudo descobriu que o acesso à terra pode melhorar a condição nutricional na China, porque serve não só como meio de geração de renda, mas também como fonte de calorias baratas relativamente ao mercado (Burgess, 2000). Outro estudo descobriu que na China rural a riqueza, especialmente da terra, está distribuída com maior igualdade (coeficiente Gini de 0,31) do que a renda (coeficiente Gini de 0,34). A principal fonte de desigualdade de renda rural é a renda salarial, mais do que os retornos da terra, um padrão atípico para um país em desenvolvimento (McKinley, 1996).

A reforma agrária é contenciosa e politicamente difícil. A reforma agrária assistida pelo mercado emergiu nos anos recentes como uma alternativa para a tradicional, e está sendo implementada pelo Brasil, Colômbia e África do Sul. A idéia básica é que o Estado dê a pessoas qualificadas, mas sem terra, uma ajuda ou um empréstimo subsidiado para que possam comprá-la. Esta abordagem assistida pelo mercado difere das reformas agrárias totalmente compensadas em dois modos: não existem nem alvos explícitos para a distribuição da terra, nem esquemas de tempo fixo. Além do mais, as reformas são demandas dirigidas; a maioria das pessoas que querem a terra virá para comprá-la. Alguns pesquisadores sustentam que a reforma agrária assistida pelo mercado tem vantagens, especialmente se combinada com microcrédito, programas extensivos e ações complementares que facilitem as cooperativas agrícolas e pequenos cultivos (Banerjee, 1999). O sucesso do programa pode ser melhorado se acompanhado de esforços para tornar os mercados de terra mais transparentes e fluidos, conseguindo envolver o setor privado (Deininger, 1999). Enquanto é ainda muito cedo para tirar conclusões definitivas sobre os custos e benefícios destas reformas, alguns outros estudos descobriram que esse tipo de abordagem beneficia grandes latifundiários, porque os preços da terra estão, provavelmente, para lançar as ofertas, requerendo que o pobre pague preços elevados (López & Valdes, 2000).

Distribuir Capital Eqüitativo e Fomentar Competição

Um acordo pode ser também feito para melhor distribuição da igualdade por meio do emprego de planos de propriedade. Nos países industrializados, o estoque de planos de propriedade empregados foi positivamente associado

a desempenhos das empresas. As empresas dos Estados Unidos empregaram planos de posse na reestruturação. Por exemplo, a United Airlines negociou significativas concessões de salário em troca de uma maior eqüidade de financiamento para os empregados. Comunicando os benefícios do plano reestrutural a seus investidores reempregados, a companhia reduziu o seu custo de reestruturação frontal, aumentando os efeitos da reestruturação, criando, com isso, o valor dos acionistas adicionais. Tanto os investidores como os empregados saíram beneficiados (Gilson, 1995).

Nos países atingidos pela recente crise financeira, a venda igual de ações para os empregados pode fornecer um caminho para recapitalizar companhias com uma necessidade de capital desesperada e pode igualmente redistribuir riquezas e riscos. Onde a reestruturação leva a economias, aos trabalhadores desligados podem ser dadas ações eqüitativas em lugar do último pagamento, e, assim, eles se beneficiam da reestruturação e da recuperação das companhias. Planos de posse podem ajudar a reduzir a resistência dos trabalhadores à reestruturação (Claessens et al., 1999). Prover microfinanciamento para os trabalhadores desligados do trabalho, a fim de que possam estabelecer novas pequenas empresas, é outro modo de habilitá-los a construir capital físico e financeiro.

A privatização oferece oportunidades adicionais para redistribuir igualdade. Como as empresas públicas foram construídas utilizando-se de rendas vindas de impostos, uma determinada proporção da eqüidade pode, justificadamente, ser distribuída ou vendida para os pagadores de impostos durante a privatização. Programas de privatização propriamente designados podem reduzir desigualdades de bens e a pobreza; por exemplo, utilizando procedimentos da privatização das maiores empresas do Estado, a Bolívia estabeleceu um fundo comum de bens financeiros destinado a criar um fundo de pensão mínima para todos no país. Enquanto a quantia fornecida é pequena, o programa atingirá as pessoas mais vulneráveis da sociedade: os pobres mais velhos, incapacitados de poupar para a aposentadoria. A Hungria utilizou-se de suas receitas vindas da privatização para reembolsar dívidas externas, o que aumentou sua taxa de débito soberanamente, reduziu seus pagamentos de capital e beneficiou todos os cidadãos (Kornai, 2000).

A privatização acarreta ganhos em eficiência tanto quanto perdas sociais, e a sociedade deve manter equilíbrio entre a eficiência dos ganhos sociais e as perdas (e compensar os perdedores); seus ganhos devem ser sustentáveis. Depois da privatização no México, houve aumento de 24% na razão da operação renda para vendas. Daqueles ganhos em lucratividade, 10% foram devidos aos mais altos preços dos produtos, 33% para transferência de trabalhadores demitidos e o restante, 57%, para ganhos em lucratividade (La Porta & López-De-Silanes, 1999). Para compensar aqueles que sofrem perdas como resultados da privatização, as porções iguais no lugar da indenização poderiam ser distribuídas para os demiti-

dos ou outras formas de transferência de renda poderiam ser financiadas pela taxação.

Competição e regulamentação são vitais para uma economia de mercado. A eficiência de uma economia de mercado depende tanto da propriedade privada como dos mercados competitivos, mas muitas economias de transição em desenvolvimento são carentes de ambas. Antes e durante a privatização, a competição e uma estrutura reguladora devem ser introduzidas (Stiglitz, 1999). A evidência vinda do Reino Unido mostra que, quando grandes empresas públicas foram privatizadas, regulamentações antitrustes foram cruciais para assegurar alocações transparentes, eqüitativas e eficientes dos recursos (ver também Herrera, 1992). Privatizar grandes empresas públicas que possuem monopólio natural sem primeiro estabelecer regulamentações antitruste, como se deu na Rússia, pode piorar a distribuição de riqueza e renda. E poderia criar interesses poderosos e entrincheirados que minassem a possibilidade de uma regulamentação viável e competição no futuro, bloqueando posteriores medidas de reforma de base ampla (Kornai, 2000).

Combinar Capital Humano com Oportunidades nos Mercados Abertos

A criação de oportunidades de trabalho é criticamente importante para a utilização produtiva do capital humano e para a redução da pobreza. O *World Development Repport 1990* (World Bank, 1999) propôs uma estratégia de base ampla, crescimento de trabalho intensivo para gerar oportunidade de ganho de renda para os pobres. Algumas economias perseguiram esta estratégia e mais – combinaram investimentos em ganho na educação com abertura, formando um círculo virtuoso. Exemplos incluem Japão e Hong Kong na década de 1950; Taiwan, Coréia e Cingapura a partir da década de 1960 até 1980.

O acúmulo de conhecimento influencia o comércio de um país e sua competitividade e o comércio aumenta o acúmulo de conhecimento especialmente mediante importação. Lucas (1993) notou que, para sustentar o acúmulo de conhecimento, uma nação deve ser orientada para o exterior e um exportador significativo. Young (1991) e Keller (1995) descobriram que o comércio em si não é uma máquina de crescimento, mas deve operar por meio de algum mecanismo, tal como a formação de capital humano, para afetar o crescimento.

A abertura de mercado facilita o progresso tecnológico e a capacidade de construção por meio de vários modos de aprendizagem, tal como a importação do capital e dos bens intermediários, aprender fazendo, e treinamento no trabalho. Foster & Rosenzweig (1995) descobriram uma forte evidência do aprender-fazendo e expansões de aprendizagem: as próprias expe-

riências dos agricultores e a de seus vizinhos com altas variedades de produção aumentaram significativamente a lucratividade. Agricultores com vizinhos experimentados são significativamente mais lucrativos que outros, e o efeito da expansão associado com a aprendizagem de outros é pequena, mas não sem importância.

A ligação entre políticas econômicas gerais e o impacto da educação é clara. O *World Development Repport 1991* (World Bank, 1991) descobriu que, entre sessenta países em desenvolvimento de 1965 a 1987, as taxas de crescimento econômico eram especialmente altas para aqueles com altos índices de educação, estabilidade macroeconômica e abertura de mercado. O impacto da abertura comercial sobre o crescimento a longo prazo depende, assim, de quão bem as pessoas podem absorver e utilizar a informação e a tecnologia que acompanham o comércio e o investimento estrangeiro.

Aumentos no estoque de capital humano tendem a acelerar o crescimento durante as reformas de mercado e sob uma estrutura econômica orientada para o exterior, mas, em sua ausência, a educação não tem nenhum impacto significativo no crescimento. O efeito do crescimento de uma interação entre abertura e educação foi robusto (López et al., 1998; ver também Capítulo 2 e Anexo 2). De forma similar para 1.265 dos projetos do Banco Mundial, Thomas & Wang (1997) descobriram que a taxa de retorno era três pontos percentuais mais alta nos países tanto com uma força de trabalho mais educada quanto com uma economia mais aberta do que nos países que tinham apenas uma ou outra (Figura 3.12 e Anexo da Tabela A3.4).[8]

Proteger os Trabalhadores Contra o Choque

Os pobres urbanos habitualmente são desprovidos de capital humano adequado para tudo, menos o trabalho não especializado. Com a abertura aumentada e a globalização, as oportunidades de trabalho para trabalhadores não especializados tornaram-se mais raras e as rendas mais voláteis. Diwan (1999) descobriu que as divisões de trabalho no PIB vêm caindo há mais de vinte anos na maioria das regiões. Coerente com esta evidência, as taxas de emprego na América Latina subiram desde o fim da década de 1980. Em 1989, apenas cinco ou seis de cem latino-americanos disponíveis para o trabalho estavam desempregados: por volta de 1996, aproximadamente oito de cada cem não estavam trabalhando.

O desemprego cresceu nos países da Ásia oriental atingidos pela recente agitação financeira, de prévios níveis modestos para 4,5% na Tailândia, 5,5% na Indonésia e 7,4% na Coréia urbana (World Bank, 2000a, p.59). Talvez ainda pior foi a queda dos salários reais, porque os pobres não tinham condições de ficar desempregados. Os salários reais caíram em 16 dos

22 episódios de recessão na América Latina durante as décadas de 1980 e 1990. Em 18 casos, depois de dois anos os salários reais permaneceram mais baixos que os seus níveis anteriores à crise (Lustig, 1999). Na Ásia oriental, os salários reais de manufaturação caíram 4,5% na Tailândia, 10,6% na Coréia e 44 % na Indonésia entre 1997 e 1998 (World Bank, 2000a, p.57). Como resultado tanto do declínio dos salários reais como do crescimento de emprego, a divisão de trabalho no PIB caiu drasticamente, seguindo as crises financeiras, talvez por o trabalho ser menos móvel que o capital; sendo assim, é forçado a suportar uma ampla divisão do ônus financeiro da resolução da crise (Diwan, 1999).

Trabalhadores urbanos não especializados são muito vulneráveis aos choques externos, ajuste estrutural e reveses econômicos. Na falta de capital humano adequado, são freqüentemente incapazes de se ajustar às mudanças na demanda do mercado de trabalho. O problema é exacerbado pelas distorções do mercado de trabalho e instituições frágeis, que posteriormente atrapalham os ajustes desse mercado. As distorções do mercado

Educação e abertura interagem e aumentam os retornos de investimentos

Figura 3.12 – Educação, Abertura e Taxas Econômicas de Retorno em 1.265 Projetos do Banco Mundial

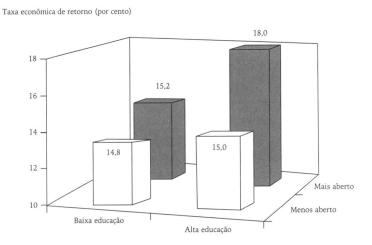

Nota: As taxas econômicas de retorno derivam da base de dados avaliativos do Departamento de Avaliação de Operações do Banco Mundial. A educação é avaliada pelo nível médio de escolaridade da força de trabalho, e a abertura pelo logaritmo do câmbio estrangeiro *premium* do mercado.
Fontes: Thomas & Wang (1997); Anexo 3.

de trabalho precisam ser checadas: a existência de trabalho infantil e as estruturas de salários distorcidas desencorajam a demanda pela educação. Os governos precisam elaborar instituições de mercado de trabalho e fornecer as informações que os pobres precisam sobre esse mercado.

É necessário, também, treinar e retreinar trabalhadores deslocados e aumentar a mobilidade através dos setores. Gana treinou mais de quatro mil pessoas em escolas vocacionais ou programas de aprendizagem, que ofereceram treinamento em atividades como costura, eletrificação e carpintaria. Os participantes receberam certificados e ferramentas depois de completar o treinamento, dando-lhes capital humano e físico para começar a trabalhar de imediato como autônomos. Muitos centros de troca de trabalho foram estabelecidos na China para retreinar e deslocar trabalhadores de setores estatais para setores privados. Alguns dos procedimentos para liquidar os bens das empresas estatais falidas foram usados para redobrar o número de operários desempregados. Tais medidas ajudaram a facilitar o crescimento de tensões sociais e a desigualdade durante períodos de transição.[9]

Conclusões

Para que o crescimento tenha impacto na redução da pobreza, os bens dos pobres precisam ser aumentados. Isto pode ser realizado tanto por meio de investimento em novos bens, especificamente o capital humano, como de redistribuição dos bens existentes. Este capítulo focou-se no investimento em novos bens examinando a qualidade e a distribuição da educação e suas causas e conseqüências, assim como os remédios para amplas dispersões na conclusão educacional. Quando a qualidade da escolaridade é baixa e a desigualdade educacional é alta, os pobres são mais atingidos porque o capital humano freqüentemente é seu principal bem. Investimento inadequado no capital humano dos pobres exacerba e perpetua a pobreza e a desigualdade de renda.

Melhorar a alocação dos gastos públicos na educação é a chave. Apesar de envidar esforços com esta finalidade, muitos países não foram capazes de concentrar investimento público na educação primária e na secundária. Alocações inadequadas dos gastos públicos levaram à conclusão da média baixa por dólares gastos nos estudantes, o que afeta principalmente os pobres. Os governos precisam realocar o gasto público em direção à educação básica, enquanto ao mesmo tempo capacite os setores público e privado e os parceiros públicos/privados para aumentar os esforços na educação superior. Os países têm razões coercitivas para fortalecer a educação em todos os níveis. Ela pode aumentar o aspecto de redução da pobreza do crescimento e, além disso, melhorar diretamente o bem-estar. Ela capacita os países a participarem efetivamente na economia global.

MELHORANDO A DISTRIBUIÇÃO DE OPORTUNIDADES

Apenas o fato de investir na educação não irá garantir o desenvolvimento bem-sucedido nem a redução da pobreza. Assim, este capítulo foi além da educação para questões relacionadas à utilização do capital humano, principalmente a distribuição da terra e outros bens produtivos e políticas de economia ampla. Para reduzir a pobreza, os países precisam de uma estratégia multidimensional centrada no povo. É preciso assegurar o acesso à educação e a serviços de saúde e distribuí-los bem, para facilitar o uso total do capital humano dos pobres e para habilitar o pobre com terra, eqüidade de capital, treinamento e oportunidades de trabalho tornadas possíveis pela abertura ao comércio internacional, investimento e idéias.

Notas

1. Sobre a importância da distribuição de bens, ver, por exemplo, Ahluwalia (1976); Birdsall & Londoño (1997); Chenery et al. (1974); Deininger & Squire (1998); Kanbur (2000); Knight & Sabot (1983); Lam & Levison (1991); Lanjouw & Stern (1989 e 1998); Li et al. (1998); Ram (1990); Ravallion & Datt (1999); e Sen (1980 e 1988). Ver Tabela A3.5 anexa para evidência adicional.

2. Alguns argumentos aplicam-se aqui para a saúde, mas, devido a limites de espaço, este capítulo focaliza apenas a educação.

3. Algumas afirmativas concentram-se aqui. Esta conclusão se sustenta se há um mercado competitivo e dois fatores de produção: capitais físico e humano. Também é verdade se o capital humano for decomposto para trabalho especializado e não especializado.

4. Tais medidas, contudo, são sensíveis a políticas de promoção nacional. Placares sobre testes internacionalmente comparáveis representam uma melhoria sobre os indicadores tradicionais, mas são disponíveis para apenas uns poucos países em desenvolvimento, e não são comparáveis no decorrer do tempo. Em razão destes problemas, não são aqui utilizados.

5. O mesmo é verdade quanto aos países industrializados. Um estudo estimativo do custo dos diferentes tipos de classes nacionais abrange políticas de redução nos Estudos Unidos e descobriu-se que os custos operacionais podiam ser tão amplos como US$ 2 bilhões a US$ 7 bilhões ao ano (Brewer et al., 1999).

6. Houve um debate acalorado sobre "a eqüidade de quê?". Sen (1980) encara os níveis individuais das funções, tais como alfabetização e nutrição, como atributos a serem equalizados. Outros vêem as oportunidades que o povo enfrenta como atributos a serem equalizados (Arneson, 1989; Cohen, 1989; Roemer, 1993). Outros, ainda, consideram a quantidade de recursos como o atributo a ser equalizado (Dworkin, 1981).

7. Muitos estudos compararam renda, terra e riqueza. Os coeficientes Gini (por exemplo, Leipziger et al. (1992) para a Coréia). Contudo, nenhum estudo comparou os coeficientes Gini para a educação com os de renda ou terra. Os coeficientes Gini para a renda estão disponíveis apenas para alguns anos seletos (Deininger & Squire, 1996):

	1970	1977	1983	1990	1992		1970	1976	1980	1985	1988
Índia	0,30	0,32	0,31	0,32	0,32	Coréia	0,33	0,39	0,39	0,35	0,34

8. Os dados de nível projetados através do país incluíram variáveis na educação, renda *per capita*, abertura, gastos governamentais e projeto de desempenho. Os dados projetados cobriram 3.590 projetos de empréstimo em 109 países avaliados pelo Departamento de Avaliações Operacionais para 1974-1994, com uma taxa de desempenho geral (não satisfatória) e taxas econômicas de retorno.

9. Para maiores discussões sobre mercado de trabalho e questões de proteção social, ver Basu et al. (1999); Kanbur (2000); World Bank (1994) sobre a crise antiga, e World Bank (2000i).

CAPÍTULO 4

SUSTENTAR O CAPITAL NATURAL

Se realmente nos importamos com o futuro do nosso planeta, devemos parar de deixar para os "outros" resolverem todos os problemas. Depende de nós salvar o mundo para amanhã, depende de você e de mim.

— Jane Goodall, *Reason for Hope*

O capital natural tem contribuído enormemente para o bem-estar e o desenvolvimento humano. O termo capital natural abrange as funções encobertas, ou seja, ar e água como meios receptivos para a poluição gerada pelos humanos e as funções-fonte, ou seja, produção baseada nas florestas, pescas e minérios minerais; proteger as funções encobertas é essencial para a saúde humana. Proteger as funções-fonte ou produtivas é crucial para a segurança econômica de muitos que dependem desses recursos para suas vidas. A alta qualidade do capital natural contribui indiretamente para o bem-estar como parte essencial da produção sustentada dos bens econômicos e serviços. Também contribui para o bem-estar diretamente, quando as pessoas tiram prazer dos arredores intocados, florestas de crescimento antigo, rios e lagos limpos nos quais nadar e pescar.

O Capítulo 2 demonstrou a importância dos capitais humano, natural e físico para o crescimento econômico e o bem-estar. Em decorrência da substituição imperfeita, estes bens precisam crescer a taxas não distorcidas e muito bem equilibradas para realizar o crescimento econômico sustentável. O crescimento desequilibrado ou distorcido – marcado pelo acúmulo especialmente rápido do capital físico, acumulação lenta de capital humano e queda delineada do capital natural – aumenta a volatilidade do crescimento, atingindo desproporcionalmente os pobres. Uma economia que fomente

o crescimento desequilibrado provavelmente sofrerá estagnação a longo prazo (ver Anexo 2).

Economias que tiram muito de sua renda dos recursos naturais não podem sustentar o crescimento substituindo acúmulo de capital físico para deteriorar o capital natural (López et al., 1998). É provável que a degradação ambiental seja mais devastadora para os pobres, que freqüentemente dependem dos recursos naturais para sua renda, com poucas possibilidades para substituir outros bens. Especialmente a longo prazo, as abordagens do crescimento que dão atenção à qualidade ambiental e uso dos recursos contribuem eficientemente para acúmulo, investimento, crescimento econômico e bem-estar humano (Munasinghe, 2000).

Ainda, países pelo mundo todo superexploraram suas florestas, pescas e riquezas minerais e poluíra sua água e seu ar em acelerado crescimento econômico a curto prazo, com agentes de política ressaltando que sua abordagem aumentaria o bem-estar de seus cidadãos. Enquanto muito capital natural tem sido sacrificado com desmatamento, perda de biodiversidade, degradação do solo e poluição do ar e da água, o acesso à água de qualidade e a facilidades de tratamento de esgoto e saneamento freqüentemente tem demonstrado melhorias quando a economia cresce. Este capítulo examina as razões pelas quais o capital natural tende a ser usado de forma abusiva e a ser superexplorado, especialmente durante o crescimento econômico rápido, e que medidas podem ser tomadas para corrigir a espiral negativa do declínio ambiental.

A adequação de ações corretivas dependerá da natureza do problema e do cenário econômico e institucional. Por exemplo, a qualidade do ar pode ser melhorada com a cobrança de um imposto sobre as emissões industriais de poluentes, enquanto a eficiência produtiva baseada nos recursos naturais pode ser aumentada por medidas como a concessão de direitos de propriedade claros para a terra, ou pela concessão de cotas transferíveis aos pescadores. Resultados de sucesso requerem uma intervenção ativa, seletiva pelo Estado, em colaboração com o setor privado e a sociedade civil.

Perdas Extensivas

A poluição do ar pelas emissões industriais, escapamentos dos carros e combustíveis fósseis queimados nas residências mata mais de 2,7 milhões de pessoas a cada ano, principalmente por dano respiratório, doenças do coração, pulmão e câncer (UNDP, 1998). Dos que morrem de modo prematuro, 2,2 milhões são pobres camponeses expostos à poluição do ar interior pela queima de combustíveis tradicionais. A poluição do ar também reduz os resultados econômicos em conseqüência da perda de dias de trabalho produtivos. (Ver Tabela 4.1 para entender a magnitude das perdas em razão da poluição do ar em diferentes partes do mundo. Os nú-

meros simplesmente estão aqui para ilustrar os possíveis impactos da poluição ambiental; eles estão longe de constituir estimativas não-controversas de dano ambiental.)

Custos de saúde associados com doenças provenientes da água e da poluição da água também são profundos. Em 1992, mais de dois milhões de crianças com menos de cinco anos morreram em decorrência de doenças causadas por água contaminada. A Tabela 4.2 relata os achados de alguns estudos sobre o ônus na saúde causado pela água, relatando deficiências no saneamento e efeitos poluentes.[1]

Efluentes tóxicos (dioxinas, pesticidas, organoclorinas, graxa, petróleo, ácidos, alcalóides, e metais pesados como cádmium e condutores) de fábricas, minas e indústrias químicas contaminaram grandes quantidades de água em todas as partes do mundo. Trabalhadores, agricultores e demais pessoas que entraram em contato com os contaminantes apresentam pro-

Tabela 4.1 – Custos Anuais de Saúde Associados com a Poluição do Ar

Região e cidade	Impacto	Custo
China: 11 principais cidades	Custos econômicos da mortalidade prematura e custo de doenças	Mais de 20% da renda urbana
Ásia oriental: Bangcoc, Jacarta, Seul, Kuala Lumpur, Manila	Número de mortos prematuros devido à poluição acima dos limites de segurança definidos pela WHO	15.600
Ásia oriental: Bangcoc, Jacarta, Kuala Lumpur	Custos econômicos da mortalidade prematura e custo de doenças	Mais de 10% da renda urbana
Estados independentes recentes: Federação Russa (Volgograd); Armênia (áreas urbanas); Azerbaijão (nacional); Cazaquistão (nacional)	Número de mortos prematuros devido à poluição acima dos limites de segurança definidos pela WHO	14.458

Nota: As estimativas são baseadas em diferentes estudos que aplicam diferentes metodologias e não são comparáveis. Em muitos casos, a mortalidade excessiva é estimada utilizando-se funções de resposta para economias industrializadas para mudanças marginais de poluição, mas, então, aplicadas para mudanças não marginais que tendem a superestimar as reduções de mortalidade. Alguns estudos utilizam a boa disposição ajustada do PPP para pagar dados das economias industrializadas; outros utilizam a abordagem do custo das doenças.
Fonte: World Bank (1997a, 1999f).

Tabela 4.2 – Custos Anuais da Saúde Associados com Doenças Provindas da Água e da Poluição

Região e cidade	Impacto	Custo
Vietnã	Morte de crianças evitadas anualmente pelo fornecimento de acesso à água limpa e saneamento	50.000
China	Mortes prematuras devido a doenças relacionadas com a água, tais como diarréia, hepatite, parasitoses intestinais	135.000
Ásia oriental	Custo de doenças provenientes da água	US$ 30 bilhões por ano
Moldova	Mortes prematuras Perda de dias de trabalho devido a doença	980-1.850 2-4 milhões por ano

Fonte: World Bank (1997a, c; 1999f).

blemas de saúde severos. Assim como em relação à poluição do ar, os pobres são os que mais sofrem; 25 milhões de pobres trabalhadores na agricultura no mundo em desenvolvimento (11 milhões só na África) são envenenados por pesticidas a cada ano e centenas de milhares deles morrem (UNDP, 1998). As pescas, que fornecem o recurso principal de proteína para os pobres, também estão sendo destruídas pelas descargas industriais e a poluição da água. Na Baía de Manila, os produtos da pesca declinaram 40% nos últimos dez anos (UNDP, 1998). Para uma descrição perturbadora da degradação ambiental na Índia, como relatado na imprensa, ver Quadro 4.1.

Estimativas recentes utilizando DALYs sugerem que a morte prematura e as doenças decorrentes dos principais riscos de doenças ambientais representam aproximadamente um quinto dos custos totais da doença no mundo em desenvolvimento (Murray & López, 1996).[2] Entre os principais riscos ambientais, que incluem pobres suprimentos de água, saneamento inadequado, poluição interna do ar, poluição urbana do ar, malária, e produtos químicos agroindustriais e devastamento, 14% do total dos custos de doenças é provocado por pobres suprimentos de água, saneamento inadequado e poluição interna do ar. Afetam predominantemente as crianças e as mulheres de famílias pobres (Lvovsky et al., 1999).

Superexploração e degradação dos recursos naturais também são problemas preocupantes. A degradação do solo constitui problema em todos

---

Quadro 4.1 – Degradação Ambiental na Índia

Numa questão especial, *O envenenamento da Índia, India Today* (1999) relatou a seguinte informação:

- O ar respirado na Índia urbana é equivalente a fumar vinte cigarros por dia. Na capital, Nova Delhi, o nível de partículas de matérias suspensas é mais que duas vezes o limite de segurança especificado pela WHO. Medidas recentes da poluição do ar em Nova Delhi indicam que o nível do total de partículas suspensas pode ser tão alto quanto cinco vezes o limite considerado seguro pela WHO.
- A cada ano mais de quarenta mil pessoas morrem prematuramente pelos efeitos da poluição do ar.
- Mais de 30% do lixo gerado nas cidades é deixado intocado, transformando-se num solo fértil para doenças.
- Apenas oito das 3.119 cidades e aldeias da Índia

possuem coleta moderna de esgoto e facilidade de tratamento, outras 209 possuem facilidades rudimentares, e o restante absolutamente nenhuma.
- Um terço da população urbana não tem acesso aos serviços sanitários. Em Lucknow, 70% da população manda seu lixo para o rio Gomti.
- A maioria dos serviços de esgoto data dos tempos coloniais; logo, 93% do esgoto de Mumbai é lançado ao mar sem tratamento, matando virtualmente a ampla vida marinha ao longo da costa.
- Diclorodifeniltricloretano, comumente conhecido como DDT, e exaclorino de benzeno, o BHC, ajudaram muito com quase 40% do total de pesticidas utilizados na Índia. Ambos são neurotoxinas que prejudicam o sistema nervoso central e causam distrofia muscular. Análises químicas revelam sua presença em quantidades crescentes no leite, nos legumes, nos cereais e nas frutas.

Fonte: Robby (1999).

os lugares, principalmente na Ásia e na África. Na China, os custos podem chegar a 5% do PIB (ADB, 1997), e para vários países africanos os custos anuais são de 1% a 10% do PIB agrícola (Bojo, 1996). Enquanto as perdas anuais são preocupantes, os efeitos cumulativos são alarmantes. Estima-se que a desertificação, uma conseqüência direta da degradação do solo, custa US$ 42 bilhões ao ano apenas na perda da produtividade agrícola, isto colocando cerca de 250 milhões de pobres em risco de fome (UNDP, 1998).

Pelo menos de 10 a 12 milhões de hectares de terras florestais desaparecem a cada ano. Práticas de desmadeiramento e conversão de florestas para agricultura e pastoreio concorrem para o volume das perdas (Brown et al., 1998; World Bank, 1999d). A diminuição da produção de produtos florestais de madeira, ou não, reduziu igualmente os serviços de preservação do solo e da água e acarretou a perda do carvão anulando as funções deste. Isso resultou em uma rede de perdas econômicas no valor de US$ 1 a 2 bilhões por ano para a economia global (dados calculados com base em informações do World Bank). Em 1997, um incêndio florestal provocou danos de nevoeiro e fumaça relacionados no total de US$ 4 bilhões na Indonésia e dano extensivo nas vizinhas Malásia e Cingapura (EEPSEA, 1998). As gerações futuras irão sentir os custos dessa associação de perda na biodiversidade, mesmo que difícil de ser quantificada.

Como os incêndios florestais na Indonésia, os impactos da negligência ambiental local não estão confinados às políticas de fronteiras. Testemunham a crescente desertificação, zona costeira de degradação, mudança climática global, chuva ácida transfronteiriça e esgotamento da camada de ozônio (GEF, 1998; Watson et al., 1998). A mudança do clima global durante o século XXI poderia resultar em aumentos na intensidade e freqüência de inundações e estiagens, inundação das áreas costeiras baixas, mais freqüente aparecimento de doenças infecciosas e morte acelerada das florestas. A mudança climática também irá atingir a segurança de alimentos, reduzindo resultados agrícolas nos países em desenvolvimento e colocando uma ameaça para a segurança e a saúde humanas. Poderia custar para a economia mundial mais ou menos US$ 550 bilhões ao ano e é provável que os países em desenvolvimento irão agüentar uma proporção desigual dos custos (Furtado et al., 1999).

"Poupanças genuínas" fornecem um conceito útil para captar a degradação do capital natural, que pode ser utilizado para financiar a saúde ambiental dos países. Poupanças genuínas equalizam poupanças internas brutas, menos depreciação do capital físico, menos esgotamento de minerais e energia, menos esgotamento de florestas, menos danos de poluição, mais investimentos no capital humano. Para o mundo em desenvolvimento como um todo, em 1997 as poupanças internas brutas perfaziam 25% do PIB. Poupanças internas em rede (depois da correção para depreciação do capital físico) eram em torno de 16% do PIB, mas, corrigidas posterior-

mente pelo esgotamento do capital natural (tais como floresta, energia e minerais) e pelos danos causados em razão das emissões de dióxido de carbono, as poupanças internas eram pouco mais de 10% do PIB (World Bank, 1999e). Depois de incluir o investimento no capital humano, as poupanças genuínas cresceram em torno de 14%. Isto inclui o Nepal, onde só o esgotamento florestal foi estimado em 10,3%, superando as poupanças internas brutas do país de 10%, e a Federação Russa, onde o esgotamento dos recursos energéticos (petróleo, carvão, gás natural) reduziu as poupanças em mais de 9% ao ano.

Benefícios Significativos da Ação Ambiental

De um ponto de vista econômico, nem toda poluição deve ser totalmente controlada, nem toda degradação dos recursos naturais deve ser totalmente revertida. Poluição e degradação dos recursos naturais devem ser controladas ao ponto em que os danos marginais (sociais) equivalem aos custos marginais (sociais), custos de redução ou controle, ou seja, o nível ótimo de proteção ambiental.

O atual custo descontado de fornecimento de água limpa a todos na China, dentro de dez anos, por exemplo, será de US$ 40 bilhões, e o atual valor do benefício é de US$ 80 bilhões a US$ 100 bilhões (World Bank, 1987a). Fazer o mesmo na Indonésia custaria cerca de US$ 12 bilhões a US$ 15 bilhões, com benefícios correspondentes de US$ 25 bilhões a US$ 30 bilhões. Para prover Moldova de água encanada de qualidade, custaria de US$ 23 milhões a US$ 38 milhões, mas traria benefícios de US$ 70 milhões a US$ 120 milhões (World Bank, 1999f). Controlar a poluição do ar na China custaria cerca de US$ 50 bilhões, mas produziria benefícios de aproximadamente US$ 200 bilhões com a redução de doenças e mortes (World Bank, 1997a).

Com pagamentos tão grandes, por que será que a degradação ambiental e a destruição continuam?[3] A razão principal é que os retornos privados sobre os investimentos na proteção ambiental são significativamente menores que os custos privados (Dasgupta & Mäler, 1994; Hammer & Shetty, 1995). Muitos dos benefícios são distribuídos amplamente para a sociedade, agora e no futuro, mais do que ao agente privado que faz os investimentos. Logo, os indivíduos que vêem apenas seus ganhos privados a curto prazo raramente fatoram o custo da degradação – que espalha desigualdade através da geração atual e afeta igualmente as futuras gerações – com suas tomadas de decisão. O caso clássico de externalidades de falência de mercado fornece uma forte justificativa para ações políticas públicas destinadas a criar mercados ou condições parecidas com a de mercado que alinhe os incentivos privados aos custos sociais e os benefícios de fornecer serviços ambientais.

Distorções políticas que refletem subavaliação do meio ambiente contribuem para a poluição e a degradação (Dasgupta & Mäler, 1994). Por exemplo, subsídios agrícolas em entradas e suporte de preços para saídas tornam a administração das florestas não competitiva, e cria pressão para converter florestas em pastos. Os subsídios energéticos para manter os preços ao consumidor contribuem pouco para o supraconsumo e a poluição excessiva. As isenções de impostos, subsídios a empresas operando em terras de fronteira, construção de estradas em áreas ecologicamente frágeis e um hóspede ou outro de políticas de curta visão também levam à degradação e má administração dos recursos e ameaçam as populações vulneráveis que vivem nestas áreas (Chomitz & Gray, 1996; Cropper et al., 1997). Remover subsídios e impor reformas ambientais podem diminuir distorções e permitir que os preços atinjam seu nível ótimo.

Vários outros fatores contribuintes e falsas noções permanecem no caminho da administração eficiente do capital natural: o modo de pensar "cresça agora e limpe mais tarde", corrupção, direitos de propriedade mal definidos e fundos inadequados para administração do meio ambiente. Freqüentemente, as brechas de informação impedem o completo entendimento das causas e conseqüências da degradação ambiental e a indiferença pública cerceia sua resolução. A ação internacional é difícil, apesar de existir um momento para a proteção ambiental (Quadro 4.2). A relativa contribuição destes fatores difere de país para país e precisa ser taxada antes que as ações públicas efetivas possam ser determinadas.

O Nexo do Crescimento do Capital Natural e do Bem-Estar

Após dissipar a idéia disseminada de que a degradação ambiental pode esperar por reparação até que sejam feitas outras reformas mais urgentes (a ideologia do "cresça agora e limpe depois"), exploraremos a evidência empírica que liga o crescimento à qualidade do capital natural.

Cresça Agora e Limpe Depois

A evidência do crescimento, ao contrário, não tem difundido a percepção de que o meio ambiente é um luxo produtivo, que exigirá aumento de rendas com o crescimento econômico. Como um dos resultados, os países em desenvolvimento tendem a ignorar os interesses ambientais, enquanto o foco dos agentes de política se dirige quase que exclusivamente para o crescimento econômico acelerado. Sustentam sua posição, citando exemplos de países industrializados que deram pouca atenção à degradação ambiental nas fases iniciais de seu crescimento e reprimiram e

Quadro 4.2 – Esforços pelo Mundo Afora para Ação Ambiental

Em junho de 1992, representantes de 178 nações reuniram-se no Rio de Janeiro para acordar medidas que assegurassem um desenvolvimento ambiental e socialmente sustentável. A Cúpula da Terra captou o interesse do governo para transformar objetivos políticos amplos, em ações concretas. O compromisso dos líderes de todo o mundo com o desenvolvimento sustentável foi cultuado na Agenda 21, documento-chave da cúpula. As atividades da Agenda 21 são organizadas sob temas ambientais e desenvolvimentistas: qualidade de vida, utilização eficiente dos recursos naturais, proteção dos bens comuns globais, administração dos assentamentos e crescimento econômico sustentável. A Agenda 21 reconhece que a persistência de pobreza aguda em várias partes do mundo caminha lado a lado com um padrão de vida baseado no desperdício do consumo dos recursos, em outras partes é incompatível com a sustentabilidade, e que a administração ambiental precisa igualmente ser praticada pelos países em desenvolvimento e industrializados. Chegou-se ao consenso que, para implementar a Agenda 21, os países preparariam uma estratégia de desenvolvimento sustentável nacional.

Em 1987, doadores da agência de desenvolvimento internacional iniciaram os planos de ações ambientais nacionais para todas as agências tomadoras de empréstimos. Antes de receber os fundos, requisitava-se dos tomadores de empréstimos que apresentassem uma estratégia de longo prazo para a manutenção do meio ambiente natural do país, a saúde e a segurança da população e sua herança cultural durante os esforços para o desenvolvimento econômico. Esta prática espalhou-se para outros países e cem nações preparam estratégias nacionais de desenvolvimento sustentável ou planos de ação ambientais nacionais para guiar seu pensamento sobre o gerenciamento ambiental. Estes planos foram úteis ao identificar problemas ambientais, alimentando a propriedade nacional e o planejamento ambiental e criando o clima político necessário para encorajar uma ação efetiva para reformas políticas. Foram também úteis ao identificar estruturas políticas do país e desenhar uma visão estratégica para o meio ambiente (Bojo & Segnestam, 1999).

Enquanto essencial para focalizar importantes questões ambientais, as estratégias e os planos são menos efetivos na identificação de prioridades para a ação e a realização de resultados desejáveis. A documentação e a disseminação de casos bem-sucedidos e de experiências específicas no gerenciamento ambiental tornam-se cruciais. O Banco Mundial tem desempenhado um papel de facilitação importante mediante esforços para a integração do meio ambiente no diálogo político do banco (Warford et al.,1994; Warford et al., 1997).

Fonte: World Bank (1997d).

---

reverteram o problema mais tarde. Contudo, ignoram a enormidade potencial dos custos econômicos, sociais e ecológicos e a realidade; algumas vezes, o dano é irreversível.

Enquanto os níveis de poluição do ar e da água parecem ser reversíveis, seus impactos no bem-estar humano freqüentemente não o são. Promessas de uma ação reparadora futura dificilmente podem compensar as perdas de bem-estar pela geração atual. Apenas uma política de crescimento limpo é coerente com a eqüidade intergeracional. Além do mais, investir no controle direto da poluição irá produzir retornos positivos em outras áreas. Por exemplo, melhoria nos resultados de saúde podem conduzir a um acúmulo mais favorável do capital humano e a um crescimento mais sustentado.[4]

Uma abordagem "cresça agora e limpe depois" também tende a ser injusta; os pobres e desfavorecidos sofrem o impacto da poluição ambiental

e a degradação dos recursos. Por exemplo, quando os efluentes tóxicos industriais e outros poluentes degradam a qualidade da água, falta aos pobres o acesso aos suprimentos municipais de água purificada e os recursos para investir em filtros de água e outros sistemas de purificação. A poluição do ar também atinge desproporcionalmente os pobres, uma vez que eles tendem a viver próximos às estradas, onde os níveis de poluição são mais altos, e não podem mudar para combustíveis mais limpos para uso interno (UNDP, 1998). Estes impactos distribucionais agravam as desigualdades de renda e podem conduzir a sérios conflitos sociais. Logo, prestar atenção ao meio ambiente enquanto se acelera o crescimento é totalmente coerente com a estratégia de redução da pobreza.

A perda irreversível de material genético e a ameaça potencial do colapso do ecossistema fornecem outras razões coercitivas para rejeitar uma abordagem do tipo "cresça agora e limpe depois". Alguns danos nunca podem ser desfeitos. A destruição do hábitat resultou em perda irreversível de biodiversidade terrestre e aquática por todo o mundo. A poluição dos mares e as técnicas destrutivas de pesca causaram danos de larga proporção nos recifes de corais na Ásia oriental e constitui séria ameaça à vida das plantas e animais do oceano (Loh et al., 1998).

As experiências dos países de alta renda mostram que os custos de saúde, do controle de poluição postergados podem exceder os custos de prevenção, embora, comparando-os, a diferença no tempo de sua ocorrência e a incerteza de resultados deveriam ser idealmente contabilizados. Por exemplo, o custo da limpeza e da compensação para as vítimas da doença Itai-Itai, causada por envenenamento pelo cádmium, da asma de Yokaishi, resultado da exposição excessiva às emissões sulfúricas, e da doença Minamata, ou envenenamento por mercúrio, são de 1,4 a 102 vezes o custo da prevenção (Kato, 1996). Não obstante, além dos impactos sobre a saúde humana, os altos custos da limpeza, do *dumping* amplamente difundido e do lixo tóxico pelas empresas industriais dos Estados Unidos exemplificam outra limitação da abordagem "cresça agora e limpe depois" (Harr, 1995).

Será que o Crescimento Econômico Mais Rápido ou Mais Lento Garante a Proteção do Capital Natural?

Tanto as economias de crescimento rápido como lento experimentaram a degradação do meio ambiente, mas em diferentes graus. A análise de crescimento do PIB e um índice da qualidade do capital natural mostram um coeficiente de correlação negativo (ver Figura 1.5). Observando-se a ligação entre crescimento rápido e vários componentes da degradação do capital natural num nível mais agregado, pode-se ter uma idéia melhor da força e da direção de relacionamentos.

Os registros falsos dos fenômenos da Ásia oriental do crescimento econômico e redução da pobreza é o registro mais pobre do seu meio ambiente. Em 1995, a China foi a sede de 15 a vinte metrópoles mais poluídas do mundo, como medida pela concentração do total de partículas suspensas (World Bank, 1999e). A poluição do ar, especialmente altos níveis de total de partículas suspensas, resultou em mortes prematuras e severos danos à saúde em áreas urbanas, tais como Bangcoc, Jacarta, Manila e várias metrópoles chinesas (ver Tabela 4.1). Os países que experimentaram crescimento rápido no contexto de reformas econômicas na década de 1980 – China, Coréia, Malásia e Tailândia – viram as emissões de dióxido de carbono *per capita* dobrarem ou triplicarem depois das reformas e aceleração do crescimento (Tabela 4.3).

Os recursos naturais alimentaram-se igualmente de modo muito pobre. As taxas de desmatamento foram altas e permanecem assim na maioria dos países (Tabela 4.3). Cerca de 20% da terra produtiva na Ásia oriental sofre de degradação do solo, causada por inundação, erosão e excesso de pastagem. A degradação severa da terra na China, Tailândia e Vietnã ameaça

Tabela 4.3 – Comércio, Crescimento, Pobreza e Degradação do Meio Ambiente, em Anos Seletos

(por cento, a menos que indicado de outro modo)

Região e economia	Comércio	Crescimento	Pobreza	Indicadores de capital natural		
	Crescimento anual do volume de mercadorias exportadas, 1980-94	Crescimento anual do PNB per capita, 1970-95	Porcentagem da população vivendo com menos de US$ 1 por dia (PPP) (vários anos)	Desmatamento anual (mudança percentual) 1990-95	Total de partículas suspensas nas principais cidades (microgramas por metro cúbico)	Porcentagem de emissão de dióxido de carbono per capita, 1980-96
Ásia oriental						
China	12,2	6,9	29,4 (1993)	0,1	377	86,7
Hong Kong, China	15,4	5,7	<1	0,0	–	15,6
Indonésia	9,9	4,7	14,5 (1993)	1,0	271	100,0
Coréia	11,9	10,0	<1	0,2	84	172,7
Malásia	13,3	4,0	5,6 (1989)	2,4	85	180,0
Filipinas	5,0	0,6	27,5 (1988)	3,5	200	12,5
Cingapura	13,3	5,7	<1	0,0	223	63,6
Tailândia	16,4	5,2	<1	2,6	223	277,8
América Latina						
Argentina	1,9	-0,4	–	0,3	97 (Córdoba)	0,2
Bolívia	-0,3	-0,7	7,1 (1989)	1,2	–	62,5
Brasil	6,2	–	28,7 (1989)	0,5	86 (Rio=139)	13,3
Chile	7,3	1,8	15,0 (1992)	0,4	–	36,0
Costa Rica	6,6	0,7	18,9 (1989)	3,0	–	27,3
México	13,0	0,9	14,9 (1992)	0,9	279	2,7
Peru	2,4 -	1,1	49,4 (1994)	0,3	–	-21,4
Uruguai	0,9	0,2	–	0,0	–	-15,0
Venezuela	1,1	-1,1	11,8 (1991)	1,1	53	10,7

– Não disponível.

Fontes: World Bank (1997a, 1999e); ver também Anexo 4.

vários ecossistemas com danos irreversíveis (World Bank, 1999b). A biodiversidade, em 50% a 75% das linhas costeiras e áreas marinhas protegidas na Ásia oriental, é classificada como altamente ameaçada.

Nem todos os indicadores mostram piora nas condições ambientais entre as economias de crescimento mais rápido na Ásia. O acesso à água limpa e ao saneamento cresceu rapidamente na China, Coréia, Malásia e Tailândia. Em 1995 a fatia da população com acesso à água de qualidade cresceu de 71% em 1982 para 89% na Malásia, de 66% a 89% na Tailândia, de 39% para 55% na Indonésia, e de 65% para 83% nas Filipinas. A disponibilidade de serviços de saneamento cresceu de 46% para 96% na Tailândia, de 30% para 35% na Indonésia, e de 57% para 77% nas Filipinas (World Bank, 1999e). Embora ainda em baixos níveis no Camboja, na República Democrática do Lao e no Vietnã, o acesso à água pura e ao saneamento tem aumentado de modo firme com o crescimento econômico (World Bank, 1999b, e).

Contudo, se não é apenas o crescimento rápido que conduz a problemas da degradação do capital natural, como nos países da Ásia oriental, o crescimento lento dos países latino-americanos conheceu melhorias no acesso à água tratada e ao saneamento (World Bank, 1999e), mas sofreu igualmente deterioração do meio ambiente. A maioria desses países experimentou desmatamento extensivo, especialmente pesca exagerada e poluição da água nas zonas costeiras. A contaminação da água por produtos agroquímicos e envenenamento por pesticidas das pessoas e criações. Enquanto a poluição do ar não é um problema tão disseminado quanto na Ásia, em parte devido ao crescimento relativamente lento da industrialização (Tabela 4.3), constitui um problema sério na Cidade do México, no Rio de Janeiro e em Santiago. Em decorrência do crescimento lento, altamente tendencioso das distribuições de renda, investimentos inadequados na educação e na saúde e da instabilidade política, a pobreza permaneceu teimosamente alta, criando ciclos viciosos de aumento da degradação dos recursos naturais e posterior perda de renda (ver também Quadro 4.3).

Logo, nem o crescimento rápido nem o lento são aliados automáticos do capital natural (Thomas & Belt, 1997). Por exemplo, na década de 1980, as diferenças na poluição do ar e congestionamento de tráfego entre a Manila de crescimento lento e a Bangcoc de crescimento rápido era mínimo (Hammer & Shetty, 1995). Contudo, o crescimento rápido com crescente urbanização, expansão industrial e exploração de recursos renováveis e não-renováveis pressiona o meio ambiente, de modo que muitos indicadores apresentam um declínio na qualidade do capital natural durante os períodos de crescimento.

Ainda assim, o crescimento assegura condições para melhoria do ambiente ao criar demanda por melhor qualidade do meio ambiente e fazer com que se destinem recursos disponíveis para supri-los. Será que isso implica a existência de uma curva Kuznets do meio ambiente? Enquanto as rendas crescem, será que a qualidade do meio ambiente primeiro deteriora

Quadro 4.3 – População, Pobreza e Meio Ambiente

A análise do nexo pobreza-população-meio ambiente é complexa. O crescimento da população sempre foi acusado como responsável pela pobreza ou pela degradação do meio ambiente (Cropper & Giffiths, 1994; Pearce & Warford, 1993). Contudo, o argumento de debate afirma que a pobreza e a degradação ambiental são as causas do crescimento populacional, não as conseqüências dele. Ambas as posições são parciais; precisa ser reconhecido que os três fatores estão interligados (Cleaver & Schreiber, 1994; Dasgupta, 1995; Ekbom & Bojo, 1999; Mink, 1993). A força destas ligações irá diferir de situação para situação e as recomendações políticas dependerão de uma legião de fatores, inclusive do tipo de recurso, densidade e taxa de crescimento populacional, preparativos institucionais e leis que regulem a utilização do recurso (López, 1998b). Como resultado, não há nenhuma conclusão geral a respeito das ligações entre população, meio ambiente e pobreza está disponível.

O exemplo seguinte tirado de Dasgupta (1995) lança alguma luz na complicada natureza do nexo. Nos cenários rurais, muito trabalho é preciso mesmo para tarefas simples, tais como coletar água limpa ou lenha para cozinhar. Além disso, os membros das famílias rurais dedicam tempo a produzir comida e lavrar para a criação e produzir produtos mercadológicos simples. As crianças são necessárias como trabalhadores extras, mesmo quando os pais são jovens. Famílias pequenas são simplesmente inviáveis; cada uma precisa de muitos braços. Como os recursos da comunidade estão esgotados, mais braços são necessários para juntar combustível e água para o uso diário. Mais crianças são produzidas, causando danos posteriores ao meio ambiente, o que fornece um incentivo para aumentar ainda mais a família.

Os fatores que influenciam a demanda dos pais por filhos podem reverter esta espiral destrutiva. A política mais potente irá utilizar muitos dos fatores simultaneamente. Boas políticas econômicas, direitos de posse seguros, estabilidade política podem juntos diminuir as pressões populacionais. Oferecer combustível barato e água potável irá reduzir a necessidade de braços extras e diminuir a demanda por filhos. Serviços de planejamento familiar, aliados a serviços de saúde e reprodutivo que ajudarão a ligar as necessidades impróprias para a contracepção, e uma alfabetização e emprego dirigido para mulheres que se habilitam nas decisões do tamanho da família tornam-se fundamentais.

---

e depois começa a melhorar? Se os bens do meio ambiente são bens de consumo normais, com elasticidade de renda positiva da demanda, que é maior do que a unidade em determinados níveis de renda, conseqüentemente a qualidade irá melhorar além do patamar do nível de renda. López (1997) sugere que os bens do meio ambiente, tais como ar e água puros e tratamento de esgotos, que afetam diretamente a saúde e geram externalidades locais, provavelmente devem ser bens normais com uma elasticidade de demanda de alta renda. Logo, provavelmente devem melhorar depois de um período de declínio, durante um período de crescimento.

A maioria dos estudos empíricos focaliza indicadores de função ocultos da qualidade do meio ambiente, tais como a concentração de partículas suspensas no ar e a demanda bioquímica de oxigênio da água, o nível das emissões de dióxido de carbono e dióxido sulfúrico e a prevalência de poluentes inorgânicos industriais (Galeotti & Lanza, 1999; Grossman & Krueger, 1995; Ravallion et al., 1997; Roberts & Grimes, 1997; Selden & Song, 1994; Shafik, 1994; Stern et al., 1996), descobrindo algum apoio para uma curva Kuznets ambiental.

Hettige et al. (1998), utilizando-se de dados internacionais, mediram o relacionamento entre poluição da água a partir de descargas industriais e renda *per capita*. O estudo mostrou que a poluição primeiro cresce com o desenvolvimento, tendo um pico de renda *per capita* de cerca de US$ 12 mil, em seguida nivela todos os valores observáveis. Os autores concluíram que "o desenvolvimento econômico permanece bem longe do estilo Kuznets e final feliz no setor hídrico" (p.26) e sugerem que as emissões totais permanecerão constantes com o crescimento da renda, a menos que outros fatores intervenham.[5]

É menos provável que a qualidade dos recursos naturais siga uma curva Kuznets padrão do que é a poluição porque, mais que bens de consumo, são fatores tipicamente de produção. Além do mais, as externalidades associadas com a destruição dos recursos naturais são principalmente globais, portanto, menos provável serem internalizadas na demanda local (López, 1997). Como conseqüência, uma economia crescente impõe demandas ainda maiores dos recursos naturais e tornam-se cruciais as intervenções administrativas.[6]

Os países não precisam esperar até que as rendas atinjam o ponto decisivo da curva de Kuznets. São Paulo refreou a severa poluição no tempo de uma geração, mesmo que enquanto isso milhões permanecessem pobres. O crescimento rápido de Xangai, a maior base industrial da China, tem produzido quantidades de dióxido sulfúrico mais baixas do que Sishuan, de crescimento lento (World Bank, 2000d). Esses e outros casos exemplificam métodos que incluem características, tais como regimes reguladores apropriados, instrumentos centralizados baseados no mercado – para preservação ambiental –, estruturas legislativas e políticas, capacidade institucional, e opções tecnológicas que ajudem a prevenir a poluição e proteger os recursos (Panayotou, 1997).

A evidência sugere que a flexibilidade da curva de Kuznets é tanto possível quanto necessária.[7] Se as economias são de crescimento rápido ou lento, muitos indicadores de recursos naturais – desmatamento, esgotamento da pesca, degradação do solo, poluição da zona costeira – têm sido deteriorados. Porque os recursos naturais são importantes como fatores de produção, um crescimento crescente tende a colocar demandas igualmente crescentes sobre eles. Muitas das externalidades associadas com sua superexploração, como o confisco do carvão e as perdas da biodiversidade, são globais. Como conseqüência, os governos locais não levam em consideração as repercussões do mau uso ou exaustão de seus recursos.

Outros componentes do capital natural, como a qualidade da água e o acesso a serviços de esgoto e saneamento, são tipicamente bens de consumo normais. Para esses bens com uma elasticidade de renda maior do que a unidade, o crescimento de renda está, provavelmente, associado a melhorias na qualidade. Embora algumas evidências empíricas sugiram a existência de curvas Kuznets ambientais para um limitado conjunto de indicadores, os

custos da inação podem ser extremamente elevados, porque muitos países em desenvolvimento não conseguem atingir a inversão dos níveis de renda durante décadas.

Dois indicadores, acesso à água limpa e saneamento, surgem para melhorar tanto nos cenários de crescimento rápido quanto nos de lento, e testemunham a eficácia das intervenções, mas requer-se um olhar mais atento para os benefícios e custos, a fim de verificar se o andamento das melhorias é ótimo.

Desigualdade na Vantagem de Renda e a Qualidade do Capital Natural

Uma distribuição mais eqüitativa da renda e das vantagens poderia ser associada às melhorias nos indicadores-chave da qualidade ambiental, tais como desmatamento e poluição da água. Por exemplo, se agricultores em pequena escala devem usar a terra improdutiva porque os latifundiários de grande escala ocupam as melhores terras, a injusta distribuição de terras pode dirigir o desmatamento (Ekbom & Bojo, 1999). A adoção de combustíveis limpos e de tecnologias mais eficientes de energia implica que a propensão marginal para emitir dióxido de carbono declina enquanto a renda sobe. Logo, a redistribuição de renda pode acelerar a redução das emissões (Holtz-Eakin & Selden, 1995). Em um estudo de 42 países, Ravallion et al. (1997) estimaram um coeficiente positivo amplo entre emissões de dióxido de carbono *per capita* e o coeficiente Gini da desigualdade de renda. Este estudo sugere que o crescimento que reduz a desigualdade de renda e da pobreza poderia levar ao declínio nas taxas de emissão.

O Crescimento Pode Complementar a Proteção do Capital Natural

Um diagrama pode ajudar a mostrar que o crescimento e a proteção do capital natural complementam-se (Figura 4.1). Consideremos uma economia pré-industrial com uma baixa taxa de crescimento e um meio ambiente intocado, representado como ponto A. O país tenta acelerar o crescimento econômico investindo na indústria e explorando o potencial da globalização. Numa situação ideal, procuraria equilibrar o crescimento acelerado com alta qualidade ambiental, que pode ser representado graficamente como um movimento vertical rumo ao ponto E ou para um à sua direita. Contudo, mesmo uma estratégia ambiental bem administrada, que poderia ser mostrada como movimento do ponto A para o ponto F, pode não eliminar totalmente a deterioração qualitativa tanto nas funções ocultas como em fontes, embora o impacto negativo sobre o capital natural fosse relativa-

SUSTENTAR O CAPITAL NATURAL

Muitas combinações de crescimento e qualidade ambiental são possíveis

Figura 4.1 – Caminhos do Crescimento e Qualidade Ambiental

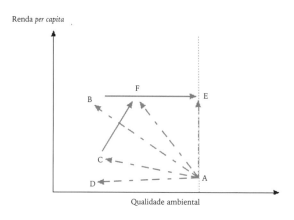

Fonte: Autores.

mente pequeno e reversível.[8] Enquanto países embarcam num caminho de desenvolvimento sustentável que pode incorporar políticas ambientais diretamente em sua estratégia econômica a qualquer tempo, a maioria dos países seguiu a abordagem do "cresça agora e limpe depois" (Tabela 4.4).

Os maiores crescedores entre os países em desenvolvimento, tais como China, Indonésia, Coréia e Tailândia, experimentaram uma situação que poderia ser representada por um movimento a partir do ponto A para o ponto B, onde pagaram severamente pela deterioração da qualidade ambiental. Muitos dos crescedores mais lentos, tais como Gana e Nepal, mostraram um movimento do ponto A para o ponto C na Figura 4.1 e sofreram igualmente dano ambiental considerável. Outros ainda na América Central, na América do Sul e na África seguiram políticas que falharam em estimular o crescimento enquanto continuam a degradar o ambiente; suas ações seriam simuladas por uma flecha desde o ponto A para o ponto D.[9]

As economias representadas nos pontos B, C e D sofreram sérias perdas a partir do dano do ecossistema: doenças, mortes, florestas degradadas e extensões de água e ar poluídos, entre outros. As economias em desenvolvimento e as industrializadas que ignoraram a degradação de seu capital natural aprenderam que a estratégia do "cresça agora e limpe depois" criou custos que são difíceis de recuperar. Por exemplo, os Estados Unidos precisaram gastar dezenas de bilhões de dólares para restaurar o dano causado aos pântanos da Flórida pelo desenvolvimento dos canais de irrigação para o cultivo da cana-de-açúcar.

Tabela 4.4 – Classificação de Países Seletos pela Trajetória do Crescimento Ambiental

A para B: alto crescimento e degradação ambiental		A para C: médio crescimento e degradação ambiental		A para D: baixo crescimento e degradação ambiental		A para F: crescimento com proteção ambiental	
Desmatamento	Emissão de dióxido de carbono	Desmatamento	Emissão de dióxido de carbono	Desmatamento	Emissão de dióxido de carbono	Desmatamento	Emissão de dióxido de carbono
Indonésia	China	El Salvador	El Salvador	Argélia	México	Botswana	
Malásia	Índia	Gana	Paquistão	Camarões			
Sri Lanka	Indonésia	Guatemala	Panamá	Haiti			
Tailândia	Coréia	Moçambique		México			
	Malásia	Nepal		Nicarágua			
	Tailândia	Paquistão		Zâmbia			
		Panamá					

Nota: As taxas de desmatamento foram desenhadas pelas médias anuais para 1990-1995; as emissões de dióxido de carbono são de 1980 até 1996. Crescimento alto é definido como crescimento de renda *per capita* de mais de 2,3% ao ano, tanto na década de 1980 como na de 1990; crescimento médio inclui países que mantiveram crescimento positivo da renda *per capita* em ambas as décadas, ou melhoraram o crescimento de pelo menos dois pontos percentuais ao ano, mais alto na década de 1990 do que na de 1980; o restante é classificado como países de baixo crescimento.
Fonte: World Bank (2000c).

Incorporar a Sustentabilidade Ambiental a Políticas de Crescimento

Muitos países integraram interesses ambientais e políticas de crescimento. Os quatro casos seguintes mostram como isso pode ser feito. Eles foram escolhidos para ilustrar histórias de sucesso na administração da poluição e preservação dos recursos naturais e para acentuar os tipos de intervenções requeridas para realizar objetivos ambientais específicos. Para mais estudos de casos dos instrumentos perseguidos com sucesso por cenários particulares, ver Thomas et al. (1998) e World Bank (1997e, 2000d).

Costa Rica: Preservar as Florestas e Atenuar a Mudança Climática

A rica biodiversidade da Costa Rica atrai ecoturistas de alto poder aquisitivo de todo o mundo; ainda assim, na década de 1980 as taxas de desmatamento subiram para mais que 3% ao ano. Para proteger este valioso recurso natural, a Costa Rica desenvolveu um dos sistemas mais inovadores e funcionais de proteção florestal no mundo. Observando os benefícios dos serviços ambientais marcados e não marcados das florestas, o sistema identificou quem suporta os custos e quem recebe os benefícios (Tabela 4.5). Calculou os valores anuais por hectare de US$ 29 para US$ 87 para florestas primárias e de US$ 21 para US$ 63 para florestas secundárias. A análise

Tabela 4.5 – Serviços Ambientais das Florestas Costa-Riquenhas e seus Beneficiários

Tipo de benefício	Beneficiários		
	Latifundiário	País	Mundo
Produção sustentável de madeira	X		
Potencial de produção hidroenergética		X	
Purificação dos suprimentos de água		X	
Estabilização do solo e regulação do fluxo hidrológico		X	
Beleza do cenário, utilização do ecoturismo, valor existencial		X	X
Confisco de carbono			X
Preservação da biodiversidade			X

Fonte: Castro et al. (1997).

mostrou que os latifundiários ou o governo (no caso de parques nacionais) suportavam os custos da preservação do hábitat, enquanto benefícios substanciais foram para interesses estrangeiros. Logo, a Costa Rica decidiu-se a criar mercados para alguns benefícios ambientais (Castro et al., 1997).

Dos vários benefícios ambientais fornecidos pela floresta, a Costa Rica tem sido mais bem-sucedida na captura do confisco do carbono e na proteção das nascentes. O governo atua como intermediário na venda destes serviços para os compradores internacionais e do país. Os fundos provenientes das vendas (e de um imposto sobre combustível sinalizado em 5%) vão para os latifundiários para a preservação da cobertura florestal em suas terras. Contratos para mais de cinqüenta mil hectares de proteção florestal foram estabelecidos em 1997. Antes desse período, as áreas protegidas cumulativas abrangiam apenas 79 mil hectares.

A Costa Rica também atraiu investimentos internacionais para compensar os latifundiários que promovem o confisco do carbono pela manutenção das florestas. As compensações comercialmente certificáveis podem ser utilizadas para vender compensações aos gases do efeito estufa no mercado internacional. O primeiro lote foi vendido em julho de 1996. Entre 1996 e 1998, as vendas foram negociadas bilateralmente, mas recentemente a Costa Rica começou a trabalhar com empresas de corretagem em Chicago e Nova York para estabelecer o comércio certificável como uma *commodity* livremente comerciável, similar ao comércio das emissões de dióxido sulfúrico nos Estados Unidos (Chomitz et al., 1998).

A Costa Rica demonstra o sucesso prático de se criarem mercados verdes e implementarem impostos verdes para reduzir o dano ao meio ambiente. O potencial para a réplica em todos os outros lugares é bom, mas depende em grande parte de um acordo internacional completo acerca das compensações sobre o carbono e a aceitação por todas as partes da *Clean Development Mechanism of the Framework Convention on Climate Change.*

China: Controlar a Poluição da Água com um Imposto

O imposto sobre poluição, e a carga de emissões cobrindo centenas de fábricas na China, é um dos poucos instrumentos econômicos com uma longa história documentada num país em desenvolvimento. Embora o imposto tenha sido utilizado durante várias décadas, estudos sérios sobre sua eficácia surgiram apenas recentemente (Wang & Wheeler, 1996).

O sistema vem-se expandindo desde 1982; implementado na maioria das metrópoles chinesas, inclui trezentas mil fábricas que são responsabilizadas por suas emissões. Os regulamentos da agência de proteção nacional ao meio ambiente especificam as variações em padrões de efluentes por setor e taxa de poluidores. Qualquer empresa cuja descarga de efluentes exceda o padrão legal deve pagar imposto. Os impostos recaem apenas sobre as mais poluentes emissões de cada fonte. O imposto difere de taxa, que deveria cobrir cada unidade de poluidores, não apenas aqueles que excedem um certo padrão.

Entre 1987 e 1993, a poluição orgânica da água caiu para as indústrias reguladas pelo Estado, que relataram descargas à Agência de Proteção Ambiental Nacional (Wang & Wheeler, 1996). Com o crescimento de resultados de 10% ao ano, a China experimentou um declínio especialmente impressionante na poluição por unidade de saída. Enquanto o total de descargas provincianas declinou a uma taxa média de 22% ao ano, as intensidades poluidoras caíram a uma taxa média de 50%. Análises econométricas mostram que muito do declínio era tributável ao imposto.

Variação significativa nos impostos através de províncias é explicada por taxas locais de impactos poluidores e capacidades locais para melhorar os padrões nacionais. Admitir tais diferenças regionais aumentou a viabilidade e a efetividade do sistema de impostos de poluição.

Desde 1991, as autoridades coletaram mais de US$ 240 milhões por ano em impostos.[10] Aproximadamente 60% dos fundos financiam e controlam a prevenção da poluição industrial e representam mais ou menos 15% do investimento total nessas atividades, fornecendo um incentivo adicional para que as empresas possam abater. O restante destina-se às agências locais para desenvolvimento institucional e cursos administrativos (Wang & Chen, 1999). Para ajudar a regrar a poluição, os impostos também ajudaram a construir capacidades de monitoração e regulamentação de agências de melhorias locais e reforçam os incentivos para regulamentação efetiva.

Indonésia: Combater a Poluição com Informação

O governo pode estabelecer padrões para os níveis máximos de poluição permitidos com relativa facilidade, mas monitorar e melhorar a concordância pode ser difícil. A *Environment Impact Management Agency*, da Indonésia,

encarou os desafios da concordância no fim da década de 1980 e recorreu a acordos não judiciais e outras abordagens *ad hoc* que tiveram impacto limitado sobre o controle da poluição.

Procurando uma abordagem mais sustentável, a agência desenvolveu o Programa para o Controle da Poluição, Avaliação e Taxação (PROPER), que recebe os dados poluidores das fábricas, analisa e taxa seu desempenho ambiental, e dissemina as taxas para o público (Wheeler & Afsah, 1996; World Bank, 2000d). A Agência esperou que a publicação das taxas de *performance* encorajasse as comunidades locais a pressionar fábricas próximas que registraram baixas taxas para limpar suas operações. Também esperou influenciar os poluidores, por meio de mercados financeiros, dos quais se esperava que reagissem às taxações. Para encorajar as empresas a melhorar suas *performances*, também estabeleceu um programa para reconhecimento das práticas excelentes de controle da poluição ambiental.

A agência decidiu centralizar-se primeiramente na poluição da água. Ela juntou dados sobre a poluição da água das fábricas, mediante questionários e rigorosas inspeções *in loco*. O governo compilou informações sobre 187 fábricas altamente poluentes e classificou as companhias pelo nível das emissões. Os dados foram combinados numa única taxa de desempenho em cinco categorias-chave: dourado, verde e azul significavam concordância, e o vermelho e o preto representavam a não-concordância.

A Agência abriu os resultados em estágios, primeiro reconhecendo publicamente os melhores desempenhos e dando aos demais seis meses para limpar, antes que suas taxas ruins fossem reveladas. Esta abordagem por fases deu às fábricas tempo para se ajustarem ao programa, e aumentar a probabilidade de concordância. Entre junho e setembro de 1995, metade das empresas que tinham sido taxadas como não-concordantes observou os novos mandatos. Isto sugere que o PROPER criou incentivos poderosos para o controle da poluição. Em muitas instâncias, as empresas compreenderam que um gerenciamento melhor do meio ambiente reduz os custos de produção ao criar incentivos adicionais para que eles limpassem suas práticas de produção. Encorajados por estes esforços iniciais, a Agência planejou taxar duas mil plantas por volta de 2000.

O PROPER da Indonésia vai além do comando e do controle tradicionalmente utilizados com sucesso limitado para regular os poluidores. O sistema de imposto é único em que isso permite múltiplos resultados. A escolha final fica com a empresa e depende de seus recursos para o controle da poluição, os benefícios percebidos para limpeza e sua estratégia corporativista global. O PROPER baseia-se na abertura pública e na pressão pública para que as empresas poluidoras se alinhassem com as regulamentações ambientais. O PROPER envolve as pessoas afetadas pela poluição, garante um equilíbrio de barganha entre as empresas e os investidores. O papel do governo é estabelecer as regras do jogo, monitorar o nível das descargas, adotar ações punitivas quando necessário e agir como último árbitro.

A Campanha da Bandeira Azul Européia: Aumentar a Consciência do Meio Ambiente Costeiro

A Campanha Européia da Bandeira Azul, operando por meio de uma rede de organizações nacionais, é coordenada pela Foundation for Environmental Education in Europe (Fundação para Educação sobre o Meio Ambiente na Europa) (Thomas et al., 1998). Ela encoraja a compreensão e a avaliação dos cidadãos do meio ambiente costeiro e a incorporação de interesses ambientais nas tomadas de decisão das autoridades costeiras. A Comissão Européia financia aproximadamente 25% do orçamento da campanha, que chega atualmente a mais de US$ 1 milhão; patrocinadores particulares financiam o restante.

Uma praia ou marina recebe uma Bandeira Azul se preencher três conjuntos de critérios relacionados com a qualidade ambiental da localidade, gerenciamento e segurança e educação ambiental e informação. Os recebedores devem obrigatoriamente cumprir os critérios e diretrizes.

Baseado em mapas, fotografias, amostras de água e num questionário completo, um júri nacional designa locais para um júri europeu, que faz a seleção final dos recebedores de Bandeira Azul por votação unânime. Os resultados são anunciados no começo de junho, antes que o principal período de férias se inicie. A campanha atraiu vários patrocinadores comerciais, juntamente com escolares, que limparam as praias locais para manter os altos padrões requisitados pelos juízes da Bandeira Azul. Ao longo dos anos os padrões de qualidade ambiental necessários para vencer ou ganhar o prêmio foram sucessivamente aumentados, objetivando prover incentivos dinâmicos para uma melhor administração ambiental. Mais de mil localidades costeiras, a maioria delas na Dinamarca, na Grécia e na Espanha, receberam a Bandeira Azul.

Os governos encaram o Programa da Bandeira Azul como um meio eficiente para promover a consciência ambiental e aumentar os lucros do turismo. Do ponto de vista dos patrocinadores privados, ele é uma oportunidade para atrair mais turistas. A iniciativa leva o governo, os setores público e privado a parcerias que geram competições entre as jurisdições, que levantam os padrões ambientais para níveis cada vez mais altos.

Repensar o Papel do Estado

Atribuir a degradação ambiental às políticas distorcidas, subsídios danosos, carência de mercados, externalidades e conhecimento público e completo coloca o Estado na posição de um catalisador para a proteção e o gerenciamento ambiental. Contudo, o registro misto das intervenções governamentais tem motivado um repensar extensivo das políticas que o Estado deveria alimentar. Para conseguir maior impacto, o governo deveria intervir de maneira seletiva (ver Quadro 4.4).

Quadro 4.4 – O Desenvolvimento e o Meio Ambiente

O *World Development Report 1992* (World Bank, 1992, p.2) lançou o desafio de encontrar o equilíbrio correto entre desenvolvimento e meio ambiente.

A proteção do meio ambiente é uma parte essencial do desenvolvimento; sem proteção ambiental adequada, o desenvolvimento é minado; sem desenvolvimento os recursos serão inadequados para os investimentos necessários, e a proteção ambiental irá falhar ... O crescimento traz consigo o risco de dano ambiental assustador. De modo alternativo, poderia trazer consigo melhores proteções ambientais, ar e água mais limpos e a virtual eliminação da pobreza aguda. As escolhas políticas farão a diferença.

O relatório acentuou dois conjuntos de políticas para o desenvolvimento sustentável. O primeiro se constrói sobre elos positivos de vencer ou vencer, tais como remover os subsídios ambientalmente danosos;

esclarecer direitos de propriedade; acelerar a provisão do saneamento, fornecer água limpa, garantir educação especialmente para as meninas e habilitar o povo do local. A segunda procura romper os laços negativos entre meio ambiente e desenvolvimento mediante, por exemplo, o estabelecimento de padrões, utilizar instrumento baseados no mercado como impostos verdes e assumir abordagens colaborativas com o gerenciamento da poluição.

O relatório enfatizou que, embora os custos da proteção adequada do meio ambiente fossem amplos, os custos da inação seriam monumentais. É racional agir mais cedo que mais tarde.

Oito anos depois, as prescrições do relatório ainda são válidas. A experiência com gerenciamento de recursos e proteção ambiental mostra que encontrar as parcerias de políticas corretas para o desenvolvimento sustentável do meio ambiente é ainda mais viável hoje se lhe derem uma prioridade alta.

Subsídios Aerodinâmicos e Implementação de Impostos Ambientais

Em princípio, os subsídios sustentam as rendas dos pobres; na prática, freqüentemente aumentam as desigualdades, drenam o orçamento público, aceleram o esgotamento dos recursos naturais e degradam o meio ambiente. O custo global dos subsídios da agricultura, da energia, do transporte rodoviário e da água é estimado em US$ 800 bilhões ao ano, com cerca de dois terços dos gastos incorridos nos países da OECD (De Moor & Calamai, 1997). Em anos recentes, os subsídios têm baixado com uma rapidez notável, particularmente nos países em desenvolvimento. Na China, os subsídios ao carvão caíram de US$ 750 milhões em 1993 para US$ 250 milhões em 1995 (UNDP, 1998). As taxas de subsídios caíram de 61% em 1984 para 11% em 1995 (World Bank, 1997e). A remoção de subsídios perversos acarreta três benefícios: reduz a degradação ambiental, promove a igualdade e preserva os recursos orçamentários.

Nem todos os subsídios produzem maus resultados, e os bons subsídios deveriam ser encorajados. Inacessibilidade para serviços de água e saneamento concorre para uma significativa perda de vida, particularmente entre mulheres e crianças de famílias pobres. Os estudos mostram que essas famílias têm uma grande vontade de pagar por suprimentos adequados e confiáveis desses serviços. Subsídio que tenha como alvo essas famílias para

aumentar os serviços de água e saneamento, talvez vindo do setor privado, constitui, provavelmente, uma intervenção de custo efetivo para a diminuição dos impactos negativos sobre a saúde e para a redução da pobreza pela promoção do acúmulo de capital humano.

Em contrapartida, os impostos verdes sobre atividades que provocam a degradação ambiental fornecem meios poderosos para combater a poluição e o esgotamento de recursos. Os impostos verdes podem ser particularmente úteis na administração das emissões que contribuem para a poluição da água e do ar. Pode-se, por exemplo, taxar a utilização do carvão pela indústria ou pelas emissões e aumentar os lucros dos impostos; logo, os impostos verdes podem fornecer uma abordagem de vencer ou vencer para gerenciar a qualidade ambiental com o crescimento (World Bank, 1997d). As taxas de poluição são mais efetivas quando uma estrutura reguladora bem estabelecida, com normas de emissões e um sistema eficiente de monitoração e imposição, estão no lugar. Impostos verdes efetivos também encorajam a utilização de fontes energéticas mais limpas, como a energia solar.

Uma mudança de renda para os impostos de consumo também pode beneficiar o meio ambiente e o crescimento. A produção e o consumo de bens de luxo sempre provocam drásticas demandas sobre os recursos ambientais e naturais. Os impostos sobre o consumo podem dobrar a superexploração desses bens. Impostos de consumo progressivo também promovem a eqüidade e, mediante o encorajamento de poupanças, promove o crescimento econômico (Frank, 1998).

Além disso, impostos verdes podem gerar os fundos necessários para promover o gerenciamento ambiental. O setor público precisa de dinheiro para o seu papel de facilitador, mas os fundos sempre estão longe das necessidades. Qualquer estratégia para o gerenciamento ambiental deve identificar fontes de financiamento adequadas. Muitos países em desenvolvimento baseiam-se mais atualmente em impostos verdes para criar fundos para melhorias ambientais do que o fizeram no passado (World Bank, 1999f).

Sair do Controle Central para Parcerias

No passado, os governos baseavam-se muito no controle central, o que requeria monitoração extensiva da concordância para o gerenciamento ambiental. A combinação da política de comando e controle e recursos inadequados para a monitoração e a imposição garantiram a falência do programa. Os agentes de política estão aprendendo que os membros da comunidade afetados pela poluição podem complementar a regulamentação. O envolvimento das comunidades locais e da sociedade civil tem outras vantagens. Particularmente nas áreas rurais, ele é tanto a fonte-chave da informação quanto os curadores do conhecimento tradicional do meio ambiente.

Logo, podem identificar e implementar estratégias que equilibrem o crescimento com a proteção ambiental.

Onde a subavaliação de um recurso pode conduzir à sua degradação, a avaliação própria de seus benefícios econômicos e sociais pode garantir que sua contribuição seja totalmente levada a sério nas tomadas de decisões (Dixon & Shermann, 1990; Pearce & Warford, 1993; Ruitenbeek, 1989). Aferições do "produto nacional bruto do verde" e poupanças genuínas estão ganhando proeminência como um meio para incorporar a sustentabilidade no planejamento econômico tradicional (Hamilton & Lutz, 1996; World Bank, 1997d). A distância estimada entre o valor econômico total e a avaliação privada atual não pode ser facilmente percorrida, mas a evidência sugere que o Estado pode fazê-lo, criando mercados ou estabelecendo instituições e estatutos legais apropriados que criem condições semelhantes às de mercado e pela geração adequada de fluxos financeiros (ver o caso ilustrativo da Costa Rica).

Baseando-se em dados para 77 países em desenvolvimento, foi encontrada uma associação positiva significativa entre gastos educacionais e aumento na cobertura florestal (matriz correlacional disponível a pedido). Isto sugere que ímpetos acrescentados à sustentabilidade ambiental podem partir do Estado e cooperação dos setores privados para aumentar a conclusão de educação da população.

Reconhecendo as limitações da intervenção estatal e a necessidade de parcerias ativas no gerenciamento ambiental, os governos estão procurando novos meios para promovê-lo. A disseminação, para todos os investidores, do conhecimento sobre as conseqüências totais do desprezo ambiental, juntamente com uma estrutura clara de responsabilidade e habilidades ambientais, pode ter impactos poderosos (Thomas et al., 1998). As alianças entre as agências reguladoras do Estado e as empresas industriais estão ajudando a controlar a poluição em muitos países (Hanrahan et al., 1998; Schmidheiny & Zorraquim, 1996). No Zimbábue, o programa CAMPFIRE promove a aliança entre governos provinciais, o setor privado e os habitantes locais no gerenciamento da vida selvagem em prol da preservação da biodiversidade dentro de uma estrutura legal estabelecida pelo governo central (Thomas et al., 1998).

Na África, na Ásia oriental e na América Latina, a sabedoria convencional de que as práticas agrícolas de corte e queima aplicadas pelos pobres são a causa do desmatamento em ampla escala foi quebrada pela compreensão de que a mudança macroeconômica, empresas comerciais e desenvolvimento infra-estrutural freqüentemente têm maiores impactos sobre o desmatamento (Chomitz & Gray, 1996; Deininger & Minten, 1996; Mamingi et al., 1996). Uma extração insustentável de madeira por grandes companhias madeireiras comerciais conduz ao desmatamento, comunidades indígenas pobres perdem suas fontes de lenha, forragem, plantas medicinais, e até mesmo seus meios de sobrevivência. As comu-

nidades pobres que dependem das florestas deveriam ser o foco da ação pública que garante uma utilização melhor e sustentável das florestas. A melhor oportunidade de um acordo negociado está com uma parceria tripartite do Estado, comunidades locais e companhias madeireiras. O desafio para os países em desenvolvimento é aumentar tais parcerias o mais rapidamente possível.

Esclarecer os Direitos de Propriedade, Posse de Recursos e Responsabilidades Ambientais

A relação empírica entre direitos de propriedade claros e qualidade ambiental é forte (Dasgupta et al., 1995). Fazendeiros com escrituras de terra têm mais possibilidade de investir na preservação do solo, técnicas de cultivo sustentável e outras práticas de proteção ambiental (Feder, 1987). Com o capital de direitos de propriedade investido, as comunidades locais reflorestaram terras degradadas na Índia e no Nepal (Lynch & Talbott, 1995). Estabeleceram direitos de utilização para água, pescas e de madeira, e forneceram um incentivo claro e meios para o gerenciamento dos recursos (World Bank, 1997e).

Sem direitos de propriedade melhorados para os recursos naturais, interesses exteriores tiram vantagem do acesso aberto e sem nenhuma responsabilidade por suas ações, superexploram o capital natural com pescas e pastagens excessivas, utilizando de forma exagerada os lotes de madeira das aldeias e extraindo quantidades excessivas da água do solo. Enquanto as experiências variam, o investimento em direitos de propriedade comum nestes recursos parece diminuir as pressões para a superexploração. O grupo comunitário desenvolve mecanismos para restringir o acesso por forasteiros, distribuindo responsabilidades gerenciais, alocando direitos de uso entre os membros do grupo e monitorando-os. Exemplos de sistemas de gerenciamentos comunitários incluem aqueles para as florestas no Japão; as pescas na Turquia; a água de irrigação no sul da Índia; pastos nos Alpes suíços, no Himalaia e nos Andes (World Bank, 1992).[11]

A segurança do título de posse para os habitantes urbanos também pode melhorar a qualidade do ambiente, simplificando a identificação e a coerção de responsabilidade pela poluição do ar e da água, e uma disposição química tóxica sólida e causal (World Bank, 1997e). Um estudo do relacionamento entre os direitos de propriedade e o meio ambiente urbano descobriu que, quando as pessoas passam do *status* de grileiros para uma segurança moderada, a probabilidade de conseguirem serviços de coleta de lixo aumenta em 32%, ao passo que, ao mudar para alta segurança de propriedade (segurança de propriedade mais alta é caracterizada pela propriedade da terra acompanhada de uma escritura legal), a probabilidade de comprar a remoção de lixo cresce em 44% (Hoy & Jimenez, 1947). Logo, estabelecer

direitos de propriedade e de posse claros e identificar as responsabilidades ambientais poderiam ser as mais importantes contribuições do Estado rumo à realização da sustentabilidade ambiental.

Melhorar o Governo e Reduzir a Corrupção

A procura por arrendamentos e a corrupção atingem a eficiência econômica e inviabilizam resultados desejáveis até mesmo quando boas políticas para o gerenciamento ambiental existem no papel (Bhagwati, 1982; Krueger, 1974; Rose-Ackerman, 1997a). Funcionários públicos corruptos minam os esforços para monitorar e melhorar as medidas ambientais, das descargas de efluentes industriais e das emissões dos automóveis a cortes permissíveis de madeira (Quadro 4.5). Encontra-se que o controle da corrupção está associado de um modo significativo a, por exemplo, uma redução na poluição da água (Anexo 1, Figura A1.1). Coletar conhecimento e partilhá-lo amplamente pode combater a corrupção e fomentar um bom governo, com resultados benéficos para o crescimento econômico e o gerenciamento ambiental. Particularmente, a abordagem dos diagnósticos

---

Quadro 4.5 – Lucro Privado a Expensas do Gasto Público: Corrupção no Setor Florestal

A corrupção é desmedida na derrubada de árvores e corte de madeira em todos os níveis das tomadas de decisões relacionadas às florestas. A maior parte dos danos com os recursos florestais refere-se ao mau uso dos recursos públicos para ganhos privados pela elite política. Juntando-se à degradação e ao mau uso das florestas, a corrupção priva os governos e comunidades locais de recursos que poderiam ser utilizados para o desenvolvimento e melhoria do gerenciamento florestal. Práticas de corrupção incluem venda secreta e permissões de corte, depreciação ilegal da madeira por companhias para apressar a transferência e falsos certificados de espécie ou volumes cortados das florestas públicas e o madeiramento ilegal. Exemplos de todo o mundo prevalecem.

- A transferência de preços era tão prevalente na Papua-Nova Guiné que até 1986 nem sequer uma única companhia declarou lucro, apesar do comércio explosivo da madeira.
- Em Gana, 11 companhias estrangeiras estavam implicadas em fraude e outras más práticas,

custando para a economia cerca de US$ 50 milhões.
- Na década de 1980, as Filipinas perderam cerca de US$ 1,8 bilhão por ano em corte ilegal de madeira.
- Em 1994, o Departamento Florestal da Indonésia admitiu que o país estava perdendo cerca de US$ 3,5 bilhões por ano, ou um terço de seus lucros potenciais, devido ao corte ilegal de madeira.
- Em 1994, o governo russo coletou apenas de 3% a 20% dos lucros potenciais estimados derivados das taxas sobre madeira; ou seja, US$ 184 milhões ao invés dos US$ 900 milhões a US$ 5,5 bilhões.

A World Commission on Forestry and Sustainable Development enfatizou a necessidade de mecanismos de participação pública e resoluções de conflito, para expor casos de corrupção e penalizar as corporações e indivíduos ofensivos. Agindo sob esta recomendação, o Banco Mundial deu início a um programa de melhoria da lei florestal, enfocado principalmente no sul da Ásia, para corrigir a corrupção.

Fonte: World Commission on Forestry and Sustainable Development (1999).

de corrupção tem mostrado esperança de reduzir a corrupção e promover a integridade em vários países (Capítulo 6, neste volume; e Kaufmann el al., 1998).

Logo, os países em desenvolvimento deveriam dar prioridade máxima para reprimir a corrupção e melhorar o governo.

Questões Ambientais Globais Devem Ser Confrontadas

Muitas questões de gerenciamento ambiental são em escala global, embora em causas locais.[12] O efeito estufa e a mudança climática global estão claramente ligados às atividades humanas (ver Quadro 4.6). A queima de combustível fóssil é a maior fonte dos gases da estufa. O desmatamento também contribui para o problema, em razão da perda das funções ocultas

---

Quadro 4.6 – Cooperação Internacional para Mitigar a Mudança Climática Global

A Primeira Conferência Mundial sobre o Clima, realizada em 1979, reconheceu a mudança climática como um sério problema e explorou a forma como essa mudança poderia afetar as atividades humanas. A declaração da conferência conclamou os governos do mundo a predizer e prever mudanças climáticas produzidas pelo homem que poderiam causar impactos adversos sobre o bem-estar da humanidade. O painel intergovernamental sobre a mudança climática, estabelecido pela Organização Meteorológica Mundial e pelo Programa Ambiental das Nações Unidas, liberou seus primeiros relatórios de taxação em 1990 e confirmou a evidência científica para a mudança climática. A Segunda Conferência Climática Mundial, em 1990, apelou para um tratado estrutural sobre a mudança climática. A Convenção Estrutural das Nações Unidas sobre a Mudança Climática, que foi aberta pela assinatura da Cúpula da Terra do Rio de Janeiro em junho de 1992 e entrou em vigor em março de 1994, fornece o contexto para um esforço internacional acordado para responder à mudança climática. Há 166 signatários e 167 partidos para a convenção.

A Conferência dos Partidos, que substituiu o Comitê Intergovernamental de Negociação para a Convenção Estrutural, tornou-se a autoridade máxima da convenção. Isto sustentou sua primeira sessão em Berlim, em 1995. A segunda, realizada em Genebra em 1996, compreendeu o estoque de progresso e outras questões. Funcionários públicos participantes sublinharam a necessidade de conversações aceleradas sobre como fortalecer a Convenção a respeito da mudança climática. A Declaração de Genebra endossou o segundo relatório de taxação do Painel Intergovernamental sobre Mudança Climática como o imposto mais abrangente autorizador da ciência da mudança climática, seus impactos e as opções disponíveis de resposta.

O protocolo de Kyoto, adotado na Terceira Conferência dos Partidos em dezembro de 1997, é reconhecido como um passo histórico em direção às limitações obrigatórias das emissões em 39 economias industrializadas e de transição. Estas emissões são reduzidas a pelo menos 5,2% abaixo dos níveis de 1990 no período de comprometimento de 2008 a 2012. Isto é um desenvolvimento significativo, porque a projeção para os Estados Unidos, por exemplo, indica que sem tais compromissos de proibição suas emissões poderiam ser 30% acima dos níveis de 1990, por volta de 2010.

Apesar do progresso significativo, os detalhes da junta de implementação, as emissões comerciais e as obrigações dos países em desenvolvimento ficam ainda para ser resolvidas.

da floresta, que transformam dióxido de gás carbônico em biomassa. Atividades agrícolas, mineração de carvão e vazamento de gás natural dos tubos de transmissão também juntam-se aos gases da estufa pela liberação de metano.

Como esses problemas são originados por um amplo número de atividades econômicas consideradas essenciais para o crescimento, o seu controle esbarra em uma série de dificuldades. A maioria das nações em desenvolvimento depende da queima do combustível fóssil, do carvão e do petróleo para a produção econômica, sendo improvável que mudem para combustíveis menos poluentes e mais caros.

No entanto, a mudança para combustíveis menos poluentes pode conduzir a melhores resultados de saúde, o que é bom para os objetivos econômicos nacionais. Como conseqüência, uma tensão natural existe entre os dois objetivos, e muitos países optam por mais crescimento em vez de melhor saúde (Munasinghe, 2000). Assistências financeira e técnica vindas da comunidade internacional, em retorno para ceifar os benefícios da mudança para combustíveis menos poluentes, pode capacitar a compreensão conjunta tanto dos interesses globais como dos nacionais.

A cooperação entre países ricos e pobres também pode ajudar a controlar o desmatamento. Apesar das externalidades que gera, os países em desenvolvimento vêem o desmatamento como uma conseqüência inevitável de seu desenvolvimento econômico. Como acontece com seus combustíveis menos poluentes, a comunidade internacional precisa lidar com a ameaça da mudança climática global mediante a transferência de recursos, inclusive tecnologia para controlar o desmatamento (Kishor & Constantino, 1994; López, 1997). Sob a iniciativa da Convenção Estrutural das Nações Unidas sobre Mudança Climática, vários esquemas bilaterais de preservação florestal estão sendo testados em diferentes partes do mundo. Pilotos bem-sucedidos serão reaplicados numa escala maior.

A Facilidade Ambiental Global é a principal instituição que erige interesses ambientais globais. Como o mecanismo financeiro provisório da Convenção sobre Diversidade Biológica e Mudança Climática, erigem-se problemas ambientais globais mediante a colaboração entre países em desenvolvimento e industrializados, que beneficiam ambas as partes. Por exemplo, países industrializados podem diminuir as emissões de gás para o efeito estufa de um modo barato, e os países em desenvolvimento podem beneficiar-se de transferências tecnológicas e financeiras na proteção de seus recursos-base que promovem o desenvolvimento econômico.

Prevenir a mudança climática global e gerenciar suas conseqüências será um dos maiores desafios do século XXI. Convenções globais, tratados e acordos foram importantes por identificar problemas comuns, desenvolver soluções e alocar responsabilidades. A consciência nacional e o comprometimento são crescentes, e a implementação deve ser encorajada para garantir os objetivos nacionais globais. Exemplos bem-sucedidos deste casamen-

to entre objetivos nacionais e globais precisam ser reaplicados amplamente (Castro et al., 1997; Watson et al., 1998).

Conclusões

Para o mundo em desenvolvimento, o esgotamento do capital natural (florestas, energias e minerais) e o dano causado pelas emissões de dióxido de carbono são estimados em 5,8% do PIB. Os riscos para a saúde ambiental chegam a 20% dos custos globais de doença. Além disso, os enormes custos dos problemas ambientais globais precisam ser fatorados nas políticas de desenvolvimento nacionais. Os pobres, particularmente as mulheres e as crianças pequenas, freqüentemente carregam muito do peso da degradação ambiental. Assim, o capital natural é fundamental para o crescimento sustentado, e sua conservação e aumento são cruciais para estratégias desenvolvimentistas internacionais e nacionais.

Três descobertas-chave emergem da evidência apresentada neste capítulo:

- Vários indicadores da qualidade de capital natural, com a notável exceção do acesso à água de qualidade e às facilidades de saneamento em alguns países, tendem a piorar tanto nas economias de rápido como nas de lento crescimento, impor custos pesados e prospectos diminutos para o crescimento futuro. Contudo, o crescimento mais rápido torna disponíveis mais recursos para investir na melhoria do capital natural. Logo, a ideologia do "cresça agora e limpe depois", assumida por muitos países industrializados ou em crescimento, precisa mudar para uma de crescimento da sustentabilidade do capital natural.
- O Estado desempenha papel crucial no gerenciamento ambiental, mas precisa ser seletivo e eficiente em suas intervenções. Deveria centrar-se em abordagens colaborativas com as comunidades locais e o setor privado.
- Os problemas ambientais globais são enormes, mas oferecem oportunidades para levantar simultaneamente problemas nacionais se a cooperação internacional puder ser garantida. O desenvolvimento de transferência de mecanismos para recursos a pagar pelas externalidades globais é fundamental.

Os países precisam centrar-se em estratégias para realizar um crescimento de alta qualidade, que é sustentável e compatível com a estabilidade financeira interna e externa, ou seja, crescimento que sustente o pobre e o vulnerável e não degrade excessivamente a atmosfera, os rios, as florestas e os oceanos, ou qualquer parte da herança comum da humanidade. As estimativas de custo-benefício sustentam uma estratégia de

SUSTENTAR O CAPITAL NATURAL

crescimento saudável e todos os exemplos neste capítulo mostram que tal estratégia é viável.

Notas

1. Alguns estudos do Banco Mundial atribuíram 100% de todas as doenças originárias da água à falta de conexões de água encanada e facilidades de saneamento. Contudo, estudos epidemiológicos raramente mostraram declínio de mais de 40% em doenças decorrentes de intervenções de acesso à água (Esrey et al., 1990). Logo, os benefícios de saúde relacionados com um suprimento de água tratada e melhoria nos serviços de saneamento podem estar descritos de forma exagerada na Tabela 4.2.

2. O trabalho realizado sob a Iniciativa do Ônus Global das Doenças utiliza-se de uma medida padronizada de resultados de saúde, os DALYs; mediante o cruzamento de várias causas de doenças e mortes, dão um modo-padrão para quantificar algumas perdas aqui descritas (Murray & López, 1996).

3. Muitas estimativas utilizam-se de taxas de desconto no âmbito de 6% a 10% para calcular o valor atual dos benefícios. Se as taxas de desconto atual são mais altas, digamos de 20% a 25% como a evidência que alguns países em desenvolvimento sugerem, então o valor atual dos benefícios será muito mais baixo. De modo semelhante, assume-se que o custo da oportunidade de capital disponível para financiar melhorias ambientais deve ser muito mais baixo do que aquele que os países em desenvolvimento realmente enfrentam. O resultado líquido da aplicação de "verdadeiros" valores reduziria a distância dos benefícios sobre os custos, embora reduza o investimento requerido para um gerenciamento ambiental ótimo, ou mesmo reduza os benefícios abaixo dos custos, tornando tais investimentos improfícuos. Isso aponta para a necessidade de levar a cabo uma análise sensível a respeito de mudanças nas taxas de desconto para identificar, de modo confiável, as áreas de prioridade para a intervenção (Kishor & Constantino, 1994).

4. Proteger o meio ambiente enquanto se acelera o crescimento também pode ter impactos benéficos no acúmulo de capital natural. Se as autoridades anunciam padrões ambientais mais rígidos, adiantados aos dados quando eles se tornam proibitivos, os investimentos que encarnam os padrões melhorados podem ser realizados durante um período de tempo, embora reduza a obsolescência do capital ou a necessidade por um retroajuste de custos para encontrar padrões ambientais, por exemplo, a experiência com os padrões de emissões e conversores catalíticos para carros.

5. Mesmo onde uma curva ambiental Kuznets parece ser sustentada, isto não implica que o gerenciamento ambiental seja desnecessário. Vejamos o caso das emissões de dióxido sulfúrico, onde Grossman & Krueger (1995) estimaram momento de decisão para as emissões diminuírem a um nível de renda *per capita* de US$ 4,053. Mesmo com uma taxa de crescimento alta de 5% ao ano, a Índia, por exemplo, levará várias décadas para alcançar

este nível de renda. A Índia e muito do resto do mundo em desenvolvimento não poderiam continuar a sofrer as conseqüências deste tipo de poluição enquanto esperam para "crescer sem problemas".

6. O desmatamento parece seguir um caminho da curva de Kuznets (Cropper & Griffths, 1994), mas com um momento de decisão de US$ 5,420 de renda *per capita* para a América Latina. Políticas proativas são absolutamente necessárias.

7. Claramente, as ligações entre poluição e crescimento dependem de muitos fatores e uma análise de caso a caso é absolutamente necessária. Na China, por exemplo, o desenvolvimento da cidade privada e as empresas industriais da vila eram o motor principal do crescimento na década de 1990, tirando mais de cem milhões de pessoas da pobreza. Estas empresas são freqüentemente mais eficientes, com melhores tecnologias de controle de poluição que as empresas estatais. Contudo, como um resultado da expansão das empresas privadas, é provável que o crescimento acelerado esteja associado a intensidades declinantes de poluição.

8. Mover-se de A para F implica que a qualidade ambiental se deteriorou desde seu estado primitivo. Isto responde à taxa ótima de proteção ambiental a que se referiu anteriormente. Para a função oculta do ambiente, pode ser justificado no solo que "pequenas" quantidades de poluição do ar, poluição da água, e assim por diante, não colocam riscos para a saúde nem tornam irregular a habilidade para que os recursos se "renovem"; e os ganhos econômicos resultantes das atividades geradoras de poluição são amplos. Para a função-fonte, uma certa quantidade de desmatamento de floresta, por exemplo, é justificada enquanto o uso alternativo da terra fornece retornos sociais maiores e o desmatamento não ocorre nos lugares "errados", tal como barrancos ao longo de bacias fluviais, e assim por diante.

9. A Ásia oriental fornece um caso interessante. A recente crise econômica mergulhou a Tailândia e a Indonésia de B para C. Como conseqüência, esses dois países têm a dura tarefa de implementar políticas para limpar o meio ambiente enquanto aumentam o crescimento econômico, ou seja, movem-se de C para F.

10. Cerca de dois bilhões de iuanes, à taxa de 8,3 iuanes o dólar, a China unificou seu regime de câmbio dual em 1994; daqui para a frente, esta quantia deveria ser encarada como aproximada.

11. Áreas protegidas, parques nacionais, e outras terras públicas que oferecem serviços ambientais críticos, tipicamente não desfrutam das vantagens do gerenciamento comunitário. Como resultado, a migração, os abusos, a extração ilegal e outras forças continuam a degradar as terras gerenciadas pelo governo em muitas áreas.

12. Watson et al. (1998) classificam as questões ambientais globais em duas categorias: aquelas que envolvem os bens comuns globais (atmosfera, água, e assim por diante) e aquelas de importância mundial, mas que não envolvem diretamente a tributação dos bens globais

comuns (biodiversidade, esgotamento da terra, e assim por diante). Com base na atual taxação científica, as questões globais ambientais mais importantes para este século, e que requerem ação urgente, são a mudança climática global, o esgotamento da camada de ozônio, a perda de biodiversidade, o desmatamento e o uso não sustentável das florestas, a desertificação e a degradação da terra, a degradação da água doce, do meio ambiente marinho e dos recursos e os poluentes orgânicos persistentes. As interligações entre estas questões e a necessidade de equilibrá-las simultaneamente também são enfatizadas. Sem desmerecer a importância de outras questões ambientais globais, esta seção centraliza-se na mitigação da mudança climática global e no gerenciamento florestal para ilustrar os desafios com os quais nos defrontamos nesta área.

CAPÍTULO 5

TRATAR COM RISCOS FINANCEIROS GLOBAIS

Tempos difíceis inspiram-nos a rever os ideais pelos quais vivemos.

— Michael J. Sandel, Democracy's Discontent: *America in Search of a Public Philosophy.*

A crise financeira de 1997-1999, que afetou de maneira mais severa o Brasil, a Federação Russa e alguns países da Ásia oriental, sublinhou a importância da estabilidade financeira como um contribuinte para a qualidade do crescimento. Assim como aconteceu com a sustentabilidade ambiental, a educação e o bom governo, administrar os riscos da estabilidade financeira, particularmente aqueles fluxos de capital através do país, pode estimular o crescimento sustentável pela redução da desigualdade econômica, aumentando a estabilidade social pelo fortalecimento das tendências democráticas e suas instituições. Sem estabilidade social e política, "nenhuma quantidade de dinheiro juntado em pacotes financeiros irá nos dar a estabilidade financeira" (Wolfensohn, 1998).

A integração financeira global possui benefícios inegáveis para os países em desenvolvimento e os industrializados, mas também expõe países a vicissitudes dos mercados de capital internacional, tais como a volatilidade nos valores correntes, as taxas de juros, a liquidez e os volumes de fluxos de capitais, com importantes conseqüências macroeconômicas e de crescimento. Esses riscos são visíveis e onerosos, como foi demonstrado recentemente pela perda e geração de empregos, colapsos bancários e corporativos e aumento da pobreza nos países atingidos pela crise, particularmente nos países onde as estruturas reguladoras e institucionais para mercados de capital aberto não estão totalmente no devido lugar.

Os altos custos econômicos e sociais, associados à instabilidade financeira, são inaceitáveis e fazem um grande estardalhaço para divisar me-

lhores rumos para lidar com os riscos financeiros e garantir um crescimento estável. O Capítulo 2 mostra como as distorções políticas, subsídios e inúmeras garantias podem causar superinvestimento em determinados capitais financeiros e físicos, mas subinvestimentos em outros bens. Este capítulo volta-se para os fatores que influenciam a volatilidade dos fluxos de capital para os países em desenvolvimento e investimentos subótimos associados que poderiam levar a um aumento de vulnerabilidade, à turbulência financeira. Depois de uma breve revisão dos benefícios e dos riscos da integração do mercado financeiro, o capítulo examina as causas e conseqüências da volatilidade do fluxo de capital e suas implicações para os pobres. Logo, revisa os arranjos políticos e institucionais para a gestão do risco e sugere uma estrutura ampla para gerenciamento do risco que integra vislumbres da prática e a teoria política do gerenciamento moderno do risco financeiro com a política econômica de mercados abertos de capital.

Para que o crescimento seja relativamente estável, os governos podem considerar um espectro de ações como as que se seguem:

- Eliminar políticas distorcivas e garantias subsidiadas implícita ou explicitamente, que fornecem incentivos a curto prazo, das afluências de capital estrangeiro, o que pode acentuar a vulnerabilidade a choques financeiros.
- Fortalecer o regulamento interno e a supervisão dos bancos e outros intermediários financeiros e melhorar o governo corporativo e sua transparência.
- Erguer uma ampla estrutura para o gerenciamento do risco, baseada em uma abertura de modo ordeiro dos mercados de capital combinadas com medidas para o controle dos fluxos de capital de curto prazo.
- Manter o sustento público para os mercados de capital aberto, a fim de fornecer amortecedores contra riscos, seja ou por meio do mercado, seja mediante políticas distributivas em uma rede de segurança social.

Expansão dos Mercados de Capital e Volatilidade dos Fluxos de Capital

Por qualquer medida, o crescimento nos mercados financeiros internacionais ao longo dos anos 90 foi surpreendente. O empréstimo internacional a médio e longo prazos, a penhora e os empréstimos bancários atingiram US$ 1,2 trilhão em 1997, subindo de US$ 0,5 trilhão em 1988 (BIS, vários anos). O mercado mundial de bens e serviços, embora crescendo significativamente desde o início de 1970, agora está nanico em decorrência das transações financeiras internacionais de mais de cinco vezes o valor do mercado mundial (Figura 5.1).

As transações alfandegárias da OECD em depósitos de igualdades, menos que 10% do PIB em 1980, atingiram mais que 100% do PIB em 1995. A média diária de rotatividade dos mercados de troca de câmbio alcançou US$ 1,6 trilhão em 1995, subiu US$ 0,2 trilhão em 1996, e o comércio de bens anuais em bens e serviços alcançou US$ 6,7 trilhões em 1998. A capitalização do mercado global dos mercados de estoque relativos ao PIB mundial cresceu de 23:1 em 1986 para 68:1 em 1996, enquanto os mercados derivativos se expandiram de US$ 7,9 trilhões em 1991 para US$ 40,9 trilhões em 1997 (Tabela 5.1).

O fluxo líquido de capital estrangeiro privado para países em desenvolvimento também cresceu drasticamente de US$ 43,9 bilhões em 1990 para US$ 299 bilhões em 1997; a maior parte do capital veio do investimento estrangeiro direto (FDI) e de mercados internacionais de capital, que incluem fluxos de igualdade de carteiras de ações, empréstimos bancários comerciais e questões de depósitos em mercados abertos. Fluxos de FDI para os países em desenvolvimento aumentaram mais que seis vezes entre 1990 e 1998 e uma parte do fluxo do FDI global para os países em desenvolvimento cresceu de 18% na metade da década de 1980 para 24% em 1991 e 36% em 1997. Contudo, quando a crise financeira se abateu sob a Ásia no início de 1997, os fluxos de capital dos mercados de capital internacional para as economias de mercado emergentes sofreram um golpe

Figura 5.1 – O Tamanho do Mercado Financeiro Global e o Comércio Mundial, 1980-1996

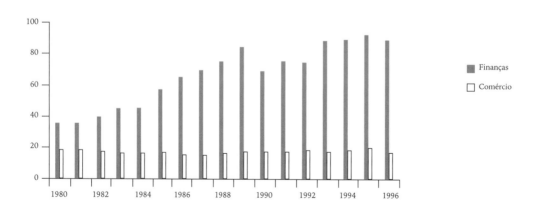

Nota: O tamanho do mercado financeiro refere-se ao estoque de mercado mundial de capitalização mais o estoque de depósitos e empréstimos bancários internacionais importantes. Figuras comerciais são a média de importação e exportação.
Fontes: BIS (1997, 1998); International Financial Corporation (vários anos).

Tabela 5.1 – Crescimento dos Mercados Derivativos, 1991-1997

Valores estimados em bilhões de dólares

	Instrumentos comercializados nas trocas					Instrumentos à mostra (OTC)				
Ano	Taxas de juros futuras	Opções de taxas de juros	Moeda corrente e opções	Estoque de mercado índices futuros e opções	Total comercializado nas trocas	Opções de taxas de juros	Trocas de taxas de juros	Trocas de moedas correntes	Total	Total
1991	2.157	1.073	81	109	3.420	577	3.065	807	4.449	7.869
1992	2.913	1.385	98	238	4.635	635	3.851	860	5.346	9.980
1993	4.959	2.362	110	340	7.771	1.398	6.177	900	8.475	16.246
1994	5.778	2.624	96	366	8.863	1.573	8.816	915	11.303	20.166
1995	5.863	2.742	82	502	9.189	3.705	12.811	1.197	17.713	26.901
1996	5.931	3.278	97	574	9.880	4.723	19.171	1.560	25.453	35.333
1997	7.489	3.640	85	993	12.207	5.033	22.116	1.585	28.733	40.940

Fonte: BIS (vários anos).

pesado, caindo a seu ponto mais baixo desde 1992 – US$ 72,1 bilhões –, enquanto o FDI permaneceu elástico (Figura 5.2) (World Bank, 1999c).

Causas e Conseqüências da Volatilidade do Fluxo de Capital

A larga expansão nos fluxos de capital privados para os países em desenvolvimento de 1990 a 1997 foi afetada positivamente por avanços na comunicação e tecnologias da informática, que reduziram os custos das transações alfandegárias.[1] Os avanços que facilitam os fluxos de capital alfandegários incluíram a criação no mercado de dinheiro para a moeda corrente Euro, a disseminação de derivados e a rápida expansão dos fundos alfandegários. Além disso, países industrializados e em desenvolvimento abriram seus mercados financeiros, removendo as barreiras para os fluxos de capital alfandegário.[2] Contudo, várias garantias governamentais implícitas ou explícitas oferecidas aos bancos, corporações e investidores, em setores financeiros liberalizados mas inadequadamente regulamentados, abasteceram o superinvestimento em certos setores industriais nos países da Ásia oriental, de um lado, e criando perigo moral e um comportamento de risco excessivo entre os investidores, de outro.[3] O acúmulo de responsabilidades governamentais contingentes e endividamentos corporativos podem contribuir para a vulnerabilidade, para a perda de confiança do investidor e para a erupção da recente crise financeira. Do ponto de vista histórico, as mudanças nos suprimentos de capital externo para os países em desenvolvimento foram causadas por fatores exógenos, tais como aumento nos preços do petróleo na década de 1970, baixa taxa de investi-

Figura 5.2 – Ascensão e Queda de Fluxos de Capital Internacional, 1990-1999

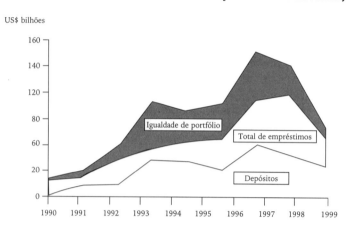

Nota: O fluxo do mercado de capital internacional para os países em desenvolvimento (inclusive a Coréia) consiste em uma igualdade da carteira de ações, depósitos bancários e empréstimos privados.
Fonte: World Bank (2000g).

mento, desregulamento dos investidores institucionais nos países industrializados e a inovação institucional e a competição dos anos 90.

O desmantelamento das barreiras aos fluxos de capital mediante fronteiras nacionais, tais como controles de capital e restrições para o câmbio externo, foi acelerado nos países da OECD na década de 1980, disseminando-se para os mercados emergentes. Os países da OECD liberalizaram quase todos os movimentos de capital, inclusive as transações de curto prazo pelas empresas e pelos indivíduos, em concordância com o Código da OECD de Liberação dos Movimentos de Capital. O Reino Unido completou toda a convertibilidade do capital em 1979, e, em 1992, Grécia, Irlanda, Portugal e Espanha tornaram-se os últimos países da OECD a abolir totalmente seus controles de capitais (OECD, 1990). No início da década de 1990, os montantes de capital dos países da OECD foram abertos em amplo espectro de transações financeiras através do país, em operações do mercado monetário, operações adiantadas, trocas e outros derivativos.[4]

Muitas economias de mercado emergentes também reformaram seus mercados financeiros e liberaram movimentos de capital alfandegário. Baseado num índice de abertura financeira construído para 96 países, desde 1977, 46 podem ser classificados como abertos e dez como semi-abertos (Quadro 5.1 e Anexo 5). Enquanto os países liberalizavam, os bancos e os tomadores de empréstimo corporativistas tiveram acesso a um menu mais amplo de financiamento externo. O desejo por capital de longo prazo, particularmente para projetos de fundos de infra-estrutura, forneceu uma vantagem competitiva forte para o capital externo, particularmente nos

Quadro 5.1 – Abertura para Fluxos de Capital Internacional

A evidência sobre a abertura de economias de mercado emergentes para fluxos de capital alfandegários é escassa e fragmentada. Problemas de informação e metodologia impedem o desenvolvimento de medidas quantitativas adequadas. A maioria dos estudos afere a incidência dos controles de capital mais que a intensidade das restrições e controles (ver, por exemplo, Alesina et al., 1994; Razin & Rose, 1994). Contudo, nem todas as transações estão sujeitas a todos os controles, e a maioria das medidas deve influenciar os incentivos para determinadas atividades. Os controles organizam-se desde limites quantitativos diretos sobre algumas transações ou transferências associadas, para tais medidas indiretas tais como imposto de renda, ou reserva de requisições sobre bens externos e responsabilidades. Tais controles também poderiam aplicar-se às transferências de fundos associadas com transações financeiras ou às próprias atividades de negócio.

Não existe nenhuma medida isolada de abertura. Qualquer medida de abertura financeira viável precisa incorporar as distinções entre a severidade dos controles e os tipos de transações. O índice de abertura financeira, mostrada no Anexo 5 (Tabela A5.5), levanta o relacionamento entre tipos de controle e transações. Utiliza-se de medidas desagregadas de controles de capitais baseados nas classificações e informações contidas no *Annual Report on Exchange Arrangements and Exchange Restrictions* do Fundo Monetário Internacional. Com base no código metodológico desenvolvido por Quinn & Toyoda (1997), a medida é um índice composto de regras, regulamentações e procedimentos administrativos que afetam os fluxos de capital para 27 transações nos montantes de capital correntes da balança de pagamentos para 96 países.

países com uma taxa de câmbio atrelada ao dólar americano. Maior acesso ao capital externo nos países em desenvolvimento abre possibilidades para financiar um conjunto mais amplo de projetos de investimento, ambos de riscos concretos.

Apesar do potencial positivo do capital externo, a fragilidade na política interna e medidas de liberalização, incluindo garantias subsidiadas, criaram incentivos para um comportamento imprudente pelos bancos, corporações e investidores que levaram ao superinvestimento em capital físico (para exemplos, ver Demirgüç-Kunt & Detragiache, 1998; Williamson & Mahar, 1998).

As garantias governamentais assumiram muitas formas, tais como taxas de câmbio atreladas, empréstimos diretos, políticas grandes demais para fracassar e depósito de garantia. Garantias governamentais implícitas ou explícitas sobre responsabilidades encorajaram a tomada de riscos excessivos, influenciando tanto os investidores do país como os internacionais (ver Mckinnon & Pill (1997) para um modelo analítico). Em essência, tal fragilidade resultou numa depreciação do risco e na baixa de margens sobre a moeda corrente externa, denominada dívida para as economias de mercados emergentes, até pouco antes do início da crise da Ásia oriental.

A Facilidade Bancária Internacional de Bangcoc, estabelecida em 1993 durante a liberalização financeira, capacitou bancos e empresas tailandesas a tomar empréstimos em moeda corrente estrangeira com vencimento a curto prazo, que é um processo denominado empréstimo de fora para den-

tro. Em decorrência dos tratados de impostos bilaterais entre Japão e Tailândia, os bancos japoneses estavam desejosos de absorver o imposto de renda e emprestar a taxas reduzidas para as companhias tailandesas. Esta injeção de dinheiro japonês resultou num crescimento rápido da Facilidade Bancária Internacional de Bangcoc do empréstimo de fora para dentro. Os empréstimos em moeda corrente estrangeira nos bancos tailandeses cresceram para US$ 31,5 bilhões, 17% dos empréstimos do setor privado, por volta do fim de 1996 (Alba et al., 1998).

O governo coreano emprestou diretamente para os *chaebols*, que levaram o superinvestimento a indústrias privilegiadas, tais como as de semicondutores, automóveis, aço e construção naval. Na Coréia, a média da razão dívida-para-eqüidade dos trinta maiores *chaebols* era de mais de 500% por volta do fim de 1996, e o retorno do capital investido ficou abaixo do custo do capital para dois terços dos maiores *chaebols* (Park, 2000).

Com a tomada excessiva de empréstimos externos a curto prazo, induzida em parte pelas garantias subsidiadas, as responsabilidades contingentes do governo acumularam-se. Quando os investidores compreenderam que o governo não era mais capaz de pagar suas obrigações, tomaram a rota de saída. Uma vez iniciada a crise em um país, o comportamento semelhante ao do rebanho e o contágio disseminaram-se por meio do comércio internacional e ligações financeiras, o que resultou em reversões de fluxo de capital privado e considerável ampliação dos empréstimos para quase todas as economias de mercado emergentes (ver também Calvo, 1999; Reinhart & Kaminsky, 1999; Van Rijckeghem & Weder, 1999).

Benefícios e Riscos dos Mercados de Capital Aberto

Os benefícios dos mercados de capital aberto são indiscutíveis; o debate político está em saber se os benefícios suplantam os riscos. Os governos podem também considerar instrumentos de emprego para minimizar tais riscos.

Os mercados de capital aberto trazem muitos benefícios tanto para os países credores como para os tomadores de empréstimo. Eles oferecem aos países em desenvolvimento fontes mais amplas de investimento financeiro para complementar as poupanças internas. Também resultam num aumento de eficiência nas instituições financeiras internas e numa condição mais inclinada da política macroeconômica. Além disso, ao facilitar coerções financeiras, os mercados de capital aberto dão tempo aos países para que façam negociações de pagamento para corrigir desequilíbrios que foram criados em resposta a choques externos.[5] Os mercados de capital aberto oferecem aos países credores maiores mercados de capital de investimento e risco e chances de diversificação, especialmente quando suas po-

pulações com fundos de pensão crescentes procuram mais altos e seguros retornos de seus investimentos.

Montantes de capital aberto também sustentam o sistema de comércio multilateral, expandindo as oportunidades para a diversificação das carteiras de ações e para a alocação eficiente de poupanças e investimentos globais (Fischer, 1998). Uma questão importante de direito de propriedade voltada para as finanças internacionais também atraiu a atenção de acadêmicos e agentes de política. Cooper (1998, p.12) nota a visão que encarna o pensamento que subjaz a ordem do mundo liberal: "Os indivíduos deveriam ser livres para dispor de sua renda e riqueza à sua vontade, desde que, assim fazendo, não façam mal aos outros". Outros argumentam que a abertura aos fluxos do capital internacional é altamente relacionada com medidas de liberdade política e civil. A evidência empírica sobre a importância da abertura financeira e do governo democrático é coercitiva, embora a direção e a natureza do elo precisem de estudo (ver Figura A5.1 no Anexo 5).

A abertura também traz consigo aumento de riscos. A volatilidade nos fluxos de capital cria incerteza nas condições econômicas, aumenta o custo do capital, podendo adversamente afetar o investimento e o crescimento a longo prazo, e diminui os esforços para redução da pobreza. Com base em dados de noventa países em desenvolvimento, constata-se que existe uma forte correlação entre a volatilidade dos fluxos de capital e a volatilidade do crescimento, como aferido por um desvio-padrão das taxas de crescimento anuais no PIB real (Figura 5.3). Além disso, utilizando dados de 130 países ente 1960 e 1995, Easterly & Kraay (1999) descobriram que a volatilidade de crescimento baseada num desvio-padrão do crescimento do PIB tem efeito negativo (-0,18) na média do crescimento *per capita*.

Duas categorias de amplo risco – aquelas relacionadas com políticas internas distorcidas e aquelas associadas com fatores externos – podem criar problemas econômicos para investidores estrangeiros e agentes de política. Políticas internas distorcidas e ambientes institucionais reguladores frágeis fornecem incentivos aos bancos e corporações para construir responsabilidades externas de curto prazo excessivas relativas a seus bens de curto prazo, ou posições de câmbio externo ilimitadas. Exemplos de fontes internas de tais riscos incluem garantias governamentais explícitas e implícitas, taxas de câmbio atreladas, empréstimo direto para os projetos de investimento e crescentes responsabilidades de contingentes. Dooley (1996) argumentou que a adoção de taxas de câmbio fixas e depósito de garantia, no contexto de um setor financeiro regulado, liberalizado mas fracamente regulamentado, pode induzir os investidores estrangeiros a colher taxas privadas mais altas de retorno que não beneficiam os países tomadores de empréstimo. Esta depreciação dos verdadeiros riscos de investimentos subjacentes deve ser levantada para assegurar investimento

Figura 5.3 – Relacionamento Entre Variabilidade do Crescimento Econômico e Volatilidade nos Fluxos de Capital Privado Externo, 1975-1996

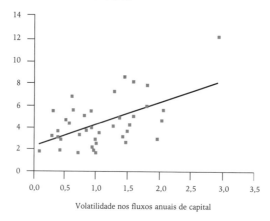

Nota: y =2,02x + 2,15, r = 0,57.
Fonte: Ver Anexo 5 para fontes e definições.

equilibrado que poderia estimular o crescimento a longo prazo e a redução da pobreza dos países tomadores de empréstimo.

A segunda categoria de risco relaciona-se ao funcionamento dos mercados financeiros internacionais, fatores externos e mudanças de sentimentos, crenças e confiança de emprestadores e investidores estrangeiros que não estão necessariamente relacionadas com a credibilidade a longo prazo de um país. Logo, Calvo, Leiderman et al. (1994) descobriram que os fatores externos, tais como as taxas de juros americanos e a volatilidade no crescimento OECD, poderiam explicar de 30% a 60% da variação nos fluxos de capitais para a América Latina. As mudanças nos sentimentos e crenças dos investidores, como refletidas em uma aguda reviravolta nos fluxos de capitais e/ou em uma ferroada nos custos de tomada de empréstimos nas economias de mercados emergentes, podem ser provocadas pela coordenação das falências de parte dos credores. Este problema de coordenação poderia acontecer devido a uma informação incompleta entre credores, que poderia transformar suas decisões em corrida ou fuga de um determinado país, dependendo do comportamento dos outros. Esta dependência pode gerar uma corrida análoga à corrida bancária em cenários internos, juntando-se a um prêmio de não cooperação no alto de outros prêmios de risco do país (veja Haldane (1999) para posterior elaboração desta questão).

Os países precisam estar preparados para lidar com os riscos associados com integração financeira e volatilidade do fluxo do capital. Porque a preparação do país varia e a edificação das instituições leva tempo, os governos

podem considerar um espectro de ações políticas e reguladoras quando se abrem para os fluxos de capitais internacionais de modo ordenado.

A Volatilidade do Crescimento e os Pobres

As crises financeiras são extremamente onerosas. A América Latina perdeu uma década de progresso econômico-social que se seguiu à crise de débito no início dos anos 80. Os países da Ásia oriental perderam estimados US$ 500 bilhões, baseados nos preços e nas taxas de câmbio de 1996, em uma saída interna agregada entre 1997-1999, como aferido pelo desvio de tendências históricas ou aproximadamente 1,3 vez a dívida externa destes países em 1996 (ver Anexo 5 para o método do cálculo). Além disso, a comunidade financeira internacional estendeu assistência financeira substancial por meio de empréstimos de resgate multilateral e bilateral aos países afetados pela crise na década de 1990.

Em particular, a volatilidade de crescimento tem severas conseqüências para os pobres que não possuem bens para minimizar seu consumo durante as reviravoltas econômicas.[6] Os custos sociais associados com as crises nas economias de mercado emergentes têm sido substanciais. Em apenas um ano, o subemprego dobrou na Tailândia e triplicou na Coréia, enquanto os padrões de vida caíram 14% e 22%, respectivamente. A Indonésia também sofreu um declínio de 25% em seu padrão de vida (Stiglitz & Bhattacharya, 1999) e um agudo aumento no número de pobres. Por volta do terceiro trimestre de 1998, a renda real do salário dos trabalhadores tailandeses caiu 24,8% nas tendências de taxa antes da crise (Krongkaew, 1999). Levinsohn, Barry & Friedman (1999) estudaram as altas dos preços no custo de vida das famílias pobres e descobriram que na Indonésia os pobres eram, de fato, atingidos mais duramente em comparação a outros grupos. Devido ao drástico aumento dos preços dos alimentos, o custo de vida para os de renda mais baixas aumentou mais de 130% depois da crise. Os pobres urbanos sem acesso à terra e que não são proprietários de suas casas foram os mais adversamente atingidos pela crise. Logo, em conseqüência das crises, os países da Ásia oriental viveram reversões agudas em suas realizações anteriores na redução da pobreza (ver World Bank, 2000a).

Gerenciamento do Risco Passado e Presente

Para proteger seu crescimento e ganho na redução da pobreza, os países em desenvolvimento devem estar mais bem preparados para lidar com os riscos associados à integração financeira e à volatilidade do fluxo de capital. O risco financeiro global e as estratégias para gerenciá-lo mudaram subs-

tancialmente durante os últimos cinqüenta anos e necessita-se de novas abordagens para lidar com estes novos riscos.

Mecanismos e Arranjos Antecipados para Gerenciamento do Risco

Visto da perspectiva do gerenciamento financeiro do risco, o período de Bretton Woods (1945-1973) apresentou alto grau de estabilidade pelas taxas de câmbio fixas, combinando judiciosamente com o controle de capital do lado externo, os macroeconomistas keynesianos e as posições estatais de bem-estar do lado interno.[7] A abordagem de Bretton Woods deu prioridade às taxas de câmbio fixas e à autonomia política nacional. Os controles de capital foram uma norma aceita do sistema monetário internacional nas décadas de 1950 e 1960. Somente até setembro de 1997, o comitê interino do Fundo Monetário Internacional concordou que os artigos de fundo do acordo "deveriam ser emendados para fazer a promoção da liberalização do montante de capital, um propósito específico do Fundo e para dar ao Fundo uma jurisdição adequada sobre os movimentos de capital" (Fischer et al., p.47).[8] Com as economias relativamente fechadas aos fluxos de capital, os governos poderiam exercitar a política monetária fiscal na perseguição de objetivos nacionais, tal como pleno emprego e igualdade social, sem medo da fuga de capitais. Este alto grau de autonomia política também serviu à causa da democracia, particularmente na Europa ocidental.[9]

Na década de 1970, uma vez que os países da Europa ocidental tinham completado a convertibilidade em moeda corrente em seus montantes de moeda corrente, o movimento livre de capital através das fronteiras nacionais começou a emergir como uma política prioritária importante. O colapso do sistema de Bretton Woods entre 1971 e 1973, o movimento rumo a um regime de taxa de câmbio flutuante, aumentando os preços do petróleo, a inflação crônica e a queda global das condições econômicas intensificaram os riscos da taxa de juros em moeda corrente nos mercados financeiros globais. As respostas foram principalmente soluções baseadas no mercado exemplificadas pela tendência para uma diversificação do capital internacional e a rápida expansão dos mercados derivativos (a taxa de juros e a moeda corrente para frente, opções e trocas). A política macroeconômica nos países da OECD mudou de uma ênfase sobre o pleno emprego para maior atenção à estabilidade macroeconômica, definida com déficits fiscais menores e inflação e taxas de juros mais baixas.

O Gerenciamento do Risco Financeiro na Década de 1990

Na década de 1990, numerosas crises de liquidez e moeda corrente surgiram tanto nos países industrializados como nos em desenvolvimento: o

sistema monetário europeu durante 1992 e 1993, México entre 1994 e 1995, Ásia oriental em 1997, Federação Russa em 1998, e Brasil e Equador em 1999. Todas estas economias emergentes de mercado experimentaram um aumento nos fluxos de capital (do início à metade da década de 1990), e então caíram vítimas de reveses repentinos; a Ásia oriental experimentou reveses da ordem de 10% do PIB. A crise da década de 1990 expôs graves fragilidades nos mercados financeiros internacionais:

- Os mercados de capitais mundiais faliram em vários níveis. Os países tomadores de empréstimo não estavam monitorando a alta exposição de seus bancos e corporações nacionais para o risco da moeda corrente estrangeira. Agências de taxação de crédito e outros jogadores maiores internacionais falharam em avaliar corretamente o risco do país no ambiente financeiro globalizante na década de 1990. Os reguladores falharam devido às frágeis estruturas supervisoras e reguladoras. Os especialistas em gerenciamento do risco financeiro subestimaram as correlações positivas entre a qualidade do setor de crédito privado e a qualidade do crédito soberano, e, assim, falharam em identificar as causas do contágio nas economias de mercado emergentes.
- Os fluxos de capital em muitos países em desenvolvimento foram canalizados por meio de instrumentos bancários de curto prazo, devido às garantias governamentais implícitas para os bancos. Muitos participantes do mercado sucumbiram ao perigo moral nestas garantias governamentais percebidas. Os padrões de crédito e os projetos de estimativas prudentes foram freqüentemente comprometidos, levando a superinvestimento nos setores com aumento da capacidade ou demanda declinante. O resultado foi simultaneamente o colapso do sistema bancário interno e crises de liquidez externas com taxas de câmbio fixas.
- As primeiras fontes de instabilidade foram no montante do capital, não no montante corrente, uma situação que as instituições Bretton Woods estavam designadas a prevenir. No ambiente financeiro global de hoje, a folha de balanço total de um país, definida por seus bens e seus débitos e responsabilidades eqüitativas, deveria ser a medida de sua posição de pagamentos externos.

As fragilidades refletem mudanças mais importantes no cenário financeiro global, que pode ser caracterizado pela internacionalização dos negócios bancários; a quebra dos limites tradicionais entre funções financeiras e de segurança; as novas chances de investimento nos mercados emergentes, e as bases mais amplas dos investidores em economias de mercados emergentes, tais como bancos comerciais, fundos de pensão, fundos de barreira e indústrias de segurança. Estas mudanças criaram novas demandas sobre

o gerenciamento do risco; os governos devem empregar estratégias mais judiciosas em níveis internacionais, institucionais (instituições financeiras e corporativas) e nacionais.

Uma Ampla Estrutura do Gerenciamento do Risco

Muita atividade atual no gerenciamento do risco refere-se a como manipular melhor, mediante uma prevenção mais adequada da crise, os riscos dos fluxos de capital para os países em desenvolvimento, e por meio da contenção e das resoluções ordenadas quando as crises ocorrem.

Nós apresentamos uma estrutura ampla dividida em duas partes para o gerenciamento do risco que favorece um ponto de vista moderado. Uma estrutura reguladora adequada e instrumentos relacionados para o controle dos fluxos de capital de curto prazo deveriam acompanhar uma abertura ordenada dos mercados financeiros. O apoio público para a abertura deveria ser mantido pela provisão governamental dos amortecedores contra riscos, tais como redes de segurança social e redistribuições políticas bem designadas e de custo efetivo.

Política Internacional e Reações Reguladoras

Com a memória da crise de débito da década de 1980 e sua resolução prolongada ainda fresca, os governos implementaram imediatamente uma política internacional e reações reguladoras para as crises de 1997-1999. Os principais países industrializados facilitaram a política monetária, estenderam empréstimos de resgate a longo prazo, desenvolveram padrões internacionais de boa prática e divulgação, e estabeleceram comitês de alto nível para fortalecer a solidez dos bancos e outras instituições financeiras (ver Drage & Mann (1999) para mais exemplos de resolução de crise).

Em fevereiro de 1999, o G-7 (que inclui Canadá, França, Alemanha, Itália, Japão, Reino Unido e os Estados Unidos), ministros e diretores de bancos centrais endossaram a criação do Fórum de Estabilidade Financeira. Na nova mesa-redonda, o G-7 reuniu autoridades monetárias nas principais agências reguladoras e instituições multilaterais, para avaliar as vulnerabilidades no sistema financeiro global e identificar reações institucionais.

Reações Institucionais

O gerenciamento do risco financeiro no nível institucional avançou de modo significativo no fim da década de 1990. Atualmente, as instituições

financeiras e não financeiras utilizam-se das técnicas quantitativas de aferição do risco, tal como valor no risco, na volatilidade em medidas beta, e modelos de fixação de preços optativos, em razões Sharpe. Utilizando-se desses instrumentos, as instituições financeiras têm a habilidade para aferir de modo sistemático e controlar o risco relacionado ao mercado sob volatilidade normal. Além disso, a rápida expansão nos mercados derivativos de crédito está alterando fundamentalmente os negócios bancários, fornecendo oportunidades para riscos de crédito comerciais. O gerenciamento do risco no nível corporativo move-se rumo a uma abordagem de ampla companhia integrada que abrange crédito, mercado e riscos de liquidez.

Reações Nacionais: Reconciliar a Integração Financeira e a Autonomia Política Nacional

A integração nos mercados financeiros impõe uma coerção muito mais severa na escolha da política nacional do que outros aspectos da globalização, tais como o comércio dos bens e os serviços sobre os quais os esforços de liberalização concentraram-se desde a Segunda Guerra Mundial. A integração dos mercados de capitais reduz a habilidade dos governos nacionais para conduzir a política, principalmente a política macroeconômica, devido à saída do capital de risco. Aqueles que adotam este ponto de vista, baseado no modelo de Robert Mundel e J. Marcus Fleming de uma macroeconomia aberta, contestam que os países podem atingir apenas duas das três condições seguintes: mobilidade de capital, taxas de câmbio fixas e autonomia política monetária.

Redistribuição para diminuir o risco. Sociedades democráticas precisam resolver a tensão entre integração do mercado financeiro e autonomia política nacional para perseguir suas metas sociais e econômicas definidas de forma democrática. Esta tensão relaciona-se com a habilidade dos governos nacionais para regular impostos para objetivos redistributivos e divisão do risco enquanto seguem a disciplina necessária em um cenário global. Em um mundo de alta mobilidade internacional do capital, sociedades democráticas abertas devem equilibrar a ameaça da saída do capital tornada mais fácil pelos mercados abertos de capital, com demandas políticas pela intervenção e pela voz governamental, pelas deslocações de amortecedores do mercado. Investidores descontentes com as políticas dos países anfitriões ou com o clima de investimento prevalente consideram fácil mudar os recursos financeiros para outros países e regiões com uma subseqüente distribuição desproporcional dos custos nascidos por fatores menos móveis da produção, ou seja, trabalho e terra. Logo, a motivação para a redistribuição como segurança de renda – distinta do altruísmo e outros motivos relacionados com a redução da pobreza – é induzida pela volatilidade e insegu-

rança em condições econômicas subjacentes e quando os cidadãos são avessos ao risco. O risco da saída de capital intensifica a insegurança econômica e o risco para uma grande parte da sociedade. Porque é mais provável que os ricos sejam beneficiados relativamente a partir da liberalização do mercado de capitais, pelo menos de início, enquanto os pobres podem suportar os custos, a dimensão política da liberalização do mercado de capital requer uma atenção cuidadosa.

Gastos do setor social, abertura e liberdade política. O contrapeso para a ameaça da saída de capital é a voz política de cidadãos que exigem proteção contra os riscos externos por meio da redistribuição, da segurança social, dos programas de rede e de outras medidas de segurança.[10] Na ausência de um mercado para tal segurança de risco, os cidadãos nacionais irão estruturar instituições não mercadológicas para reduzir as perdas de bem-estar decorrentes da volatilidade nas condições econômicas. Logo, nesta interpretação, a voz pertence à esfera política e a forma como ela é exercida constitui uma função das instituições políticas subjacentes e, em particular, a força da democracia e o grau correspondente de liberdades civis e políticas: quanto mais alto o grau de democracia, maior a necessidade de equilibrar a ameaça da fuga de capital com exigências políticas, o que inclui incentivos políticos para aumentar a intervenção governamental, amortecendo o deslocamento do mercado. É justo dizer que a voz política dos cidadãos que exigem proteção, mediante redistribuição, redes de segurança social e outras medidas de cunho securitário, tem sido crítica ao facilitar a tensão entre políticos e abertura financeira dos países da OECD. O gasto governamental com saúde, educação, segurança social e bem-estar em países de alta renda entre 1991 e 1997 atingiu a média aproximada de 25% do PIB, para os que gastaram relativamente menos, os países europeus abertos como Dinamarca, Noruega e Suécia gastando até 30%.[11] Existe uma associação positiva entre redistribuição, abertura financeira e liberdade política e civil para uma ampla amostra de países (Tabela 5.2). A análise estatística confirma que a abertura financeira, democracia (como definida pelas liberdades políticas e civis)[12] e o gasto social do governo vão em conjunto (Tabela 5.3, Figuras 5.4, 5.5 e 5.6).

Ainda assim, porque a redistribuição freqüentemente precisa ser financiada pelos impostos discricionários, os agentes de política precisam avaliar os custos macroeconômicos e fiscais associados.

Quase todas as democracias modernas avançadas estão abertas aos movimentos de capital internacional. O relacionamento entre abertura financeira e democracia parece ser principalmente uma função de renda *per capita*: com poucas exceções, os países ricos têm governos democráticos e estão abertos ao movimento de capital internacional porque possuem um alto grau de desenvolvimento do setor financeiro e desfrutam de estabilidade macroeconômica, expectativas estáveis de mudança prática de regime, regra

Tabela 5.2 – Países Agrupados pela Abertura Financeira

	Categoria	Aberto	Amplamente aberto	Amplamente fechado	Fechado
1	Índice de democracia[a]	0,81	0,71	0,63	0,48
2	Liberdades civis[b]	2,28	3,30	3,38	4,55
3	PIB *per capita*, 1990-1997	13.147	3.051	2.317	1.557
4	Gastos sociais (% do PIB)[c]	22,30	23,50	12,50	6,70
5	Gastos totais do governo (% do PIB)[d]	26,00	19,90	23,40	27,70
6	Consumo geral do governo (% do PIB)[e]	16,10	17,90	15,50	14,70
	Número de países	46	10	34	11

Nota: A tabela dispõe as médias de grupo computadas pelos países com dados. Definição de variáveis:

a. Abarca de 0 (mais baixo) a 1 (mais alto), calculado com base nos índices de direitos políticos e liberdades civis (ver a nota final 11 para detalhes).

b. Uma medida de respeito e proteção dos direitos dos cidadãos de um país, religiosos, étnicos, econômicos, lingüísticos e outros, inclusive gênero e direitos familiares, liberdades individuais e liberdade de imprensa, crença e associação.

c. A soma de saúde, educação e segurança social e bem-estar; média 1991-1997.

d. A média dos montantes orçamentários e do governo central mais governo provincial ou estatal, 1990-1997.

e. Todos os gastos correntes para o consumo de bens e serviços em todos os níveis do governo, excluindo a maioria das empresas governamentais, 1990-1997.

Fonte: Anexo 5.

Tabela 5.3 – Resultados Estimados do Modelo Lógico Binomial Sobre a Probabilidade dos Países Pertencerem a Altas Categorias de Abertura Financeira

Variável independente	Coeficiente	Margem de erro	Efeito marginal [a]
Constante	-11,234**	2,7500	-2,0296
Registro (razão de gasto social do PIB)	1,534*	0,6146	0,2772
Registro do PIB *per capita*	0,795*	0,3156	0,1436
Número real de países no grupo-alvo	28		
Número previsto de países no grupo-alvo[b]	20		
Número atual de países em outros grupos	39		
Número previsto de países em outros grupos	32		
Registro de probabilidades	-27,744		

* $p \leq 0,05$.

** $p \leq 0,01$.

Nota: A variável dependente recebe o código 1 se o país cair na abertura financeira, alta democracia, e 0 se for de outro modo.

a. Mudança marginal na probabilidade de resultados de uma mudança infinitesimal na variável explicativa.

b. Grupo-alvo refere-se a países com alto nível de direitos políticos e alta abertura financeira.

Fonte: Anexo 5.

interna de direito e instituições estáveis que garantem as liberdades políticas e civis (para uma discussão mais detalhada do laço entre democracia e abertura financeira, ver Dailami, 2000).

Contudo, o elo entre democracia e abertura financeira prova ser mais complexo; a análise revela que mais do que apenas a renda influencia este elo. A coordenação na política internacional, na regulação financeira e política macroeconômica e na supervisão é parte da resposta. Tem sido fundamental na redução dos desequilíbrios de pagamento, na estabilização das

Transferências e gasto social facilitam a tensão entre a abertura financeira e a política

Figura 5.4 – Relacionamentos Entre Abertura Financeira e Democrática, Mobilidade de Capital e Gastos Sociais do Governo

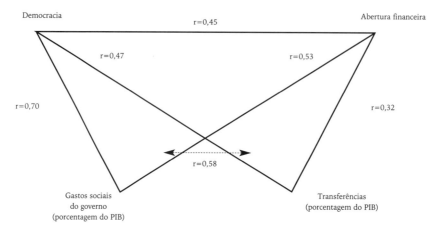

Nota: Os dados através do país, com amostras abrangendo de 70 para 140, mostram resultados significativos do ponto de vista estatístico a 1% (exceção para a correlação entre transferências e abertura financeira que é significativa a 5% para todos os relacionamentos).
Fonte: Anexo 5 (Tabela A5.5).

Figura 5.5 – Relacionamento Entre Abertura Financeira e Gastos Sociais
(Controle de renda *per capita*)

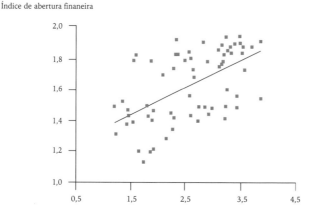

Nota: y = 0,17x + 1,17.
R^2 = 0,32.
Fonte: Ver Anexo 5 para descrição dos dados.

Figura 5.6 – Classificação por País: Direitos Políticos e Abertura Financeira

Abertura financeira

		Baixo	Alto
Democracia	Baixo	23	9
	Alto	32	37

Nota: O nível de democracia deriva-se dos índices de direitos políticos e liberdades civis desde o estudo da Freedom House no *Freedom in the World*. O nível da abertura financeira é definido por um *score* de mais de 1,6 no índice de abertura financeira (ver Tabela A5.2 no Anexo 5).
Fonte: Cálculos dos autores.

expectativas para a moeda corrente e movimentos das taxas de juros, e em minorar a volatilidade dos fluxos de capitais alfandegários. A coordenação da regulamentação bancária internacional em países industrializados, tais como o Basel Capital Accord (1992) e o subseqüente Core Principles for Effective Banking Supervision, também foi fator significativo ao promover a estabilidade econômica para as democracias OECD.[13]

Análises empíricas das classificações dos países ao longo dos dois eixos da democracia e abertura financeira sustentam o ponto de vista que a distribuição política contribui para as democracias e abre mercados (Figura 5.6 e Tabela 5.3). Utilizando a análise logit pode-se demonstrar que a renda *per capita* e a razão dos gastos sociais para o PIB estão estatisticamente relacionados com a probabilidade de que um país será aberto tanto democrática quanto financeiramente (ver Anexo 5 para o modelo de especificação e estimativa, e Dailami (2000) para uma análise mais detalhada). Depois do controle para a renda na análise, a política redistributiva, que inclui programas para o gasto público com a segurança social, saúde, moradia, bem-estar, educação e transferências, figura em lugar proeminente na ligação entre democracia e abertura financeira.

Controles de Capital como Instrumento de Gerenciamento do Risco. Os controles de capital podem ser empregados como uma abordagem alternativa para resolver a tensão entre integração do mercado de capital e autonomia política nacional. O interesse nesta abordagem foi remodelado pelas crises financeiras na Ásia e América Latina nos anos de 1997-1999. Os controles de capital, particularmente nos fluxos de curto

prazo, são desejáveis para reduzir a volatilidade sob algumas circunstâncias, tais como fragilidade nos mercados financeiros locais, comportamento eufórico ou pânico pelos investidores estrangeiros, e equilíbrio estrutural dos problemas de pagamentos.

Muitas intervenções políticas estão disponíveis para gerenciar os fluxos de capital, inclusive impostos e instrumentos baseados no mercado, como facilidade de liquidez contingente e pedidos de saque remunerado ou não remunerado nos fluxos de risco a curto prazo. A Argentina e o México têm utilizado um contingente de facilidades de liquidez e pedidos de liquidez remunerada para os bancos, e o Chile utilizou pedidos de saque não remuneráveis e afluência de capital de risco a curto prazo entre 1991 e 1998.

Os controles sobre o capital de curto prazo no Chile atraíram interesses consideráveis, em parte porque são baseados no mercado, transparentes e mais fáceis de parar gradualmente do que os controles quantitativos (Quadro 5.2). Os controles foram efetivos na mudança da composição da dívida pela redução das afluências de capital de curto prazo enquanto aumentavam os fluxos de capital a longo prazo e abriam um espaço maior entre as taxas de juros externos e internos. As medidas, contracíclicas, foram impostas em 1991 depois de uma maré de crescimento

---

Quadro 5.2 – Chile: Abertura, Controles de Capital e Proteção Social

Com o restabelecimento da democracia em 1990, o Chile perseguiu uma estratégia explícita de crescimento com eqüidade, mantendo uma estrutura política orientada para o mercado ao mesmo tempo que mantinha uma estrutura política orientada para o mercado. O governo assumiu muitas medidas para gerenciamento do risco em um comércio aberto e regime de investimentos.

Os investimentos sociais do Chile foram extremamente lentos no final da década de 1980. Não mediram os níveis de gastos dos regimes pré-militares. Contudo, desde 1990 o Chile implantou um sistema altamente direcionado de assistência social nas áreas como saúde, educação e habitação. Utilizou-se também de transferências de renda para melhorar as condições afetas ao capital humano. Os investimentos sociais aumentaram para 75% entre 1987 e 1994, o que contribuiu positivamente para a redução da pobreza.

Em reação à rápida expansão das afluências de capital entre 1988 e 1990, em 1991 o Banco Central do Chile impôs um pedido de saque não remunerado sobre afluências seletivas. Ao mesmo tempo, o governo levantou controles administrativos severos sobre os defluxos, inclusive nos tetos de tomadas de bens estrangeiros pelos bancos, companhias de seguro e fundos de pensão e o pedido de que os exportadores entregassem seus procedimentos de exportação para o Banco Central. O pedido de saque não remunerado aumentou o escopo para uma política monetária independente. O pedido de saque contribuiu para mudar a composição dos defluxos em rumo aos vencimentos a longo prazo. Contudo, a queda nos fluxos a curto prazo foi apenas parcialmente compensada pelo aumento das afluências de longo prazo. O pedido de saque não parece ter afetado o padrão das taxas de câmbio reais: aumentar as taxas de juros a curto prazo, contudo, afetou adversamente o investimento que contribuiu diretamente para isso. Além do mais, envolveu custos de transação na monitoração dos bancos comerciais.

Fontes: Ferreira & Litchfield (1999); Gallego et al. (1999); World Bank (1997b). Ver também Ariyoshi et al. (1999) e Edwards (1999) para uma visão geral das experiências do país sobre os controles de capital.

das afluências de capital, entre 1988 e 1990, e cessadas gradualmente em setembro de 1998, quando não eram mais necessárias durante as crises financeiras globais.

Conclusões

Os países defrontaram-se com dois desafios ao integrar seus mercados de capitais. O primeiro diz respeito ao andamento em que os países desmantelam os controles administrativos sobre os fluxos de capital e movem-se em direção à convertibilidade do montante do capital. O segundo refere-se ao sistema de incentivo e regulamentação dos fluxos financeiros internacionais para minimizar riscos e pânicos. Os países necessitavam de mecanismos apropriados para equilibrar tanto os benefícios como os riscos da integração financeira. Os avanços tecnológicos e o simples tamanho dos mercados financeiros tornam o risco do pânico e da crise sempre presente. Contudo, os governos têm várias opções para reduzir significativamente esse risco.

Perseguir políticas macroeconômicas sólidas é um primeiro passo óbvio, mas não o suficiente. A experiência recente mostra que a estabilidade macroeconômica não é suficiente para garantir resultados duradouros e crescimento sustentável. Para garantir o crescimento sustentável, deve ser reforçada por ações que removam políticas distorcivas que fornecem incentivos para as afluências de capital estrangeiro de curto prazo, que poderiam levar a uma vulnerabilidade financeira elevada. A regulamentação interna e a supervisão dos bancos e outros intermediários precisam ser aumentadas e melhorada a governabilidade corporativa.

Com o movimento em direção à democracia pelo mundo afora, os mecanismos para prover os cidadãos com segurança contra os riscos da mobilidade de capital, tanto por meio da praça do mercado como de políticas redistributivas, são igualmente importantes se a pressão política pelo controle de capital deve ser evitada. A longo prazo, a globalização do capital requer uma estrutura institucional aberta para garantir montantes transparentes, direitos de propriedade seguros e licenças para contratos impositivos, regulamentos e mecanismos para gerenciar os riscos. Estabelecendo uma tal estrutura, será assegurado que os mercados financeiros abertos irão contribuir completamente para o crescimento estável e a redução da pobreza.

O notável confronto econômico nos países atingidos pela crise durante os meses passados, reforçados por medidas já tomadas no nível internacional para fortalecer a arquitetura dos mercados financeiros internacionais, fizeram bom agouro para os prospectos de maior estabilidade financeira e comprometimento coletivo com um sistema financeiro internacional aberto e liberal no novo milênio.

Notas

1. Uma grande parte da bibliografia desenvolveu-se nos últimos poucos anos discutindo causas e conseqüências das recentes crises financeiras nas economias de mercado emergente. Ver Calvo & Mendoza (1996); Corsetti et al. (1998); Krugman (1998); Obstfeld (1996); Radelet & Sachs (1998); e Sachs Tornell & Velasco (1996). Sobre as causas da volatilidade do fluxo do capital, ver Dooley (1996); López-Mejia (1999); Montiel (1998); e World Bank (1997f).

2. De uma perspectiva histórica, a globalização das finanças na década de 1990 é equivalente ao nível atingido durante o período do padrão-ouro de 1870-1914. Contudo, durante o padrão-ouro, apenas uns poucos países industrializados estavam envolvidos com os fluxos de capital (ver Verdier, 1998).

3. O perigo moral é um conceito-chave na economia da informação assimétrica. Ele ocorre quando os atores econômicos cobertos por alguma forma de segurança assumem mais riscos do que poderiam tomar se não fosse assim. Exemplos típicos incluem um motorista segurado que dirige imprudentemente, ou um banqueiro não segurado envolvendo-se com práticas de empréstimo imprudentes.

4. Ver também Helleiner (1994) para um cômputo de como em 1974 os Estados Unidos levantaram as restrições temporárias de capital na metade da década de 1960.

5. Os mercados fornecerão margem de segurança apenas se os emprestadores perceberem que os países estão fazendo ajustes que fundamentalmente se direcionam para os desequilíbrios prospectivos e existentes. De outro modo, os mercados irão eventualmente exercer uma disciplina que pode encurtar brutalmente o tempo permitido ao reajuste (Dailami & Ul Haque, 1998).

6. Veja, por exemplo, Diwan (1999); Krongkaew (1999); Levinsohn, Berry & Friedman (1999); Lustig (1999).

7. Esta mistura política é mencionada por Ruggie (1983) como "um compromisso do liberalismo embutido". Ele conota um comprometimento com uma ordem liberal diferente tanto da economia nacionalista dos anos 30 como do liberalismo do padrão-ouro. Para elaboração posterior, ver Garrett (1998). Sally (1998) também referiu-se ao liberalismo não encaixado como "sistema de pensamento misto". Ver também Dailami (2000).

8. Refletindo a compreensão do tempo, Keynes expressou sucintamente a questão em seu freqüentemente citado discurso nº 1944 ao Parlamento, afirmando: "Não meramente como uma característica da transição, mas como um arranjo permanente, o plano outorga a todo membro do governo o direito explícito de controlar todos os movimentos de capital. O que costumava parecer uma heresia agora é aceito como ortodoxo ... Segue-se que nosso direito a controlar o mercado interno de capital é assegurado em fundações mais firmes que nunca e é formalmente aceito como uma parte dos Acordos Internacionais ajustados" (Gold, 1977, p.11).

9. Contudo, na era de Bretton Woods havia um equilíbrio periódico de crises de pagamento, desvalorização da taxa cambial e episódios de crescimento intermitentes.

10. A idéia da distribuição como segurança tem uma longa tradição nas economias de bem-estar que remontam a Harsanyi (1953), Lerner (1944) e Rawls (1971). Mais recentemente, esta questão foi analisada da perspectiva da economia política constitucional (ver Mueller, 1998; Wessels, 1993).

11. Focalizando a globalização por meio do comércio, Rodrik (1997b) também enfatizou o relacionamento entre redistribuição e abertura.

12. De modo mais preciso, uma medida da democracia, de acordo com a bibliografia recente explorando o papel da democracia sobre o crescimento econômico, níveis de renda e salários, define a democracia como um índice compósito e delineado sobre a Freedom House de política e liberdade civil; ou seja:

$$\text{Democracia} = \frac{14 - \textit{direitos civis} - \textit{direitos políticos}}{12}$$

O índice será definido a partir de 0 a 1, com 0 indicando baixa democracia e 1 indicando alta democracia. Os índices de liberdade política e civil são do *Comparative Survey of Freedom* que a Freedom House forneceu sobre uma base anual desde 1973.

13. Ver Bryant & Hodgkinson (1989) e Webb (1994) para uma discussão da Coordenação Política Internacional em ternos macroeconômicos e Kapstein (1989) para a informação sobre a coordenação internacional da regulamentação bancária. Para leituras seletivas na volumosa bibliografia sobre a necessidade de melhor regulamentação e supervisão, ver Alba et al. (1998); Caprio & Honohan (1999); Claessens, Djankov & Klingebiel (1999); e Stiglitz (1993).

CAPÍTULO 6

GOVERNO E ANTICORRUPÇÃO

Assim como é impossível não experimentar o mel ou o veneno que se pode encontrar na ponta da língua de alguém, também é impossível para aquele que lide com fundos governamentais não experimentar pelo menos um bocadinho da riqueza do rei.

— Kautilya, *The Arthashastra*

Escrito na Índia antiga há mais de dois mil anos, *Arthashastra* é a visão detalhada de uma sociedade que tece em conjunto as variáveis socioeconômicas, institucionais e políticas. Nos escritos contemporâneos sobre desenvolvimento, notáveis como Hirschmann, Myrdal, Coase, Stiglitz, North, Olson e Williamson forneceram uma visão ampla da interação das variáveis econômicas institucionais e convencionais. Em anos mais recentes, tem-se dado crescente atenção à corrupção, começando por Rose Ackerman e Klitgaard, em certa medida devido à consciência crescente de suas horríveis conseqüências para o desenvolvimento. Contudo, a maior parte do trabalho* sobre desenvolvimento contemporâneo tem subestimado a primazia do governo, definido amplamente, para o crescimento e o desenvolvimento. Falta muito fre-

---

* O trabalho, neste capítulo, aproveita-se de um número de iniciativas de colaboração entre o autor do capítulo e a equipe do World Bank sobre as questões de governo, inclusive Aart Kraay, Sanjay Pradhan, Randi Ryterman, Pablo Zoido, assim como a colaboração com Joel Hellman e Girainet Jones, no Banco Europeu para Reconstrução e Desenvolvimento, e Luis Moreno Ocampo da Transparência Internacional, e das entradas da equipe do Instituto sobre o governo do Banco Mundial e o grupo do setor privado do banco. Os dados utilizados neste capítulo originam-se de vários projetos de pesquisa e estudos (assim como de agências de especialistas sobre impostos externos) e estão sujeitos a margem de erro. Seu objetivo não é o de apresentar classificações objetivas através do país, mas ilustrar as características do desempenho do governo. Daí não se pretender nenhuma classificação dos países, nem pelo autor do capítulo, do Banco Mundial, ou sua equipe de diretores. Para detalhes posteriores de "desvelamento" empírico do governo e da corrupção, os dados e as questões metodológicas, ver Anexo 6 e visitar o site http://www.worldbank.org/wbi/governance.

qüentemente o reconhecimento de que um governo efetivo e transparente, operando dentro de uma estrutura de liberdades civis e bom governo, é fundamental para ganhos de bem-estar sustentados e mitigação da pobreza. Falta também uma visão integrada de governo e corrupção. De fato, a corrupção deveria ser encarada como um sintoma da fragilidade fundamental do Estado, não como uma determinante básica ou ímpar dos males da sociedade.

Este capítulo não apresenta uma abordagem abrangente ao estudo do governo e da corrupção. Em vez disso, dissecamos as noções de governo – e de corrupção e arrecadação do Estado – e apresentamos aspectos relevantes ao crescimento e desenvolvimento das nações para extrair idéias e estratégias que permitam melhorar o governo. Faltam-nos muitas respostas, as lições emergentes do sucesso e do fracasso estão sendo filtradas. Contudo, têm sido feitos progressos no entendimento conceitual, empírico e prático destas questões. Alguns desses progressos pertencem à agudeza e ao "desvelamento" das noções de medidas de governo e corrupção. Este desvelamento permite entender de maneira mais clara as causas e conseqüências do mau governo, ajudando a fornecer melhor aconselhamento político.

O Governo Afeta a Qualidade do Crescimento

A evidência pelo mundo afora sugere que um Estado capacitado com instituições governamentais boas e transparentes está associado ao alto crescimento da renda, saúde nacional e realizações sociais. Rendas mais altas, investimento e crescimento, assim como uma maior expectativa de vida, encontram-se em países com instituições governamentais efetivas, honestas e meritocráticas, com aerodinâmica e regulamentações claras, e também onde o papel do direito é aplicado de maneira justa, onde as políticas e a estrutura legal não foram tomadas pelos investimentos de capital da elite, e onde a sociedade civil e a mídia têm voz independente acentuando a responsabilidade de seus governos. A experiência histórica e internacional também nos ensina que um governo honesto e capacitado não requer em primeiro lugar que o país se torne totalmente modernizado e rico. A experiência de países em via de industrialização, como Botswana, Chile, Costa Rica, Estônia, Polônia e Eslovênia, assim como a evidência sobre ao últimos vinte anos das economias de Cingapura e Espanha, exemplificam esta lição.

Os capítulos anteriores enfatizavam a necessidade de política, regulamentações em recursos públicos para promover desenvolvimento orientado para o mercado e para mitigar os impactos negativos das externalidades e falências de mercado. Com ênfase na pobreza e na distribuição de renda, eles analisaram aqueles fatores que afetam adversamente o capital humano

e o meio ambiente. Um papel-chave para o Estado consiste na entrega de serviços públicos e bens vitais para realizar um crescimento sustentado e reduzir, assim, a pobreza. Também, os governos precisam estabelecer estruturas de fazer política, políticas de boas condições de mercado e estruturas reguladoras eficientes e aerodinâmicas, assim como eliminar as regulamentações desnecessárias sobre as empresas, tais como controle de preços, restrições comerciais, alvarás para as empresas e os entraves burocráticos.

Contudo, freqüentemente o governo tem dado atenção insuficiente às regulamentações governamentais referentes ao trabalho infantil, segurança do trabalhador, monopólios infra-estruturais, supervisão do setor financeiro e meio ambiente. Além disso, em muitos cenários houve uma tendência quanto ao tamanho, composição e entrega dos gastos públicos e investimentos para beneficiar os interesses das elites, freqüentemente resultando em subinvestimento no capital humano e nos resultados que atingem os pobres. Esses interesses da elite, freqüentemente também conduzem à captação de políticas legal e reguladora. O estudo do governo e da construção inadequada de uma instituição é essencial para que se entendam estes resultados.

Um processo político determina as políticas públicas e a alocação dos benefícios e gastos públicos. Seu sucesso depende de um governo responsável, da participação da comunidade, e de uma voz forte para o povo e as empresas competitivas. A adoção efetiva e o uso de políticas e gastos requerem um bom governo. As empresas precisam operar dentro de uma estrutura contratual e legal que proteja os direitos de propriedade e facilite as transações, que detenha as tentativas das empresas da elite de capturar o Estado e permita que as forças de mercado competitivas determinem os preços e salários, e que as empresas entrem e saiam do mercado. O setor público pode fazer muito para baixar os custos das transações para fazendas e empresas, sustentando-as com informação e instituições e exterminando o mau governo e a corrupção.

Definir e Desvelar Corrupção e Governo

A corrupção é comumente definida como o abuso da administração pública com fins de ganhos privados. Os debates sobre se determinadas atividades podem ser classificadas como corruptas ou não, e a necessidade de desvelar a corrupção, os exemplos vividos no cotidiano na imprensa e nas conversas, circunscrevem a discussão do que constitui a corrupção. Contudo, governo é um conceito mais amplo que corrupção. Definimos governo como o exercício da autoridade mediante tradições e instituições formais e informais para o bem comum. Governo engloba o processo de seleção, monitoração e substituição dos governos. Também inclui a capacidade de formular e implementar políticas sólidas e o respeito dos cidadãos

para com o Estado pelas instituições que governam as interações econômicas e sociais entre eles.

A partir desta noção, podemos dividir o governo em seis componentes, organizados em torno de três categorias amplas como se segue: (a) voz e responsabilidade, que incluem liberdades civis, liberdade de imprensa e estabilidade política; (b) eficácia governamental, que inclui a qualidade dos agentes de política e entrega do serviço público, e a falta de ônus regulador; e (c) regra de direito, que inclui a proteção dos direitos de propriedade e independência do judiciário e controle da corrupção (Kaufmann; Kraay et al., 1999a, b).

Todavia, no desvelamento do governo, colocamos que a corrupção é um entre os seis componentes bem entrelaçados do governo. Governo afeta o bem-estar e a qualidade de vida mediante canais diretos e indiretos complexos que ainda não entendemos completamente. Uma melhoria em um componente do governo, tal como as liberdades civis, sublinha diretamente a qualidade de vida para o povo de um país, mesmo quando todos os outros fatores socioeconômicos permaneçam constantes. Logo, o governo pode ser uma entrada direta no bem-estar da população.

Contudo, efeitos indiretos importantes também estão em jogo. Por exemplo, o desgoverno pode atingir a taxa de crescimento das rendas e do capital humano, e aumentar a taxa de esgotamento dos recursos naturais – freqüentemente, os resultados do capital investido dos políticos e da elite. Além do mais, Estados mal governados tendem a exibir um conjunto distorcido das políticas econômicas e institucionais que faz decrescer o fator de produtividade, crescimento e diminuição da pobreza. Contudo, por meio dos mecanismos diretos e indiretos, um governo eficiente e claro é vital para a implementação e a sustentação de políticas institucionais e econômicas sólidas e para promover o desenvolvimento do capital humano e a diminuição da pobreza.

As Medidas Empíricas de Governo

Estudos empíricos recentes sugerem a importância das instituições do governo para resultados de desenvolvimento. Knack & Keefer (1997) descobriram que o ambiente institucional para a atividade econômica determina, em larga medida, a habilidade dos países pobres para convergir para os padrões dos países industrializados. Por sua vez, La Porta et al. (1999) estudaram as determinantes da qualidade de governos, entre outras coisas, e descobriram que o tipo dos regimes legais importa tanto quanto outros fatores históricos.

A definição de governo, como apresentada na parte anterior, é ampla o suficiente para que uma larga variedade de indicadores através do país possa lançar luz sobre seus vários aspectos. Aplicando uma definição ampla como

esta, Kaufmann, Kraay e Zoido-Lobatón analisaram centenas de indicadores pelo país como substitutos para vários aspectos de governo. Estes indicadores originaram-se de uma variedade de organizações, inclusive agência de taxa de risco comercial, organizações multilaterais, uma "fábrica de cérebros",* e outras organizações não governamentais (ONGs). São baseados em estudos de especialistas, empresas e cidadãos e cobrem um amplo espectro de tópicos: as percepções da estabilidade política, o clima de negócios, os pontos de vista sobre a eficácia da provisão do serviço público, as opiniões a respeito da regra do direito e um relato sobre a incidência de corrupção.[1] (Ver Anexo 6 para uma descrição da metodologia de Kaufmann, Kraay e Zoido-Lobatón.)

As reações céticas levantaram-se naturalmente a respeito dos dados sobre a riqueza no governo. Seriam dados informativos? O que podem os analistas de negócios de Wall Street possivelmente saber sobre a corrupção no Azerbaijão, em Camarões, na Moldávia, em Myanmar ou na Nigéria? Seriam coerentes os dados? Será que as taxas relatadas pelas empresas sobre pressões dos servidores civis e seus tempos de espera pela liberação alfandegária contam-nos alguma coisa sobre a eficácia do governo em geral ou medem totalmente coisas diferentes? Serão comparáveis os dados? Será que a contagem de três (entre quatro) nas economias de transição pode ser comparada com uma contagem de sete (entre dez) nos países asiáticos? Além disso, de acordo com estes critérios, será que os dados podem ser úteis para uma análise econométrica rigorosa da corrupção ou para objetivos de aconselhamento político?

Essas questões, levantadas detalhadamente nas duas referências e no Anexo 6, motivaram a estratégia empírica para medir o governo: os dados estão mapeados para os seis subcomponentes do governo e expressos em unidades comuns. Os dados são informativos, dentro de limites mensuráveis, mas a imprecisão nas estimativas requer cuidados em sua apresentação e utilização para aconselhamento político. Estes seis indicadores distintos que agregam o governo são assim desenvolvidos, impondo alguma estrutura sobre variáveis disponíveis e melhorando a confiabilidade do componente governamental mensurado, o que significativamente excede a precisão de qualquer medida governamental única.

Por exemplo, consideramos em primeiro lugar as questões de aferição para um dos seis componentes compostos do governo: regra de direito. Na Figura 6.1, a barra vertical descreve intervalos de confiança específica do país para a estimativa dos níveis de governo ("ponto estimativo"). Os intervalos de confiança (linhas verticais) refletem o desacordo, ou margem de erro (entre as fontes individuais originais fornecidas pelas várias organizações externas) sobre a aplicação da regra de direito.[2]

---

* *Think tanks*, no original, ou seja, grupo organizado, no governo ou nos negócios, para fazer pesquisa intensiva e resolver problemas, especialmente com o auxílio de computadores e equipamentos sofisticados. (N. E.)

A QUALIDADE DO CRESCIMENTO

Figura 6.1 – Qualidade do Indicador da Regra de Direito: A Abordagem Apresentacional dos "Sinais de Tráfego"

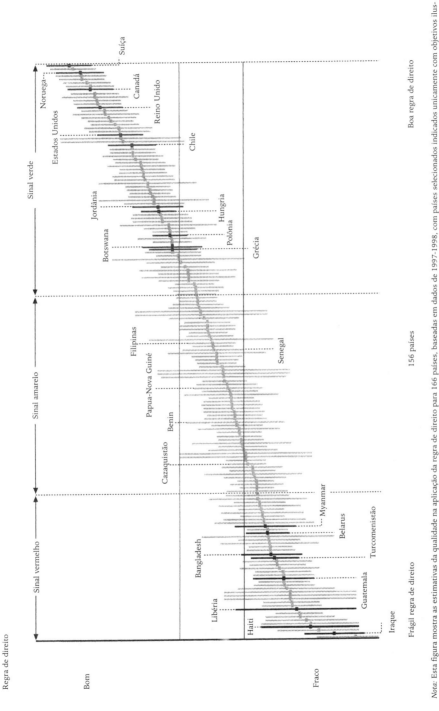

Nota: Esta figura mostra as estimativas da qualidade na aplicação da regra de direito para 166 países, baseadas em dados de 1997-1998, com países selecionados indicados unicamente com objetivos ilustrativos. As barras verticais mostram o escopo provável dos indicadores do governo para cada país, e os pontos intermediários destas barras indicam um valor mais provável. A extensão desses escopos varia com a quantidade de informações disponíveis para cada país e na medida em que percepções das diferentes fontes de corrupção coincidam. Países com barras verticais sólidas (na área do sinal vermelho) ou nas barras verticais verde-escuras (na área do sinal verde) são aqueles para os quais o indicador do governo é estatisticamente significativo tanto no terceiro abaixo (sinal correto) ou no terceiro acima (sinal verde) de todos os países. Países com barras verticais sinal verde (na área de sinal amarelo) não incidem em nenhum dos grupos anteriores. Logo, nenhuma classificação precisa pode ser realizada. As taxações do país de nenhum modo refletem os pontos de vista oficiais do Banco Mundial.

Fontes: Kaufmann et al. (1999a, b). Para maiores detalhes, incluindo dados gerais e metodologia, consultar http://www.worldbank.org/wbi/governance. Para uma síntese do documento, ver Kaufmann et al. (2000) em http://www.imf.org/fandd.

As diferenças entre mais de 160 países são amplas para a regra de direito, tanto quanto para as outras cinco medidas. Os países são ordenados ao longo do eixo horizontal, de acordo com suas (admitidamente imprecisas) classificações, enquanto o eixo vertical indica as estimativas de governo para cada país; as margens de erro para cada país descritas na linha vertical fina pode ser considerável. Logo, é enganoso ter países que "correm" pelo mundo todo, de modo semelhante a precisas "corridas de cavalo", para verificar sua classificação em vários indicadores governamentais. Em vez disso, a abordagem seguinte que agrupa os países dentro de três categorias amplas, semelhante a sinais de tráfego para cada dimensão governamental, é mais apropriada e estatisticamente garantida:

- Sinal vermelho: Países nesta categoria poderiam ser considerados como estando numa crise de governo naquele componente particular. De fato, apesar das margens de erro nos dados disponíveis, é ainda o caso em que um grupo de aproximadamente trinta a quarenta países exibe uma probabilidade extremamente alta de estar em crise onde a regra do direito (ou das outras medidas de governo) foi avaliada.
- Sinal amarelo: Os países estão vulneráveis ou em risco de cair em uma crise governamental num componente governamental específico.
- Sinal verde: os países têm melhor governo e não estão em risco.

Ao mover-se para longe do falso sentido de precisão, comum nos índices que classificam internacionalmente os países (que estão sujeitos a consideráveis margens de erro), esta abordagem alternativa de amplos agrupamentos categóricos sinaliza vulnerabilidades onde um país cai para grupos de sinal verde ou de sinal amarelo. Para outro componente governamental, neste caso aferindo o controle de corrupção (também baseado nos dados do fim da década de 1990), os países selecionados são apresentados com tal estrutura ilustrativa de sinais de tráfego na Figura 6.2.

Efeitos de Governo

Os dados através do país indicam uma simples e significativa correlação entre o governo e os resultados socioeconômicos. Para explorar o efeito do governo sobre as variáveis socioeconômicas, estimamos dois estágios de pequenos quadrados de regressão da variável socioeconômica (por exemplo, renda *per capita*) num componente governamental constante e assim por diante, utilizando indicadores históricos como instrumentos (de acordo com a abordagem de Hall & Jones, 1999). De acordo com tal abordagem, interesses quanto ao erro de medida e variáveis omitidas foram igualmente dirigidos (ver Kaufmann et al. (1999b) para maiores detalhes). A evidência desafia o argumento de que apenas os países ricos podem dar-se ao luxo de ter um bom governo.

Figura 6.2 – Controle de Corrupção: A Abordagem Apresentativa dos "Sinais de Tráfego"

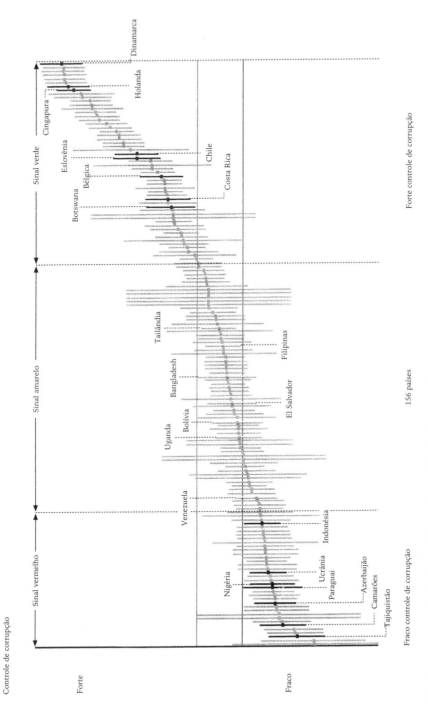

Nota: Esta figura mostra estimativas de controle de corrupção para 155 países, baseadas em dados de 1997-1998, com países selecionados indicados para objetivos ilustrativos. As barras verticais mostram o escopo provável do indicador governamental para cada país e os pontos médios dessas barras mostram o valor mais provável. O alcance dessas classificações varia com a quantidade de informações disponíveis para cada país e na medida em que percepções de diferentes fontes de corrupção coincidam. Países com barras verticais sólidas (na área de sinal vermelho) ou barras verticais verde-escuras (na área de sinal verde) são aqueles para os quais o indicador governamental é estatisticamente significativo nos dois grupos anteriores. As posições relativas dos países estão sujeitas a significativas margens de erro e refletem as percepções de uma variedade de organizações dos setores público e privado pelo mundo afora. Logo, nenhuma classificação precisa pode ser realizada. As taxas dos países de modo algum refletem pontos de vista do Banco Mundial.

Fontes: Kaufmann et al. (1999a, b). Para mais detalhes a respeito dos bancos de dados sobre o governo geral, ver Kaufmann et al. (2000); http://www.imf.org/fandd/2000/06/Kauf.htm; http://www.worldbank.org/wbi/governance.

A análise empírica sugere grande efeito direto partindo do melhor governo para os melhores resultados de desenvolvimento. Considerar uma melhoria (de um desvio-padrão) na regra de direito a partir dos baixos níveis na Federação Russa, atualmente, aos níveis médios na República Tcheca ou uma redução na corrupção semelhante àquela da Indonésia para a da Coréia. Nesta estrutura, aumenta os resultados *per capita* de duas a quatro vezes, reduz a mortalidade infantil numa grandeza similar, e melhora a alfabetização de 15 a 25 pontos percentuais a longo prazo. E considera que as diferenças de governo para estes dois pares de países não são muito grandes. Melhorias muito maiores na eficácia governamental dos níveis no Tajiquistão (no grupo do sinal vermelho) para aqueles no Chile (no grupo do sinal verde) nesta estrutura quase dobraria os impactos de desenvolvimento mencionados há pouco.

Os relacionamentos entre resultados de desenvolvimento e as quatro medidas de governo são ilustradas na Figura 6.3. A altura nas barras verticais mostra as diferenças de resultados de desenvolvimento nos países com governo fraco, médio e forte, que ilustram a forte correlação entre bons resultados e bom governo. Depois de controlar a causalidade reversa e os efeitos de outros fatores não governamentais no desenvolvimento, as linhas sólidas representam o impacto estimado do governo sobre os resultados do desenvolvimento: "dividendo desenvolvimentista" de melhoria do governo.[3]

Indicadores de governos compósitos, baseados em fontes de dados múltiplas e exteriores, chamam a atenção poderosamente para as questões governamentais. Elas são igualmente indispensáveis para pesquisa através do país nas causas e conseqüências do mau governo.

Por exemplo, este amplo conjunto de dados desmascara que países maiores são mais corruptos (uma construção estatística resultante destes testes com um número menor de países). Contudo, estes novos indicadores governamentais fornecem apenas uma primeira e grosseira bancada em que os países permanecem relativos um ao outro nas questões governamentais, e constroem uma ferramenta sem corte para uma ação informada para melhorar o governo. Para fazer indicadores compósitos mais específicos e úteis dentro de um país, é necessário saber muito mais sobre o modo como as percepções dos dados sobre o desgoverno são refletidas nas falhas políticas e institucionais. Os instrumentos de diagnóstico de profundidade de governo são necessários dentro de um país para fornecer dados significativos e informações para a formulação e as reformas governamentais. Contra este pano de fundo, o restante do capítulo levanta as seguintes questões: Como a corrupção e o mau governo minam o desenvolvimento? Quais são as causas subjacentes da corrupção? Que tipos de vislumbre podem derivar-se pelo desvelamento da corrupção em componentes distintos? Que tipos de instrumento de diagnóstico e abordagens estratégicas podem servir melhor ao intento do país em fazer progresso rumo a um governo honesto e bom?

A QUALIDADE DO CRESCIMENTO

Figura 6.3 – O Dividendo Desenvolvimentista do Bom Governo

Mortalidade infantil e corrupção

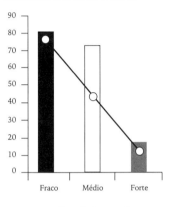

Renda per capita e ônus regulatório

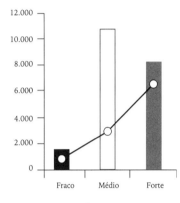

Alfabetização e regra de direito

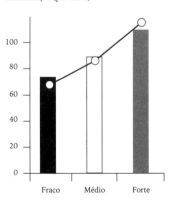

Expectativa de vida, voz e responsabilidade

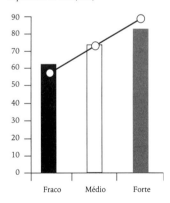

Nota: A altura das barras verticais mostra as diferenças na média dos resultados do desenvolvimento, nos países com governo frágil, médio e forte. As linhas sólidas mostram o efeito estimativo do governo nos resultados do desenvolvimento. Para mais detalhes sobre testes econométricos (sintetizados nas linhas sólidas), ver nota final 3 neste capítulo e a Tabela A6.1 no Anexo 6.
Fontes: Kaufmann et al. (1999b, 2000); http://www.imf.org/fandd.

A Corrupção Solapa
o Crescimento e o Desenvolvimento

Muitos estudos apontaram o efeito pernicioso da corrupção sobre o desenvolvimento. Mauro (1997) mostrou que a corrupção retarda a taxa de crescimento dos países. Ele descobriu que, se reduzisse a corrupção ao nível de Cingapura e a taxa de crescimento fosse de 4% ao ano, a média anual de Bangladesh para o crescimento PIB *per capita* entre 1960 e 1985 teria sido 1,8 ponto percentual mais alto, um ganho potencial de 50% na renda *per capita*.

Estes são alguns dos muitos canais pelos quais a corrupção pode enfraquecer o crescimento econômico:

- Deslocamento de talento (Murphy et al., 1991), incluindo subutilização dos segmentos-chave da sociedade, tais como as mulheres.
- Níveis mais baixos de investimento doméstico e estrangeiro (Mauro, 1997; Wei, 1997).
- Desenvolvimento e crescimento empresarial distorcido da economia informal (Johnson et al., 1998).
- Gastos públicos e investimentos distorcidos e estrutura física deteriorada (Tanzi & Davoodi, 1997).
- Lucros públicos mais baixos e menos provisão da regra de direito como um bem público (Johnson et al., 1997).
- Exagerada centralização governamental (Fismann & Gatti, 2000).
- Captação estatal pela elite corporativa das leis e políticas ("compradas") do Estado, solapando o crescimento das saídas e dos investimentos do setor empresarial (Hellman et al., 2000a; ver Anexo 6 para maiores detalhes).

Investimento Mais Baixo

Evidência de uma ampla interseção dos países sugere que a corrupção reduz de modo significativo o investimento estrangeiro e interno. Se as Filipinas pudessem reduzir a corrupção a um nível muito mais baixo do que em Cingapura, aumentaria seus investimentos para a razão PIB em 6,6 pontos percentuais (Mauro, 1997). Observando para o FDI bilateral no início da década de 1990, de 14 países-fonte para 41 países recebedores de empréstimo, Wei (1997) descobriu a evidência de que a corrupção desencoraja o investimento. Reduzir a corrupção a seu nível mais baixo em Cingapura teria o mesmo efeito sobre investimentos estrangeiros para um país corrupto como reduzir a taxa corporativa marginal para mais de 20 pontos percentuais. Muitos países atingidos pela corrupção também oferecem taxas de incentivos substanciais para atrair empresas multinacionais. Mediante o

controle da corrupção, poderiam atrair pelo menos o mesmo número de investimentos estrangeiros sem tais incentivos de impostos.

Má Distribuição dos Gastos Públicos

Alguns dos pioneiros dos estudos das economias de corrupção têm acentuado o efeito da corrupção sobre a alocação das finanças públicas (Klitgaard, 1988; Rose-Ackerman, 1989). Tanzi & Davoodi (1997) descobriram que a corrupção aumenta o investimento público porque cria chances para manipulação pelos funcionários públicos desonestos, de alto nível. Distorce igualmente a composição do gasto público para longe das operações necessárias e manutenção de gastos, e dirige-o para a compra de novos equipamentos, reduzindo, desse modo, a produtividade do investimento público, particularmente na infra-estrutura. Sob um regime corrupto, funcionários públicos afastam-se de programas de saúde porque oferecem um escopo menor para desvio de verba. A corrupção também pode reduzir as taxas de lucro porque compromete a capacidade do governo para receber impostos e tarifas.

Calcado nas descobertas de Tanzi e Davoodi, Wei (1997) mostrou que um aumento na corrupção, comparável ao nível de corrupção de Cingapura crescendo para a do Paquistão, iria aumentar os gastos públicos da razão PIB em 1,6 ponto percentual e reduzir o lucro governamental para a razão PIB em 10 pontos percentuais. Além do mais, um aumento na corrupção reduziria a qualidade das rodovias e aumentaria a incidência de racionamento de energia, falhas nas telecomunicações e perdas de água.

Johnson et al. (1998) também mostraram que a corrupção reduz os rendimentos dos impostos, principalmente por meio da economia informal. Sobrecarregadas pela burocracia e associadas ao desvio de verba na economia oficial, as empresas movem-se para a economia informal e pagam menos impostos. Tal rendimento de imposto reduzido está associado com uma provisão mais baixa dos bens públicos-chave, tais como regra de direito e crescimento posterior da economia informal, desequilibrando finanças públicas.

Impacto Sobre os Pobres

Onde a corrupção prevalece o crescimento é desequilibrado, acarretando um enorme efeito sobre a pobreza. Conseqüentemente, os pobres recebem menos serviços sociais, como saúde e educação.

A corrupção desvia o investimento infra-estrutural contra os projetos que ajudam os pobres e desequilibra a utilização dos meios de pequena escala, para fugir da pobreza. Ainda pior, regimes corruptos freqüentemente preferem contratos defensivos sobre clínicas de saúde e escolas rurais, um

viés político que piora a distribuição de renda e de diversos recursos, e desvia os recursos do campo para as cidades.

Gupta et al. (1998) mostram que a corrupção aumenta a desigualdade de renda e a pobreza, por meio de canais como crescimento mais baixo, impostos regressivos, menor direcionamento efetivo dos programas sociais, acesso desigual à educação, vieses políticos que favorecem a desigualdade na posse de bens, gastos sociais reduzidos e altos investimentos de risco para os pobres. Como sugerido na Figura 6.3, Kaufmann et al. (1999b) também descobriram que a corrupção aumenta a mortalidade infantil e reduz a expectativa de vida e a alfabetização. Não obstante a análise do índice de pobreza humana do UNDP, mostra-nos dados que sugerem que ele é negativamente associado a vários índices de governo e corrupção mesmo depois do controle do PIB *per capita*. Os mecanismos mediante os quais o governo afeta a pobreza são vários, complexos e ainda não totalmente entendidos. A Tabela 6.1 sugere alguns dos efeitos complexos da corrupção sobre a pobreza por meio de uma variedade de canais.

A análise do país utilizando novos instrumentos de diagnósticos governamentais ilustra como a corrupção regressiva funciona como um imposto. Por exemplo, famílias pobres no Equador precisam gastar três vezes mais em propinas como uma parte de suas rendas do que famílias de mais altas

Tabela 6.1 – Uma Matriz-Síntese: Corrupção e Pobreza

Causas "imediatas" da pobreza	Como a corrupção afeta a causa "imediata" da pobreza
Crescimento e investimento mais baixo	Economia instável/políticas institucionais devidas ao investimento de capital Alocação distorcida dos gastos/investimentos públicos Baixo acúmulo de capital humano Interesses corporativos da elite capturam leis e distorcem a feitura das políticas Ausência de regra de direito e de direitos de propriedade Obstáculos governamentais para o desenvolvimento do setor privado
Os pobres ficam com a fatia menor do crescimento	Captura do Estado pelas políticas governamentais e alocação de recursos pela elite A regressividade da "taxa" da propina sobre pequenas empresas e sobre os pobres A regressividade nos gastos públicos e nos investimentos Distribuição de renda desigual
Acesso desigual aos serviços públicos	A propina impõe taxa regressiva e acesso desigual de qualidade dos serviços básicos para os serviços de saúde, educação e justiça Captação política pelas elites do acesso aos serviços particulares
Falta de saúde e educação	Baixo acúmulo de capital humano Qualidade mais baixa de educação e serviços de saúde

Fonte: Autores.

Figura 6.4 – A Corrupção É Regressiva: Resultados dos Estudos Diagnósticos

Propina paga por empresas no Equador, 1999

Propina paga pelos negócios domésticos no Equador, 1999

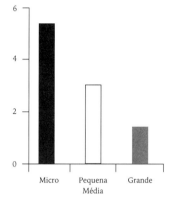
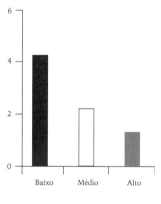

Nota: Estimativas sujeitas a margem de erro.
Fonte: World Bank (2000e).

rendas para ter acesso aos serviços públicos (Figura 6.4). De modo semelhante, em vários estudos de diagnóstico dos funcionários públicos na América Latina no fim da década de 1990, os burocratas dessas agências abundam em corrupção e falta de meritocracia, sendo responsáveis por discriminar os pobres por meio da limitação do acesso aos serviços básicos e por falhar na busca da diminuição da pobreza – em contraste com melhor acesso para os pobres pelas agências com menos corrupção e meritocracia (Figura 6.5).

Impacto da Corrupção Sobre o Comércio e Influência Corporativa Sobre o Governo Nacional

Um argumento comum encontrado na bibliografia contesta que as propinas para burlar os controles do mau governo são como um desregulamento informal e pode ter efeitos positivos, tais como promover o desenvolvimento empresarial (Huntington, 1968; Leff, 1964; Liu, 1985). Este ponto de vista – propina como graxa para as engrenagens do comércio – pode abranger conceitualmente apenas um sentido muito estreito se as más regulamentações foram fixadas independentemente do comportamento dos funcionários públicos. Ainda assim, na realidade, os funcio-

GOVERNO E ANTICORRUPÇÃO

Figura 6.5 – Corrupção e Ausência de Meritocracia nas Repartições Públicas Desigualam os Acessos aos Serviços para os Pobres: Estudos Diagnósticos dos Resultados dos Funcionários Públicos

Controle da corrupção nas repartições públicas do Paraguai e acesso aos serviços pelos pobres

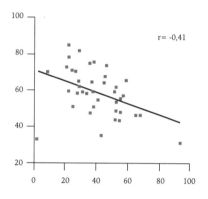

Serviço civil e meritocracia nas municipalidades do Paraguai e acesso aos serviços pelos pobres

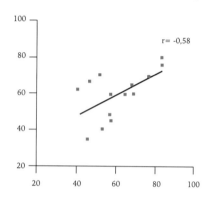

Controle da corrupção nas municipalidades da Bolívia e acesso aos serviços pelos pobres

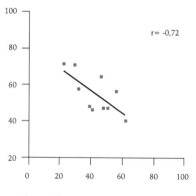

Serviço civil e meritocracia nas municipalidades da Bolívia e acesso aos serviços pelos pobres

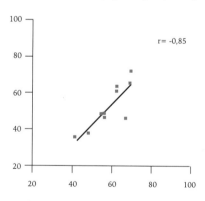

Nota: Cada observação descrita (ponto) representa uma repartição pública ou municipalidade no país pertinente. Baseados no estudo dos funcionários públicos do governo, "impacto de alívio sobre pobreza" representa a porcentagem de casos nos quais o funcionamento dos serviços públicos é proveitoso para reduzir a pobreza, e a "acessibilidade para os pobres" representa a porcentagem em casos nos quais os serviços públicos oferecidos são acessíveis aos pobres, como relatado pelos funcionários públicos no estudo do diagnóstico.
Fonte: World Bank (2000e).

nários freqüentemente são discretos no tipo e na quantidade de incômodos e regulamentações aplicados sobre as empresas individuais. Os fiscais de impostos podem sobrecarregar a renda tributada (Hindriks et al., 1999), e os fiscais de incêndio podem decidir quantas vezes checar uma empresa por "violações" de segurança. Utilizando dados de estudos independentes em mais de seis mil empresas em 75 países, Kaufmann & Wei (1999) mostraram que as empresas que pagam mais propinas administrativas gastam mais tempo com os burocratas do que as empresas que não pagam propinas.

Logo, a evidência empírica sugere que uma firma comprometida com propina administrativa insignificante (por exemplo, para alvarás ou papeladas burocráticas) não se beneficia necessariamente do pagamento de propinas; nem a comunidade ou sociedades de negócios de modo geral. A evidência da pesquisa sobre os custos da corrupção para o desenvolvimento dos negócios gerais está crescendo. Por exemplo, Fisman & Svensson (1999) descobriram que em Uganda a corrupção administrativa reduz a propensão de uma empresa para investir e crescer, e Hellman et al. (2000a) descobriram que naquelas economias em transição onde "grande" corrupção é mais prevalente, o crescimento e a taxa de investimento do setor empresarial é muito menor, enquanto a segurança dos direitos de propriedade é desigual.

A corrupção não apenas faz mancar o desenvolvimento empresarial dinâmico, mas afeta empresas menores e novos participantes, em particular. Empresas mais novas e menores tendem a suportar o impacto da "taxa" de propina, como evidenciado por uma recente análise de três mil empresas nas economias de transição.[4] De modo similar, empresas menores são preparadas para pagar significativamente mais impostos do que suas similares maiores, para que suas propinas sejam reduzidas.

Esta pesquisa sobre as economias de transição fornece também idéias sobre o elo entre influência política, corrupção maiúscula (de modo mais específico, roubando o Estado) e desempenho empresarial. Em um número de países na antiga União Soviética, o estudo descobre que as empresas (inclusive muitas com FDI) que compraram leis parlamentares, decretos presidenciais e a influência nos bancos centrais se beneficiaram a curto prazo (nos lucros e investimentos da própria empresa). Ainda assim, como afirmamos anteriormente, suas ações infligem um grande custo indireto sobre o desenvolvimento do restante do setor empresarial. Estas descobertas demonstram que, enquanto as empresas individuais se comprometem na captação do Estado, podem beneficiar privadamente (em contraste com a corrupção administrativa, Figura 6.6); uma tal forma de corrupção maiúscula impõe um custo social particularmente pernicioso ao desenvolvimento empresarial (consultar o Anexo 6 para detalhes sobre desvelamento da medida da corrupção na captação estatal, restituições de licitações públicas e corrupção administrativa).

Causas da Corrupção

Os estudos empíricos das causas da corrupção são razoavelmente novos. Ainda assim, a evidência emergente sugere que algumas determinantes são importantes. A pesquisa disponível sustenta a noção de que a corrupção é um sintoma de profunda fragilidade institucional.

A Ausência dos Direitos Políticos e das Liberdades Civis

Os direitos políticos, que incluem eleições democráticas, uma legislatura, partidos opostos, liberdades civis que incluem direitos à mídia independente e livre e liberdade de reunião e discurso, são negativamente correlatadas com a corrupção.

A Figura 6.7 mostra a estreita correlação entre liberdades civis e liberdade de imprensa com a corrupção. Aumentando os pontos de evidência para a habilitação da sociedade civil, dirige-se efetivamente para a corrupção

Figura 6.6 – "Pequenas Propinas" *versus* Captação Estatal: Será que Comprometer-se com a Corrupção Beneficia a Empresa?

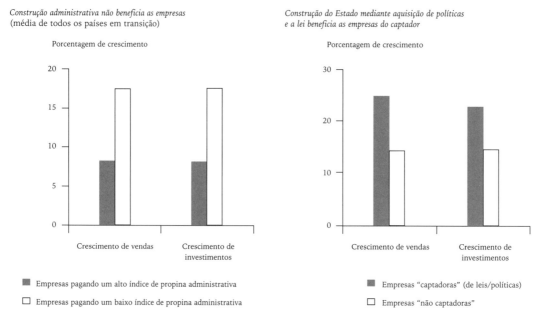

Fontes: Hellman et al. (2000a). Maiores detalhes no Anexo 6 e http://www.worldbank.org/wbi/governance.

(Figura 6.7). A evidência do estudo empresarial das economias de transição também sugere que a captação das políticas do Estado e das leis pelos interesses corporativos está associada com a ausência de liberdades civis íntegras (Hellman et al., 2000a). A evidência empírica pelo mundo afora também sugere que a inclusão das mulheres, se aferidas como representação parlamentar ou direitos sociais, ajuda a completar tal habilitação (Kaufmann, 1998). Devolução, tal como a descentralização fiscal (Collier, 1999; Fisman & Gatti, 2000), sobre as circunstâncias corretas também pode ajudar o controle da corrupção. Além disso, pontos de evidência para uma correlação significativa entre a corrupção e a regra de direito.

Regulamentação e Finanças Públicas

A corrupção é mais alta nos países com alto grau de intervenção do Estado na economia, na regulamentação excessiva e impostos, aplicação arbitrária das regulamentações e restrições comerciais. Economias monopolizadas também tendem a apresentar maior grau de corrupção.

As liberdades civis e uma imprensa livre podem ajudar a controlar a corrupção

Figura 6.7 – Corrupção e Direitos Civis

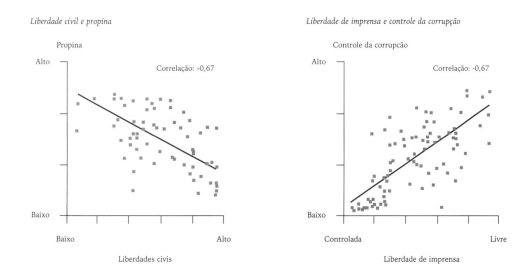

Fonte: Kaufmann (1998).

Serviço Civil

O profissionalismo do serviço civil, que inclui sistemas de treinamento, emprego e promoção, também está associado com menos corrupção. Contrariamente à sabedoria convencional, a evidência do pagamento do serviço civil é freqüentemente ambígua. Melhores salários setoriais públicos, por si sós, podem não explicar uma significativa redução na corrupção. Por exemplo, as agências do setor público equatoriano que oferecem melhores salários aos empregados não têm uma incidência menor de corrupção. Em muitos cenários, uma pequena minoria dos mais antigos políticos e funcionários públicos freqüentemente causa a corrupção mais danosa. Enquanto em alguns países aumentar salários de pessoal civil-chave selecionado pode ser garantido, é improvável que isso dê frutos sem medidas complementares. Entre essas medidas, a meritocracia na contratação, promoção e demissão dentro de um departamento está associada com menos corrupção (Figura 6.8). Os resultados contrastantes entre o baixo impacto dos salários mais altos de um lado, e o significativo efeito da meritocracia de outro, exemplificam a necessidade de conduzir em profundidade diagnósticos empíricos com o propósito de países formularem programas sérios de combate à corrupção.[5]

Uma Estratégia Anticorrupção Multifacetada

Dado o que se conhece sobre as principais determinantes de corrupção e bom governo, que tipos de programa podem ter algum impacto?[6] Melhorar o governo requer um sistema de checagem e equilíbrio na sociedade que restringe a ação arbitrária e o incômodo burocrático pelos políticos e burocratas, promove a voz e a participação da população, reduz os incentivos para a elite corporativa envolver-se na captação estatal e alimenta a regra de direito. Não obstante a pesquisa em andamento sobre a captação estatal sublinhar a necessidade de verificações e balanços no setor corporativo da elite, por meio da promoção de um mercado econômico competitivo e de uma sociedade civil ativa. Uma administração meritocrática e orientada para o serviço público é outro ponto alto da estratégia.

Reformas-Chave

A Figura 6.9 sintetiza a estratégia das reformas-chave para melhorar o governo e combater a corrupção. Contudo, como combinar e seqüenciar estas reformas para provocar maior impacto sobre a corrupção é particularmente um desafio desencorajador, como é a tarefa de detalhar e adaptar uma estratégia para a realidade específica de cada país. Por exemplo, um

Figura 6.8 – A Meritocracia Pode Reduzir a Corrupção: Evidência para Cada Repartição Pública com Base em Estudos dos Funcionários Públicos em Três Países

Corrupção em algumas repartições públicas do Equador está associada com falta de meritocracia

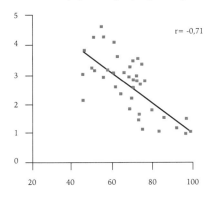

Corrupção em algumas municipalidades está associada com falta de meritocracia

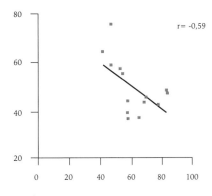

Corrupção em algumas repartições públicas da Bolívia está associada com falta de meritocracia

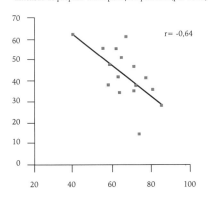

Corrupção em algumas municipalidades da Bolívia está associada com falta de meritocracia

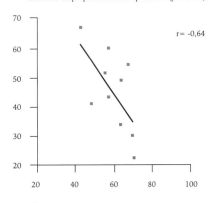

Nota: Cada observação descrita (ponto) representa uma repartição pública ou municipalidade no país pertinente. A extensão da propina é aferida pela porcentagem relatada dos serviços públicos e dos contratos que são afetados pela propina numa repartição pública ou municipalidade. O índice meritocrático (de 0 a 100) é construído com a utilização de questões de análise relatadas para o gerenciamento pessoal numa repartição pública ou municipalidade como relatado pelos funcionários públicos.
Fonte: World Bank (2000e). As contribuições de Ed Buscaglia, Maria Gonzales de Assis, Turgul Gurgur, Akiko Terada, Youngmei Zhou e Pablo Zoido-Lobatón para esta linha de pesquisa sobre funcionários públicos são conhecidas.

país que foi sujeito à captação estatal pela elite corporativa irá requerer uma estratégia diferente da de um país em que a principal fonte de mau governo origina-se nas estruturas políticas ou na burocracia. Questões específicas sobre reformas governamentais, contudo, incluem os tipos de mudança sobre que condições políticas e como as reformas seriam priorizadas dentro das realidades corporativa, política, civil e social de cada país cenário.

Competição e entrada. Em alguns países em desenvolvimento, em fase de transição, uma grande fonte de corrupção é a concentração de poder econômico e de monopólios que manipulam a influência política sobre o governo para benefícios particulares. O problema é particularmente agudo nos países ricos em recursos naturais, em que os monopólios em petróleo, gás e alumínio, por exemplo, manipulam um poder econômico político considerável, que leva a diferentes formas de corrupção: não-pagamento de impostos, cálculos amplos não transparentes, licenças e alvarás e compra de votos e decretos que restringem entrada e competição. Desmonopolização, desregulamentação, facilitação de entrada e saída (mediante a liquidação de bens e procedimentos de bancarrota efetiva), além da promoção da competição, são vitais.

Responsabilidade da liderança política. Medidas estão sendo implementadas em vários países que fornecem verificações e balanços para a liderança política e os funcionários públicos mais antigos em seu comprometimento para bom governo e anticorrupção, por meio da divulgação pública e da transparência de suas próprias ações, finanças, rendas e bens. Em vários países, isso envolveu:

- divulgação pública dos votos no Parlamento;
- rescisão de imunidade parlamentar incondicional;
- divulgação pública das fontes e quantias do financiamento dos partidos políticos;
- divulgação pública das rendas e bens dos servidores públicos mais antigos e seus dependentes-chave;
- regulamentações contra conflitos de interesse para cargos públicos;
- proteção do pessoal e segurança do emprego para os funcionários públicos que revelem abuso no ministério público por outros (estatutos atiçadores).

Administração Pública Meritocrática e Orientada para o Serviço. Recrutar e promover por mérito, como oposto ao apadrinhamento político ou filiação ideológica, está positivamente associado tanto com a efetividade governamental como com o controle da corrupção. As reformas nesta área incluíram a criação de instituições independentes e profissionais com verificações e balanços (por exemplo, uma comissão de recrutamento para o

Figura 6.9 – Estratégias Multidentadas para Combater a Corrupção e Melhorar o Governo – Reconhecer a Economia Política

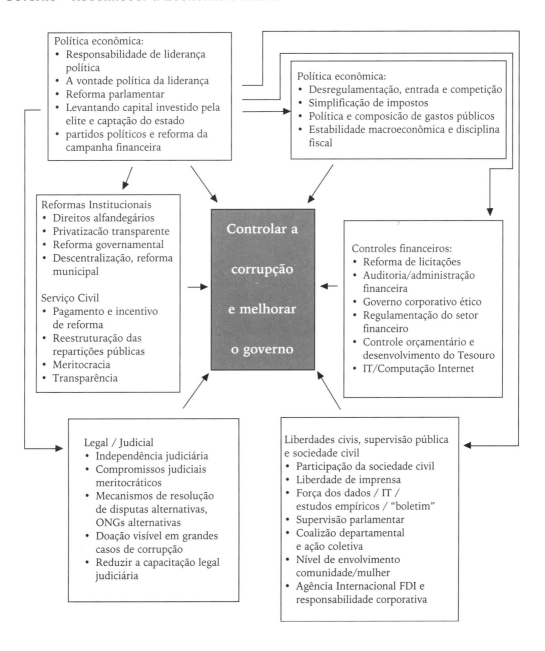

IT: Informação tecnológica.
Fontes: Autores, em colaboração com o World Bank's Public Sector Group.

serviço civil) e a introdução de um sistema de gerenciamento performático abrangente com pagamento e promoção ligados ao desempenho. Na Malásia e na Tailândia isso conduziu a um recrutamento crescente e à retenção da equipe gerencial e profissional e para uma maior efetividade no desempenho civil. Além disso, condições de benefícios não em dinheiro freqüentemente precisam ser simplificadas, monetarizadas e tornadas transparentes. Deve-se exercitar o cuidado necessário para evitar o aumento de salário em grande escala como uma panacéia.

Transparência e Responsabilidade no Gerenciamento dos Gastos Públicos.[7] Os sistemas básicos de responsabilidade na alocação e no uso dos gastos públicos constituem um pilar fundamental para o bom governo. O gerenciamento da responsabilidade nos gastos públicos requer: um orçamento abrangente e um processo consultativo do orçamento; transparência na utilização dos gastos públicos; licitação pública competitiva; e uma auditoria externa independente.

O orçamento deve, em primeiro lugar, ter uma cobertura abrangente das atividades de um governo. Muitos países se defrontam com problemas de transparência orçamentária, em que as maiores áreas dos gastos do orçamento não passam por um sistema de tesouraria e há um recurso substancial para fundos extra-orçamentários e nenhum sistema eficaz de compromissos do controle de gastos. Vários países em transição, tais como Hungria e Latíbia, fizeram progressos ao levantar esses problemas com programas abrangentes de reforma do Tesouro.

Em segundo lugar, a divulgação é importante. Muitos países industrializados (por exemplo, Austrália e Reino Unido) publicaram estruturas para estratégias de gastos públicos que são, ao mesmo tempo, o principal instrumento para explicar as escolhas e os meios de realçar a transparência dos objetivos políticos, e os alvos das saídas, calçando os orçamentos anuais. Mais recentemente, a África do Sul desenvolveu a estrutura de gasto a médio prazo, revisada anualmente e publicada na Web como meio de esclarecer escolhas estratégicas e estabelecer objetivos publicamente calculáveis para os gastos públicos.

Em terceiro lugar, uma licitação pública transparente e competitiva é a chave para limpar o governo. Reduzir a corrupção requer a adesão a uma disciplina estrita quanto à licitação competitiva e transparente dos contratos principais, maximizando o escopo da visão geral pública e uma revisão detalhada. A revolução da tecnologia da informação está provando ser um catalisador. De fato, para tornar o processo de licitação governamental mais eficaz e reprimir a curva de corrupção, três países latino-americanos – Argentina, Chile e México – adotaram recentemente sistemas eletrônicos de compras governamentais. Todas as notícias sobre licitações e seus resultados são colocados num site da Web disponível ao público. Outras importantes inovações relacionadas com monitoração externa dos

ativistas estão igualmente se estabelecendo. As ONGs estão cada vez mais desempenhando um papel para encabeçar as audiências públicas, para ter uma voz mais forte no estabelecimento das regras do jogo para projetos de licitação em grande escala (tal como no sistema metroviário de Buenos Aires) e pela transparência do próprio processo de licitação nos locais onde, por exemplo, ONGs como a Transparência Internacional inovaram. O Banco Mundial também assumiu um papel ativo em perseguir agressivamente as empresas comprometidas em má licitação nos projetos; por exemplo, firmas eliminadas de processos de licitação nos projetos subsidiados pelo Banco, por terem se comprometido em licitações corruptas, estão em lista publicamente disponível no site da instituição.

Em quarto lugar, estabelecer auditorias externas independentes é importante. Várias economias de transição e emergentes, tais como a República Tcheca e a Polônia, estabeleceram instituições de auditorias supremas, que são genuinamente independentes e têm impacto construtivo sobre sistemas de gerenciamento financeiro público. Na República Tcheca, os relatórios das auditorias são publicados, apresentados ao Legislativo e discutidos no gabinete, juntamente com um plano proposto para ações corretivas, na presença da instituição de auditoria suprema e ministros relevantes.

Promover a Regra de Direito. De acordo com o *New Palgrave Dictionary of Economics and the Law*, a regra de direito é definida opondo a regra dos poderosos. Isto sintetiza o desafio em muitos países, onde políticos poderosos, e líderes, interesses da elite ou oligarquias freqüentemente influenciam as operações práticas do Parlamento, do Judiciário e das instituições de aplicação da lei, tal como a polícia. Estes países freqüentemente possuem um conjunto de leis adequado nos livros, ainda que a falência esteja em sua eficaz aplicação e vigência. E em alguns países, tais leis foram tomadas pelos interesses da elite. A evidência de uma disposição vasta dos dados pelo mundo afora (sintetizado na Figura 6.1) sugere que há uma crise da regra de direito em muitos países da antiga União Soviética, na África, assim como em alguns da América Latina. A disfunção institucional em tais países fica em agudo contraste com os outros, onde, embora de modo imperfeito, a capacidade das instituições legais e judiciárias está melhorando. Ilustrando o desempenho dos tribunais em diferentes países, a Figura 6.10 mostra quão honestos, confiáveis e justos os tribunais são considerados pelo setor empresarial na Estônia e na Hungria. Como contraste, em países como a Federação Russa e a Ucrânia eles são considerados corruptos, muito parciais e injustos, não confiáveis e não fazem vigorar a lei.

O mau governo no Judiciário e nas instituições legais nem sempre se originou tão-somente no setor público. Em alguns países, os interesses corporativos da elite exerceram pressões corruptas igualmente, como também compilaram com base nos estudos empresariais recentes dos países em

Figura 6.10 – Alta Variação na Qualidade dos Tribunais em Economias Seletas

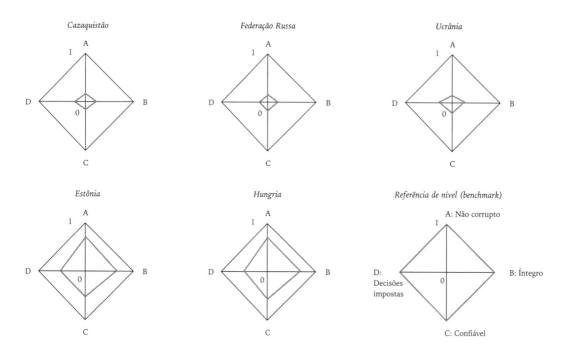

Quadro de medidas de dimensões de qualidade: A – não corrupto; B – íntegro; C – confiável; D – decisões impostas.
Nota: Um diamante com quatro pontas numa escala de 0 a 1, na qual 1 indica 100% da empresa em julgamento dando a mais alta taxa em cada dimensão qualitativa do Tribunal relevante. O painel direito mais baixo do campo seria um *benchmark* hipotético ideal, se 100% das empresas apresentassem contagens perfeitas.
Fontes: Hellman et al. (2000); ver também Anexo 6. Baseado em um exame de empresas de 1999 das economias em transição.

transição e ilustrados na Figura 6.11, que sugere a extensão da tomada (pelas empresas, inclusive o FDI) dos sistemas legais e judiciários em alguns países.

Logo, mesmo se as instituições legais fossem totalmente equipadas por juízes e pessoal treinados, eles podem estar sujeitos à tomada pelos políticos ou interesses corporativos corruptos. Neste contexto, as instituições legais do setor público são parte integral do problema governamental e não uma parte da solução.

Isto reduz a importância do aconselhamento convencional sobre melhoria de governo por meio da criação de instituições dentro do setor público (como um escritório de ética e um departamento anticorrupção), aprovando lei anticorrupção, fornecendo assistência técnica na forma de computadores ou outros *hardwares*, ou juízes estabelecidos para treinamento ou "viagens de estudo". Em vez disso, mecanismos inovadores para melhorar o governo são fre-

Figura 6.11 – Captação Legal e Judiciária pelo Setor Corporativo em Algumas Economias de Transição Seletas

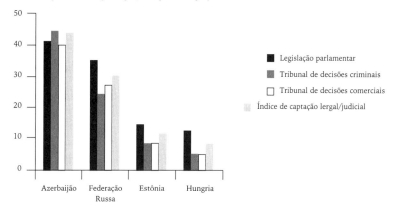

Nota: O índice de captação legal e judiciária é a média simples das empresas que relatam o efeito da compra corporativa da legislação parlamentar, de decisões dos tribunais criminais e das decisões dos tribunais comerciais. Estimativas sujeitas a margem de erro.
Fontes: Hellman et al. (2000a, b); para maiores detalhes, as colunas 1, 4 e 5 na Tabela A6.1 do Anexo 6. Dados de 1999.

qüentemente necessários, tal como uma disputa alternativa de mecanismos de resolução, provendo uma participação mais sistemática das ONGs e outros arranjos institucionais alternativos, estratégias de disseminação pela mídia e explorando de modo mais completo e transparente o poder dos dados e da informação dentro e fora do setor público. De igual importância, o desafio de maior relevância de realizar a captação legislativa em muitos países freqüentemente requereria reformas parlamentares e políticas, tais como divulgar publicamente todos os votos parlamentares, eliminar as leis de imunidade para membros do Parlamento e a reforma político-financeira.

Estudo dos Instrumentos Diagnósticos para uma Avaliação Governamental Dentro do País

A coleção, a análise e a disseminação de dados específicos de um país sobre a corrupção estão alterando o diálogo político sobre a corrupção e habilitando a sociedade civil por meio da ação coletiva. Ainda que desafios importantes permaneçam, incluindo o refinamento dos métodos em andamento que transformam a evidência do estudo em prioridades de reforma e como melhor complementar em profundidade os exames diagnósticos empíricos com o foco aprofundado nos grupos de metodologias – envolvendo completamente os investidores nos desafios-chave do governo dentro do país. Um

desafio-chave envolve o desenvolvimento de uma estratégia efetiva para a implementação da agenda de reformas. Uma vez que os dados dos exames e suas análises estão disponíveis, os países onde a vontade política está presente devem começar a tarefa mais difícil da priorização de medidas de acordo com a realidade do país e introdução de reformas para eliminar as fontes de corrupção.

Sustentar o esforço reformador com uma participação de base abrangente que envolva todos os ramos do governo, a sociedade civil e a comunidade de negócio constitui outro desafio à corrupção e à agenda de melhoria do governo (Quadro 6.1). Em cooperação vinda do setor privado e das ONGs, o governo pode alavancar a reforma permitindo a competição privada juntamente com a provisão pública de alguns serviços, por exemplo, a adoção de formas privadas em disputa de resolução alternativa para competir com a provisão judiciária ou privada da coleta do lixo em nível municipal. Estudos diagnósticos em profundidade de governo e anticorrupção (e suas análises de dados concomitantes) precisam ser institucionalizados, de modo que as estatísticas sobre a corrupção em departamentos específicos possam ser monitoradas e agir sobre eles periodicamente. Uma ampla disseminação das grandes quantias de estatísticas que estão sendo geradas pelos estudos diagnósticos e estudos do governo e captação pode habilitar posteriormente os investidores para que fortaleçam e sustentem a mudança institucional.

O esboço e a implementação de um departamento específico em exames de diagnósticos em profundidade para os funcionários públicos (Figuras 6.5 e 6.8), famílias ou usuários (Figura 6.4) e empresas (Figuras 6.4 e 6.11) constituem numa inovação que fornece entradas tangíveis para os países comprometidos com a capacidade de implementar a construção de programas e mudanças institucionais. Novos instrumentos de análise podem coletar informações detalhadas sobre o comportamento até nos departamentos governamentais de funcionamento mais ineficiente na entrega dos serviços públicos. Por exemplo, as comparações do preço pago pelo sal comprado por diferentes hospitais, depois de contabilizar o transporte e outros custos idiossincráticos, pode mostrar se existe a corrupção nos hospitais públicos. Utilizado juntamente com outros esquemas empíricos, tais estudos diagnósticos podem focalizar-se sobre o diálogo político em áreas concretas para reformar e recuperar a sociedade civil por detrás dos esforços reformadores.

Tais dados autodiagnosticados de um país, utilizados por uma variedade de investidores de dentro do país e disseminado pelas oficinas participativas, mobilizaram uma sustentação mais ampla para a elaboração do consenso e a ação coletiva para as reformas institucionais. Países como Albânia,[8] Bolívia, Geórgia e Latíbia realizaram progressos mediante o uso de diagnósticos para assumir ações concretas. A Bolívia está enfatizando o serviço civil e as reformas de licitação. A Latíbia tem dado prioridade à reforma dos impostos e direitos alfandegários. Na Geórgia, seguindo os resultados do exame abissal relativo ao estado do Judiciário, o presidente Chevardnadze decidiu que todos os juízes deveriam passar por uma nova

Quadro 6.1 – Governo e Instrumentos para Estudos Diagnósticos: O Poder dos Empíricos

O primeiro conjunto de estudos diagnósticos em profundidade no governo e na corrupção dos funcionários públicos, empresas e cidadãos foi realizado na Albânia, na Geórgia e na Latíbia em 1998. Mais recentemente, a implementação de versões refinadas e disseminadas desses estudos diagnósticos foi realizada em outros países, focando mais amplamente no complexo governo dos departamentos-chave num país e avaliando as principais determinantes institucionais do mau governo e da corrupção. Desafiando a sabedoria convencional, os novos estudos dos funcionários públicos, empresas e cidadãos encontraram os interrogados desejosos de fornecer informações detalhadas sobre o mau governo que eles haviam observado e experimentado (como oposição a meramente indicar suas vagas percepções sobre a corrupção por todo o país, por exemplo).

O relatório do estudo dos interrogados traz informações sobre desvio de fundos públicos, roubo da propriedade estatal, suborno para diminuir o tempo processual, propina para obter poder de monopólio e propina na licitação. Por exemplo, em 1998, no desvio de fundos públicos na Geórgia e na corrupção no Judiciário, entre outras coisas foi identificado um sério problema. Naquele tempo, o roubo da propriedade estatal foi identificado como um problema particular na Albânia. A propina na licitação e na alfândega é um desafio comum na maioria dos cenários nos quais estes estudos diagnósticos foram levados a cabo. A fragilidade no Judiciário foi identificada como uma das principais causas da corrupção na Albânia, enquanto os fracassos reguladores são muito menos importantes naquele país do que na Geórgia e na Latíbia, por exemplo. Nestes estudos diagnósticos, estatísticas detalhadas são coletadas sobre a freqüência e custos das propinas pagas pelas empresas a reguladores em diferentes departamentos, assim como chegadas a curto prazo da entrega do serviço público e outros indicadores eficazes de desempenho. Uma multiplicidade de dimensões governamentais está incluída nestes diagnósticos, permitindo uma análise em profundidade de questões como a meritocracia, a discricionarlidade, a transparência orçamentária e o foco e o impacto na diminuição da pobreza. A análise dessas estatísticas serve, assim, como uma entrada vital para priorizar a formulação de uma melhoria do programa reformador governamental.

Uma fatia significativa das propinas administrativas é paga a funcionários públicos para evitar os impostos, deveres alfandegários e outros compromissos financeiros com o Estado. Algumas propinas – tais como pagamentos de restituição aos funcionários públicos para a feitura de leis e decisões judiciais, ou para a licitação pública – descobriu-se serem particularmente onerosas. Os resultados do estudo indicam que os departamentos e as atividades vistas pelos funcionários públicos particularmente corruptos comandam os mais altos preços para garantir trabalho, sugerindo que assegurar tais posições públicas é visto como um investimento privado com uma significativa espera de retorno privado.

Quando os dados foram apresentados nas oficinas a membros da comunidade de negócios, a maioria da sociedade civil, e os ramos executivos e legislativos, o debate político abruptamente mudou de vago, não substancial e freqüentes acusações pessoais para um discurso centrado na evidência empírica e nas fragilidades sistêmicas que precisavam ser corrigidas. Programas de ação foram formulados e a implementação das reformas institucionais começou.

Fontes: Kaufmann et al. (1998). Para um guia mais detalhado sobre a implantação do diagnóstico governamental e anticorrupção consultar, http://www.worldbank.org/wbi/governance.

---

avaliação, o que foi transmitido ao vivo pela televisão. Dois terços dos juízes fracassaram na avaliação e foram substituídos.

Em outros países, esforços para uma melhoria de governo semelhante são efetuados num nível municipal. Por exemplo, em numerosas cidades ucranianas, ações específicas para melhorar a eficácia do governo local no fornecimento de serviços públicos estão sendo levadas a efeito seguindo os estudos diagnósticos. Tendo começado em Bangalore, na Índia, no início da

década de 1990, o estudo sobre o hoje bastante conhecido cartão do cidadão usuário permite que os cidadãos avaliem a qualidade dos serviços do governo local (Quadro 6.2). Em Campo Elias, na Venezuela, graças à liderança da prefeita, uma mulher corajosa que acredita no poder dos dados do governo para informar e mobilizar para a ação, a incidência de corrupção relatada foi reduzida à metade (Gonzalez de Asis, 2000).

Assim, os dados são poderosos para mobilizar a sustentação para as reformas, mas os obstáculos apresentados pela enorme corrupção e a captação do Estado pelos capitais investidos que resistem a essa reformas também são poderosos. Contudo, a liderança política, a sociedade civil, os investidores do setor privado e a comunidade doadora precisam construir sobre idéias e momentos gerados pelo diagnóstico e utilizar e disseminar estatísticas em conjunção com a promoção das liberdades civis e com o envolvimento da mídia, resultando em uma maior responsabilidade e mais ações contra a corrupção.

Transparência Por Meio da Voz e da Participação

A corrupção pode produzir conhecimento e uma cidadania informada. De fato, a habilitação da sociedade civil com informações mais rigorosas e con-

---

Quadro 6.2 – A "Voz" Como um Mecanismo para Fazer Valer a Transparência e a Responsabilidade

Os estudos dos clientes e cidadãos que incorporam a realimentação dos cidadãos ajudaram a melhorar o desempenho do setor público em muitos países. O método do boletim que começou por San Paul, em Bangalore, na Índia, encarna esta abordagem. Vincula avaliações periódicas dos cidadãos de municipalidades locais e seus cálculos dos serviços públicos, propina e extorsão. Existe evidência de que as repartições públicas em Bangalore deram passos concretos para melhorar a entrega do serviço.

Em Mendoza, na Argentina, os cidadãos participaram na criação de regras transparentes relacionadas à licitação pública. Um número de localidades por todo o mundo abraçou processos participativos semelhantes. Como parte de seu sistema pioneiro de orçamento participativo, Porto Alegre, no Brasil, reúne grandes assembléias nas quais as prioridades de gastos para educação, saúde, transporte, desenvolvimento, taxação, organização da cidade e o desenvolvimento urbano são discutidos. As Assembléias elegem então membros para um conselho orçamentário participativo de toda a cidade, que decide o seu plano de investimentos. Evidências preliminares mostram que mais estradas foram pavimentadas e o número de estudantes matriculados nas escolas primária e secundária dobrou.

De modo crescente, a voz e a transparência acentuando as reformas têm sido implementadas por intermédio da revolução da Internet e não apenas em áreas como a licitação, discutida anteriormente. No Chile, apenas durante o ano passado, a fatia da população pagante de impostos preenchendo o formulário via Internet aumentou de 5% para 30%. Ademais, a combinação das tecnologias de ponta estatística, computacional e da Internet também está promovendo uma maior responsabilidade nas eleições políticas, como se pôde testemunhar recentemente nas contagens extremamente eficazes, precisas e rápidas na Argentina, no Chile e no México, em agudo contraste com as eleições em numerosos países.

fiáveis é um pilar-chave da reforma. A transparência é um componente importante da habilitação e da voz pública. Como resultado, a ação política e grandes projetos públicos deveriam ser baseados na incorporação da voz e da participação dos investidores no desenvolvimento (ver Quadro 6.2 para uma discussão sobre transparência e governo). A pesquisa do Banco Mundial mostra que, quanto maior a participação dos beneficiários no esboço do projeto e sua implementação, melhores serão o projeto e o desempenho do serviço.

Importância das Liberdades Civis

Nas seções anteriores deste capítulo apresentamos a estreita associação entre liberdades civis e liberdade de imprensa por um lado, e controle da corrupção e captação do Estado por outro (Figura 6.7). Ainda, que a importância suprema das liberdades civis e políticas transcende seu valor em diminuir o nível de corrupção, ou simplesmente como um *input* para um resultado desenvolvimentista: é um bem básico que sublinha o bem-estar por si. Ao mesmo tempo, avaliar se as liberdades civis importam como uma entrada nos resultados desenvolvimentistas e financeiros é de relevância no bojo do debate na comunidade de ajuda, em relação às responsabilidades fiduciárias, para tornar a ajuda efetiva.

As evidências de mais de 1.500 projetos financiados pelo Banco Mundial sugerem que as liberdades civis e a participação do cidadão são fatores importantes para os resultados do desenvolvimento. Pesquisas centradas na aferição do impacto das variáveis civis e participativas no desempenho do projeto descobriram amplos efeitos coerentes, estatisticamente significativos, e das liberdades civis, nas taxas de retorno do projeto. Dependendo da medida das liberdades civis utilizadas, se um país fosse aperfeiçoar suas liberdades civis a partir do pior para o melhor, a taxa de retorno econômico dos projetos poderia aumentar até 22,5 pontos percentuais (Tabela 6.2). Porque os índices de liberdade civil utilizam-se de diferentes escalas, um método mais padronizado de comparação serve para calcular quanto a taxa de retorno econômico aumentaria se cada índice categórico fosse melhorado por um desvio-padrão. Como pode ser constatado na última coluna da Tabela 6.2, isto ainda dá resultados significativos, sugerindo um impacto da voz do cidadão no desempenho do governo. Não obstante, o relatório *Assessing Aid* (World Bank, 1998a) descobriu que tanto as liberdades civis como a democracia eleitoral têm efeitos benéficos no desempenho governamental, com a probabilidade de que o principal canal de influência seja a disponibilidade das liberdades civis.

No Rajastão, na Índia, uma organização popular denominada Mazdoor Kisan Shakti Sanghathan elaborou uma auditoria pública onde se expunha a apropriação indébita pelos governos locais dos fundos de desenvolvimento dirigidos aos trabalhadores locais. Isto gerou a demanda da cidade para posteriores investigações no âmbito do governo. Os governos locais, estando

GOVERNO E ANTICORRUPÇÃO

Tabela 6.2 – Impacto das Liberdades Civis Sobre o Projeto de Taxas de Retorno Socioeconômicas

Variável de liberdades civis	Especificação em variáveis independentes				Efeitos da taxa econômica de retorno sobre um aumento de desvio-padrão nas liberdades civis
	Apenas com controle de variáveis endógenas	Com simulações regionais	Com variáveis de políticas	Com variáveis de simulações regionais e políticas	
Freedom House Liberdades Civis (1978-87) (N=649)	1,81 (0,0005)	1,16 (0,079)	1,71 (0,002)	1,07 (0,114)	1,57
Humanas (1982-85) (N = 236)	0,290 (0,003)	0,299 (0,007)	0,296 (0,002)	0,289 (0,013)	5,19
Pluralismo de mídia (1983-87) (N = 448)	4,61 (0,0001)	4,45 (0,002)	3,66 (0,001)	3,43 (0,026)	3,12
Liberdade para organizar (1983-1987) (N = 448)	3,17 (0,0001)	1,81 (0,184)	2,41 (0,006)	-0,26 (0,854)	2,70

N = número de observações.

Nota: O erro-padrão está entre parênteses. A taxa média de retorno econômico nos projetos está na amplitude de 12%-16%.

Fonte: Isham et al. (1997).

sob a inquirição pública e da imprensa, foram obrigados a condescender. O governo do Rajastão reconheceu o direito popular de acesso aos documentos oficiais e decretou a legislação de demarcação de terra (Bhatia & Dréze, 1998) (ver Quadro 6.3).

Grupos governamentais e cidadãos podem fazer que sua voz venha à tona mediante estudos e dados coletados em modos mais sistemáticos. Os estudos dos clientes podem lançar luzes nas experiências dos cidadãos com os serviços do governo e identificar sugestões para melhoria do desempenho. Os estudos subseqüentes podem ser usados para garantir a responsabilidade e assegurar que as melhorias estão sendo feitas na direção desejada.

Gerar dados e disseminá-los amplamente são ações poderosas para mobilizar a sociedade civil e fazer pressão nas estruturas políticas. Por exemplo, os mapas comparativos simples, exemplificando as descobertas de corrupção, podem ajudar a mobilizar e dar voz a grupos de cidadãos anteriormente silenciosos e desiguais.

Rumo a um Contrato Social: Facilitar a Supervisão e a Participação da Sociedade Civil

A supervisão e a participação da sociedade civil sobre a tomada de decisão e o funcionamento do setor público foi um contrapeso e um instru-

Quadro 6.3 – Milhões de "Auditores" Fazem Valer a Transparência e o Governo nos Cálculos Orçamentários e Além

A transparência significa habilitar a cidadania a tornar-se milhões de auditores na sociedade, propiciando voz e acesso a uma imprensa livre. Isto capacita o fluxo das informações econômicas sociais e políticas adequadas e confiáveis sobre o uso que os investidores privados fazem dos empréstimos e a credibilidade dos tomadores de empréstimo, a provisão dos serviços de governo, políticas monetária e fiscal, e as atividades de instituições internacionais. Por contraste, falta de transparência significa que alguém, tal como um ministro do governo, instituição política, corporação ou banco, está deliberadamente impedindo o acesso ou deturpando as informações.

Em geral, falta de transparência aumenta o escopo para a corrupção por meio da criação de assimetrias informais, entre as entidades reguladas e as reguladoras.

A corrupção afeta todas as principais áreas da administração pública, arrecadação de renda como um meio de aumentar os fundos públicos e alocações de receitas públicas como uma forma de prover os bens públicos. Isto afeta a regulamentação pública como meios de diminuição das falhas de informação nos mercados, particularmente nos mercados de capital. Pesquisa empírica recente dos episódios de crise financeira indica que a probabilidade de tais crises foi significativamente mais ampla onde não havia transparência. Os diagnósticos governamentais em profundidade das repartições públicas discutidas anteriormente dentro de um país também sugerem que os departamentos com fluxos transparentes de informação tendem a mostrar uma corrupção mais baixa e melhor governo e desempenho gerais.

---

mento para combater a corrupção e melhorar o governo. Isso implica tornar o governo transparente para o público e habilitar a cidadania para desempenhar um papel ativo. Enquanto poucos países da OECD estiveram à frente das reformas de transparência, em muitas das economias de transição e emergentes o setor público da cultura é ainda um dos sigilos das tomadas de decisão. Freqüentemente, os votos parlamentares não são divulgados publicamente, o acesso público à informação governamental não é garantido e as decisões judiciais não estão normalmente disponíveis para o povo. Ademais, apesar de uma sociedade civil crescente, o governo caracteristicamente não envolve as ONGs na monitoração dos processos decisórios ou desempenhos. A posse da mídia concentrada e recentes restrições no relato fragilizaram a capacidade da mídia para garantir a responsabilidade do setor público.

Em conseqüência, mudar a cultura para uma cultura de transparência envolve uma mudança fundamental no modo como são tomadas as decisões no setor público. Os tipos de reformas transparentes que demonstraram internacionalmente ser efetivas incluem:

- garantir o acesso público a informações governamentais (liberdade de informação);
- requerer que certos tipos de reuniões governamentais sejam abertos à observação pública;
- conduzir auditorias públicas e *referenda* em esboços, decretos, regulamentações e leis;
- publicar as decisões judiciais legislativas e manter um registro;

- assegurar a liberdade de imprensa, proibindo a censura, desencorajando a utilização, pelos funcionários públicos, de leis de calúnia e difamação, para intimidar os jornalistas e encorajar a diversidade da posse da mídia;
- envolver a sociedade civil para monitorar seu desempenho em áreas tais como anticorrupção e ordem de licitações públicas em larga escala;
- utilizar os novos instrumentos baseados na Internet para transparência, divulgação, participação pública e disseminação.

O papel da sociedade civil deveria ser tanto dinâmico quanto fornecedor de uma oportunidade para os líderes políticos tentarem construir a credibilidade na instância estatal; novas atividades em muitos países para os quais o Banco Mundial fornece assistência envolvem a sustentação da equipe de trabalho coletiva da sociedade civil, a mídia, especialistas, o setor privado e os reformadores no Executivo e Legislativo nos programas de reforma de governo e anticorrupção. O processo de envolvimento pelos investidores-chave na sociedade civil cria um momento rumo à posse e sustentabilidade das reformas e constrói a credibilidade, como está ocorrendo em alguns países da Europa oriental, da África e da América Latina, por exemplo.

Conclusões

O governo deve ser entendido num contexto mais amplo do que simplesmente equilibrar a corrupção, o que é um sintoma-chave de uma das fragilidades institucionais mais fundamentais. Tanto governo quanto corrupção precisam ser rigorosamente desvelados e entendidos de modo analítico e empírico. O mau governo distorce a tomada de decisões políticas, a feitura de políticas e a alocação dos fatores de produção, que, por sua vez, retarda o crescimento de renda e bem-estar e aumenta a pobreza. As muitas capacidades fracassadas de abordagens de construção no passado não deram atenção suficiente para alimentar o bom governo, controlar a corrupção, melhorar a burocracia e o serviço civil, promover as liberdades civis e abordagens participativas, entender as origens e as conseqüências da captação do Estado, ou o conhecimento posterior sobre a economia política do edifício institucional. O governo precisa dar entrada ao estágio central da capacidade de construir estratégias de mudanças institucionais. A compreensão dos capitais particulares investidos por diferentes grupos de influência é necessária – incluindo o setor corporativo (tanto doméstico quanto FDI) –, como é o reconhecimento de que os incentivos, a prevenção e os desafios de mudança sistemática no âmbito das instituições afetam de modo vital o governo e são pelo menos tão importantes quanto os aspectos tradicionais da aplicação da lei.

O governo, a voz e a participação serão chaves fundamentais para uma abordagem melhorada à assistência técnica e capacidade de construção no futuro. Melhorar o governo deveria ser visto como um processo que integra três componentes vitais: conhecimento, com dados rigorosos e análises empíricas, inclusive diagnósticos de governo dentro do país e disseminação transparente, utilizando os instrumentos tecnológicos de informação de ponta; liderança na sociedade civil e política e na arena internacional; e ação coletiva por meio de consenso participativo e sistêmico, construindo abordagens com os investidores-chave na sociedade (para os quais a revolução tecnológica também está ajudando). A responsabilidade coletiva também implica que as corporações internacionais, o setor privado nacional e as agências internacionais precisam colaborar com os governos nacionais e liderar as tentativas de melhoria do governo.

A evidência aponta para a necessidade de uma abordagem mais abrangente e integrada para propiciar o clima para o desenvolvimento bem-sucedido. Instituições econômicas e medidas políticas, tais como o orçamento e a natureza dos programas de investimentos públicos, são importantes, assim como as liberdades civis e a participação, com as quais interagem. Isto calça a disputa para uma abordagem mais holística ao desenvolvimento que liga variáveis econômicas, institucionais legais e participativas.

A participação e a voz são vitais no crescimento da transparência, fornecendo as verificações e contrapesos necessários, e melhorando a captação do Estado pelos capitais investidos da elite. Não é o suficiente manter as políticas de economia básica só no papel; as forças da economia política em ação também devem ser reconhecidas. Essas forças irão variar de um país para outro. Em alguns países, equilibrar a reforma legal, reguladora e de licitação será fundamental para melhorar o governo e controlar a corrupção. Em outros, onde a captação do Estado é feita pela elite corporativa e quando há uma frágil vontade política para a reforma, a supervisão da sociedade civil, a competição empresarial e trabalhar para melhorar a proteção do direito de propriedade poderiam ser a chave.

Para um foco acentuado na diminuição da pobreza, uma abordagem acordada, que integra uma compreensão empírica rigorosa dos desafios do governo dentro de um país, encoraja o envolvimento ativo de todos os investidores-chave, talhado nas próprias realidades do país e defendido pela liderança local, provavelmente dará bons frutos.

Notas

1. Pletora dos indicadores que aferem os vários aspectos do governo são ordinais; ou seja, possuem um elemento qualitativo ou subjetivo. Contudo, os dados são importantes. Em primeiro lugar, para alguns aspectos do governo, estes são os únicos tipos de dados disponíveis (e é agora possível desligar o "ruído" do "sinal"). Quase por definição, os dados

pesados (numéricos cardinais) têm sido até aqui virtualmente impossíveis de se obter num formato sistemático e, para aquelas poucas dimensões governamentais onde tais dados existem, são seguidos por uma larga margem de erro e/ou questões metodológicas. Em segundo lugar, para muitos aspectos do governo, os resultados dos estudos (mesmo que contenham um elemento de percepção) importam tanto quanto os dados oficiais. Por exemplo, se o setor de negócios de um país encara o sistema judiciário como uma arma do governo e evita se utilizar dos tribunais, vai pensar duas vezes sobre decisões de investimento. Ver Anexo 6 para maiores detalhes.

2. A assimetria das barras horizontais é explicada pelas diferenças na variável dentro de cada quartilho. Enquanto as diferenças nos países são pequenas nos dois primeiros quartilhos, são maiores no terceiro e no quarto.

3. A metodologia econométrica e sua aplicação empírica sugere que as variáveis governamentais afetam diferentes variáveis socioeconômicas, tais como mortalidade infantil, alfabetização e renda *per capita* de um modo causal. Contudo, tendo estabelecido que as variáveis governamentais conjuntamente importam significativamente para os resultados socioeconômicos, é preciso ter cuidado ao desembaraçar os impactos causais independentes sobre as variáveis desenvolvimentistas de cada único subcomponente do governo. Dada a existência de multicolinearidade entre os vários subcomponentes do governo, é possível que o impacto da voz observado sobre a mortalidade infantil, por exemplo, esteja sendo escolhido por procuração de outras determinantes governamentais, tais como a corrupção ou a regra de direito. Ver também o Anexo 6 para detalhes metodológicos.

4. Hellman et al. (consultar http://www.worldbank.org/wbi/governance).

5. Outros fatores no estudo empírico das causas da corrupção também aparecem como importantes. Como esperado, a renda *per capita* e a educação têm correlação com um nível de corrupção mais baixo quando os outros fatores são mantidos constantes. As variáveis gerais do desenvolvimento são freqüentemente procurações para determinantes mais específicas da corrupção, tais como a qualidade das instituições públicas ou a regra de direito (ver Ades & Di Tella (1999) para uma revisão útil).

6. Muito deste capítulo deve-se ao trabalho colaborativo com Sanjay Pradhan, Randi, Ryterman e o Grupo do Setor Público. Ver também World Bank (2000h).

7. Grande parte deste capítulo é devida ao Gerenciamento de Gastos Públicos, no trabalho de Allistair Moon, Sanjay Pradhan e Gary Reid.

8. Em 1998 o chefe do governo, os membros do gabinete e as centenas de investidores da sociedade civil participaram da oficina sobre o governo nacional da Albânia, que ocorreu simultaneamente às semifinais do Campeonato Mundial de Futebol na França. A oficina caracterizou os principais achados dos diagnósticos em profundidade e um debate sobre as prioridades para a ação. Concluiu-se com um compromisso pela liderança com um programa pró-governo. Exemplificando a importância atribuída ao evento pela nação, no dia seguinte as primeiras páginas de todos os jornais de Tirana publicaram como manchete os resultados do diagnóstico do governo, enquanto os resultados da Copa de Futebol foram relegados a páginas secundárias. A Albânia está levando a efeito um programa anticorrupção, que inclui a reforma judicial e alfandegária, com sustentação do Banco Mundial.

CAPÍTULO 7

AGARRAR AS OPORTUNIDADES DE MUDANÇA

Devemos usar o tempo de modo criativo e compreender de uma vez que ele está sempre maduro para se fazer o correto.

— Nelson Mandela, *Higher Than Hope: The Authorized Biography of Nelson Mandela*

Este livro revisitou as experiências de desenvolvimento das décadas recentes, com um foco na década de 1990. A última década do século XX conheceu um progresso impressionante em algumas partes do mundo, mas também estagnação e reveses, mesmo em países que haviam desfrutado um crescimento rápido. Enquanto a prosperidade se espalhava e a qualidade de vida melhorava para muitos dentro da sociedade, estimava-se que a pobreza tinha persistido com muita teimosia, e piorado para alguns. As pressões maiores da população, pouco acesso à educação e a degradação dos recursos naturais tornaram os pobres cada vez mais vulneráveis à volatilidade do crescimento.

Entre 2000 e 2010, a população das economias desenvolvidas (incluindo as em transição) é projetada para um crescimento de cinco a seis bilhões de pessoas. Se os países seguissem um cenário de negócios como de hábito, o número de pessoas no mundo em desenvolvimento (excluindo a China) vivendo abaixo da linha de pobreza poderia aumentar para cerca de 130 milhões. Este livro indica modos para melhorar resultados futuros.

A Estrutura e os Temas

Os bens de capital humano, natural e físico são os principais recursos de um país para o crescimento e as melhorias do bem-estar. Sua distribuição, crescimento e produtividade determinam amplamente a renda do povo e seu bem-estar. Os pobres baseiam-se nos capitais natural e humano, além do capital físico, de modo que o acúmulo e a produtividade destes bens têm um impacto forte sobre a pobreza. Estudos mostram que "os pobres raramente falam de renda, mas centralizam-se, ao contrário, na manipulação do bens – físico, humano, social e ambiental – como um modo de lidar com sua vulnerabilidade" (Narayan et al., 2000).

O crescimento baseado no acúmulo relativamente correto (ou equilibrado) é provavelmente menos volátil e sustentado a longo prazo. Este tema é respeitado pela evidência do país no Capítulo 2. Em primeiro lugar, uma comparação dos reformadores e não reformadores mostrou que as reformas ajudaram a acelerar o crescimento na década de 1990; contudo, este crescimento (em muitas instâncias) foi baseado num agudo aumento no acúmulo de capital físico, enquanto os investimentos nos capitais humano e natural foram deixados para trás. Em segundo lugar, uma análise econométrica de vinte países com maioria de renda média mostrou que a taxa do crescimento econômico declina, enquanto o estoque de capital físico aumenta para os dados níveis dos capitais humano e natural, mas o acúmulo dos bens de capital humano, pelo acesso crescente à educação e à saúde, pode interromper este declínio. Em terceiro lugar, uma análise econométrica de setenta países em desenvolvimento confirmou as descobertas anteriores sobre o acúmulo de capital e mostrou que, quando o capital natural também é levado em consideração como um fator de produção, o capital humano pode ser substituído pelo capital natural em alguma extensão e reduzir a dependência dele como uma fonte de crescimento.

Melhorar a Distribuição das Oportunidades

Para que o crescimento reduzisse de modo efetivo a pobreza, os bens dos pobres precisariam ser aumentados. Seu principal bem é o capital humano. Assim, a desigualdade na educação está desequilibrada. Se as capacidades forem distribuídas de modo normal pela população – sem se importar se as pessoas são ricas ou pobres –, a desigualdade de acesso à educação básica e ao trabalho representaria uma das maiores perdas de bem-estar para a sociedade. Quando a qualidade da escolaridade é baixa e a desigualdade na escolaridade é alta, os pobres são, em sua maioria, atingidos pela educação inadequada. O subinvestimento no capital humano dos pobres pode ser atribuído a brechas de gênero, falta de riqueza, falência de mercado e distorções políticas.

Ademais, muitos países não têm focalizado de modo adequado o investimento público na educação básica. Realocar em direção da educação básica é fundamental para melhorar a eficácia dos gastos públicos. A educação em todos os níveis, inclusive o superior, precisa beneficiar-se dos investimentos privados e das parcerias público/privadas. Tomadas de decisão descentralizadas e escolas gerenciadas pela comunidade encarnam a grande promessa para a melhoria dos resultados da educação. Contudo, para tornar a educação mais produtiva para os pobres, eles precisam ser habilitados com terra, eqüidades de treinamento de capital e oportunidades de trabalho e mercados abertos e competitivos (Capítulo 3).

Sustentar o Capital Natural

Diversos indicadores da qualidade do capital natural, com a notável exceção do acesso à água de qualidade e saneamento, tenderam a deteriorar tanto nas economias de crescimento lento quanto nas de crescimento rápido. Para o mundo em desenvolvimento como um todo, o esgotamento do capital natural (florestas, energia e minerais) e os danos provocados pelas emissões de dióxido de carbono são estimados em 5% do PIB. Essa deterioração do capital natural impõe custos atuais significativos e diminui as perspectivas para um crescimento futuro. O crescimento mais rápido possui o potencial de deixar disponíveis os recursos a serem investidos no acúmulo de capital natural, mas é preciso que haja ações para garantir a qualidade do processo de crescimento. Logo, a abordagem da ideologia do "cresça agora e limpe depois" precisa ser substituída por uma política ambiental integrada às políticas de crescimento.

Este livro documenta com sucesso as iniciativas que incorporaram as ações de modo simultâneo, para estimular o crescimento e proteger o capital natural. Essas medidas envolvem, freqüentemente, intervenções estatais seletivas e o setor privado. Os problemas globais e nacionais podem ser levantados simultaneamente mediante a cooperação internacional, incluindo mecanismos de transferência para pagamentos destinados a compensar as externalidades globais. Como conseqüência, a busca do crescimento de alta qualidade é possível e desejável, sem uma degradação extensiva da atmosfera, das florestas e dos rios, ou quaisquer outros aspectos do capital natural (Capítulo 4).

Tratar com os Riscos Financeiros Globais

A integração com o sistema financeiro global tem trazido, inegavelmente, benefícios tecnológicos e econômicos para os países, mas isso também os expõe a choques e à grande volatilidade dos valores atuais da moeda,

das taxas de juros e dos fluxos de capitais. Os choques podem realizar importantes saídas e perdas de emprego, desastres bancários e corporativos e aumento da pobreza. Logo, os países precisam de mecanismos adequados para equilibrar os benefícios da globalização com seus riscos. Precisam reduzir os riscos do pânico e as crises, mantendo, ao mesmo tempo, seus compromissos com a abertura do mercado.

Um ambiente político macroeconômico sólido é essencial para o crescimento sustentado, mas experiências recentes mostram que a estabilidade macroeconômica não pode fazer isso sozinha. Deve ser complementada com ações para remover as garantias governamentais explícitas ou implícitas que forneçam incentivos para as afluências de capital, para fortalecer a regulação nacional e a supervisão dos bancos e de outros intermediários, para reconstruir a infra-estrutura informativa dos mercados financeiros e melhorar o governo corporativo e a transparência. Os países devem, igualmente, manter a sustentação pública para os mercados abertos de capitais. Nos países democráticos, isso acarreta fornecimento de segurança para os cidadãos – tanto por meio do mercado quanto dos gastos públicos redistributivos na educação, na saúde e transferências de pagamentos (Capítulo 5).

Melhorar o Governo e Combater a Corrupção

O governo tem o papel principal na distribuição dos bens públicos essenciais para realizar um crescimento equilibrado e sustentado e para reduzir a pobreza. Também precisa ter regimes reguladores eficazes e aperfeiçoados, para corrigir externalidades e falência no mercado. O mau governo e a corrupção distorcem a feitura da política e a alocação de fatores-chave de produção, conseqüências que alentam a renda e o crescimento do bemestar e aumentam a pobreza. Muitos projetos e investimentos em desenvolvimento falharam porque deram pouca atenção à alimentação do bom governo e das liberdades civis, controlando a corrupção, melhorando a burocracia e erigindo uma capacidade institucional.

A participação pelos beneficiários, a atenção às vozes do povo e das empresas competitivas e a responsabilidade e transparência nos governos são vitais para o controle da corrupção e melhoria do governo. Novas abordagens para o edifício da coalizão e a integração dos métodos de ponta de governo e os estudos da corrupção com novas tecnologias para análise adequada e a disseminação estão produzindo resultados encorajadores em alguns países. A ação coletiva originada desta edificação do processo participativo de um consenso, acoplada com o poder da informação, divulgação, transparência e edificação do conhecimento e da capacidade podem nutrir a vontade política e a capacidade técnica para equilibrar o mau governo e sustentar a edificação das instituições (Capítulo 6).

Ações para Garantir a Qualidade

Os temas emergentes ajudam a esclarecer quatro dimensões que formam a qualidade do processo de crescimento: distribuição de oportunidades, sustentabilidade do meio ambiente, o gerenciamento dos riscos globais e o governo (Quadro 7.1). Estes elementos contribuem diretamente para o desenvolvimento. Têm um relacionamento de mão dupla com o crescimento, juntam-se ao impacto do crescimento sobre o bem-estar, ajudam a tornar o crescimento mais sustentado e equilibram os conflitos que o crescimento poderia colocar para a sustentabilidade.

Este livro fornece evidências de um espectro de áreas e fontes que mostram que um foco centrado na quantidade não irá, por si só, garantir a qualidade. De modo que os níveis de gastos públicos não podem oferecer uma indicação adequada do impacto. Em um estudo da WHO, que classifica 191 países quanto à qualidade (incluindo eqüidade e ampla cobertura) de seus sistemas de saúde, os Estados Unidos são o 1° em gastos de saúde *per capita*, mas são o 37° no desempenho dos sistemas de saúde geral. A França

---

Quadro 7.1 – Ações para a Qualidade

Quais poderiam ser as implicações políticas para garantir a qualidade do crescimento? Este livro apresentou várias, que podem ser organizadas sob três princípios.

Políticas para um crescimento não distorcido dos capitais físico, humano e natural

- Evitar subsídios diretos ou indiretos para o capital, tais como isenção de impostos, colocação de poderes monopolistas e nos subsídios, privilégios especiais que alimentam a corrupção e garantias implícitas nas taxas de retorno.
- Investir de modo eficaz no capital humano e garantir o acesso aos pobres por meio de incentivos e da alocação de investimentos públicos na educação.
- Sustentar o capital natural esclarecendo os direitos de propriedade, evitando níveis baixos enganosos de *royalties* para os recursos naturais e a aplicação de impostos ambientais.

Atenção para com os aspectos de estabilidade e distributivos do crescimento

- Assegurar que os pobres possam ter acesso à educação, à tecnologia e a serviços de saúde, assim como à terra, ao crédito, ao treinamento para habilidades, e a oportunidades de trabalho nos mercados abertos.
- Garantir estruturas reguladoras eficazes e medidas anticorrupção para acompanhar a abertura financeira e a privatização.
- Alinhar reformas e a reestruturação para mecanismos de diminuição dos custos das crises, que provavelmente serão sofridos de maneira desproporcional pelos pobres.

Construir a estrutura governamental para o desenvolvimento

- Envolver todos os investidores – o setor privado, inclusive, as empresas transnacionais e o setor nacional privado, ONGs, a sociedade civil e o governo – na implementação de uma agenda de desenvolvimento compartilhada por todos.
- Habilitar as pessoas por meio da voz, participação e liberdades civis e políticas maiores.
- Sustentar a liberação econômica por meio da promoção do desenvolvimento institucional e de melhor governo.

– 4º em gasto *per capita* – é o 1º em desempenho; a Colômbia é o 22º; o Chile, 33º; Costa Rica, 36º; e Cuba, 39º (WHO, 2000).

Este livro mostra, igualmente, os efeitos das falhas do mercado. Sobre a habilidade dos pobres para construir o capital humano. Sobre a subavaliação e subseqüente superexploração do capital humano. E sobre a indevida instabilidade dos mercados financeiros. Um foco sobre a qualidade sublinha o papel das políticas reguladoras e dos gastos públicos ao lidar com estas falhas de mercado.

A resposta não deve necessariamente aumentar o ônus regulador da economia ou os gastos públicos. Em vez disso, deve realocar os gastos públicos de acordo com novas prioridades e mudar a natureza da regulação – eliminando regulamentações que são contraprodutivas e melhorar aquelas para corrigir as falhas de mercado. Quais deveriam ser as novas prioridades dos gastos públicos? Fazer mais para promover a edificação do capital humano, especialmente entre os pobres. Investir mais para prevenir a degradação posterior do capital natural e reduzir os subsídios regressivos que beneficiem o capital físico. Visar às regulamentações das falhas nos mercados financeiros e nos mercados que afetam a utilização dos recursos ambientais.

Onde as Políticas para Qualidade Funcionam – Ou Não?

Não há nenhum cenário onde os atributos da qualidade foram enfatizados com sucesso uniforme. Contudo, as experiências dos quatro países que se seguem ilustram a busca dos aspectos qualitativos do crescimento, com graus de eficácia variáveis.

Investir com Eficiência na Educação Básica: A República da Coréia

Começando com uma economia de guerra dilacerada e uma base pobre em recursos naturais, a Coréia teve uma média anual de PIB *per capita* de mais de US$ 500, baseado em PPP dólares de 1980, no fim da década de 1950. Então, o PIB *per capita* dobrou em cada uma das três décadas seguintes, dirigido por um crescimento de base ampliada, orientada pela exportação. O crescimento foi acompanhado por uma rápida redução da pobreza e uma distribuição de renda relativamente eqüitativa (Leipziger, 1997).

A Coréia gastou uma média de 3,4% do PNB na educação pública na década de 1980, que estava alinhada com a média regional. Contudo, diferentemente dos outros países em desenvolvimento, a Coréia gastou dois

terços de seu orçamento educacional em educação básica compulsória na década de 1960 e no início da de 1970. Na década de 1990, os subsídios públicos para estudantes da escola primária eram duas ou três vezes aquele para os estudantes universitários. A educação superior era financiada principalmente por gastos privados. A Coréia estava apta para expandir rapidamente a educação básica e reduzir a desigualdade educacional, ou, segundo a medida do coeficiente Gini para a educação, de 0,55 em 1960 para 0,22 em 1990.

O governo coreano sustentou indústrias favorecidas por empréstimos diretos, subsídios e garantias. Em ambientes liberalizados mas inadequadamente regulados, estas medidas levaram a tomadas de empréstimo estrangeiro e investimentos perdulários pelo setor corporativo e a uma fragilidade financeira intensificada. Tanto as lições positivas como as caucionárias podem ser esboçadas a partir da experiência coreana.

Crescimento de Base Ampla Dentro de uma Agenda Incompleta: Kerala, Índia

Sobre tais dimensões do desenvolvimento social como educação, saúde, lacuna de gênero, liberdades civis e políticas, redução da pobreza e desigualdade, o desempenho do desenvolvimento de Kerala, na Índia, é comparável àquele de muitas economias mais ricas. Uma criança nascida em Kerala pode esperar viver mais do que uma nascida em Washington, D.C. Contudo, o crescimento econômico medido de Kerala tem sido, até recentemente, mais baixo do que a média entre os estados indianos.

Kerala deu atenção aos aspectos qualitativos do desenvolvimento enquanto negligenciava os de primeira geração: políticas orientadas para o crescimento. Para um crescimento equilibrado dos bens, as políticas econômicas das boas condições de mercado precisam complementar as iniciativas sociais. A falta de progresso ao implementar um ambiente aberto e competitivo para as atividades econômicas atrapalhou o crescimento econômico em Kerala. Uma vez que foram implementadas estas reformas políticas de primeira geração, o alto nível de desenvolvimento social deveria oferecer uma base para o crescimento sustentado de alta qualidade.

Ravallion & Datt (1999) descobriram que o impacto do crescimento na redução da pobreza varia com a alfabetização inicial, a produtividade agrícola e o padrão de vida nas áreas rurais, relativos àqueles nas áreas urbanas. Nos estados com taxas altas de alfabetização e educação básica distribuída eqüitativamente, cada ponto percentual adicional de crescimento tem um forte impacto sobre a redução da pobreza, maior do que em outros estados. A elasticidade da redução da pobreza para o crescimento não agrícola em Kerala foi a mais alta de todos os estados na Índia. Se todos os estados indianos tivessem a elasticidade da redução da pobreza de Kerala, a parcela de seu povo na pobreza teria caído quase três vezes mais rápido – a 3,5% ao ano, e não 1,3%.

Equilibrar o Crescimento Econômico
e o Capital Natural Sustentado: Costa Rica

A Costa Rica tem uma taxa de alfabetização alta, estabilidade política e econômica, e nenhum orçamento militar. A distribuição de renda pelos indicadores sociais está entre os melhores na América Latina. Contudo, ainda assim, o país precisava corrigir vários problemas ambientais, desde poluição urbana, utilização excessiva de agroquímicos e superexploração dos pescados, para a perda de biodiversidade e uma taxa de desmatamento que na década de 1980 era estimada em 3% ao ano.

A Costa Rica reagiu com um sistema inovador e abrangente de proteção florestal. Um sistema de compensação por meio dos mercados para o confisco do carbono, a preservação das bacias hidrográficas e a proteção da biodiversidade ajudou a proteger as florestas. O sistema gera seus próprios recursos mediante um imposto sobre combustíveis aplicado aos consumidores domésticos, contratos com as empresas de energia hídrica e pagamentos pelos partidos internacionais para os deslocamentos das emissões de gás carbônico.

O Ministério do Meio Ambiente e Energia sustentou as reformas políticas baseadas em pesquisas para programas de proteção e educação ambientais para escolares. As avaliações do impacto ambiental são imperativas para a maioria dos projetos, inclusive construção comercial e residencial e mineração. A lei estabelece diretrizes estritas sobre a proteção dos recursos hídricos, pântanos, monumentos naturais, áreas naturais protegidas e recursos costeiros e marinhos. Ela estabelece, igualmente, diretrizes para todos os tipos de poluição e abuso da terra e remoção imprópria do lixo. Atualmente, o plano é aumentar a eficácia das leis, fortalecer a capacidade das instituições responsáveis pela aplicação e entrar em parceria com os setores civil e privado da sociedade (Thomas, 1998).

Abertura Equilibrada, Gerenciamento
do Risco e Proteção Social: Chile

Depois de uma década de rápida abertura dos mercados e um crescimento volátil na década de 1980, o país tomou medidas para o gerenciamento do risco na década de 1990. Em primeiro lugar, o Chile implementou um sistema altamente dirigido de assistência social, mediante programas de saúde, educação, habitação e divisão de rendas. Os investimentos sociais do governo aumentaram perto de 75% entre 1987 e 1994, que, complementando um crescimento econômico robusto, deram contribuições sólidas para a redução da pobreza. Em segundo lugar, como os fluxos de capital tornaram-se mais voláteis, o Banco Central independente implementou controles de capital seletivo sobre afluências de capital de curto

prazo entre 1991 e 1998. De modo discutível, eles ajudaram a aumentar a fatia entre taxas de investimento nacional e estrangeiro e a mudar a composição das afluências de capital em direção a vencimentos mais longos (Gallego et al., 1999).

Estas e outras políticas contribuíram para o rápido crescimento econômico, com um declínio significativo na pobreza. A incidência da pobreza caiu de 41% da população em 1987 para 23% em 1994, enquanto a incidência de pobreza aguda (baseada sobre uma linha de pobreza/indigência mais baixa) caiu de 13% para 5%. A desigualdade de renda parece ter se estabilizado desde 1987, depois de subir durante a maior parte do período de 1960-1985 (Ferrera & Litchfield, 1999). Além disso, os recursos naturais foram subprotegidos e superexplorados. A distribuição da educação tornou-se menos eqüitativa, como refletido por uma brecha crescente nos anos de escolaridade entre ricos e pobres (World Bank, 1997b).

Economia Política de Quantidade *versus* Qualidade

As variadas experiências das economias sugerem que uma ênfase na qualidade é essencial em três pontos. Em primeiro lugar, qualidade promove diretamente o bem-estar ao influenciar uma distribuição mais uniforme da educação e dos cuidados de saúde e uma melhoria ambiental. Crescimento e aspectos qualitativos – ligados um ao outro numa relação de mão dupla – necessitam de atenção conjunta.

Em segundo lugar, o andamento do crescimento é menos volátil e mais sustentável quando os aspectos qualitativos são levados em consideração. Onde as taxas de crescimento são altamente variáveis ao longo do tempo, os impactos negativos são especialmente pronunciados para os pobres.

Em terceiro lugar, as economias que se focam na qualidade podem lidar melhor com acordos difíceis. Um acordo mencionado neste livro é a tentação de subsidiar o capital físico ou superexplorar o capital natural em um esforço para promover o crescimento. Neste caso e em casos similares, o foco nos aspectos qualitativos do crescimento ajuda a gerenciar os acordos.

A maioria dos países – e muito aconselhamento político – sublinhou a estabilização e a liberalização macroeconômica em primeiro lugar. Nesse ínterim, as ações sobre os aspectos qualitativos, tais como a distribuição da educação e a utilização sustentável do capital natural, são adiadas. A evidência aqui apresentada mostra as limitações fundamentais desta abordagem e os benefícios da ação conjunta.

De vez em quando, os reformadores acharam isso necessário para tirar vantagem de janelas de oportunidades para liberalização, quando o capital investido e a oposição à liberalização foram silenciados. Se as dimensões qualitativas também recebem prioridade, podem depender de outras con-

dições, inclusive da expansão das instituições democráticas. Num cenário cada vez mais crescente e participativo, um país não deveria querer adiar os aspectos qualitativos importantes do crescimento para um tempo em que os custos para corrigi-los terão se multiplicado.

Algumas vezes as dificuldades políticas podem impedir o progresso, mesmo quando a importância dos aspectos qualitativos é clara. Os grupos de interesse podem dirigir um calço entre o esboço político e sua implementação. Um conluio entre os políticos e a elite pode distorcer a dotação de recursos públicos para recompensar os donos do capital físico. Por exemplo, as isenções de impostos, garantias implícitas de infra-estrutura, poderes monopolistas e fácil acesso aos recursos naturais freqüentemente beneficiam os ricos, mas atingem os pobres.

A economia política das reformas, menos explorada que outros aspectos do crescimento, é uma área difícil de ser avaliada – ainda que algumas iniciativas pareçam ser indiscutivelmente dignas de valor. Alimentar a participação do beneficiário, encorajando o domínio dos programas de reformas, e promover a representação política dos pobres é um bom começo.

Seguir em Frente

Como podem os países atribuir maior prioridade às dimensões qualitativas do crescimento? E como podem financiar e sustentar tais objetivos na prática? Várias observações esboçadas a partir da discussão neste livro podem conduzir os esforços neste sentido:

- Uma atenção explícita para assegurar a transparência e reduzir a corrupção e o desvio de verba não irá apenas aumentar a poupança nacional e o investimento e promover um crescimento sustentado, mas também ajudará a distribuir seus frutos de maneira mais eqüitativa.
- Algumas dimensões qualitativas prestam-se à taxação ou avaliação do custo total, ambos gerando recursos públicos.
- Outras medidas para garantir a qualidade requerem a realocação dos gastos públicos – redução de subsídios e distorções em algumas áreas e o aumento do investimento público em outras.
- Dar atenção à qualidade não significa mais intervenção governamental, mas, antes, pode significar maior envolvimento do setor privado, das organizações não governamentais e da sociedade civil na implementação de metas compartilhadas.
- Um alcance civil mais amplo pode nutrir as liberdades civis e os processos participativos, que, por sua vez, podem ajudar a sustentar as mudanças políticas.
- Tudo isso, no entanto, requereria um foco muito maior sobre as

habilidades e o desenvolvimento tecnológico e a capacidade de construir, assim como a eficácia com a qual isto é feito.

A evidência neste livro fornece uma forte motivação para centralizar o
foco nos aspectos qualitativos, marcando a habilidade do povo para dar
forma às suas vidas – por exemplo, a igualdade de oportunidades para o
desenvolvimento humano, a sustentabilidade do meio ambiente, o gerenciamento do risco global e o modo de governar – juntamente com as facetas
tradicionais do crescimento. Os governos não têm e nem deveriam assumir
o ônus total, por dar maior prioridade às dimensões qualitativas.

Antes de requerer mais intervenção governamental, a evidência neste
livro requer maior amplitude de voz e participação do setor privado, ONGs
e sociedade civil. Um envolvimento mais amplo por meio do qual todos
podem mudar a ênfase do desenvolvimento, além do crescimento do PIB
medido para incluir o progresso social e ambiental, maior habilitação e voz,
e melhor governo. Esta realocação das prioridades irá aprimorar a contribuição dos aspectos qualitativos do processo de crescimento e focar o
holofote naquilo que o desenvolvimento verdadeiramente significa.

ANEXO 1

OBJETIVOS AMPLOS E OS INSTRUMENTOS

A valorização contínua do progresso desenvolvimentista e das políticas requer uma estrutura mais ampla que a habitual, mesmo que todos os elementos não sejam quantificáveis. Aqui, observamos as metas do desenvolvimento e os instrumentos políticos e formulamos algumas hipóteses sobre os elos entre eles. Um modelo formal e a discussão dos resultados empíricos encontram-se no Capítulo 2 e no Anexo 2.

O povo vale pelo menos em três dimensões da vida na atualidade, e nos tempos futuros. Ele recebe satisfação direta por meio da educação e de outros aspectos do capital humano, tais como expectativa de vida ou alfabetização; a partir da água e do ar não poluídos e outros estoques de capital natural; e por fluxos de consumo de bens, tais como comida e moradia. Ele também se preocupa com o bem-estar das gerações futuras e seu desfrute de todos os aspectos da vida (com alguma taxa de desconto). Uma sociedade tentará tirar o máximo dos capitais humano, natural e físico, sujeitos à coerção dos recursos totais. Juntos, os aumentos nestas dimensões significam crescimento qualitativo.

As associações simples entre as metas e as políticas, na forma de correlações e mapas espalhados, são aqui apresentados. O Anexo 2 apresenta uma análise econométrica que complementa uma ampla bibliografia nesta área.

Metas e Medidas Políticas

Construímos índices compósitos para o desenvolvimento humano e a sustentabilidade ambiental, capacitando-nos a que nos centralizemos nas três medidas de qualidade do crescimento, preferivelmente a um número amplo: desenvolvimento humano, crescimento econômico e sustentabilidade ambiental. Os instrumentos políticos incluem aqueles enfatizados no

World Development Repport (World Bank, 1991), juntamente com vários outros. As correlações entre políticas e metas são mostradas na Tabela A1.1. Estas correspondem às Figuras 1.2 e 1.5 no Capítulo 1. As associações entre as políticas e os indicadores componentes que formam os índices não são mostradas. Os esboços disseminados para as combinações escolhidas de metas políticas são mostrados na Figura A1.1, depois de controlar os efeitos do período inicial da renda.

As metas e as variáveis aproximadas utilizadas são:

- *Indicadores do desenvolvimento humano.* Construímos um índice de desenvolvimento humano com base nos dados de reduções na mor-

Tabela A1.1 – Relacionamentos Entre Objetivos do Desenvolvimento em Instrumentos Políticos, 1981-1998

	Metas								
	Desenvolvimento humano			Crescimento PIB			Desenvolvimento sustentável		
Instrumentos	Coeficiente de correlação	Nível de significância	Número de países	Coeficiente de correlação	Nível de significância	Número de países	Coeficiente de correlação	Nível de significância	Número de países
Gasto educacional/ PIB	0,04	0,72	87	-0,02	0,84	88	0,17	0,21	56
Gastos com saúde/ PIB (1990-98)	-0,01	0,95	70	*-0,28*	0,02	71	0,18	0,23	49
Excedente de orçamento	0,12	0,40	55	*0,27*	0,05	55	0,01	0,97	39
Razão comércio/ PIB	0,07	0,50	89	0,07	0,50	90	-0,05	0,69	56
Mudança na tarifa média	0,05	0,82	26	-0,09	0,65	26	-0,10	0,65	25
Índice de abertura do cálculo de capital (1988)	0,21	0,22	36	0,00	0,99	36	-0,22	0,23	31
Índice de repressão financeira (1996)	-0,16	0,50	21	0,26	0,26	21	-0,35	0,12	21
M2/PIB	*0,36*	0,00	89	*0,29*	0,01	90	-0,08	0,58	56
Ação ambiental (variável simulada)	-0,16	0,15	80	*0,24*	0,03	81	-0,10	0,47	56
Ação ambiental internacional (variável simulada)	0,11	0,35	80	0,08	0,49	81	*-0,24*	0,08	56
Índice regra do direito (1997-98)	*0,34*	0,00	86	*0,41*	0,00	87	0,18	0,19	55
Índice de eficácia do governo (1997-98)	*0,35*	0,00	81	*0,27*	0,00	82	0,05	0,73	55

Nota: A melhoria no desenvolvimento humano é definida com base no índice Borda da redução da mortalidade infantil, redução do analfabetismo e aumento na expectativa de vida entre as décadas de 1980 e 1990. A melhoria no desenvolvimento sustentável é definida com base no índice Borda das diminuições das emissões de dióxido de carbono, desmatamento e poluição da água entre as décadas de 1980 e 1990. As correlações significativas, pelo menos no nível de 10%, são mostradas em itálico bold.

Fontes: World Bank (2000c); cálculos dos autores.

Relacionamento entre objetivos e instrumentos

Figura A1.1 – Objetivos Desenvolvimentistas e Instrumentos Políticos

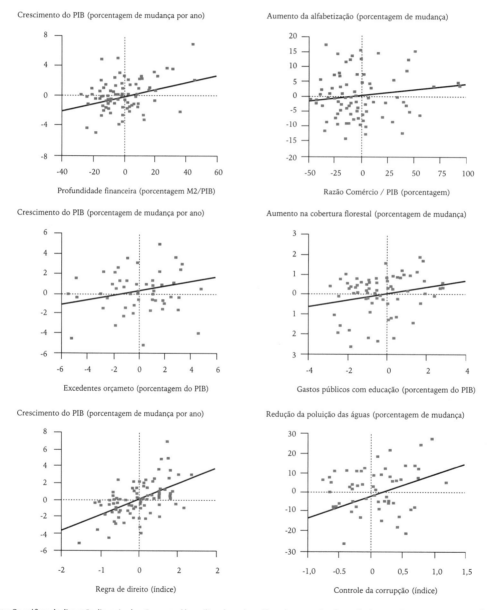

Nota: Os gráficos de dispersão disseminados são construídos utilizando-se de resíduos das regressões das variáveis respectivas – pertencente a ambos os eixos – contra o PIB *per capita* em 1981.
Fontes: World Bank (2000c); cálculo dos autores.

talidade infantil, reduções na taxa de analfabetismo e aumento de expectativa de vida. O período sobre o qual as mudanças foram computadas corresponde ao início da década de 1980 até o fim da década de 1990. Queríamos incorporar no índice variáveis refletindo a distribuição de renda, a redução na incidência da pobreza e a brecha de gênero na formação educacional, mas não o fizemos porque os dados não estavam disponíveis para muitos países.

- *Indicadores de desenvolvimento sustentável.* Construímos um índice compósito da taxa negativa anual de desmatamento, redução nas emissões de dióxido de carbono *per capita* e redução na poluição da água *per capita*. O período utilizado foi novamente a partir do início dos anos 80 para o fim dos anos 90. Queríamos incluir no índice uma medida de poluição do ar nas maiores cidades dos países em desenvolvimento, mas os dados comparativos só estavam disponíveis para os anos mais recentes.

- *Crescimento de renda.* Utilizamos taxas de crescimento PIB entre 1981 e 1998 e indicadores intermediários, como estoque e crescimento FTP, utilizados em muitos estudos empíricos, tais como aqueles empregados por Barro (1990), Easterly (1999a), Easterly et al. (1993), Nehru e Drareshwar (1993), Pritchett (1998), Banco Mundial (1991) e Young (1992).

Os instrumentos políticos foram representados pelos seguintes:

- *Gastos sociais com educação e saúde.* Eles foram expressos como porcentagens do PIB, com média calcada em valores disponíveis para o período: 1981-1997 para os gastos com educação, e 1990-1998 para os gastos com saúde. Em decorrência das limitações de dados, não pudemos incluir dotação de gastos na educação básica e nos serviços preventivos de saúde (Filmer et al., no prelo; López et al., 1998).

- *Compromisso ambiental.* Utilizamos duas variáveis de modelo, para representar o compromisso ambiental: uma para ação nacional baseada na formulação estratégica ambiental e perfilamento ambiental, e outros para a ação internacional, baseada na assinatura do Tratado Global sobre Mudança Climática. Desafortunadamente, indicadores mais completos de políticas de governo para o desenvolvimento sustentado ainda não estão disponíveis.

- *Política macroeconômica.* Utilizamos excedentes de orçamento como uma porcentagem do PIB (Barro, 1990; Fischer, 1993).

- *Abertura.* Utilizamos a razão de comércio para PIB, prêmio do mercado paralelo, mudança na principal tarifa e uma medida de controle de capital baseada em Quinn (1997) e Quinn & Toyoda (1997) (um valor mais alto do índice representa um grau maior de abertura para as afluências de capital; ver Anexo 5).

- *Profundidade financeira, prudência e gerenciamento do risco.* Utilizamos

profundidade financeira como medida pela razão de M2 para o PIB e um índice de repressão financeira (baseado em Williamson & Mahar, 1998; um valor mais baixo do índice representa um sistema financeiro mais liberal).

* *Indicadores de governo.* Seis indicadores de governo – regra do direito, eficácia governamental, controle da corrupção, voz e responsabilidade, ônus regulador e a instabilidade e violência políticas – foram examinados neste livro. Desta lista, os três primeiros foram utilizados neste Anexo. Para análise e detalhes posteriores, ver o Capítulo 6 e o Anexo 6.

Índices Compósitos do Desenvolvimento Humano e do Desenvolvimento Sustentável

Utilizamos a técnica de classificação de Borda para construir um índice único para o desenvolvimento humano, e um para o desenvolvimento sustentável. Os indicadores para o índice de desenvolvimento humano são:

* redução na mortalidade infantil entre as décadas de 1980 e 1990;
* redução no analfabetismo adulto entre as décadas de 1980 e 1990;
* aumento da expectativa de vida entre as décadas de 1980 e 1990.

Os indicadores para o índice do desenvolvimento sustentável são:

* Diminuição nas emissões de dióxido de carbono *per capita* entre as décadas de 1980 e 1990;
* diminuição na emissão de poluentes orgânicos da água (quilogramas por dia por trabalhador) entre as décadas de 1980 e 1990;
* a taxa da média anual negativa de desmatamento medida durante o período 1980-1995.

O procedimento de classificação de Borda envolve atribuir a cada país um ponto igual à sua classificação em cada critério componente. Os pontos de cada país sobre todos os componentes são calculados pela média, e as médias são utilizadas para reclassificar os países. O processo permite a agregação de indicadores com unidades diferentes de medida e coberturas de diferentes períodos e países, ou seja, permite comparações entre países por meio de categorias, mesmo quando o número de países estudados varia pela categoria. Para maiores detalhes sobre as técnicas de classificação de Borda, ver Fine & Fine (1974a, b), Goodman & Markowitz (1952), Smith (1973) e Thomas & Wang (1996).

Também tentamos um método alternativo de agregação, que transformasse cada variável componente em um placar-padrão, com média em 0

(zero) e um desvio-padrão de 1 (um), e então ponderá-los. Nos coeficientes correlacionais significativos, os resultados foram substancialmente similares.

ANEXO 2

ESTRUTURA E EVIDÊNCIA

Este anexo fornece uma estrutura e uma evidência empírica para o Capítulo 2.

Uma Função de Bem-Estar

Definir um aditivo e uma função de bem-estar separável, U, para uma sociedade que consiste em N indivíduos

$$(A2.1) \quad U = \sum_{i=1}^{N} u(c_i) + \sum_{i=1}^{N} v(h_i; R),$$

onde c_i é o consumo do indivíduo; i, h_i é o capital humano do indivíduo i, e R, o nível (agregado) dos recursos ambientais. R assume-se que seja um bem público puro, e daí sua distribuição entre a população é irrelevante. Igualmente, $u(\cdot)$ e $v(\cdot)$ estão aumentando e estritamente côncavos em seus argumentos. Uma aproximação de segunda ordem de U avaliado pelos valores médios ou cálculos de c e dos rendimentos h.

$$(A2.1) \quad U \approx Nu(\bar{c}) + \sum_{i=1}^{N} u'(\bar{c})(c_i - \bar{c}) + \frac{1}{2} \sum_{i=1}^{N} u''(\bar{c})(c_i - \bar{c})^2$$

$$+ Nv(\bar{h}; R) + \sum_{i=1}^{N} v'(\bar{h}; R)(h_i - \bar{h}) + \frac{1}{2} \sum_{i=1}^{N} v''(\bar{h}; R)(h_i - \bar{h})^2$$

onde $\bar{c}$ é a média ou consumo *per capita*, $\bar{h}$ é a média ou capital humano *per capita*, $u'(\bar{c})$, $v'(\bar{h}; R)$ são os primeiros derivativos com respeito ao c e ao h, respectivamente, avaliados em valores médios $\bar{c}$ e $\bar{h}$ e $u''(\bar{c})$ são derivativos secundários. Examinando as expectativas, obtemos a média de bem-estar por indivíduo i,

$$(A2.1) \quad E(U) \approx u(\bar{c}) + \frac{1}{2} u''(\bar{c})\sigma_c^2 + v(\bar{h}; R) + \frac{1}{2} v''(\bar{h}; R)\sigma_h^2,$$

onde σ_c^2 é a variação consumo por meio da população e σ_h^2 é a variação da distribuição do capital humano por meio da população. Pela concavidade estrita de $u(\cdot)$ e $v(\cdot)$, temos que $u'' < 0$ e $v''(\cdot) < 0$. Logo, o bem-estar agregado ou esperado está aumentando em $\bar{c}$ e $\bar{h}$ e diminuindo em σ_c^2 e σ_h^2. Além do mais, devido a $v(\cdot)$ estar aumentando em R, $\partial v''/\partial R \approx 0$ é suficiente para obter que $E(U)$ também está crescendo em R.

A partir da definição no texto, o crescimento sustentado requer que a expansão do capital físico ao longo do tempo seja acompanhada pelo crescimento positivo do capital humano, sem piorar sua distribuição. Igualmente, é provável que o crescimento sustentado diminuirá a pobreza, e não é coerente com uma piora na distribuição de renda. O crescimento sustentado aumenta $\bar{c}$ e $\bar{h}$ e reduz, ou pelo menos não aumenta, σ_c^2 e σ_h^2. Logo, é provável que o crescimento sustentado aumente o bem-estar, $E(U)$ na equação (A2.3), enquanto R não cair ou cair de modo suficientemente lento.

A Otimização do Setor Privado

Como foi indicado no texto, o capital humano (h) e o capital natural (R) estão sujeitos a duas externalidades possíveis associadas ao consumo e à produção. As externalidades de consumo originam-se do fato de que os efeitos diretos positivos de h e R sobre a função do bem-estar podem ser apenas parcialmente consideradas pelo setor privado em suas decisões de dotações de recursos. Externalidades de produção crescem porque muito da expansão tecnológica positiva associada a h não pode ser levada em consideração pelo setor privado. Além do mais, parte do valor de R como um recurso produtivo também pode ser ignorado pelo setor privado, particularmente nos casos em que os direitos de propriedade do capital natural não estão bem definidos.

Neste ponto, procedemos a uma suposição extrema: que todos os valores de consumo direto de h e R sobre a função do bem-estar (assim como os efeitos distributivos representados pelo σ_c^2 e σ_h^2) são ignorados pelas decisões do setor de produção privado. Além disso, assumimos que as externalidades de produção estabelecem um calço entre os produtos marginais privados de h e R e os verdadeiros produtos marginais desses recursos. Ou seja, o setor privado só considera uma fração da contribuição de h e R para a produção. Assumimos, ainda, que um nível mínimo de consumo de subsistência c_s existe. A representatividade doméstica precisa de um nível de consumo c_s para sobreviver e não permitirá que o consumo atinja níveis abaixo de c_s. Ou seja, impomos uma coerção de subsistência, $c - c_s \geqslant 0$.

Sob estas suposições, o problema relevante é a maximização do valor atual descontado de $u(\hat{c})$ – como oposição àquele do $E(U)$ – sujeito às seguintes coerções:

(A2.4) (i) $\dot{k} = G(k, h; R; A(k, h); p) - c - I_h^g - I_h^p - I_R^g$

(ii) $c - c_s \geqslant 0$

(iii) $\dot{h} = I_h^g + I_h^p$

(iv) $\dot{R} = \phi(R) + \beta I_R^g - \psi[G(\cdot)]$,

(v) $k(0) = k_0;\ \ h(0) = h_0;\ \ R(0) = R_0$

onde k é o capital físico *per capita*, $G(\cdot)$ é a função PIB *per capita* da economia, $A(\cdot)$ é um índice de produtividade, p representa as variáveis da política e fatores exógenos, I_h^g é o investimento do governo no capital humano, I_h^p é o investimento privado no capital humano, β é um parâmetro, I_R^g é o investimento do governo no capital natural, $\phi(R)$ é uma função de crescimento dos recursos renováveis através do tempo e $\psi(\cdot)$ é uma função crescente do PIB que reflete o possível impacto direto negativo da atividade econômica aumentada no capital natural. Assumimos que a população N é fixa de modo que, utilizando as unidades apropriadas, pode ser normalizada para 1, daí a distinção entre variáveis totais de *per capita* na Equação (A2.4) tornar-se irrelevante. Igualmente, para uma simplicidade algébrica, assumimos uma taxa zero de desvalorização de k e h. Assumir uma taxa de depreciação logarítmica constante para esses bens, como é atualmente feito, não afeta nenhum dos resultados.

Vários comentários sobre a Equação (A2.4) estão ordenados:

- Assume-se que I_h^g e I_R^g são variáveis políticas.
- Assume-se que o efeito do PIB sobre o capital natural não é absolutamente interiorizado pelo setor privado, e que, como conseqüência, o setor privado não irá investir no capital. Logo, na Equação (A2.4) a equação (iv) só é utilizada como uma identidade calculada, e não é diretamente levada (e *ex ante*) em consideração nas decisões do setor privado, mesmo que a evolução de R atinja suas decisões futuras.
- O efeito de h sobre $G(\cdot)$ é apenas parcialmente incorporado às decisões do setor privado. O governo pode preencher uma parte, ou toda a extensão da brecha de subinvestimento no capital humano deixada pelo setor privado.
- Permitimos que k e h afetem o conhecimento representado pela função produtiva $A(\cdot)$. Assume-se que o conhecimento é um bem público que qualquer empresa pode ter acesso a custo zero. Alinhados com a hipótese do "aprender fazendo", seguimos Arrow (1962) e Romer (1986) e assumimos o aprender fazendo por meio do investimento de cada empresa em k. Contudo, especificamos que aprender

fazendo requer capital humano, ou que o capital humano facilite e aumente a eficácia deste processo. Logo, a função $A(\cdot)$ é assumida como sendo crescente em seus argumentos e o efeito marginal de k sobre A aumenta com h, ou seja $\partial^2 A/\partial k \partial h > 0$.

- A Equação (A2.4) (i) implica que o investimento público no capital humano é financiado fora das poupanças totais, pela soma dos impostos da massa informe. Uma abordagem alternativa deve assumir que os investimentos públicos são financiados por uma taxa de renda proporcional ao PIB, como em Barro (1993).

- Assume-se que a produção do capital humano deve ser gerada por alguns processos produtivos, tanto de capital físico como de bens de consumo. Esta suposição tem sido freqüentemente usada na bibliografia (ver, por exemplo, Barro, Sala-I-Martin, 1995). De modo alternativo, pode-se postular uma função de produção separada de h, como em Lucas (1988) ou Rebelo (1991). Embora a última seja uma abordagem mais realista, a suposição de uma função produtiva comum para consumidores de todos os bens de investimento reduz de modo considerável a álgebra e não altera as conclusões básicas.

O Caso de uma Economia de Renda Média com um Consumo Inicial Muito Acima da Subsistência

Em primeiro lugar, assumimos que a coerção (A2.4) (ii) não está comprometendo; a economia é suficientemente rica para permitir $c > c_s$ em todas as vezes. Analisaremos o papel da coerção de subsistência no caso da economia pobre.

Pode-se mostrar que o setor privado, neste modelo, investe apenas em k se o produto do capital físico $G_k(\cdot)$ for mais alto que o produto do capital humano marginal, como percebido pelo setor privado, $G_h^p(\cdot)$.[1] Ele investirá tanto em k quanto em h se o $G_h^p = G_k$ e só irá investir em h se $G_h^p > G_k$. Logo, ao assumir que k é de início relativamente baixo, $I_h^p = I_R^p = 0$ e $\dot{k} > 0$. Sem dúvida, a principal razão pela qual o setor privado investe apenas em um fator é nossa hipótese de que todos os fatores sejam produzidos fora de uma função produtiva comum. Se permitirmos uma função de produção diferente para h, o setor privado pode ser mostrado investindo tanto em k quanto em h, mesmo fora do equilíbrio de longo prazo. Contudo, o ponto essencial é que o setor privado tende a subinvestir nos capitais humano e natural, com relação ao capital físico. Ou seja, o setor privado tende a ter uma carteira de investimentos muito estreita, enquanto os efeitos externos positivos associados a h e R são maiores do que aqueles associados ao k, sem se importar se h ou R possuem funções produtivas separadas. Em certo sentido, a extrema especificação (fora da simplificação da álgebra)

ajuda a sublinhar o fato de que a economia de mercado tende a operacionalizar-se em escolha de investimentos e superespecializar suas escolhas de investimento.

A partir das condições de primeira ordem do problema citado, pode-se derivar a taxa de crescimento da economia no modo habitual se $G_k > G_h^p$. O crescimento econômico é uma função crescente da brecha entre um retorno marginal para o capital e seu custo marginal, $b(\cdot)$. Sob a afirmação habitual da aversão do risco constante – por exemplo, que $-u''(c) \cdot c/u'(c)$ $\phi > 0$, é uma constante – e onde $u(c)$ é definido na Equação (A2.3), a taxa do crescimento econômico é

(A2.5) $\dot{c}/c = \dfrac{1}{\phi} [G_k (k, h; R, A; p) - b(r; p)],$

onde $\dot{c}/c$ é a taxa de crescimento de consumo *per capita* (suprimimos a barra sobre c), $G_k(\cdot)$ é uma função que reflete um produto marginal do capital físico para um dado nível de A e r é a taxa de desconto.[2]

Há quatro casos possíveis:

i.   *O crescimento sustentado requer um crescimento absolutamente equilibrado dos bens.* Este caso ocorre se a função de produção agregada $G(\cdot)$ for sujeita a constantes retornos na escala (CRS); por exemplo, os efeitos da expansão de k e h sobre $A(\cdot)$ são desprezíveis. Em conseqüência, G_k é uma função apenas de razões fatoriais. Vamos pressupor que h e R permaneçam constantes enquanto $\dot{c}/c > 0$ e $\dot{k}/k > 0$. Neste caso, o setor privado não investe em R e h. Logo, o crescimento será desequilibrado, baseando-se exclusivamente no acúmulo de k. Por causa de CRS, $G_k(\cdot)$ declina enquanto k aumenta. Logo, a expressão entre colchetes em (A2.5) declina e o "curso lento" aplica-se. Uma taxa de crescimento positiva não pode ser sustentada, a menos que o governo invista em h e/ou R. (O crescimento declina se, certamente, R cair mais rápido como uma conseqüência do crescimento.) Assim, neste caso, o crescimento sustentado só pode ser realizado pelo governo que invista em h e R, de modo que $\dot{k}/k = \dot{c}/c = \dot{R}/R$. Um crescimento absolutamente equilibrado destes três recursos é exigido para sustentar uma taxa de crescimento positiva.

ii. *O crescimento sustentado pode ser realizado com crescimento desequilibrado dos recursos.* Este caso pode ocorrer se as amplas expansões tecnológicas associadas com o acúmulo de capital existirem. Nesta hipótese, é possível que o produto marginal de k não decline porque A está aumentando em k. Agora, mesmo se h e R não aumentarem ou se diminuírem numa taxa suficientemente baixa, a taxa de crescimento ainda poderá ser sustentada. Assim, neste caso, podemos ter um crescimento sustentado, ainda que desequilibrado,

baseado puramente no crescimento do capital físico e nas expansões tecnológicas.

iii. *O crescimento sustentado pode ser obtido com uma expansão de recursos semi-equilibrada.* Isto poderia acontecer se houvesse um alto grau de substituição entre h e R na função G_k. A substituição entre h e R permite dois subcasos possíveis como $h > h^c$, onde h^c representa um nível crítico do capital humano:

    a. Sob CRS sem efeitos expansivos, o crescimento pode ser sustentado se h e k cresceram em taxas idênticas, ou seja, a razão k/h permanece constante. *Um crescimento absolutamente semi-equilibrado de recursos é necessário para produzir este cenário.*

    b. Os efeitos expansivos que implicam efetivamente que a função de produção demonstre retornos crescentes na escala em k e h, mas que o produto líquido marginal de k seja decrescente em k. Neste caso, h pode crescer em um andamento mais lento que k, ou seja, é necessário um *crescimento relativamente semi-equilibrado de recursos.*

    Neste caso, $\partial G_k/\partial R$ diminui enquanto h aumenta e $\partial G_k/\partial R \approx 0$ enquanto $h \geqslant h^c$, em que h^c está num nível determinadamente crítico. Ou seja, enquanto h aumenta sobre h^c, o crescimento econômico torna-se independente de R, embora R ainda tenha um produto marginal positivo. Observe-se que a substituição relevante é para o produto marginal de função k, não para a função produtiva, como geralmente se pressupõe. Isto implica que a substituição relevante entre h e R se relaciona aos efeitos de terceira ordem e não aos efeitos de segunda ordem como as elasticidades habituais de substituição de Hixxen ou Allen implicam.

iv. *O crescimento sustentado pode ser realizado com um relativo crescimento equilibrado dos recursos.* Este caso pode ocorrer se as expansões tecnológicas dependerem tanto de k quanto de h, com um relacionamento fortemente complementar na função A e $h < h^c$. Discutimos neste texto que não é possível as expansões tecnológicas associadas com capital físico serem grandes nos países em desenvolvimento, que não possuem um nível de crescimento suficientemente alto da educação geral. Ou seja, a elasticidade de substituição entre h e k na função $A(\cdot)$ é pequena. Se h for muito baixo, o efeito de k sobre A será pequeno. Neste caso, o crescimento sustentado pode ser realizado apenas se h e R crescerem de modo que $G_k(\cdot)$ não caia, enquanto k aumenta. Isso implica que o crescimento sustentado pode ser realizado com relativo, antes que absoluto, crescimento equilibrado de recursos. Uma economia pode sustentar uma taxa de crescimento positiva quando o setor público investe em h e R numa taxa geralmente mais baixa do que a taxa de acúmulo de capital físico.

Os resultados empíricos apresentados no texto permitem-nos excluir o primeiro e o segundo casos. Ou seja, embora um equilíbrio de recursos completos ou absolutos não seja necessário para o crescimento sustentado, um crescimento baseado apenas sobre um acúmulo de capital físico também não é sustentável. De acordo com descobertas empíricas, os últimos dois casos são empiricamente os mais relevantes. Os países pobres, que não possuem amplos níveis de capital humano, requerem que os capitais natural e humano cresçam em uma determinada taxa, que é geralmente mais baixa do que aquela do capital físico, para sustentar o crescimento. Ou seja, o último caso reflete melhor a situação para as economias pobres que ainda não desenvolveram uma base sólida de capital humano. O terceiro caso, especialmente o subcaso (iii)b é o mais relevante para os países de renda média que já possuem um nível significativo de capital humano.

A Figura A2.1 exemplifica processos de crescimento equilibrado e desequilibrado sob a pressuposição de que não há economias de escala ou expansões tecnológicas associadas ao acúmulo de capital e que $h > h^c$ implica que mudanças em R não desempenham nenhum papel no crescimento econômico. O produto marginal $G_k(G_h)$ está diminuindo (aumentando) no capital físico para a razão do capital humano. Na figura, G_h é o verdadeiro produto marginal do capital humano, x é a contribuição marginal do capital humano para o bem-estar como um bem de consumo, e, em conseqüência, $G_h + x$ é a contribuição total e verdadeiramente marginal social no capital humano. G_h^p é a contribuição marginal do capital humano como percebido pelo setor privado.

Para uma economia que cresce a partir de uma razão baixa de k/h, o produto marginal de k cai ao longo da tabela G_k, enquanto k/h aumenta. Na ausência de intervenção, uma economia de *laissez-faire* continuará acumulando capital físico até atingir o ponto B, em cujo momento crítico não ocorre nenhum crescimento posterior; k/h não crescem. Neste ponto, $G_k = b$ onde b é o custo marginal; e daí para a frente o crescimento pára. No quadrante mais baixo da Figura A2.1 relacionamos o crescimento do consumo, $\dot{c}/c$, ao nível de k/h. Na ausência de intervenção, $\dot{c}/c$ declina de modo continuado até atingir o ponto L em $(k/h)^0$ onde $\dot{c}/c = 0$. (Este caso representa o padrão de crescimento 1 discutido no Capítulo 2.)

Se o setor público investir no capital humano, contudo, o crescimento a longo prazo será possível. Uma intervenção ótima envolveria um investimento do setor público no capital humano, uma vez que a economia atingisse $(k/h)^*$ ou o ponto D, enquanto o produto marginal G_k do capital físico é igual ao produto marginal social do capital humano G_h+x. Neste ponto, $G_k = G_h +x >b$, de modo que a economia continua crescendo. Contudo, como o crescimento agora é equilibrado com $\dot{k}/k = \dot{h}/h$, k/h permanece constante em $(k/h)^*$. No quadrante inferior a intervenção ótima implica que o k/h pára de crescer em $(k/h)^*$ no ponto d. Temos aqui uma

taxa de crescimento de consumo positiva e sustentável igual a $\dot{c}/c^*$. (Esta situação reflete o padrão de crescimento 3 no Capítulo 2.)

De modo alternativo, o governo pode escolher subsidiar os investidores de capital físico, reduzindo b ou aumentando G_k ao longo do tempo (veja a Equação A2.5). Contudo, estes subsídios devem ser financiados. Pressupondo-se que sejam financiados por uma soma de taxas em efeito cascata, o orçamento apertado, Equação A2.4 (i), implica que o governo deve reduzir I_h^g e/ou I_R^g. Contudo, isto significa que a economia se torna cada vez mais dependente de subsídios como meios para sustentar o crescimento. Na Figura A2.1 este padrão de crescimento pode ser mostrado mediante uma mudança para a direita da tabela G_k em razão dos subsídios de capital (ou por uma queda de b). Mas o aperto do orçamento implica que o governo possui menos recursos para investir no capital humano. Logo, para preservar o crescimento (manter uma brecha positiva entre G_k e b), os subsídios devem ser continuamente aumentados com o passar do tempo. Ou seja, a tabela G_k deveria estar se mudando constantemente para a direita mediante subsídios crescentes e permanentes. O crescimento econômico torna-se dependente dos subsídios cada vez mais crescentes para donos de capital com um conseqüente impacto negativo na distribuição de renda e nos capitais humano e natural. (Este é o padrão de crescimento 2 discutido no Capítulo 2.)

O Caso de Uma Economia Pobre

Aqui, consideramos uma economia pobre em que o nível inicial de consumo está apenas levemente acima da subsistência e encontra-se em processo de crescimento rumo a um nível estacionário. Denominamos isto como uma economia de semi-subsistência. A idéia é que os pobres constituam por si mesmos uma subeconomia em que a maior parte do crescimento ocorre a partir de seus próprios esforços para poupar e investir. A economia de semi-subsistência não possui contatos com os setores modernos, porque os pobres vendem parte de seus produtos aos setores modernos e porque alguns dos pobres estão aptos a migrar para os setores modernos. Pelo bem da brevidade e simplicidade, não vamos explicitar modelos de nenhum destes processos. Simplesmente, afirmaremos que a função PIB dos pobres é dependente de choques vindos dos setores ricos por meio da variável $\boldsymbol{p}$ na função $G(\cdot)$. Por exemplo, uma recessão numa economia moderna é traduzida por uma queda em $\boldsymbol{p}$, o que, por sua vez, leva as funções $G(\cdot)$ e $G_k(\cdot)$ a serem deslocadas para baixo. Um outro choque possível surge da degradação de R causada por uma expansão do setor moderno em áreas onde vivem os pobres.[3] Presumimos que a economia seja inicialmente crescente por investir principalmente em k. O crescimento de h depende 100% dos gastos governamentais com o capital humano.

Figura A2.1 – Retornos Constantes à Escala e Nenhuma Expansão Tecnológica

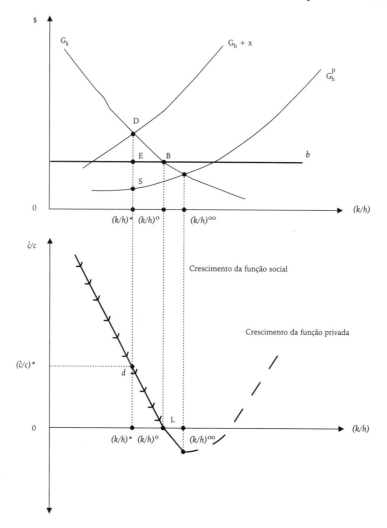

Fonte: Autores.

Definimos dois casos-limite. O primeiro é aquele em que a renda menos depreciação dos estoques de recursos seja exatamente suficiente para cobrir o nível de consumo de subsistência:

(A2.6) $\quad c^z = h_0 \{ G[\frac{k}{h}, 1 ; \frac{R_0}{h_0}, A ; p] - \delta_k (\frac{k}{h})^s - \delta_h \}$,

em que h_0 é o nível inicial do capital humano e R_0 é o nível inicial do capital natural, e agora presumimos uma taxa de depreciação positiva para k e h (δ_k e δ_h).

Ou seja, para um determinado nível de R_0, h_0, e variáveis de política exógena p, há um único nível $(k/h)^s$, que permite que a economia satisfaça exatamente seu consumo mínimo de subsistência. Se $k/h > (k/h)^s$, a economia está acima da subsistência com potencial para poupanças líquidas positivas e crescimento. Se $k/h < (k/h)^s$, a economia não é capaz de cobrir a depreciação de seus estoques de capital e, em conseqüência, com consumo real igual a c^s, os estoques estão sendo reduzidos. Isto é, a economia está exaurindo seu capital. Isto causa um crescimento negativo como as quedas em k/h.

O outro caso-limite dá-se quando a economia mal pode satisfazer seu consumo de subsistência, a menos que utilize sua saída total sem permitir qualquer substituição de estoques:

$$(A2.7) \quad c^s = h_0\, G[(\frac{k}{h})^{ss},\ 1;\frac{R_0}{h_0},\ A;\ p].$$

Uma vez que $k/h = (k/h)^{ss}$, as famílias precisam utilizar toda sua saída para consumo. Em $(k/h)^{ss}$ a economia torna-se inviável.

Observe-se que tanto $(k/h)^s$ quanto $(k/h)^{ss}$ dependem dos níveis de h_0, R_0, A, e p. Pode-se ver facilmente que $(k/h)^s$ e $(k/h)^{ss}$ estão ambos diminuindo em h_0, R_0, A e p (presumindo que $G(\cdot)$ está aumentando em p, ou seja, p representa fatores exógenos positivos). Logo, num choque negativo devido, por exemplo, a uma recessão na economia moderna que reduz os termos do comércio dos pobres ou o nível de R em decorrência da intrusão de interesses comerciais nos recursos naturais pertencentes aos pobres (o que ironicamente é mais provável que aconteça durante períodos de explosão no setor moderno), $(k/h)^s$ irá aumentar.

Suponhamos que a economia esteja inicialmente em $(k/h)_0$ maior que $(k/h)^s$ Isto é, está crescendo em direção a $(k/h)^*$ (ver Figura A2.2). Imaginemos agora que ocorra uma recessão no setor moderno que reduz p. Isto fará com que $(k/h)^s$ cresça. Se o novo $(k/h)^s$ é agora maior ou igual a $(k/h)_0$, então a economia de semi-subsistência é lançada numa armadilha de subsistência que poderia levar a um crescimento negativo, conduzindo k/h rumo a $(k/h)^{ss}$.

Consideremos o caso em que o choque inicial ocorre no tempo t e é eventualmente revertido e p é levado de volta a seu nível original no tempo $t + \tau$. Aqui há duas possibilidades:

- A queda de k/h entre os tempos t e $t + \tau$ não é tão ampla e $(k/h)^s_t$ $> (k/h)_{t+\tau} > (k/h)^s_{t+\tau}$. Isto é, em $t + \tau$, quando a política retorna ao seu nível original, o crítico (que é igual ao nível original $(k/h)^s_0$) está ainda em nível mais baixo de $(k/h)_{t+\tau}$ (que é mais baixo que o nível inicial $(k/h)_0$). Neste caso, o choque teve apenas um efeito negativo

temporário sobre o crescimento. Mas uma vez que p é devolvido a seu nível original, a economia de semi-subsistência retoma seu trajeto de crescimento.

- A queda de k/h entre t e $t + \tau$ é ampla de modo que $(k/h)_t^s > (k/h)_{t+\tau}^s > (k/h)_{t+\tau}^s$. Isto é, enquanto p volta ao seu nível original em $t + \tau$, o nível de $(k/h)_{t+\tau}$ caiu tanto que agora está mais baixo que o nível crítico original. Neste caso, temos aquilo a que nos referimos como *"hysterisis"*: o choque temporário tem um efeito permanente na economia e, mesmo que esse choque desapareça, a economia não volta a seu nível original. O efeito do choque causa um retrocesso irreversível da economia pobre. A economia cai num ciclo de pobreza, conduzindo k/h a uma queda contínua em direção a $(k/h)^{ss}$, ponto no qual deixa de existir como economia viável.

A Figura A2.2 pode ajudar a esclarecer esses pontos. A figura mostra caminhos possíveis para a economia pobre. Se inicialmente a razão de k/h está acima do $(k/h)^s$ crítico, a economia está num caminho de acúmulo, seguindo a linha FJ na metade do painel na Figura A2.2 em direção a $(k/h)^*$. Durante este caminho, o consumo *per capita* é continuamente crescente, embora numa taxa decrescente. Eventualmente, a economia atinge $(k/h)^*$, em cujo ponto cresce a uma taxa constante indefinidamente. O painel inferior mostra a evolução do nível de consumo, que cresce de modo permanente. Imaginemos agora que um choque negativo ocorra enquanto a economia está no percurso de FJ. Isto leva as tabelas G_k e $G_h + x$ a deslocar-se para baixo com uma nova interseção em um ponto mais baixo que D, o que implica uma taxa inferior de crescimento a longo prazo. Mas a conseqüência mais importante é que $(k/h)^s$ irá mover-se para a direita, enquanto aumenta por causa do nível reduzido de G implicado por um choque negativo. A questão-chave é saber se a razão inicial (k/h) está agora abaixo ou acima do novo $(k/h)^s$ crítico, depois do choque. Se (k/h) está abaixo do novo $(k/h)^s$, o percurso da economia reverte durante um percurso de estagnação como o percurso NM no painel inferior da figura. Isto é, a economia que estava originalmente crescendo fica estagnada e, eventualmente, quando atinge o ponto M, torna-se inviável.

Suponhamos que o k/h inicial seja suficientemente baixo de modo que a economia entre numa fase de estagnação, com uma razão k/h declinante, mas que depois de um período de tempo o nível de p seja restabelecido em seu nível original. A questão é saber se o novo $(k/h)^s$ está, ou não, acima da razão k/h habitual. Se estiver acima, então a economia não retoma seu percurso de crescimento original. Continua na espiral descendente, posteriormente reduzindo sua riqueza. Ou seja, a reversão do processo de crescimento torna-se permanente e um choque puramente temporário teve um efeito permanente, irreversível, provocando um ciclo vicioso de pobreza e desacumulação de recursos.

Figura A2.2 – Subsistência, Crescimento e Armadilhas da Pobreza Entre os Pobres: O Caso de Retornos Constantes à Escala e Nenhuma Expansão

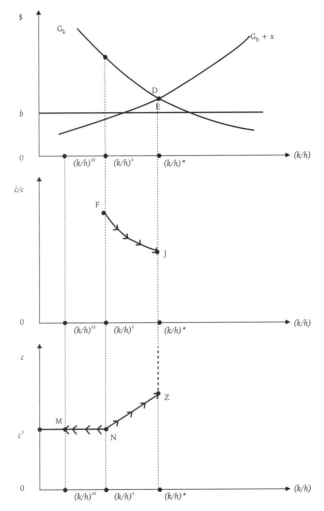

Fonte: Autores.

Especificação Econométrica Utilizada para Avaliar Funções de Crescimento

Uma equação comportamentista básica que surge tanto dos modelos de crescimento neoclássicos como endógenos é a seguinte:

(A2.8) $g = \phi \; [F_k(K, H, R; A, p) - C_k(r, \delta, p)]$,

em que g é a taxa do crescimento PIB *per capita*; K, H e R são capitais físico, natural e humano, respectivamente; p é um vetor de variáveis políticas e de preços; A é um fator de produtividade; F_k é o retorno marginal para k; C_k é o custo marginal do capital que depende tipicamente da taxa de desconto (r), da taxa de depreciação (δ) e, presumivelmente, da variável política p (tais como subsídios ao investimento); e $\phi(\cdot)$ é uma função monotônica e crescente.

A Equação (A2.8) indica que o crescimento depende da brecha entre os retornos marginais ao capital e seu custo marginal. Se tal brecha for positiva, o crescimento também é positivo. E o crescimento chega a uma pausa, se tal brecha desaparecer. Além disso, sob determinadas circunstâncias geralmente supostas, o crescimento é diretamente proporcional a essa brecha.

Logo, essa expressão comportamentista básica relaciona o crescimento econômico ao nível dos estoques de recursos, produtividade fatorial total, taxas de desconto e variáveis políticas. Contudo, estudos sobre crescimento mais empíricos não utilizam essa abordagem comportamentista mas, ao contrário, baseiam-se em várias formas de crescimento computando identidades que relacionam crescimento a *mudanças* nos estoques de recursos, em vez de seus níveis como sugere um modelo teórico de crescimento.

Nossa análise empírica é baseada na Equação (A2.8). Se incluímos tempo numa forma discreta, é natural postular que o crescimento em um período depende dos estoques de recursos no final do período anterior. Logo, uma expressão mais operacional para a Equação (A2.8) é:

$$(\text{A2.9}) \quad g_{it} = \phi[F_k(K_{it\text{-}1}, H_{it\text{-}1}, R_{it\text{-}1}; A, P, \alpha_{it}) - C_k(r^i, \delta_{it}, p_{it}; \alpha_i)],$$

em que i representa um país e t é o tempo. Pressupomos que r^i e α_i são as características fixas de um país que influenciam tecnologia e custos. Isto é, os países diferem em suas taxas de descontos, r^i, e características tecnológicas ou institucionais, α_i (por exemplo, direitos de propriedade e regra do direito).

Notamos que na Equação (A2.9) o crescimento em tempo t é dependente de *níveis de estoque de recursos atrasados*, em vez de *fluxo corrente de mudanças de recursos*, como assumido em muitos estudos empíricos. Isto é, esta equação de crescimento teórico fornece variáveis "instrumentais" naturais, postulando o crescimento como uma função dos níveis de estoque do último período. Isto acontece de algum modo em vieses decrescentes, surgindo das correlações contemporâneas entre variáveis explanatórias e o prazo do erro em razão da endogeneidade de tais variáveis. *Níveis* de estoque atrasados são muito menos prováveis de ser endógenos às taxas de crescimento do que às *mudanças* de estoque contemporâneas.

Já que estamos relacionando crescimento atual ao estoque atrasado de recursos, temos que $K_{it\text{-}1} = (1 - \delta)\, k_{it\text{-}2} + I_{it\text{-}1}$, onde $I_{it\text{-}1}$ é o investimento *per capita* no período $t - 1$. Assim, substituindo isto na Equação (A2.9), desco-

brimos que utilizar níveis de estoque atrasados na regressão do crescimento é equivalente a crescimento regressivo em duas vezes estoques e investimentos em atraso. Se repetirmos este processo substituindo k_{it-2}, utilizando uma expressão similar, poderemos voltar ao primeiro ano do estoque de recursos. Assim, a equação estimativa (A2.9) é equivalente ao crescimento estimativo dos níveis de investimento atrasados *per capita* de cada recurso e o nível "inicial" de cada recurso. Daí, esta especificação utiliza implicitamente o nível inicial de renda (dado que o nível inicial de renda é uma função de todos os recursos iniciais) como um fator explanatório. Isto é, poderíamos, em princípio, relacionar o coeficiente estimado dos recursos para análises de convergência das taxas de crescimento através dos países.

Também pressupomos que o fator total de produtividade descuidado está relacionado com estoques de recursos e outras características do país, por exemplo, A_{it} $(K_{it-1}, H_{it-1}, R_{it-1}, \alpha_1)$. Isto é, mesmo se F_k for declinante em K_{it-1}, a taxa de crescimento pode ser crescente ou não decrescente em K_{it-1}, se as expansões tecnológicas e de escala forem suficientemente poderosas. Ou seja, se o efeito parcial de K_{it-1} sobre A_{it} for positivo e de magnitude suficiente de modo a que $dF_k/dK_{it-1} = \partial F_k/\partial K_{it-1} + (\partial F_k/A_{it})(\partial A_{it}/K_{it-1}) > 0$. Logo, estimamos uma forma reduzida da Equação (A2.9) permitindo efeitos fixos para países

$$(A2.10) \quad g_{it} = \psi[K_{it-1}, H_{it-1}, R_{it-1}, P_{it}] + \beta_i + f_t +, \mu_{it},$$

em que $\psi(\cdot)$ é uma função geral bem definida, β_i é um coeficiente que capta o efeito fixo do país, relacionado aos efeitos de α_i e r^i na Equação (A2.9), e μ_{it} é um distúrbio aleatório. O coeficiente f_t corresponde a efeitos de tempo. A estimativa empírica utiliza várias formas funcionais para que o $\psi(\cdot)$, incluindo um logaritmo 1 e uma forma translogarítmica para permitir inter-recursos e interações políticas.

A utilização dos efeitos fixos do país lida com vieses que surgem de variáveis omitidas correspondentes a números possivelmente amplos de variáveis específicas do país que não são observadas. Logo, a especificação na Equação (A2.10) ajuda a reduzir vieses decorrentes tanto da endogeneidade das variáveis explanatórias pela utilização de estoques de recursos atrasados variáveis como instrumentos, como de variáveis omitidas por utilizar efeitos fixos.

Evidências Originadas dos Países em Desenvolvimento

A Tabela A2.1 apresenta a evidência empírica para a seção "Evidência Econométrica: Vinte Países de Renda Média"; e as Tabelas A2.2 e A2.3 mostram resultados empíricos para a seção "Evidência Econométrica: Setenta Países em Desenvolvimento". A tabela A2.4 traz alguns estudos empíricos sobre o impacto e o tamanho dos subsídios de capital.

Notas

1. Coerente com a discussão apresentada, $G_{bh} < G_h$, onde G_h é o produto marginal verdadeiro do capital humano.

2. A função de custo marginal, b, é igual $r + \delta$, em que δ é a taxa de depreciação do capital. Aqui nós permitimos que políticas p afetem o custo marginal de capital.

3. Isto é coerente com um fato estilizado que é válido para vários países tropicais, particularmente na América Latina e na Ásia: embora os pobres sejam mais dependentes dos recursos naturais, a maior parte da destruição desses recursos é provocada pelos grandes interesses comerciais que invadem os recursos possuídos pelos pobres (ver a ampla evidência empírica destas questões fornecidas por Kates & Haarmann, 1992).

Tabela A2.1 – A Equação do Crescimento Sob Várias Especificações
(Variável dependente: crescimento PIB *per capita*)

Variáveis	Efeitos fixos		Efeitos aleatórios	
	Equação 1	*Equação 2*	*Equação 3*	*Equação 4*
Média de escolaridade	0,005	0,004	-0,012	-0,013
	(0,025)	(0,020)	(0,009)	(0,009)
Escolaridade x variável simulada de reforma	0,084**	0,084**	0,049**	0,049**
	(0,024)	(0,024)	(0,018)	(0,018)
Estoque capital *per capita*	-0,21*	-0,021**	-0,012**	-0,009**
	(0,012)	(0,010)	(0,005)	(0,004)
Capital x variável simulada de reforma	-0,016**	-0,016**	-0,008**	-0,008**
	(0,005)	(0,005)	(0,004)	(0,004)
Simulado 1982-85	-0,019**	-0,019**	-0,017**	-0,018**
	(0,005)	(0,005)	(0,005)	(0,005)
Força de trabalho	-0,001	n.a.	-0,006	n.a.
	(0,067)	n.a.	(0,006)	n.a.
Desvio padrão do logaritmo de escolaridade	-0,018	-0,018	-0,034**	-0,033**
	(0,019)	(0,016)	(0,012)	(0,012)
Homoscedasticity (Teste Breusch-Pagan)	Rejeitado em 5%	Rejeitado em 5%	Não rejeitado em 5%	Não rejeitado em 5%
Teste de especificação de White	Rejeitado em 5%	Rejeitado em 5%	n.a.	n.a.
Teste de Hausman: efeitos fixos x aleatórios	n.a.	n.a.	Não rejeitado em 5%	Não rejeitado em 5%

n.a.: não aplicável.
* Significativo no nível de 10%.
** Significativo no nível de 5%.
Nota: Todas as variáveis estão em forma de logaritmo. Todas as variáveis explanatórias estão atrasadas por um período. Os erro-padrão dos coeficientes estão entre parênteses. São apresentados dados de vinte países. Os erro-padrão da "heteroscedasticity-consistent" de White são relatados sob efeitos fixos.
Fonte: López et al. (1998).

Tabela A2.2 – Taxas do Crescimento do PIB Regressadas nos Estoques por Operário, Utilizando Todos os Países com Dados Disponíveis de 1965 a 1990

Variáveis	Sem produtos cruzados: efeitos fixos (com simulações de país)	Sem produtos cruzados: efeitos fixos (com simulações de país e tempo)	Translogaritmo: efeitos fixos (com simulações de país e tempo)
Observações	335	335	335
Países	67	67	67
Logaritmo de probabilidade	-631,70	-606,30	-605,80
1n (capital/trabalho)	10,34	11,36	13,21
	(4,79)	(5,67)	(3,19)
1n (área florestal/trabalho)	-1,31	-0,54	8,86
	(-0,68)	(-0,31)	(2,15)
1n (educação)	-19,56	-21,41	-12,32
	(-5,68)	(-6,60)	(-2,42)
$[1n\ (capital/trabalho)]^2$	-0,74	-0,95	-1,11
	(-6,34)	(-6,93)	(-4,88)
$[1n\ (área\ florestal/trabalho)]^2$	0,31	0,36	0,09
	(2,74)	(3,25)	(0,62)
$[1n\ (educação)]^2$	1,36	1,44	0,84
	(5,52)	(6,20)	(1,64)
1n (capital/trabalho) x 1n (área florestal/trabalho)	n.a.	n.a.	0,108
	n.a.	n.a.	(-0,54)
1n (capital/trabalho) x 1n (educação)	n.a.	n.a.	0,467
	n.a.	n.a.	(0,78)
1n (área florestal/trabalho) x 1n (educação)	n.a.	n.a.	-0,596
	n.a.	n.a.	(-2,03)

n.a.: não aplicável.

Notas:

1. t-estatísticas estão entre parênteses.
2. A variável dependente é anual *per capita* e o crescimento PIB computado durante um intervalo de cinco anos utilizando dados anuais. A regressão está em 1n(PIB)= $a + bt + e$, onde e é o resíduo. Taxa de crescimento igual 100*[exp(b)-1].
3. Os parâmetros foram computados por repetidos viáveis e generalizados menos quadrados (FGLS) e, em conseqüência, seria equivalente à estimativa da probabilidade máxima.
4. A correção para AR(1) selecionou um parâmetro único para a totalidade dos países.
5. A correção para o heteroscidasticity da forma do grupo foi feita computando uma variação de grupo para cada país.
6. As medidas do PIB *per capita* e trabalho foram extraídas de Summer's and Heston's Penn World Tables Mark 5.6. Medidas da educação foram extraídas de Barro & Lee (1997). Elas representam a média de anos de educação para pessoas de 25 anos e mais velhas. Medidas de capital per capita foram extraídas de King & Levine (1993). Medidas de área florestal (estoque de recursos) foram extraídas do disco de dados do World Resources (1996-1997), e é originalmente de FAO-STAT. As tabelas de Pen World podem ser obtidas em http://www.nuff.ox.ac.uk/Economics/Growth/. Os conjuntos de dados de Barro-Lee e King-Levine podem ser pesquisados na página da Web do World Bank em http://www.worldbank.org/html/prdmg/grthweb/ddkile93.htm. Os dados florestais podem ser extraídos de Food and Agriculture Organization of the United Nations na página da Web http://apps.fao.org/.

Fonte: López et al. (1998).

Tabela A2.3 – Elasticidades para os Estoques por Operário, nas Taxas de Crescimento do PIB *per capita*

Variáveis	Elasticidade		
	Valor mínimo	*Valor máximo*	*Média*
Sem permissão para produtos cruzados			
Capital/trabalho	0,038	-0,081	-0,040
	(0,019)	(0,022)	(0,009)
Área florestal/trabalho	0,007	0,071	0,047
	(0,046)	(0,027)	(0,022)
Educação (média de escolaridade da força de trabalho)	-0,056	0,056	0,018
	(0,011)	(0,020)	(0,011)
Função translogarítmica			
Capital/trabalho	0,046	-0,093	-0,045
	(0,022)	(0,026)	(0,012)
Área florestal/trabalho	0,034	0,050	0,044
	(0,049)	(0,029)	(0,023)
Educação	-0,031	0,035	0,012
	(0,028)	(0,022)	(0,013)

Notas:
1. As elasticidades são computadas pela conversão da taxa percentual de crescimento para o logaritmo da taxa de crescimento dividindo a porcentagem por 100.
2. Os efeitos marginais são computados utilizando a regressão dos efeitos fixos com simulações de tempo e país, corrigida para a forma do grupo pela heteroscedasticity para todos os países, e um termo comum AR(1) para a autocorrelação. Os dados são para todos os países, 1965-1990.
3. Os valores marginais (dy/dx) computados para cada x não logaritmado são simplesmente o exponencial de seus respectivos valores registrados. Isto significa que a barra de x não é a média verdadeira.
4. Os valores marginais para a formulação translogarítmica utiliza-se dos valores médios do logaritmo do termo cruzado.
5. Os erro-padrão estão entre parênteses, e são baseados na variabilidade apenas da estimativa dos parâmetros (incluindo covariações entre parâmetros) e não em qualquer variabilidade na média variável mínima ou máxima.
6. A elasticidade do trabalho é computada como negativa da soma das elasticidades para capital/trabalho e recursos/trabalho.
Fonte: López et al. (1998).

Tabela A2.4 – Estudos Empíricos Seletos Sobre o Impacto e a Extensão dos Subsídios de Capital

Autores	Métodos	Principais descobertas
Studies on the impact of subsidies. Bergström (1998). "Capital Subsides and rhe Performance of firms".	Os estudos examinam os efeitos no FTP nos subsídios dos capitais públicos para empresas na Suécia entre 1987 e 1993. Foram utilizados painéis de dados.	"Em muitos países, governos concedem subsídios de capital diferentes aos setores de negócio que prometem crescimento ... Os resultados sugerem que os subsídios podem influenciar o crescimento (em um curto prazo), mas parece haver pouca evidência de que os subsídios afetam a produtividade." (p.1)
Bregman et al.(1999). "Effect of Capital Subsidization on Productivity in Israeli Industry".	Utiliza-se de um conjunto de microdados e de um perfil temporal para 620 firmas em Israel.	"A política de subsídio de investimentos no capital físico foi utilizada em muitos países ... Estimamos que entre os anos de 1990 e 1994, esta política resultou em deficiências de produção que variam entre 5% e 15% para firmas subsidiadas." (p.77)
Harris (1991). "The Employment Creation Effects of Factor Subsidies".	Utiliza a função de produção CES (elasticidade constante da substituição) e um modelo da simulação para a indústria manufatureira da Irlanda do Norte, 1955-1983.	"Os resultados indicam que, desde que a indústria manufatureira na província tende a operar com um trabalho tecnológico intensivo, e a elasticidade de demanda para a saída é muito baixa, os efeitos de geração de emprego para os subsídios de capitais são fortemente negativos." (p.49)
Lee (1996). "Government Interventions and Productivity Growth".	Utiliza dados de quatro períodos do painel nos anos 1963-1983.	"As políticas industriais, tais como incentivos de imposto e subsídios ao crédito, não foram correlacionadas com o crescimento do fator total de produtividade nos setores promovidos."
Lim (1992). "Capturing the Effects of Capital Subsidies".	Utiliza-se do nível de dados de 3.900 – 4.900 empresas da Malásia, de 1976 a 1979.	"A maioria dos países em desenvolvimento fornece incentivos fiscais para encorajar investimentos estrangeiros e nacionais. Este estudo mostra que esses esquemas subsidiam significativamente o uso do capital e produzem uma intensidade maior de capital na manufaturação na Malásia." (p.705)
Oman (2000). "Policy Competition for Foreign Direct Investment", OECD Development Centre.	O estudo levanta três questões: (a) Com que extensão os governos competem realmente pelo FDI, (b) o efeito da competição e (c) as implicações para agentes de política.	"Incentivos baseados na competição ao FDI é um fenômeno global: os governos em todos os níveis, países OECD e não OECD, acoplam nos globais ... O efeito distorcionário dos incentivos ... pode ser significativo ... Isto pode ser contraprodutivo se os governos oferecerem incentivos dispendiosos em investimento" (p.7-9). Incentivos de investimento na indústria automobilística são mostrados em uma tabela da página 73.
Studies on the size of subsidies. Gandhi et al. (1997).	Subsídios estimados que danificaram o ambiente.	"Subsídios estimados para energia, estradas, água e agricultura aumentando as economias de transição na década de 1990 em US$ 240 bilhões por ano. Cortar esses subsídios ao meio poderia diminuir o excedente em US$ 100 bilhões para o investimento no desenvolvimento sustentável." (p.10)

ESTRUTURA E EVIDÊNCIA

Tabela A2.4 Continuação

Autores	Métodos	Principais descobertas
Moore (1999). "Corporate Subsidies in the Federal Budget".	Um testemunho sobre o Comitê do Orçamento, U.S. House of Representatives.	"Bem-estar associado é um grande componente para o crescimento do orçamento federal."(p.1) Em 1997, as corporações da Fortune 500 eram estimadas para receber quase US$ 75 bilhões de subsídio do governo.
De Moor & Calamai (1997). *Subsidizing Unsustainable Development: Undermining the Earth with Public Funds.*	Um relatório do Conselho da Terra, que estimou subsídios públicos em quatro setores.	"Em países da OECD, subsídios anuais totais em quatro setores – energia, estradas de rodagem, água e agricultura – atingiram US$ 490-615 bilhões; nos países não-OECD, US$ 217-272 bilhões. Os subsídios totais globais nos quatro setores são estimados em US$ 710-890 bilhões". (p. 93)
Gulatti & Narayanan (2000). "Demystifying Fertilizer and Power Subsidies in India".	Este relatório estima a quantidade de subsídios e examina os reais beneficiários.	"Amplamente, a metade do enorme subsídio agrícola sobre fertilizantes e energia ... abrangendo 2% do PIB, está indo tanto para a indústria, no caso de fertilizantes, ou está sendo roubado por consumidores não agrícolas, no caso da energia." (p.784)

Nota: Uma tabela mais detalhada está disponível nas solicitações aos autores.
Fonte: Autores.

ANEXO 3

DISTRIBUIÇÃO DA EDUCAÇÃO, ABERTURA E CRESCIMENTO

Teorias econômicas sugerem um forte elo causal da educação com o crescimento, mas a evidência empírica não foi unânime e conclusiva. López et al. (1998) centram seu foco em dois fatores que explicam por que os estudos empíricos não têm sustentado esmagadoramente as teorias. Em primeiro lugar, a distribuição da educação afeta o crescimento econômico; em segundo, o ambiente da política econômica afeta imensamente o impacto da educação sobre o crescimento, por determinar o que as pessoas podem fazer com sua educação. Reformas de comércio, investimento e políticas trabalhistas podem aumentar os retornos da educação. Usando os dados do painel de vinte países em desenvolvimento para 1970-1994, investigamos o relacionamento entre educação, reformas políticas e crescimento econômico e fizemos as seguintes observações:

- *A distribuição da educação é importante.* Uma distribuição excedente enviesada da educação tende a ter um impacto negativo sobre a renda *per capita* da maioria dos países. Controle para a distribuição da educação e utilização de formas funcionais apropriadas levam a efeitos de educação média positivos e significativos na renda *per capita*, enquanto o fracasso em realizar isso conduz a efeitos de educação média insignificantes ou negativos.
- *O ambiente político é extremamente importante.* Os resultados indicam que as políticas econômicas que suprimem as forças do mercado tendem a reduzir o impacto da educação sobre o crescimento econômico. Além disso, o estoque de capital físico é relacionado negativamente com o crescimento econômico para economias na amostragem, implicando um declínio da produtividade de capital marginal.

A Função de Produção Ampliada com a Distribuição da Educação

Utilizamos um modelo no qual o capital físico é totalmente comercializável, mas o capital humano não é. O nível, assim como a distribuição do capital humano, incorpora a função de produção agregada. Se a educação combinar a dispersão da habilidade, o efeito marginal da distribuição educacional sobre a renda desaparece. Se a dispersão da educação for maior do que a dispersão da habilidade, a renda *per capita* poderá ser aumentada reduzindo-se a dispersão da educação. Se a dispersão da educação for menos tendenciosa que a habilidade, então os governos devem concentrar o investimento em umas poucas pessoas com grande capacidade de aprender.

O Coeficiente Gini de Educação é calculado em duas etapas. Em primeiro lugar, uma curva de Lorenz para educação é construída com base nas proporções da população com vários níveis de escolaridade e a extensão de cada nível de escolaridade, que mostra os anos cumulativos de escolaridade com respeito à proporção da população. Então, o Coeficiente Gini de Educação é calculado como a razão da área entre a curva de Lorenz e a linha de 45 graus (igualdade perfeita) para a área total do triângulo. Uma definição alternativa do Coeficiente Gini de Educação é a razão para a média de escolaridade de metade da soma das diferenças absolutas de conclusão escolar entre todos os pares possíveis de indivíduos em um país (Deaton, 1997).[1] A Tabela A3.1 apresenta o Coeficiente Gini para vinte países e os dados preliminares estimados para 85 países estão disponíveis em Thomas et al. (2000).

Usando dados qüinqüenais de vinte dos mais importantes países de renda média, as funções de produção agregadas foram estimadas. A Tabela A3.2 relata quatro estimativas da função de produção *per capita* agregadas para 1970-1974. A primeira coluna apresenta o efeito fixo tradicional do modelo log-linear que ignora ambos os fatores explanatórios anteriores: distribuição da educação e ambiente político. Como mostra a primeira coluna, o capital humano tem um efeito significativo e negativo sobre a produção; nisso reside o "quebra-cabeça da educação".

A segunda coluna apresenta um modelo de efeito fixo em uma forma log-linear, mas a estimativa permitiu que a distribuição da educação desempenhasse um papel na função. A segunda coluna não permite nenhum efeito de país específico a partir da distribuição da educação; e mostra associações positivas entre estoque de capital humano, sua distribuição e nível de renda. Neste caso, o coeficiente da média educacional torna-se positivo e estatisticamente significativo em 5%. O efeito da distribuição educacional sobre a função de produção foi estatisticamente diferente através dos países. A diversidade através dos países do efeito da dispersão da educação é coerente com a idéia de que é provável que o *efeito da dispersão da educação varie e mude o sinal de acordo – se está abaixo ou acima de seu nível ótimo.*

DISTRIBUIÇÃO DA EDUCAÇÃO, ABERTURA E CRESCIMENTO

Tabela A3.1 – Os Coeficientes Gini de Educação para Países Seletos, em Anos Seletos

Países	1970	1975	1980	1985	1990
Argélia	0,8181	0,7683	0,7080	0,6525	0,6001
Argentina	0,3111	0,3257	0,2946	0,3182	0,2724
Brasil	0,5091	0,4290	0,4463	0,4451	0,3929
Chile	0,3296	0,3327	0,31561	0,3120	0,3135
China	0,5985	0,5541	0,5094	0,4937	0,4226
Colômbia	0,5095	0,4594	0,4726	0,4752	0,4864
Costa Rica	0,4106	0,3916	0,4059	0,4165	0,4261
Índia	0,7641	0,7429	0,7517	0,7238	0,6861
Indonésia	0,5873	0,5817	0,5051	0,4388	0,4080
Irlanda	0,2488	0,2454	0,2364	0,2377	0,2498
Coréia	0,5140	0,3942	0,3383	0,2877	0,2175
Malásia	0,5474	0,5150	0,4719	0,4459	0,4204
México	0,5114	0,4990	0,4978	0,4695	0,3839
Paquistão	0,8549	0,8450	0,8170	0,8065	0,6448
Peru	0,5048	0,5028	0,4258	0,4371	0,4311
Filipinas	0,4327	0,3578	0,3404	0,3360	0,3285
Portugal	0,4985	0,5142	0,4255	0,4350	0,4315
Tailândia	0,4185	0,4257	0,3591	0,3891	0,3915
Tunísia	0,8178	0,7589	0,6935	0,6710	0,6168
Venezuela	0,5789	0,5585	0,3919	0,3970	0,4209

Fontes: López et al. (1998). Para dados sobre países adicionais, ver Thomas et al. (2000).

A terceira coluna apresenta os resultados obtidos mediante a permissão para efeitos específicos do país da distribuição educacional. Os coeficientes da variabilidade da educação para os vários países são conjuntamente significativos a 1%. Contudo, sete dos vinte coeficientes de países específicos não são estatisticamente diferentes de zero.

A última coluna utiliza-se do desvio-padrão nos registros como outra medida de dispersão da educação. Esta medida de dispersão exerce um efeito muito maior sobre a renda *per capita*. A maioria destes coeficientes de países específicos é negativa, e oito entre vinte coeficientes são altamente significativos.

A Tabela A3.3 apresenta os resultados obtidos ao utilizar-se da especificação não-linear sugerida pelo modelo teórico. Ou seja, esta especificação lida com as duas variáveis omitidas e a forma funcional dos problemas de especificação. Em todas as três especificações, os coeficientes da média educacional são positivos e estatisticamente significativos no nível de 5%. Nesta forma funcional, a distribuição da educação está associada positivamente ao nível de renda, que é ainda coerente com o modelo que afirma que um certo nível de dispersão educacional é importante para a produção, especialmente considerando-se o progresso e a inovação tecnológica.

Tabela A3.2 – Função de Produção: Estimativa Linear
(dependente variável: registro do PIB *per capita*)

Variáveis	*Efeitos fixos, excluindo efeito da distribuição educacional*	*Efeitos fixos, a forma log-linear permitindo, para efeitos de distribuição de educação, usar coeficientes de variáveis de educação*	*Efeitos fixos, a forma log-linear permitindo, para efeitos de distribuição de educação, usar coeficientes de variáveis de educação*	*Efeitos fixos permitindo, para efeitos de distribuição de educação, usar o desvio-padrão do registro de educação*
Capital humano	-0.275**	0.491**	0,004	-0,380**
	(0.085)	(0.106)	(0,112)	(0,131)
Capital físico	1.108**	0.981**	1,066**	1,083**
	(0.033)	(0.012)	(0,022)	(0,071)
Simulação1982-85	-0.063**	-0.077**	-0,063**	-0,033**
	(0.012)	(0.012)	(0,011)	(0,009)
Efeitos de distribuição da educação		1.187**		
		(0.133)		
Brasil			2,828**	-0,423**
			(0,350)	(0,196)
Chile			-0,20	-0,320
			(0,309)	(0,279)
China			0,354**	-1,197**
			(0,139)	(0,225)
Colômbia			0,765	-0,300
			(0,916)	(0,269)
Índia			0,012	0,015
			(0,278)	(0,299)
Coréia			1,146**	0,012
			(0,089)	(0,148)
México			0,843**	-0,475
			(0,264)	(0,306)
Malásia			2,494**	-0,690**
			(0,196)	(0,304)
Peru			0,574	-0,409
			(0,559)	(0,344)
Filipinas			-2,138	-0,861**
			(2,627)	(0,275)
Tailândia			-2,478**	-0,541**
			(0,618)	(0,175)
Venezuela			1,032**	-0,109
			(0,142)	(0,330)
Argélia			-0,685*	0,818*
			(0,378)	(0,471)
Argentina			1,307**	-0,367
			(0,316)	(0,269)
Costa Rica			-3,849**	-0,666**
			(0,579)	(0,222)
Indonésia			2,081**	-1,004**
			(0,298)	(0,157)
Irlanda			1,287**	0,251
			(0,161)	(0,284)
Paquistão			-0,024	-0,292
			(0,165)	(0,321)
Portugal			-0,001	0,027
			(0,483)	(0,238)
Tunísia			0,654**	-0,065
			(0,188)	(0,484)

* Significativo no nível de 10%.

** Significativo no nível de 5%.

Nota: Um coeficiente auto-regressivo de primeira ordem foi estimado pela probabilidade máxima para cada país em separado. Esta informação foi utilizada para corrigir os dados. Erros-padrão relatados (entre parênteses) são da" heteroscedasticity-consistent" de White. Todas as variáveis estão em formas logarítmicas, exceto para as simulações.

Fonte: López et al. (1998).

Tabela A3.3 – Função de Produção: Estimativa Não-Linear
(dependente variável: registro do PIB *per capita*)

Variáveis	*Não-linear, permitindo uma distribuição de efeitos*	*Não-linear, permitindo efeitos de distribuição dentro de vários continentes*	*Não-linear, permitindo efeitos de distribuição dentro de vários continentes com diferentes níveis de variabilidade de educação*
Capital humano			0,159**
	0,369**	0,272**	(0,056)
Capital físico	(0,049)	(0,051)	0,897**
	0,842**	0,863**	(0,017)
Simulações 1982-85	(0,018)	(0,019)	-0,061**
	-0,066**	-0,065**	(0,011)
Efeitos de distribuição da educação	(0,012)	(0,12)	
Efeitos de distribuição de educação ($\rho\sigma_a$)			
Geral	7,532**	13,040**	
	(0,831)	(2,407)	
América Latina		9,541**	
		(1,611)	
Ásia		3,720**	
		(0,656)	
África		8,140**	
		(2,362)	
Europa			
Baixa variabilidade			11,416**
			(3,624)
Média variabilidade			32,595**
			(10,195)
Alta variabilidade			3,145**
			(0,533)

* Significativo no nível de 10%.
** Significativo no nível de 5%.
Nota: Um coeficiente auto-regressivo de primeira ordem foi estimado pela probabilidade máxima para cada país em separado. Esta informação foi utilizada para corrigir os dados. Todas as variáveis estão em forma de logaritmos, exceto para as simulações. Dados de vinte países foram utilizados na análise, os erros-padrão estão entre parênteses.
Fonte: López et al. (1998).

Análise Empírica em Retornos de Investimento na Educação

Baseado na experiência emprestada do Banco Mundial durante os últimos vinte anos, Thomas & Wang (1997) examinaram se educação e abertura podem melhorar o impacto desenvolvimentista de projetos de investimento. O modelo é uma função de produção do país dividida em produção para a exportação e produção para os mercados domésticos. As formas reduzidas são as seguintes:

$$P(Sat = 1)_i = \alpha \cdot \dot{E}_i + \beta \cdot \dot{X}_i + \gamma \cdot G_i + \varphi \cdot R_i + \varepsilon_i$$

$$ERR_i = \alpha \cdot \dot{E}_i + \beta \cdot \dot{X}_i + \gamma \cdot G_i + \varphi \cdot R_i + \varepsilon_i$$

em que $P(sat = 1)_i$ é a probabilidade de um projeto i que está sendo taxado como satisfatório, ERR_i é a taxa de retorno econômico para o projeto i, $\dot{E}_i$ é a mudança no nível médio de escolaridade da força de trabalho para o país em que o projeto está locado e o período em que o projeto é implementado, $\dot{X}_i$ é o vetor das variáveis indicando crescimento de exportação ou abertura, G é o vetor das variáveis indicando a potencialidade do governo e do institucional, e R inclui variáveis exógenas e simulações regionais. A primeira equação é estimada utilizando a análise de Probit porque a variável dependente é uma variável discreta (0/1), e a segunda equação utiliza o Procedimento Tobit porque ERRs estão truncadas em 5%.

Dados do Projeto

Depois que cada projeto do Banco Mundial é completado, um relatório da conclusão do projeto é escrito e duas medidas de desempenho são calculadas. A equipe do departamento de avaliação das operações avalia e atribui uma taxa de desempenho geral de satisfatório ou insatisfatório na conclusão dos objetivos desenvolvimentistas do projeto. Uma taxa de retorno econômico *ex post* (ERR) também é calculada para projetos em oito setores – infra-estrutura, agricultura, indústria, energia, água, transporte urbano e turismo –, nos quais a corrente dos benefícios do projeto podem ser quantificados. O ERR é a corrente descontada dos custos do projeto e seus benefícios durante a vida do projeto, avaliada a preços econômicos. Os ERRs *ex post* são calculados de modo aproximado de dois a três anos depois da conclusão do projeto, oportunidade em que os avaliadores conhecem os custos de investimentos reais e os custos operacionais reais e a demanda, mas eles ainda precisam estimar a corrente futura de benefícios.

Variáveis Explanatórias

Não se fez nenhuma tentativa para construir um modelo completo de determinantes do sucesso do projeto, que iria requerer informação setorial e nível de projeto, assim como informação sobre o nível do país. Quatro grupos de variáveis explanatórias foram utilizados:

- Educação, que pode ser medida por meio de três variáveis. Elas incluem mudanças na média dos anos de escolaridade, da força de trabalho, entre a aprovação do projeto e anos de avaliação; interação de educação e abertura, aferida pelos desvios das partes comerciais; e o nível inicial da educação, baseado em Nehru et al. (1995) e atualizado por Patel.
- Indicadores de abertura, incluindo o prêmio e o mercado negro de

câmbio de moeda estrangeira e os desvios nas partes comerciais, definidos pelas partes comerciais reais menos a parte comercial predita que foi estimada por um simples modelo de gravidade.

- Governo e capacidade institucional, que podem ser refletidos indiretamente por um índice para corrupção no governo (*International Country Risk Guide*, 1982-1995) pelas partes do consumo governamental em PIB, e partes do *surplus*/déficit do orçamento no PIB. A segunda e a terceira medidas podem refletir a habilidade do governo para controlar suas finanças e implementar prudência e disciplina estritas.

Os resultados da regressão são apresentados na Tabela A3.4. Os achados sugerem a importância da abertura comercial e da educação para melhorar a *performance* do projeto e os ganhos potenciais e uma aprendizagem orientada para o exterior. Bom governo e uma disciplina fiscal estrita também são considerados condutores a retornos mais elevados do projeto (ver Thomas & Wang, 1997).

Tabela A3.4 – Educação, Abertura e Desempenho do Projeto de Empréstimo

Variáveis independentes	Variável dependente = taxa de retorno econômico		Variável dependente = satisfatório ou não	
	Coeficiente Tobit	Prob > Chi	Coeficiente Probit	Prob > Chi
Variáveis educacionais				
Mudança em níveis de educação entre aprovação e anos de avaliação	3,33	0,01	0,34	0,00
Educação x abertura de mercado				
(medida por ações do comércio prediletas)	0,00	0,04	0,00	0,45
Falta de aberturas				
Registro do mercado *premium* de câmbio negro estrangeiro				
(3 anos movimentando a média)	-3,14	0,04	-0,23	0,01
Instituição e governo				
Compartilha do excedente do orçamento/déficit no PIB				
(3 anos movimentando a média)	0,26	0,05	0,06	0,04
Corrupção no governo (1 =mais, 6 = menos)				
Outros controles de variávies e simulações				
Nível inicial do PIB *per capita* na aprovação do projeto anual	0,00	0,95	-0,06	0,02
Simulação para a complexidade do projeto	-4,27	0,00	-0,45	0,00
África subsaariana	5,31	0,41	1,56	0,00
Norte da Ásia	9,13	0,15	2,56	0,00
Sul da Ásia	10,47	0,09	2,13	0,00
América Latina e Caribe	7,77	0,24	1,92	0,00
Europa, Oriente Médio e norte da África	10,80	0,09	2,20	0,00
Registro de probabilidade	-3.209,00		-1.032,00	
Número de observações	830,00		1.826,00	

Nota: Prob = 0,05 significa a rejeição do coeficiente = 0 a 95% de confiança. As regressões cobrem projetos avaliados entre 1974 e 1992.
Fonte: Thomas & Wang (1997).

Estudos Selecionados Sobre Distribuição de Recursos e Crescimento

A Tabela A3.5 inclui um conjunto seleto de estudos empíricos sobre a distribuição de recursos e o crescimento econômico, o que forneceu algumas das evidências utilizadas no Capítulo 3.

Notas

1. O Coeficiente Gini de educação pode ser calculado utilizando a fórmula a seguir:

$$\gamma = \frac{1}{\mu N(N-1)} \sum_{i>j} \sum_{j} |x_i - x_j|.$$

onde γ é o índice Gini, μ é a média da diferença em obtenção de grau escolar e N é o número total das observações (ver Deaton, 1997).

Tabela A3.5 – Estudos Empíricos Seletivos Sobre a Distribuição de Recursos, Crescimento e Pobreza

Autores	Metodologia	Maiores descobertas
Maas & Criel (1982)	Cálculo de Coeficiente Gini de Educação baseado nos dados de matrícula em 16 países do norte da África.	A desigualdade na distribuição de educação varia enormemente através dos países.
Ram (1990)	Cálculo de desvio-padrão de educação para aproximadamente cem países.	Com o nível de escolaridade aumentando, a desigualdade educacional aumenta primeiro, e, após atingir um certo pico, começa a declinar. O ponto de retorno é baseado em sete anos de educação.
O'Neill (1995)	1. Assumindo que o estoque de capital humano é o acúmulo de educação passada, insensível para o nível de renda corrente. 2. Utilizando a variação de renda e a análise dos capitais físico e humano. 3. Utilizando ambas as quantidades e avaliações de capitais humano e físico.	Entre países desenvolvidos, a convergência em níveis da educação resulta na redução da dispersão de rendas. Entretanto, as rendas globais têm divergido a despeito da convergência substancial dos níveis de educação.
Ravallion & Sen (1994)	Apresentando um caso do estudo interior na taxa de efetividade da política de redução da pobreza.	Esquemas de diminuição da pobreza em contingentes de terra em Bangladesh tem um impacto na redução da pobreza, "embora os ganhos máximos despeçam os menores" (p.823).
Deininger & Squire (1996)	Coeficiente Gini para a Terra medindo o crescimento do PIB (1960-1990).	Países com maior eqüidade na distribuição de terras tendem a crescer mais rápido.
Ravallion (1997)	Taxa de crescimento do Coeficiente Gini de Renda.	Em qualquer taxa de crescimento positiva, quanto maior a desigualdade inicial, menor a taxa de queda de renda da pobreza.
Birdsall & Londoño (1998)	Uma análise dentro do país usando um modelo tradicional de crescimento, após um controle de acumulação de capital, níveis de renda e educação e recursos naturais.	Níveis de desigualdade na educação inicial e Coeficiente Gini para a Terra têm fortes impactos negativos no crescimento econômico e crescimento de renda dos pobres.
Deininger & Squire (1998)	Dados prováveis entre países na renda e na distribuição de vantagens (terra).	"Há um drástico relacionamento negativo entre a desigualdade inicial e a distribuição de vantagem no crescimento a longo prazo; desigualdade reduzindo o crescimento de renda do pobre, mas não do rico; e dados longitudinais disponíveis fornecem um pequeno apoio às hipóteses de Kuznets."
Li et al. (1998)	Coeficiente Gini para a Terra. Coeficiente Gini de Renda.	Coeficiente Gini de Renda está positivamente relacionado com o Coeficiente Gini para a Terra.
IDB (1998)	Regressão usando dados de 19 países, Gini para a Terra, Gini de Renda, Gini de Educação e desvio-padrão de educação.	Desigualdade de renda (Gini) está negativamente relacionada com Gini para a Terra, e positivamente relacionada com desvio-padrão de educação.
López et al. (1998)	Uma função de produção "nontradable" é estimada usando dados qüinqüenais de vinte países, depois controlando capital físico, trabalho, e assim por diante. Coeficientes Gini de Educação são estimados na obtenção dos dados.	1. A distribuição da educação é importante para os níveis de renda, assim como para o crescimento. 2. Abertura financeira e reformas melhorando a produtividade do capital humano e modelos de crescimento.

Tabela continua na próxima página

A QUALIDADE DO CRESCIMENTO

Tabela A3.5 Continuação

Autores	Metodologia	Maiores descobertas
Ravallion & Datt (1999)	Utilizando vinte estudos domésticos dos 15 maiores estados da Índia em 1960-1994 para estudar a questão de "quando o crescimento é pró-pobre". Foram estimadas elasticidades de pobreza a não-agricultores.	Os processos de crescimento são mais pró-pobres nos estados com alta alfabetização inicial, alta produtividade agrícola e padrão de vida rural mais elevado do que dos moradores urbanos. Kerala tem a mais alta elasticidade de pobreza de saídas não agrícolas.

Fonte: Compilação dos autores.

ANEXO 4

AFERINDO O CAPITAL NATURAL

Uma análise sistemática quantitativa dos elos entre o estado do meio ambiente e o crescimento econômico tem sido atrapalhada por falta de dados confiáveis sobre o capital natural. Em decorrência da crescente necessidade de pesquisa rigorosa sobre o tema, numerosas iniciativas foram direcionadas para coletar dados mais confiáveis e sistemáticos pelo mundo afora: dados sobre desmatamento compilados pela Organização de Alimentação e Agricultura das Nações Unidas; aferições da poluição do ar urbana compiladas pelo WHO; estatísticas sobre o acesso ao saneamento, água limpa e muitos outros aspectos ambientais compilados pelo UNDP e o Global Environmental Monitoring System.

The World Development Indicators (WDI) é uma publicação anual do Banco Mundial e inclui um amplo corpo de dados ambientais extraídos das fontes mencionadas anteriormente, ao lado de muitas outras. Por juntar dados úteis de diversas fontes e um formato de boas condições ao usuário, o WDI tornou-se rapidamente um balcão de parada obrigatória para o acesso a dados ambientais. A maior parte dos dados ambientais utilizados no Capítulo 4 e outros lugares neste relato foi extraída das Tabelas do WDI.

Além de ser uma rica fonte de dados, o WDI também é referência útil. A publicação e suas tabelas de dados podem ser acessadas na Web em www.worldbank.org/data/wdi.

Dois índices para o capital natural foram construídos com base nos dados disponíveis no WDI, especialmente:

- *O índice do desenvolvimento sustentável para aferir resultados ambientais.* Este é um índice de mudança construído dando-se pesos iguais para taxas anuais de desmatamento entre 1980 e 1995, diminuição da poluição da água, representado pelas emissões de poluentes orgânicos da água em quilogramas por dia por operário entre os anos 80 e

225

90, e declínio nas emissões de dióxido de carbono em toneladas métricas *per capita* entre os anos 80 e 90.

- *O índice político do meio ambiente como uma medida de comprometimento de governo na proteção do capital natural.* Isto inclui duas variáveis simuladas: uma para ação interna baseada na formulação de uma estratégia ambiental nacional e de perfis ambientais e outra para a ação internacional baseada na sinalização da Convention on Climate Change.

Ambos os índices são preliminares e o trabalho está em andamento para desenvolver indicadores mais abrangentes e confiáveis. O seguinte site da Web dá uma idéia dos esforços do Banco Mundial nesta direção: http://www.esd.worldbank.org/eei.

ANEXO 5

ABERTURA FINANCEIRA

Nossa ampla medida da abertura financeira incorpora controles e/ou restrições em ambas as transações, moeda corrente e capital. É construída como a média aritmética simples de medidas quantitativas de grau, de controles ou restrições sobre 27 transações individuais relacionadas a pagamentos de importação, procedimentos de exportação, transações invisíveis e transações de cálculo de capital, como mostrado na Tabela A5.1. Esta classificação baseia-se no relatório anual do Fundo Monetário Internacional sobre *Arranjos de Câmbio e Restrições de Câmbio*.

Esta classificação, desenvolvida a partir da metodologia criada por Quinn & Incla (1997), baseia-se em uma escala de cinco categorias que abrangem de 0 a 2 para cada item, indicando o grau de abertura (0, altamente controlado; 2, altamente liberal) definido como se segue:[1]

0.0 Leis e/ou regulamentações que impõem restrições quantitativas ou outras restrições reguladoras a uma transação particular, tais como licenças ou exigências de reserva que proíbem totalmente tais transações econômicas.

0.5 Leis e/ou regulamentações que impõem restrições reguladoras quantitativas ou outras numa transação particular, tais como licença e exigências de reserva que proíbem parcialmente tais transações econômicas.

1.0 Leis e/ou regulamentações que requerem que a transação particular seja aprovada pelas autoridades ou submetida a pesadas taxas quando aplicada, seja na forma de práticas de moeda corrente múltipla ou outras taxas.

1.5 Leis e/ou regulamentações que requerem que a transação particular seja registrada, mas não necessariamente aprovada pelas autoridades e igualmente taxada quando aplicada.

2.0 Nada de regulamentações que requeiram que a transação particular seja aprovada pelas autoridades e livre de taxação quando aplicável.

Tabela A5.1 – Transações Internacionais

Categoria	Tipo de transação
Importações e pagamento de importações	Orçamento de câmbio estrangeiro
	Financiamento de requerimentos para importação
	Documentos para liberação de câmbio estrangeiro para importação
	Licença para importação e outras medidas não tarifadas
	Taxas de importação e/ou tarifas
	Monopólio do Estado sobre a importação
Exportações e exportações contínuas	Exigência de repatriação
	Exigências de financiamento
	Exigência de documentação
	Licença de exportação
	Taxa de exportação
Pagamentos para transações invisíveis e transferências correntes	Controles destes pagamentos
Continuidade para transações invisíveis e transferências correntes	Exigência de repatriação
	Restrições no uso dos fundos
Transações de capital principal	Segurança do mercado de capitais
	Instrumentos no mercado monetário
	Segurança em investimentos coletivos
	Derivativos e outros instrumentos
	Crédito comercial
	Crédito financeiro
	Garantias, segurança, cópias de segurança financeira
	Investimento direto
	Liquidez e investimento direto
	Verdadeiras transações estatais
	Movimentação de recursos próprios
	Bancos comerciais e outras instituições financeiras
	Investidores institucionais

Fonte: FMI (1998).

Aplicando esta metodologia codificada, o índice de abertura financeira estimada abrange de 1,93 para a Irlanda e Luxemburgo, a 1,12 para a Etiópia (ver Tabela A5.2).

Um índice mais estritamente definido, que capta o grau de abertura para as transações de cálculo de capital, pode ser atingido de maneira similar. O índice estrito utiliza apenas 13 transações das arroladas na categoria de transações de cálculo de capital na Tabela A5.1.

ABERTURA FINANCEIRA

Tabela A5.2 – Índice de Abertura Financeira, Países Seletos, 1997

Aberto		Amplamente aberto		Parcialmente fechado		Amplamente fechado	
País	Índice	País	Índice	País	Índice	País	Índice
Argentina	1,78	Croácia	1,54	Bahamas	1,36	Bangladesh	1,21
Austrália	1,77	Equador	1,54	Belize	1,44	Barbados	1,28
Áustria	1,92	Honduras	1,56	Benin	1,48	Bhutan	1,19
Bahrain	1,73	Israel	1,59	Botswana	1,48	Brasil	1,19
Bélgica	1,88	Mongólia	1,56	Bulgária	1,46	Etiópia	1,12
Bolívia	1,79	Filipinas	1,59	Burkina Faso	1,49	Índia	1,20
Canadá	1,92	Polônia	1,54	Burundi	1,39	Malawi	1,26
Dinamarca	1,92	Rep. Eslovaca	1,58	Camarões	1,41	Malásia	1,34
Egito	1,81	Eslovênia	1,50	Cabo Verde	1,39	Marrocos	1,27
El Salvador	1,91	Turquia	1,52	Chile	1,43	Paquistão	1,31
Estônia	1,88			China	1,37	Síria	1,20
Finlândia	1,83			Colômbia	1,38		
França	1,73			Rep. Dem. Congo	1,42		
Alemanha	1,84			Costa Rica	1,48		
Grécia	1,91			Rep. Tcheca	1,48		
Guatemala	1,73			Rep. Dominicana	1,49		
Guiana	1,72			Gana	1,43		
Islândia	1,74			Hungria	1,49		
Irlanda	1,93			Indonésia	1,46		
Itália	1,84			Coréia	1,42		
Jamaica	1,76			Lesoto	1,41		
Japão	1,73			Mali	1,49		
Kuwait	1,77			Malta	1,40		
Latíbia	1,88			Maldova	1,46		
Lituânia	1,85			Moçambique	1,41		
Luxemburgo	1,93			Namíbia	1,33		
Ilhas Maurício	1,82			Papua-Nova Guiné	1,36		
México	1,69			Romênia	1,48		
Holanda	1,87			Federação Russa	1,43		
Nova Zelândia	1,90			África do Sul	1,44		
Nicarágua	1,82			Sri Lanka	1,43		
Noruega	1,83			Tailândia	1,46		
Panamá	1,90			Tunísia	1,39		
Paraguai	1,81			Ucrânia	1,36		
Peru	1,90						
Portugal	1,84						
Cingapura	1,78						
Espanha	1,82						
Suécia	1,86						
Suíça	1,88						
Trinidad e Tobago	1,67						
Reino Unido	1,86						
Estados Unidos	1,85						
Uruguai	1,77						
Venezuela	1,84						
Zâmbia	1,79						

Nota: Aberto: nenhuma, ou mínima, regulamentação para transações exteriores e interiores e um meio ambiente geralmente não discriminatório. Amplamente aberto: algumas regulamentações são exercidas nas transações exteriores ou interiores com a necessidade de apoio documental, mas sem a necessidade da aprovação governamental. Parcialmente fechado: a aprovação e as regulamentações governamentais são requeridas para transações internas e externas e habitualmente avalizadas. Amplamente fechado: restrições substanciais e aprovações governamentais são requeridas e raramente concedidas para transações internas e externas.
Fonte: Estimativa dos autores.

Nota Sobre a Vulnerabilidade do País e Medidas de Volatilidade

A classificação de vulnerabilidade baseia-se em nossas estimativas da volatilidade nos fluxos de capital privado, orientando-se pela seguinte equação de previsão:

(A5.1) $KF_{it} = \alpha_i + \beta_i KF_{i\,(t-1)} + u_{it}$

em que KF_{it} denota fluxos totais líquidos de capital privado para o país i no ano t; e u_{it} denota o termo de erro.

A volatilidade no país i é definida como

(A5.2) $V_i = \dfrac{S(u_{it})}{GDP_{it}, 1996}$

onde $S(u_{it})$ é a menor estimativa comum de segunda potência do erro-padrão dos resíduos na Equação (A5.1) utilizando dados de seqüências temporais de 1975 a 1996 (ver Tabela A5.3 para o índice).

Nota Sobre as Brechas no Produto Interno Bruto

Os valores atuais da diferença entre o PIB potencial, extrapolado com base nas taxas de crescimento histórico da economia real no período 1980-1996, e o PIB real ou estimado de 1997 a 1999 são calculados como custo econômico devido à crise financeira. O valor atual foi calculado para valores de 1996 utilizando-se uma taxa de desconto real de 3% ao ano. Expressos como uma porcentagem do estoque de débito em 1996, os custos estimados da crise foram de 81% para a Malásia, 97% para a Indonésia, 128% para a Tailândia e 291% para a Coréia. Um cálculo similar para o Brasil rende uma estimativa de 21%. Note-se que, para a Coréia, a figura de estoque de débito utilizado é para 1997.

Tabela A5.3 – Países em Desenvolvimento Classificados por Graus de Volatilidade para Fluxos de Capital Estrangeiro

Altamente volátil		Volátil		Moderadamente volátil		Minimamente volátil	
País	Índice	País	Índice	País	Índice	País	Índice
Jamaica	3,23	México	1,54	Colômbia	0,99	Uganda	0,63
Gabão	2,93	Equador	1,50	Tunísia	0,98	Brasil	0,60
Nigéria	2,07	Quênia	1,49	Indonésia	0,95	Paraguai	0,58
Venezuela	2,04	Nicarágua	1,48	Turquia	0,93	China	0,54
Malásia	1,97	Bolívia	1,44	Argentina	0,91	Sri Lanka	0,46
Jordão	1,82	Chile	1,38	Costa Rica	0,85	Paquistão	0,44
Panamá	1,79	Etiópia	1,31	Uruguai	0,83	Guatemala	0,43
Camarões	1,60	Filipinas	1,27	Egito	0,74	República Dominicana	0,39
Zâmbia	1,59	Honduras	1,04	Tanzânia	0,72	Índia	0,38
Zimbábue	1,59	Tailândia	1,01	Marrocos	0,64	El Salvador	0,32
						Nepal	0,29
						Bangladesh	0,10

Fontes: World Bank (1999 c); cálculos dos autores.

Nota Sobre um Modelo Binomial de Logit

O modelo binomial de *logit* é usado para estimar o impacto das variáveis independentes na probabilidade de que um país cairia na categoria de alta democracia-alta abertura financeira. Neste modelo, a variável dependente é definida por uma variável aleatória dicotômica y, que assume o valor de 1 se o país i pertence à categoria de alta democracia-alta abertura financeira, e 0 caso contrário. Isto é dado por

$$y_i = p_i + e_i,$$

em que p é a probabilidade de que determinado país pertença à categoria alta democracia-alta abertura financeira e especificada como $p = F(\mathbf{a}'\mathbf{x})$, onde x é um vetor de variáveis independentes, a é o vetor correspondente de coeficiente, $F(\mathbf{a}'\mathbf{x})$ é a função de distribuição cumulativa, e e_i um termo do erro suposto para seguir a distribuição de Bernoulli.

Expressando a probabilidade para a observação por meio do modelo *logit*, obteremos a expressão

$$F(\mathbf{a}'\mathbf{x}_i) = \frac{\exp(\mathbf{a}'\mathbf{x}_i)}{1 + \exp(\mathbf{a}'\mathbf{x}_i)}.$$

De modo subseqüente, a transformação *logit* daria

$$\log \frac{p_i}{1 - p_i} = \mathbf{a}'\mathbf{x}_i.$$

Neste capítulo, centramo-nos nas variáveis explanatórias definidas como:

*   registro dos gastos sociais totais como uma porcentagem do PIB (média 1990-96) ($\mathbf{x}_1$);
*   registro do PIB *per capita*, dólares atuais dos Estados Unidos (média 1990-1996) ($\mathbf{x}_2$).

Este modelo binomial foi estimado pelo método de máxima probabilidade utilizando-se dados através do país para uma amostragem de 67 países, para os quais dados coerentes nas duas variáveis explanatórias estavam disponíveis. De modo computacional, obtivemos a máxima probabilidade utilizando o algoritmo Newton-Raphson, que adotou o procedimento STATA *logit*. Os resultados foram gerados depois de cinco iterações. Os resultados estimados são relatados no texto da Tabela 5.3. O resultado indica que tanto a renda *per capita* como a razão dos gastos socais para o PIB têm um impacto estatisticamente significativo ao explicar a probabilidade de um país cair na categoria alta-alta. O modelo também desempenha bem ao prever porcentagem de países que estão corretamente classificados como pertencentes ao grupo de alta democracia-alta abertura financeira. Ou seja, dos 27 países do grupo alta-alta, 19 foram corretamente previstos para estar naquele grupo (baseado na probabilidade limiar de 0,5), logo, produzindo uma taxa de classificação correta de 70,37%.

Estatísticas Sumárias para Variáveis Utilizadas no Capítulo 5

Várias análises estatísticas foram executadas no decorrer deste capítulo. A Tabela A5.4 fornece estatísticas sumárias das principais variáveis e suas fontes. Relacionamentos entre estas variáveis são explorados na Figura A5.1 e na Tabela A5.5.

ABERTURA FINANCEIRA

Tabela A5.4 – Estatísticas Sumárias para Países Industrializados Seletos e Países em Desenvolvimento

Variáveis	Médio	Desvio-padrão	Mínimo	Máximo	Número de países
Direitos políticos	3,42	2,18	1,00	7,00	123
Liberdades civis	3,09	1,73	1,00	7,00	138
Abertura de capital	15,39	3,62	8,50	22,00	97
Abertura financeira	38,21	6,48	21,50	48,50	99
Transferência de pagamentos	3,09	3,09	0,001	13,84	68
Gastos sociais	17,82	11,77	3,35	49,11	51
Abertura comercial	70,60	45,90	15,21	378,67	141
Renda *per capita*	5.803,00	8.645,00	91,59	37.198,00	68

Nota: Direitos políticos, extraído de *Freedom in the World*, 1998, publicado pela Freedom House; um país concede a seus cidadãos *direitos políticos* quando lhes permite formar partidos políticos que representem um significativo espectro da escolha eleitoral e cujos líderes podem competir abertamente para e serem eleitos para posições de poder no governo.

Liberdades civis, extraído de *Freedom in the World*,1998, publicado pela Freedom House; um país preserva as *liberdades civis* de seus cidadãos quando respeita e produz seus direitos religiosos, étnicos, econômicos, lingüísticos e outros, incluindo direitos de gênero e família, liberdade pessoal e liberdades de imprensa, crença e associação.

Abertura das contas de capital é uma medida do grau de controles e/ou restrições que se aplicam apenas às transações de cálculo de capital (13 transações como classificadas pelo FMI AREAER) e são definidas na Tabela A5.1

Abertura financeira é uma medida mais ampla incorporando controle e/ou restrições tanto sobre capital corrente como transações de cálculo de capital (ver Tabela A5.1).

Transferências de pagamentos, estatísticas financeiras governamentais: média de gasto central, estatal e local como porcentagem do PIB. Transferências para outros níveis de governo nacional, 1991-1997; países com o mínimo para esta variável são: Chile, Costa Rica, República Dominicana, Grécia, Irlanda, Lesoto, Panamá, Sri Lanka e Tailândia. Dinamarca tem o valor máximo para esta variável.

Gastos sociais, estatísticas financeiras governamentais e UNESCO: média de gasto central, estadual e local como porcentagem do PIB, 1991-1997; Paquistão tem o mínimo para esta variável. Dinamarca tem o valor máximo para esta variável.

Abertura comercial, Indicadores do Desenvolvimento Mundial: média comercial ou porcentagem do PIB, década de 1980.

Renda per capita, média de renda *per capita*, 1990-1997; na amostragem de países, o mínimo é de US$ 91,60 para Moçambique e o máximo é de US$ 37.199 para a Suíça.

Fontes: Freedom House (1998); FMI (1999, várias publicações); UNESCO (1998); Banco Mundial (1999f).

Notas

1. Para alguns países onde os dados sobre determinadas transações não estavam disponíveis, foram dados os valores médios de 1.

Figura A5.1 – Correlações da Abertura Financeira com Direitos Políticos e Liberdades Civis

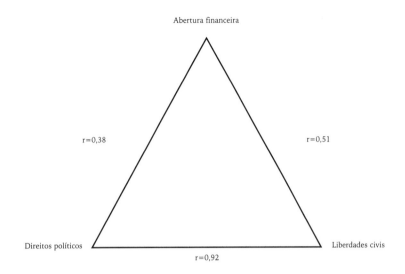

Nota: A estimativa de correlação entre os coeficientes é estatisticamente significativo a 1% (baseado no z-test).
Fonte: Cálculo dos autores.

Tabela A5.5 – Os Relacionamentos Entre Abertura Financeira, Democracia e Gastos Sociais

Variáveis	Abertura financeira	Abertura de capital	Direitos políticos	Liberdades civis	Abertura comercial	Gastos sociais	Transferência de pagamentos	Renda per capita
Abertura financeira	1,00							
Abertura de capital	0,91	1,00						
Direitos políticos	-0,32*	0,22*	1,00					
Liberdades civis	-0,55*	0,46**	0,91*	1,00				
Abertura comercial	0,18	0,21*	-0,06	-0,14	1,00			
Gastos sociais	0,52*	0,42**	-0,72*	-0,74*	0,28**	1,00		
Transferência de pagamentos	0,23	0,17	-0,19	-0,21	-0,14	0,31**	1,00	
Renda *per capita*	0,52*	0,44**	-0,54*	-0,68*	0,29*	0,67*	0,26	1,00

* Significativo ao nível de 0,01 de confiança.
** Significativo ao nível de 0,05 de confiança.
Fontes: Informações baseadas em dados da Freedom House (1998); FMI (1999, vários anos); UNESCO (1998); Banco Mundial (1999f); ver Tabela A5.4 para variáveis de explanação.

ANEXO 6

ÍNDICES DE GOVERNO E CORRUPÇÃO

MÉTODOS DE AGREGAÇÃO, MEDIDAS EMPÍRICAS NOVAS E DESAFIOS ECONOMÉTRICOS

O recente interesse pelas conseqüências dos fatores de economia política, instruções formais e informais, regra de direito, captação legal e judiciária e a corrupção tem sido acompanhado pela proliferação de dados simulando medir os vários aspectos relacionados, com o que pode ser amplamente chamado de governo. Neste anexo resumimos algumas pesquisas recentes, relacionadas com resultados empíricos e metodológicos sobre o governo e a corrupção, apresentados no texto do Capítulo 6. A primeira parte do anexo resume os desafios empíricos sobre os indicadores governamentais, enquanto a segunda apresenta o resumo do projeto de pesquisa que desvela a aferição da corrupção na propina administrativa, na captação estatal (que inclui a captação legal e judiciária) e em pagamentos de licitações públicas.

Definir e Desvelar o Governo

Entre outras coisas, este relatório desvela o conceito de governo em seis indicadores componentes agregados que foram construídos por Kaufmann et al. (1999a, b). Detalhes sobre estes agregados e a noção de governo subjacente a eles são dados no texto do capítulo.

Os indicadores agregados são baseados em mais de trezentas medidas produzidas pelas 13 diferentes organizações. As fontes incluem dados publicados e não publicados de um número de estimativas privadas e organizações de negócio de risco, reserva de pensamento, outras ONGs, e os resultados dos estudos levados a efeito por organizações multilaterais e outras. A base de dados cobre 170 países. Habitualmente, os dados são apenas

para um período: 1997-1998. Os dados e os detalhes posteriores sobre a metodologia econométrica estão disponíveis em http://www.worldbank.org/wbi/governance.

Governo, ou a maneira de governar, engloba o processo de seleção, monitoração e substituição dos governos, e refere-se à capacidade governamental de formar e implementar políticas sólidas e o respeito aos cidadãos e as condições para suas instituições. No Capítulo 6 apresentamos os seis índices componentes com os quais se mede o governo: voz e responsabilidade, estabilidade política, eficácia governamental, orçamento regulatório, regra de direito e controle da corrupção. Para cada um dos seis aspectos de governo, um grande número de índices individuais de diferentes fontes foi identificado como relevante e agregado para formar uma das seis medidas compósitas. A agregação utiliza-se de um modelo de componentes não observados. Vantagens que derivam do método incluem:

- Um grande número de indicadores e, antes de tudo, ruidosos, transformado em um único número menor de indicadores agregados mais confiáveis. Estes agregados refletem o consenso estatístico de muitas fontes diferentes e um rigoroso método de agregação que separa sinal de ruído. Como resultado, esses indicadores agregados são mais precisos que indicadores mais convencionais.
- O método computa estatisticamente sólidas margens de erro em torno das estimativas de governo para países individuais, ou seja, pode-se ter relativa confiança quanto ao grau de incerteza associado com estimativas de governo específicas do país.

A metodologia utilizada enfatiza uma limitação de indicadores atuais do governo: são incapazes de produzir medidas precisas. Em vista das margens de erro que cercam as medidas estimativas de governo, pequenas diferenças nas estimativas não serão prática ou estatisticamente significativas; seria desorientador oferecer classificações muito precisas de países de acordo com seu nível de governo. Ao invés disso, amplos agrupamentos de países, ao longo das linhas de uma abordagem de sinais de tráfego e estatisticamente defensável é apresentado no texto do capítulo.

O que acabamos de apresentar resume algumas questões metodológicas levantadas em "Aggregating Governance Indicators" (Kaufmann,1999a) e na interpretação deles. Além do mais, neste documento os autores organizam os dados de modo que, dentro de cada um dos seis grupos de governo, cada indicador individual mede um conceito básico subjacente similar de governo. Há consideráveis benefícios da combinação destes indicadores relatados num indicador de governo agregado para cada grupo, porque: os indicadores agregados medem um conjunto muito mais amplo de países que qualquer fonte individual, indicadores agregados

podem fornecer medidas mais precisas de governo que os indicadores individuais, e é possível construir medidas quantitativas de precisão tanto das estimativas de governo agregado para cada país como de seus componentes. Isto permite testar formalmente hipóteses relacionadas com diferenças através do país no governo.

Para cada um destes grupos, Kaufmann et al. combinam os indicadores componentes em um indicador de governo agregado, utilizando-se de um modelo de componentes não observados, acrescido de um termo de perturbação que capta os erros de percepção e/ou amostragem de variação em cada indicador. Assim, as estimativas são geradas de cada uma das seis medidas de sua precisão. A escolha das unidades para o governo garante que as estimativas de governo tenham uma média de 0, um desvio-padrão de 1, e um alcance de -2,5 a 2,5. Valores mais elevados correspondem a melhores resultados. Desde que a distribuição condicional do governo nos dados observados é assumida como sendo independente através dos países, é possível fazer afirmações probabilísticas comparando o governo em pares de países.

Achou-se que os conceitos subjacentes do governo em cada grupo não são estimados com muita precisão como descrito nas Figuras 6.1 e 6.2 do Capítulo 6. O preferencialmente tamanho grande destes intervalos de confiança tem importantes implicações para o uso destes indicadores de governo agregados. Pequenas diferenças de pontos estimativos do governo através dos países não são estatisticamente significativas. Como resultado, os usuários destes dados deveriam centralizar o foco no escopo de governo possível para cada país como resumido nos 90% dos intervalos de confiança mostrados na Figura 6.1 do Capítulo 6. Para dois países em pólos opostos da escala de governo dos quais 90% dos intervalos de confiança não se sobrepõem, é razoável concluir que há diferenças significativas no governo. Para pares de países que estão mais próximos e dos quais 90% dos intervalos de confiança se sobrepõem, a circunspecção está em ordem e as comparações aparentemente precisas deveriam ser evitadas.

Apesar da imprecisão destes indicadores agregados, eles são muito úteis por várias razões. Primeiro, porque desde que cada um destes indicadores agregados medem um conjunto muito maior de países do que qualquer indicador individual, é possível fazer comparações – embora imprecisas – através de um conjunto muito mais amplo de países do que seria possível com qualquer indicador simples. Segundo, cada indicador *agregado* fornece um sinal mais preciso de seu conceito mais amplo correspondente do governo do que alguns de seus indicadores componentes *individuais*, assim como um *resumo* consistente da evidência disponível. Terceiro, as medidas de precisão para cada país são igualmente úteis, porque capacitam os testes estatísticos formais das diferenças de governo através dos países – ao invés de comparações arbitrárias. Quarto, é possível utilizar informação nas estimativas de precisão de cada agregado para quantificar o efeito do erro de

aferição na análise de regressão que utiliza indicadores governamentais como variáveis (independentes) como o lado correto da mão.

Em outro trabalho, "Governance Matters", Kaufmann et al., 1999b), os autores detalham todas as fontes de dados exteriores, descrevem cada variável individual e analisam o relacionamento entre componentes governamentais e as variáveis desenvolvimentistas. Os dados através do país indicam uma correlação simples significativa entre governo e resultados socioeconômicos (alfabetização, mortalidade infantil, longevidade e renda *per capita*).

Para explorar o efeito do governo ou das variáveis socioeconômicas, padronizando para outros fatores, testes econométricos específicos foram realizados, baseados numa regressão de dois estágios menos quadrados e uma variável dependente socioeconômica particular numa componente constante de governo, utilizando indicadores de herança colonial como instrumento, seguindo a abordagem de Hall & Jones (1999). O modelo é bem especificado no sentido de que os instrumentos possuem um poder preditivo forte para o governo e as hipóteses do nulo destes instrumentos afetam as rendas apenas mediante seus efeitos sobre o governo, se não forem rejeitadas. Os interesses sobre o erro de aferição e das variáveis omitidas também estão erigidos em detalhe em Kaufmann et al. (1999b).

Aferir e Desvelar a Corrupção

Uma cobertura particular ao desafio de corrigir a corrupção foi dada no texto do Capítulo 6, em razão de sua importância dentro do governo e da emergência de achados empíricos novos. Até recentemente, a aferição da corrupção, onde era feita, seguia uma abordagem unidimensional e generalizada para este problema complexo. Progressos empíricos recentes no estudo da corrupção por meio de técnicas de estudo e abordagens melhoradas permitem um desvelamento multifacetado e em profundidade da corrupção. No texto do capítulo, relatamos a relação entre estratégias corporativas e governo nacional, e mostramos também que, enquanto no equilíbrio administrativo, a propina "não paga" por negócios. Formas "maiores" de corrupção, tal como a captação do Estado (Figura 6.11), extraem benefícios privados significativos para a empresa captadora (Figura 6.6 do Capítulo 6), embora resultando em custos sociais enormes. Detalhamos a seguir como tal desvelamento foi realizado.

O Ambiente de Negócios e o Estudo do Desempenho Empresarial: Desvelando a Corrupção

A capacidade de distinguir entre estas várias manifestações, causas e

conseqüências de diferentes tipos de corrupção deriva do efeito ajustado para desvelar empírica e conceitualmente o problema da corrupção, iniciado dentro de um estudo em grande escala de economias de transição. O ambiente de negócios e o estudo do desempenho empresarial (BEEPS) foi conduzido com base em entrevistas pessoais com gerentes ou donos de empresas em visitas *in loco* durante junho até agosto de 1999 em 22 países, e cobriu em torno de três mil empresas.

Em cada país, entre 125 e 150 empresas foram entrevistadas, com exceção de três países em que amostragens mais amplas foram utilizadas: Polônia (250), Federação Russa (550), Ucrânia (250). As questões do estudo examinam a corrupção com base em um número de ângulos diferentes que fornecem checagens coerentes nas respostas de cada empresa. Além do mais, foram conduzidos testes para detectar qualquer viés negativo ou positivo entre as respostas das empresas em qualquer país em questão.

Ao esboçar o estudo, a corrupção foi abordada como um fenômeno multifacetado, que requer um desvelamento rigoroso e, em tal base, uma tipologia para distinguir entre os padrões de países diferentes e as conseqüências a que se chegou. Uma ênfase particular foi dada às três dimensões da corrupção: corrupção administrativa, corrupção de licitação pública e captação do Estado (Hellman et al., 2000a ["Colhe o Estado, Colhe o Dia"]; Hellman et al., 2000, ["Aferição Governamental, Corrupção e Captação do Estado"] — reconhecendo que as diferentes dimensões da corrupção poderiam ter origens e conseqüências únicas.

Definições da Tipologia da Corrupção

A *corrupção administrativa* refere-se à aplicação arbitrária e distorcida e à implementação das leis existentes, regras e regulamentações para ganho ilícito privado por um funcionário público, e está sujeita a uma variedade de medidas quantitativas nos BEEPS (tais como a porcentagem de propinas administrativas pagas pela empresa ou uma parte de seus lucros totais). *A corrupção da licitação pública*, uma importante dimensão da alocação corrupta das finanças e dos recursos públicos, é aferida pela porcentagem da taxa de propina paga para garantir contratos. *A captação estatal* refere-se a ações dos agentes econômicos ou empresas, ambos dentro dos setores público e privado para influenciar a formação e a formulação de bens, regulamentações, decretos e outras políticas governamentais (isto é, as regras básicas do jogo) em seu próprio benefício – como um resultado do pagamento de agentes privados a funcionários públicos. Por exemplo, um oligarca influente na chefia de um poderoso grupo financeiro industrial pode comprar os votos dos legisladores para erigir barreira para a entrada no setor energético.

Desvelar a Captação do Estado e Calcular o Índice Geral de Captação

No interior das empresas BEEPS, perguntou-se a respeito de sua propensão para comprar a captação de influência legislativa, e pediu-se também, como um detalhe, para que relatassem sobre o impacto na empresa de diferentes dimensões da captação do Estado na economia. Para um grupo seleto de economias de transição (para detalhes e dados completos, inclusive aferição das margens de erro, ver Hellman et al., 2000a; Hellman et al., 2000c), a Tabela A6.1 apresenta as várias dimensões da captação do Estado que foram aferidas, assim como os índices gerais da captação do Estado derivados através da média simples de todos os subcomponentes nas colunas anteriores que aferem os efeitos da componente de captação do Estado. Em troca, o índice geral da captação do Estado foi utilizado no segundo painel da Figura 6.6, enquanto a medida da corrupção administrativa foi utilizada no primeiro painel daquela figura, na base dos componentes desvelados da captação do Estado; também é possível construir outros subíndices de importância. Da Tabela A6.1, o índice de captação do Judiciário pode ser calculado, por exemplo, baseado na proporção de empresas afetadas pela compra de decisões judiciárias e criminais e comerciais (colunas 4 e 5). A análise das causas e conseqüências (incluindo a ausência de liberdades civis e reformas econômicas) (ou a saída de crescimento do investimento e a proteção dos direitos de propriedade) da captação do Estado é realizada por meio de análises econométricas multivariadas (incluindo especificações *logit* e o mínimo comum dos quadrados). A análise em profundidade do FDI liga-se a captação do Estado, pagamento de licitação pública e outras formas de influência (incluindo as legais); também é baseada nos dados extraídos de BEEPS e apresentados detalhadamente em Hellman et al. (2000b).

Dos Estudos Através do País para Diagnóstico Específico em Profundidade do País

Para uma ação programática em um país, quando muito, estudos melhorados através do país não podem substituir a necessidade de realizar um diagnóstico em profundidade no governo e na corrupção dentro de um cenário particular. Tais instrumentos diagnósticos de governo de um país específico são discutidos no texto do capítulo, e referências adicionais são fornecidas no *site*.

Tabela A6.1 – Porcentagem de Empresas Afetadas pelas Diferentes Formas de Captação do Estado e Índice de Captação Geral do Estado, Países Seletos, 1999

País	Aquisição corporativa de						Índice global de captação do Estado[b] (1+ ... +6)
	Legislação parlamentar (1)	Decretos presidenciais (2)	Influência do Banco Central (3)	Decisões do tribunal criminal (4)	Decisões do tribunal comercial (5)	Finança de partidos políticos (6)	
Azerbaijão	41	48	39	44	40	35	41
Bulgária	28	26	28	28	19	42	28
Croácia	18	24	30	29	29	30	27
Estônia [a]	14	7	8	8	8	17	10
Geórgia	29	24	32	18	20	21	24
Hungria [a]	12	7	8	5	5	4	7
Latíbia	40	49	8	21	26	35	30
Moldávia	43	30	40	33	34	42	37
Polônia [a]	13	10	6	12	18	10	12
Romênia	22	20	26	14	17	27	21
Federação Russa	35	32	47	24	27	24	32
Eslovênia [a]	8	5	4	6	6	11	7
Ucrânia	44	37	37	21	26	29	32

a. A classificação da captação estatal é *média* para estes países. Para todos os outros países arrolados, a classificação de captação estatal é *alta*.

b. O índice de captação estatal é a média simples dos subcomponentes aferidos nas colunas 1 a 6. Subagrupamentos de tais componentes também permitem cálculos de um índice de captação legal ou judiciária (colunas 1, 4 e 5), as quais, sob uma interpretação ampliada, também poderiam abranger a compra de decretos presidenciais (coluna 2), um índice solitário de captação judiciária (colunas 4 e 5), ou um índice de captação legal (colunas 1 e 2).

Nota: Estimativas individuais sujeitas a margem de erro. Tais margens de erro são significativas; logo, deve-se ter cuidado na utilização de cada estimativa individual. Contudo, testamos para países específicos interrogados e não o achamos significativo (ver Hellman et al., 2000c).

Fontes: Hellman et al. (2000a); ver também http://www.worldbank.org/wbi/governance.

BIBLIOGRAFIA E REFERÊNCIAS

A palavra "processado" descreve informalmente trabalhos reproduzidos que normalmente não estão disponíveis nas bibliotecas.

ADB (Asian Development Bank). *Emerging Asia: Changes and Challenges.* Manila, 1997.

ADELMAN, I., TAFT-MORRIS, C. *Society, Politics and Economic Development: A Quantitative Approach.* Baltimore, Maryland: The Johns Hopkins University Press, 1967.

ADES, A., DI TELLA, R. National Champions and Corruption: Some Unpleasant Interventionist Arithmetic. *The Economic Journal,* n.107, p.1023-42, 1997.

_____. Rents, Competition, and Corruption. *American Economic Review,* v.80, n.4, p.982-93, 1999.

AHLUWALIA, M. S. Income Distribution and Development: Some Stylized Facts. *American Economic Review,* v.66, n.2, p.128-35, 1976.

AKIYAMA, T. Has Africa Turned the Corner? World Bank, International Economics Commodities and Policy Unit. Washington, D.C., 1995. (Processado).

ALBA, P. et al. The Role of Macroeconomic and Financial Sector Linkages in East Asia's Financial Crisis. Relatório apresentado no Centre for Economic Policy Research/World Bank conference on Financial Crisis: Contagion and Market Volatility. London, May, 1998.

ALDEMAN, I. Growth, Income Distribution, and Equity-Oriented Development Strategies. *World Development,* v.3, n.2-3, p.67-76, 1975.

ALESINA, A. et al. The Political Economy of Capital Controls. In: LEIDERMAN, L., RAZIN, A. (Eds.) *Capital Mobility: The Impact on Consumption, Investment and Growth.* Cambridge, U.K.: Cambridge University Press, 1994.

ALESINA, A., PEORTTI, R. The Political Economy of Growth: A Critical Survey of the Recent Literature. *World Bank Economic Review,* v.8, n.3, p.351-71, 1994.

ALESINA, A., RODRIK, D. Distributive Politics and Economic Growth. *Quarterly Journal of Economics,* n.108, p.465-90, 1994.

AMIN, S., PEBLEY, A. R. Gender Inequality within Households: The Impact of a Women's Development Programme in Thirty-Six Bangladesh Villages. *Bangladesh Development Studies*, v.22, n.2-3, p.121-54, 1994.

ARIYOSHI, A. et al. *Country Experiences with the Use and Liberalization of Capital Controls.* Washington, D.C.: International Monetary Fund, Monetary Exchange Affairs Department, 1999.

ARNESON, R. Equity and Equality of Opportunity for Welfare. *Philosophical Study*, n.56, p.77-93, 1989.

ARROW, K. The Economic Implications of Learning by Doing. *Review of Economic Studies*, n.29, p.155-73, Jun. 1962.

ÅSLUND, A. Why Has Russia's Economic Transformation Been so Arduous? Relatório apresentado na Annual Bank Conference on Development Economics. Washington, D.C., Apr. 28-30, 1999.

AVIATION WEEK AND SPACE TECHNOLOGY, v.151, n.6, Aug. 9, 1999.

BANERJEE, A. Land Reforms: Prospects and Strategies. Relatório apresentado na Annual Bank Conference on Development Economics. World Bank, Washington, D.C., Apr. 28-30, 1999.

BARRO, R. J. Government Spending in a Simple Model of Endogenous Growth. *Journal of Political Economy*, n.98, s103-25, 1990.

_____. Economic Growth, Convergence, and Government Policies. In: ZYCHER, B., SOLOMON, L. C. (Eds.) *Economic Policy, Financial Markets, and Economic Growth.* Boulder, Colorado; Oxford, U.K.: Westview Press, em cooperação com o Milken Institute for Job and Capital Formation, 1993.

BARRO, R., LEE, J. W. Losers and Winners in Economic Growth. *Proceedings of the World Bank Annual Conference on Development Economics 1993*. World Bank, Washington, D.C., 1994.

_____. International Measures of Schooling Years and Schooling Quality. *American Economic Review, Papers and Proceedings*, v.86, n.2, p.218-23, 1997.

BARRO, R., SALA-I-MARTIN, X. *Economic Growth*. New York: McGraw-Hill, 1995.

_____. *Convergence. Economic Growth: Theory and Evidence*, v.1. International Library of Critical Writings in Economics n. 68. Cheltenham, U.K.: Elgar Reference Collection, 1996.

BASTER, N. (Ed.) *Measuring Development: The Role and Adequacy of Development Indicators*. London: F. Cass (reimpressão). Journal of Development Studies, n.8, v.3, 1972. (Original).

BASU, K. et al. Household Labor Supply, Unemployment, e Minimum Wage Legislation. Policy Research Working Paper n. WPS 2049. Development Economics, World Bank, Washington, D.C., 1999.

BEASON, R., WEINSTEIN, D. E. Growth, Economies of Scale, e Targeting in Japan (1955-1990). *Review of Economics and Statistics*, v.78, n.2, p.286-95, 1996.

BECKER, G. S. *Human Capital*. New York: Columbia University Press, 1964.

BEHRMAN, J., BIRDSALL, N. The Quality of Schooling Quantity Alone Is Misleading. *American Economic Review*, v.73, n.5, p.928-46, 1983.

BEHRMAN, J., DEOLALIKAR, A. B. Health and Nutrition. In: CHENERY, H., SRINIVASAN, T. N. (Eds.) *Handbook of Development Economics*. Amsterdam: North-Holland, 1988. v.1.

BEHRMAN, J. et al. Schooling Investments and Aggregate Conditions: A Household-Survey-Based Approach for Latin America and the Caribbean. Global Research Project Paper. Global Development Network, 1999. (Processado).

BEHRMAN, J., KNOWLES, J. C. Household Income and Child Schooling in Vietnam. *World Bank Economic Review*, v.13, n.2, p.211-56, 1999.

BENHABIB, J., SPIEGEL, M. The Role of Human Capital in Economic Development. In: BALDASSARI, M. P., PHELPS, E. S. L. (Eds.) *International Differences in Growth Rates*: Market Globalization and Economic Areas. Central Issues in Contemporary Economic Theory and Practice Series. New York; London: St. Martin's Press; Macmillan Press, 1994.

BERGSTRÖM, F. Capital Subsidies and the Performance of Firms. Working Paper Series in Economics and Finance n. 285. Stockholm School of Economics, Stockholm, Sweden, 1998.

BERRY, R. A., CLINE, W. R. *Agrarian Structure and Productivity in Developing Countries*. Baltimore, Maryland: The Johns Hopkins University Press, 1979.

BESLEY, T. Property Rights and Investment Incentives: Theory and Evidence from Ghana. *Journal of Political Economy*, v.103, n.5, p.903-37, 1995.

BESLEY, T., CASE, A. Unnatural Experiments? Estimating the Incidence of Endogenous Policies. Working Paper n. 4956. National Bureau of Economic Research, Cambridge, Massachusetts, 1994.

BHAGAWATI, J. Education, Class Structure, and Income Equality. *World Development*, v.1, n.5, p.21-36, 1973.

_____. Directly Unproductive Profit-Seeking Activities. *Journal of Political Economy*, v.90, n.5, p.998-1002, 1982.

BHALLA, S. S. Growth and Poverty in India – Myth and Reality. Oxus Research and Investment. 2000. (Processado). Disponível em http://www. oxusresearch.com.

BHATIA, B., DRÉZE, J. For Development and Democracy. *Frontline*. Chennai, India, March 6, 1998. A versão resumida está disponível em http://www.transparency.de/documents/work -papers/bhatia-dreze.html.

BINSWANGER, H. P. Brazilian Policies That Encourage Deforestation in the Amazon. *World Development*, v.19, n.7, p.821-9, 1991.

BINSWANGER, H. P., DEININGER. K. Explaining Agricultural and Agrarian Policies in Developing Countries. *Journal of Economic Literature*. n.XXXV, p.1958-2005, Dec. 1997.

BINSWANGER, H. P. et al. Power, Distortions, Revolt, and Reform in Agricultural Land Relations. In: BEHRMAN, J., SRINIVASAN, T. N. (Eds.) *Handbook of Development Economics*. Amsterdam: Elsevier Science, 1995. v.IIIb

BIRDSALL, N. Government, Population, and Poverty: A Win-Win Tale. In: KIESSLING, K. L., LANDBERG, H. (Eds.) *Population, Economic Development, and the Environment*. Oxford, U.K.: Oxford University Press, 1994.

BIRDSALL, N., LONDOÑO, J. L. Asset Inequality

Matters: An Assessment of the World Bank's Approach to Poverty Reduction. *American Economic Review*, v.87, n.2, p.32-7, 1997.

_____. No Tradeoff: Efficient Growth via More Equal Human Capital Accumulation. In: GRAHAM, C. et al. (Eds.) *Beyond Tradeoffs*: *Market Reform and Equitable Growth in Latin America*. Washington, D.C.: Brookings Institution Press, em associação com o Inter-American Development Bank, 1998.

BIS (Bank for International Settlements). *Annual Report*. Basel, Switzerland, 1997, 1998. (Vários anos).

BLOMM, D. E., BRENDER, A. Labor and the Emerging World Economy. Working Paper n. 4266. National Bureau of Economic Research, Cambridge, Massachusetts, 1993.

BLOOM, D. E., FREEMAN, R. B. Economic Development and the Timing and Components of Population Growth. *Journal of Policy Modeling*, v.10, n.1, p.57-81, 1988.

BLOOM, D. E., WILLIAMSON, J. G. Demographic Transitions and Economic Miracles in Emerging Asia. *World Bank Economic Review*, v.12, n.3, p.419-55, 1998.

BOJO, J. The Costs of Land Degradation in Sub-Saharan Africa. *Ecological Economics*, v.16, n.2, p.161-73, 1996.

BOJO, J., SEGNESTAM, L. Towards a Common Goal: The Experience of NEAPS and Their Relationship to NSDSs. Paper submitted to the Regional Consultative Meeting on Sustainable Development in Africa, Sept. 1999, p.7-9, Abidjan.

BONILLA-CHACIN, M., HAMMER, J. S. Life and Death among the Poorest. Texto apresentado

ao World Bank Economist Forum. Washington, D.C., May 3-4, 1999.

BORENSZTEIN, E. et al. How Does Foreign Direct Investment Affect Economic Growth? *Journal of International Economics*, v.45, n.1, p.115-35, 1998.

_____. The Behavior of Non-Oil Commodity Prices. Occasional Paper n. 112. International Monetary Fund, Washington, D.C., 1994.

BOUIS, H. E. et al. Gender Equality and Investments in Adolescents in the Rural Philipines. Research Report n. 108. International Food Policy Research Institute, Washington, D.C., 1998.

BOURGUIGNON, F. Crime, Violence, and Inequitable Development. Texto apresentado na Annual Bank Conference on Development Economics. World Bank, Washington, D.C., Apr. 28-30 1999.

BREGMAN, A. et al. Effects of Capital Subsidization on Productivity in Israeli Industry. *Bank of Israel Economic Review*, n.72, p.77-101, 1999.

BREWER, D. J. et al. Estimating the Cost of National Class Size Reductions under Different Policy Alternatives. *Education Evaluation and Policy Analysis*, v.21, n.2, p.179-92, 1999.

BROWN, L. R. et al. State of the World 1998. In: *A Worldwatch Institute Report on Progress Toward a Sustainable Society*. New York: W.W. Norton, 1998.

BRUNETTI, A. Political Variables in Cross-Country Growth Analysis. *Journal of Economic Surveys*, v.11, n.2, p.163-90, 1997a.

_____. *Politics and Economic Growth*: *A Cross-Country*

BIBLIOGRAFIA E REFERÊNCIAS

Data Perspective. Paris: Organisation for Economic Co-operation and Development, Development Center Studies, 1997b.

BRUNETTI, A. et al. Credibility of Rules and Economic Growth. Policy Research Working Paper n. 1760. World Bank, Policy Research Department, Washington, D.C., 1997.

BRYANT, R. C., HODGKINSON, E. Problems of International Cooperation. In: *Can Nations Agree? Issues in International Economic Cooperation.* Washington, D.C.: The Brookings Institution, 1989.

BUCKLEY, R. *1998* Annual Review of Development Effectiveness. World Bank, Operations Evaluation Department, Washington, D.C., 1999.

BURGESS, R. Land Distribution and Welfare in Rural China. Relatório apresentado na Annual Bank Conference on Development Economics. World Bank, Washington, D.C., Apr. 20, 2000.

CALVO, G. A. Contagion in Emerging Markets: When *Wall Street* Is a Carrier. University of Maryland, College Park, 1999. (Processado).

CALVO, G. A. et al. Capital Inflows to Latin America: The 1970s and 1990s. In: BACHA, E. L. (Ed.) *Economics in a Changing World: Proceedings of the Tenth World Congress of the International Economic Association*, v.4, *Development, Trade, and the Environment*. New York; London: St. Martin's Press; Macmillan Press, em associação com o International Economic Association, 1994.

CALVO, G. A., MENDOZA, E. G. Petty Crime and Cruel Punishment: Lessons from the Mexican Debacle. *American Economic Review, Papers and Proceedings*, v.86, n.2, p.170-5, 1996.

CAPRIO, G., HONOHAN, P. Restoring Banking Stability: Beyond Supervised Capital Requirements. *Journal of Economic Perspectives*, v.13, n.4, p.43-64, 1999.

CARD, D., KRUEGER, A. B. School Quality and Black-White Relative Earnings: A Direct Assessment. *Quarterly Journal of Economics*, v.107, n.1, p.151-200, 1992.

CASTANEDA, B. An Index of Sustainable Economic Welfare for Chile. Masters Thesis. University of Maryland, College Park, Maryland, 1997.

CASTRO, R. et al. The Costa Rican Experience with Market Instruments to Mitigate Climate Change and Conserve Biodiversity. Relatório apresentado na Global Conference on Knowledge for Development in the Information Age. World Bank, Toronto, Jun. 24, 1997.

CHENERY, H. et al. *Redistribution with Growth*. New York: Oxford University Press, 1974.

CHOMITZ, K. M. et al. Financing Environmental Services: The Costa Rican Experience and its Implications. World Bank, Development Economics Research Group, Washington D.C., 1998. (Processado).

CHOMITZ, K. M., GRAY, D. A. Roads, Land Use, and Deforestation: A Spatial Model applied to Belize. Working Paper n. 3. Research Project on Social and Environmental Consequences of Growth-Oriented Policies. World Bank, Policy Research Department, Washington, D.C., 1996.

CHONG, A., CALDERÓN, C. Empirical Testes on Casuality and Feedback between Institutional Measures and Economic Growth. World Bank, Washington, D.C., 1997a. (Processado).

CHONG, A., CALDERÓN, C. Institutional Change

and Poverty, or Why Is it Worth it to Reform the State? World Bank, Washington, D.C., 1997b. (Processado).

_____. Institutional Efficiency and Income Inequality: Cross-Country Empirical Evidence. World Bank, Washington, D.C., 1998.

CLAESSENS, S. et al. Financial Restructuring in East Asia: Halfway There? Financial Sector Discussion Paper n. 3. World Bank, Washington, D.C., 1999.

CLEAVER, K., SCHREIBER, G. *Reversinf the Spiral: The Population, Environment, and Agriculture Nexus in Sub-Saharan Africa.* Directions in Development. World Bank, Washington, D.C., 1994.

COCHILCO. Annual report of COCHILCO. Report from the Senate of Chile, 2000.

COHEN, G. A. On the Currency of Egalitarian Justice. *Ethics*, n.99, p.906-44, 1989.

COLLIER, P. On the Economic Consequences of Civil War. *Oxford Economic Papers*, n.51, p.168-83, Jan. 1999.

COLLIER, P. et al. Fifty Years of Development. World Bank, Washington, D.C., 2000. (Processado).

COLLIER, P. HOEFFLER, A. On the Economic Causes of Civil Wars. *Oxford Economic Papers* 50, Oct. 1998, p.563-73.

COLLINS, C. Aid to Dependent Corporations. In: BRESLOW, M. et al. (Eds.) *Decoding the Contract: Progressive Perspectives on Current Economic Policy Debates.* Somerville, Massachusetts: Economic Affairs Bureau, 1996.

COLLINS, S. M., BOSWORTH, B. P. Economic Growth in East Asia: Accumulation Versus Assimilation. *Brookings Papers on Economic Activity*, n.2, p.135-91, 1996.

COMMANDER, S. et al. Restructuring in Transition Economies: Owership, Competition, and Regulation. Relatório apresentado na Annual Bank Conference on Development Economics. Washington, D.C., Apr. 28-30, 1999.

COOPER, R. Should Capital-Account Covertibility Be a World Objective? In: *Ensays in International Finance Series,* n.207. Princeton, New Jersey: Princeton University, Department of Economics, International Finance Section, 1998.

CORBO, V. et al. *Adjustment Lending Revisited*: Policies to Restore Growth. Washington, D.C.: World Bank, 1992.

CORNIA, Giovanni A. Rising Income Inequality and Poverty Reduction: Are They Compatible? UNU/WIDER, 1999. Projeto de pesquisa disponível em http://www.wider.unu.edu/wiid.wiid.htm.

CORSETTI, G. et al. What Caused the Asian Currency and Financial Crisis? New York: New York University, 1998. (Processado).

CROPPER, M. et al. Roads, Population Pressures, and Deforestation in Thailand, 1976-1989. Policy Research Working Paper n. 1726. World Bank, Policy Research Department, Washington, D.C., 1997.

CROPPER, M., GRIFFITHS, C. The Interaction of Population Growth and Environmental Quality. *American Economic Review*, n.84, p.250-4, 1994.

DAILAMI, M. Euphoria and Panic: Developing Countries Relationship to Private Finance. *EDI Forum*, v.3, n.2, p.1-3, 6, 1998.

_____. Financial Openness, Democracy, and Redis-

tributive Policy. Policy Research Working Paper n. 2372. Washington, D.C.: World Bank, 2000.

DAILAMI, M., HAQUE, N. ul. What Macroeconomic Policies Are "Soubd"? Policy Research Working Paper n. 1995. Washington, D.C.: World Bank, 1998.

DALY, H. E. Georgescu-Roegen Versus Solow/Stiglitz. *Ecological Economics*, v.22, n.3, p.261-6, 1997.

DASGUPTA, P. Well-Being and the Extent of Its Realization in Developing Countries. *Economic Journal*, v.100, n.4 (supplement), p.1-32, 1990a.

_____. Well-Being in Poor Countries. *Economic and Political Weekly* (India), n.25, p.1713-20, 1990b.

_____. *An Inquiry into Well-Being and Destitution*. New York: Oxford University Press, 1993.

_____. Population, Poverty, and the Local Environment. *Scientific American* (Washington, D.C.), Feb. 1995. p.40-5.

DASGUPTA, P., MÄLER, K.-G. Poverty, Institutions, and the Environmental Resource Base. Environment Paper n. 9. World Bank, Environment Department, Washington, D.C., 1994.

DASGUPTA, P., SERAGELDIN, I. *Social Capital*: A *Multifaceted Perspective*. Washington, D.C.: World Bank, 1999.

DASGUPTA, S. et al. Environmental Regulation and Development: A Cross-Country Empirical Analysis. Policy Research Working Paper n. 1488. World Bank, Policy Research Department, Washington, D.C., 1995.

DE GREGORIO, J. Growth in Latin America.

Journal of Development Economics, v.31, n.1, p.59-84, 1992.

DE LONG et al. Equipment Investment and Economic Growth. *Quarterly Journal of Economics*, v.106, n.2, p.445-502, 1991.

DE MOOR et al. *Subsidizing Unsustainable Development*: *Undermining the Earth with Public Funds*. San José, Costa Rica: Institute for Research on Public Expenditure and The Earth Council, 1997.

DEATON, A. *The Analysis of Household Surveys*: A *Microeconometric Approach to Development Policy*. Baltimore, Maryland: The Johns Hopkins University Press, em associação com o World Bank, 1997.

DEININGER, K. Making Negotiated Land Reform Work: Initial Experience from Colombia, Brazil, and South Africa. Policy Research Working Paper n. 2040. World Bank, Policy Research Department, Washington D.C., 1999.

DEININGER, K., MINTEN, B. Determinants of Forest Cover and the Economics of Protection: An Application to Mexico. Working Paper n. 10. Research Project on Social and Environmental Consequences of Growth-Oriented Policies. World Bank, Development Research Department, Washington, D.C., 1996. (Processado).

DEININGER, K., OLINTO, P. Asset Distribution Inequality and Growth. World Bank, Policy Research Group, Washington, D.C., 1999. (Processado).

DEININGER, K., SQUIRE, L. A New Dataset Measuring Income Inequality. *World Bank Economic Review*, v.10, n.3, p.565-91, 1996.

_____. New Ways of Looking at Old Issues:

Inequality and Growth. *Journal of Development Economics*, v.57, n.2, p.259-87, 1998.

DEMIRGÜÇ-KUNT, A., DETRAGIACHE, E. Financial Liberalization and Financial Fragility. Policy Research Working Paper n. 1917. World Bank, Development Research Group; and International Monetary Fund, Research Department, Washington, D.C., 1998.

DENISON, E. F. *Sources of Economic Growth in the United States and the Alternative Before Us*. New York: Committee for Economic Development, 1962.

_____. *Why Growth Rates Differ: Post-War Experience in Nine Western Countries*. Washington, D.C.: The Bookings Institution, 1967.

DEVARAJAN, S., HAMMER, J. S. Risk Reduction and Public Spending. Policy Research Working Paper n. 1869. World Bank, Public Economics, Development Research Group, Washington, D.C., 1998.

DIEWERT, W. E. *The Measurement of the Economic Benefits of Infrastructure Services*. Berlin; New York: Springer-Verlag, 1986.

DIKHANOV, Y. et al. Towards a Better Understanding of the Global Distribution of Income. World Bank, Development Economics Data Group, Washington, D.C, 2000. (Processado).

DIWAN, I. Labor Shares and Financial Crises. Working Paper. World Bank Institute, Washington, D.C., 1999.

DIXON, J. A., SHERMAN, P. *Economics of Protected Areas: A New Look at Benefits and Costs*. Washington, D.C.: Island Press, 1990.

DOLLAR, D., KRAAY, A. Growth Is Good for the Poor. Working Paper. World Bank, Policy Research Department, Washington, D.C., 2000.

DOOLEY, M. A Survey of Literature on Controls over International Capital Transactions. *IMF Staff Papers*, n.43, p.639-87, Dec. 1996.

DRAGE, J., MANN, F. Improving the Stability of the International Financial System. In: *Financial Stability Review*. 6.ed. Bank of England, 1999.

DREWNOWSKI, J. F., SCOTT, W. The Level of living Index. Report n. 4. United Nations Research Institute for Social Development, Geneva, 1966.

DRÉZE, J., SEN, A. *Hunger and Public Action*. WIDER Studies in Development Economics. Oxford, U.K.: Clarendon Press, 1995.

DUBEY, A., KING, E. M. A New Cross-Country Education Stock Series Differentiated by Age and Sex. *Journal of Educational Planning and Administration*, v.11, n.1, p.5-24, 1996.

DURAISAMY, P. et al. Is There a Quantity-Quality Tradeoff as Enrollments Increase? Evidence from Tamil Nadu, India. Policy Research Working Paper n. 1768. World Bank, Washington, D.C., 1998.

DWORKIN, R. What Is Equity: Part 2. Equality of Resources. *Philosophy & Public Affairs*, n.10, p.283-345, 1981.

EASTERLY, W. The Joys and Sorrows of Openness: A Review Essay. Texto preparado para o seminário Economic Growth and its Determinants, March 23-24, 1998, Ministry for Development Cooperation, The Hague, The Netherlands.

_____. Life during Growth. *Journal of Economic Growth*, v.4., n.3, p.239-79, 1999a.

_____. The Lost Decades: Explaining Developing Countries' Stagnation 1980-1998. Develop-

ment Economics Research Group, World Bank, Washington, D.C., 1999b.

_____. The Ghost of Financing Gap: Testing the Growth Model Used in the International Financial Institutions. *Journal of Development Economics*, v.60, n.2, p.423-38, 1999c.

EASTERLY, W. et al. Shaken and Stirred: Volatility and Macroeconomic Paradigms for Rich and Poor Countries. Michael Bruno Memorial Lecture, XIIth World Congress of the International Economics Association. Buenos Aires, Aug. 27, 1999.

_____. Good Policy or Good Luck? Country Growth Performance and Temporary Shocks. *Journal of Monetary Economics*, n.32, p.459-83, 1993.

EASTERLY, W., KRAAY, A. Small States, Small Problems? Policy Research Working Paper n. 2139. World Bank, Development Research Group, Macroeconomics and Growth, Washington, D.C., 1999.

EASTERLY, W., LEVINE, R. It's Not Factor Accumulation Stylized Facts and Growth Models. Working Paper. World Bank, Washington, D.C., 2000. Disponível em http://www. worldbank.org/html/prdmg/grthweb/ pdfiles/ fact3.pdf.

EASTERLY, W., YU, H. Global Development Network Growth Database. 2000. Disponível em http:// www.worldbank.org/research/growth/GDN data.htm.

EASTWOOD, R., LIPTON, M. The Impact of Changes in Human Fertility on Poverty. *Journal of Development Studies*, v.36, n.1, p.1-30, 1999.

EDWARDS, S. How Effective Are Capital Controls? *Journal of Economic Perspectives*, v.13, n.4, p.65-84, 1999.

EEPSEA (Economy and Environment Program for South East Asia). Interim Results of a Study on the Economic Value of Haze Damages in SE Asia. Economy and Environment Program for Southeast Asia, Singapore, 1998.

EHRLICH, P. R. *The Population Bomb*. New York: Ballantine, 1968.

EICHENGREEN, B. *Globalizing Capital: A History of the International Monetary System*. Princeton, New Jersey: Princeton University Press, 1996.

EICHENGREEN, B., MUSSA, M. (Eds.) Capital Account Liberalization: Theoretical and Practical Aspects. Occasional paper 172. International Monetary Fund, Washington, D.C., 1998.

EKBOM, A., BOJO, J. Poverty and Environment: Evidence of Links and Integration into the Country Assistance Strategy Process. Discussion Paper n. 4. World Bank, Africa Region, Environment Group, Washington, D.C., 1999.

ESREY. S. A. et al. Health Benefits from Improvements in Water Supply and Sanitation: Survey and Analysis of the Literature on Selected Diseases. WASH Technical Report n. 66. U.S. Agency for International Development, Washington, D.C., 1990.

EUROPEAN BANK FOR RECONSTRUCTION AND DEVELOPMENT. Transition Report: Ten Years of Transition. London, 1999.

EVANS, P. (Ed.) Government Action, Social Capital, and Development across the Public-Private Divide. *World Development*, v.24, n.6 (special section), p.1033-132, 1996.

FAKIN, B. Investment Subsidies during Transition. *Eastern European Economics*, v.33, n.5, p.62-75, 1995.

FEDDERKE, J., KLITGAARD, R. Economic Growth and Social Indicators: An Explorary Analysis. *Economic Development and Cultural Change*, n.46, Apr. 1998, p.455-89.

FEDER, G. Land Ownership Security and Farm Productivity: Evidence from Rural Thailand. *Journal of Development Studies*, v.24, n.1, p.16-30, 1987.

_____. The Economics of Land and Titling in Thailand. In: HOFF, K. A. B., STIGLITZ, J. (Eds) *The Economics of Rural Organizations: Theory, Practice, and Policy*. New York: Oxford University Press, 1993.

FERREIRA, F. H. G., LITCHFIELD. J. A. Calm after the Storms: Income Distribution and Welfare in Chile, 1987-94. *World Bank Economic Review*, v.13, n.3, p.509-38, 1999.

FFRENCH-DAVIS, R. et al. Liberalización Comercial y Crecimiento: La Experiencia de Chile, 1973-89. *Pensamiento Iberoamericano*, n.21, p.33-55, 1992.

FILMER, D., et al. Forthcoming. Health Policy in Poor Countries: Weak Links in the Chain. *World Bank Economic Observer*.

FILMER, D. PRITCHETT, L. Educational Enrollment and Attainment in India: Household Wealth, Gender, Village, and State Effects. *Journal of Educational Planning and Administration*, v.13, n.2, p.135-63, 1999a.

_____. The Effect of Household Wealth on Educational Attainment: Evidence from 35 Countries. *Population and Development Review*, v.25, n.1, p.85-120, 1999b.

_____. The Impact of Public Spending on Health: Does Money Matter? *Social Science and Medicine*, v.49, n.10, p.1309-23, 1999c.

FINE, B., K. FINE. Social Choice and Individual Rankings I. *Review of Economic Studies*, v.41, n.3, p.303-22, 1974a.

_____. Social Choice and Individual Rankings II. *Review of Economic Studies*, v.41, n.4, p.459-75, 1974b.

FISCHER, S. The Role of Macroeconomic Factors in Growth. *Journal of Monetary Economics*, v.32, n.3, p.485-512, 1993.

_____. Capital Account Liberalization and the Role of the IMF. In: *Essays in International Finance Series*, 207. Princeton, New Jersey: Princeton University, Department of Economics, International Finance Section, 1998.

FISCHER, S. et al. *Should the IMF Pursue Capital-Account Covertibility?* 1998.

FISHLOW, A. Inequality, Poverty, and Growth; Where Do We Stand? In: BRUNO, M., PLESKOVIC, B. (Eds.) *Annual World Bank Conference on Development Economics*. Washington, D.C.: World Bank, 1995.

FISMAN, R., GATTI, R. Decentralization and Corruption: Evidence across Countries. Policy Research Working Paper n. 2290. World Bank, Development Research Group, Washington, D.C., 2000. Disponível em www.wbln0018.worldbank.org/research/workpapers.nsf/.

FISMAN, R., SVENSSON, J. The Effects of Corruption and Taxation on Growth: Firm-Level Evidence, 1999. (Processado).

FOSTER, A., ROSEZWEIG, M. R. Learning by

Doing and Learning from Others: Human Capital and Technical Change in Agriculture. *Journal of Political Economy*, n.103, p.1176-209, 1995.

FOURNIER, G., RASMUSSEN, D. Targeted Capital Subsidies and Economic Welfare. *Cato Journal*, v.6, n.1, p.295-312, 1986.

FOX, J. The World Bank and Social Capital. Contesting the Concept in Practice. *Journal of International Development*, v.9, n.7, p.963-71, 1997.

FRANK, R. *Luxury Fever: Why Money Fails to Satisfy in a Era of Excess.* New York: Free Press, 1998.

FREEDOM HOUSE. *Freedom in the World: Political Rights and Civil Liberties.* New York, 1998.

FURMAN, J., STIGLITZ, J. Economic Crises: Evidence and Insights from East Asia. *Brookings Papers on Economic Activity.* 2.ed. School: Cambridge, Massachusetts, 1998. p.1-114.

FURTADO, J. et al. *Global Climate Change and Biodiversity: Challenges for the Future and the Way Ahead.* Washington D.C.: World Bank Institute, 1999.

GALEOTTI, M., LANZA, A. Desperately Seeking (Environmental) Kuznets. Relatório apresentado no World Congress of Environment and Resource Economists. Venice, Italy, Jun. 25-27, 1998.

GALLEGO, F. et al. Capital Controls in Chile: Effective? Efficient? Working Paper. Central Bank of Chile, Santiago, 1999.

GALOR, O., ZEIRA, J. Income Distribution and Macroeconomics. *Review of Economic Studies*, n.60, p.35-52, 1993.

GANDHI, V. et al. A Comprehensive Approach to Domestic Resource Mobilization for Sustainable Development. Relatório apresentado no Fourth Expert Group Meeting on Financial Issues of Agenda 21, Jan. 6-8, 1997, Santiago, Chile, United Nations, Department for Policy Coordination and Sustainable Development, New York.

GARRETT, G. Global Markets and National Politics: Collision Course or Virtuous Circle? *International Organization*, v.52, n.4, p.787-824, 1998.

GAZETTA MERCANTIL. An International Weekly. New York, May 21, 1999.

GEF (Global Environmental Facility). *Valuing the Global Environment: Actions and Investments for a 21st Century*, Washington, D.C., 1998. v.1.

GILSON, S. UAL Corporation. Case Study 9-295-130. Harvard University Business School, Cambridge, Massachusetts, Mar. 1995, p.784-94.

GOLD, J. *International Capital Movements under the Law of the International Monetary Fund.* Washington D.C.: International Monetary Fund, 1977.

GONZALEZ DE ASIS, M. Reducing Corruption: Lessons from Venezuela. PREM Note n. 39. World Bank, Washington, D.C., 2000.

GOODMAN, L. A., MARKOWITZ, H. Social Welfare Functions Based on Individual Rankings. *American Journal of Sociology*, n.58, 1952.

GRAY, C. W., KAUFMANN, D. Corruption and Development. *Finance and Development*, v.5, n.1, p.7-10, 1998.

GREANEY, V., KELLAGHAN, T. Monitoring the

Learning Outcomes of Education Systems. Direction in Development Papers. World Bank, Washington, D.C., 1996.

GRILICHES, Z. *Price Indexes ans Quality Changes: Studies in New Methods of Measurement.* Cambridge, Massachusetts: Harvard University Press, 1971.

_____. Education, Human Capital, and Growth: A Personal Perspective. *Journal of Labor Economics*, v.15, n.1 (part. 2), s330-42, 1997.

GROSSMAN, G. M., HELPMAN, E. Growth and Welfare in a Small Open Economy. Working Paper n. 2970. National Bureau of Economic Research, 1989.

_____. Comparative Advantage and Long Run Growth. *American Economic Review*, n.80, p.796-815, 1990.

GROSSMAN, G. M., KRUEGER, A. B. Economic Growth and the Environment. *Quarterly Journal of Economics*, n.112, p.353-78, 1995.

GULATI, A., NARAYANAN, S. Demystifying Fertilizer and Power Subsidies in India. *Economic and Political Weekly*, Mar. 4, 2000. p.784-94.

GUPTA, S. et al. Does Corruption Affect Income Inequality and Poverty? Working Paper n. WP/98/76. International Monetary Fund, Fiscal Affairs Department, Washington, D.C., 1998.

HALDANE, A. Private Sector Involvement in Financial Crisis. *Financial Stability Review*, Nov. 1999, Bank of England.

HALL, R. E., JONES, C. I. Why Do Some Countries Produce So Much More Output Per Worker Than Others? *Quarterly Journal of Economic*, v.114, n.1, p.83-116, 1999.

HAMILTON, K., LUTZ, E. Green National Accounts: Policy Uses and Empirical Experience. Environment Department Paper n. 39. World Bank, Environment Department, Washington, D.C., 1996.

HAMMER, J. S., SHETTY, S. East Asia's Environment: Principles and Priorities for Action. World Bank Discussion Paper n. 287. World Bank, Washington, D.C., 1995.

HANRAHAN, D. et al. Developing Partnerships for Effective Pollution Management. *Environment Matters Annual Review*, Fall, 1998. p.62-5.

HANUSHEK, E. Interpreting the Recent Research on Schooling in Developing Countries. *World Bank Research Observer*, v.10, n.2, p.227-46, 1995.

HANUSHEK, E. A., KIM, D. Schooling, Labor Force Quality, and Economic Growth. Research Working Paper n. 5399. National Bureau of Economic Research, Cambridge, Massachusetts, 1995.

HARR, J. *A Civil Action.* New York: Vintage Books, 1995.

HARRIS, R. I. D. The Employment Creation Effects of Factor Subsidies: Some Estimates for Northern Ireland Manufacturing Industry, 1955-1983. *Journal of Regional Science*, v.31, n.1, p.49-64, 1991.

HARRISS, J. (Ed.) Policy Arena: "Missing Link" or Analytically Missing? The Concept of Social Capital. *Journal of International Development*, v.9, n.7 (special section), p.919-71, 1997.

HARSANYI, J. C. Cardinal Utility in Welfare Economics and in the Theory of Risk-Taking. *Journal of Political Economy*, n.61, p.434-5, 1953.

HELLEINER, E. *States and the Reemergence of Global Reform*: From Brettan Woods to the 1990s. Ithaca, New York: Cornell University Press, 1994.

HELLMAN, J. et al. Seize the State, Seize the Day: An Empirical Analysis of State Capture and Corruption in Transition Economies. Relatório apresentado na Annual Bank Conference on Development Economics. Washington, D.C., Apr. 18-20, 2000a. Disponível em http://www.worldbank.org/wbi/governance/.

_____. Far from Home: Do Transnationals Import Better Governance in the Capture Economy. World Bank, Washington, D.C., 2000b. (Processado). Disponível em http://www.world bank.org/wbi/governance/.

_____. Measuring Governance, Corruption, and State Capture: How Firms and Bureaucrats Shape the Business Environment in Transition. Policy Research Working Paper n. 2313. World Bank, Washington, D.C., 2000c.

HERNANDEZ, L., SCHMIDT-HEBBEL, K. Capital Controls in Chile: Effective? Efficient? Endurable? Relatório apresentado na World Bank Conference on Capital Flows, Financial Crisis and Policies. Washington, D.C., Apr. 15-16, 1999.

HERRERA, A. The Privatization of the Argentine Telephone System. *CEPAL Review*, n.47, p.149-61, 1992.

HETTIGE, H. et al. Industrial Pollution in Economic evelopment (Kuznets Revisited). Policy Research Working Paper n. 1876. World Bank, Development Research Group, Washington, D.C., 1998.

HICKS, N., STREETEN, P. Indicators of Development: The Search for a Basic Needs Yardstick. *World Development*, v.7, n.6, p.567-80, 1979.

HILL, K. et al. *Trends in Child Mortality in the Developing World*: 1960-96. New York: United Nations Children's Fund, 1999.

HINDRIKS, J. et al. Corruption, Extortion, and Evasion. *Journal of Public Economics*, v.74, n.3, p.395-430, 1999.

HIRSCHMAN, A. O. *The Strategy of Economic Development*. New Haven, Connecticut: Yale University Press, 1958.

_____. *Exit, Voice, and Loyalty*: Responses to Decline in Firms, Organizations, and States. Cambridge, Massachusetts: Harvard University Press, 1970.

_____. *Essays in Trespassing*: Economics to Politics and Beyond. Cambridge, U.K.; New York: Cambridge Universitiy Press, 1981.

HOEFFLER, A. The Augmented Solow Model and the African Growth Debate. University of Oxford, U.K., 1997. (Processado).

HOLTZ-EAKIN, D., SELDEN, T. M. Stoking the Fires? CO_2 Emissions and Economic Growth. *Journal of Public Economics*, n.57, p.85-101, 1995.

HOY, M., JIMENEZ, E. The Impact of the Urban Environment of Incomplete Property Rights. Working Paper n. 14. Research Project on Social and Environmental Consequences of Growth-Oriented Policies. World Bank, Policy Research Department, Washington, D.C., 1997.

HUGHES-HALLET, A. J. Econometrics and the Theory of Economic Policy: The Tinbergen-

Theil Contributions 40 Years on. *Oxford Economic Papers*, v.41, p.189-214, Jan. 1989.

HUNTINGTON, S. P. Modernization and Corruption. In: HEIDENHEIMER, A. J. (Ed.) *Political Corruption*: *Readings in Comparative Analysis*. New York: Holt Reinehart, 1964.

_____. *Political Order in Changing Societies*. New Haven: Yale University Press, 1968.

IDB (Inter-American Development Bank). *Facing Up to Inequality in Latin America. Economic and Social Progress in Latin America.* 1998-1999 Report. Baltimore, Maryland: The Johns Hopkins University Press, 1998.

IMF (International Monetary Fund). Fiscal Reforms in Low-Income Countries: Experience under IMF-Supported Programs. Occasional Paper n. 160. Washington, D.C., 1998.

_____. *Government Financial Statistics*. Washington, D.C., 1999.

_____. *Exchange Arrangements and Exchange Restrictions*: *Annual Report*. Washington, D.C. (Várias edições).

INDIA TODAY. The Poisoning of India. Special Collectors issue, Jan. 1999 (Living Media India, New Delhi).

INTERNATIONAL COUNTRY RISK GUIDE. 1982-95. Computer file. Syracruse, New York: PRS Group. Disponível no World Bank and International Monetary Fund Staff em http://jolis.worldbankimflib.org/nldbs.htm.

ISHAM, J. et al. Civil Liberties, Democracy, and the Performance of Government Projects. *World Bank Economic Review*, v.11, n.2, p.219-42, 1997.

ISLAN, N. Growth Empiries: A Panel Data Approach. *The Quarterly Journal of Economics*, n.110, p.1127-70, 1995.

JAMES, E. et al. Finance, Management, and Cost of Public and Private Schools in Indonesia. *Economics of Education Review*, v.15, n.4, p.387-98, 1996.

JIMENEZ, E. et al. An Economic Evaluation of a National Job Training System: Columbia's Servicio Nacional de Aprendizaje (SENA). EDT24. World Bank, Education and Training Department, Washington, D.C., 1986.

JIMENEZ, E., PAQUEO, V. Do Local Contributions Affect The Efficiency of Public Primary Schools? *Economics of Education Review*, v.15, n.4, p.377-86, 1996.

JIMENEZ, E., SAWADA, Y. Do Community-Managed Schools Work? An Evaluation of El Salvador's EDUCO Program. *The World Bank Economic Review*, v.13, n.3, p.415-41, 1999.

JOHNSON, S. et al. The Unofficial Economy in Transition. *Brookings Papers on Economic Activity (Washington, D.C.)*, n.2, 1997.

_____. Regulatory Discretion and the Unofficial Economy. *American Economic Review*, v.88, n.2, p.387-92, 1998.

JONES, C. I. Time Series Tests of Endogenous Growth Models. *Quarterly Journal of Economics*, v.110, n.2, p.495-525, 1995.

KAKWANI, N. Performance in Living Standards: An International Comparison. *Journal of Development Economics* (Netherlands), n.41, p.307-36, Aug. 1993.

KAMINSKY, G., REINHART, C. Twin Crises: The Causes of Banking and Balance of Payments Problems. *American Economy Review*, v.89, n.3, p.473-500, 1999.

BIBLIOGRAFIA E REFERÊNCIAS

KANBUR, R. Why Is Inequality Back on the Agenda? Relatório apresentado na Annual Bank Conference on Development Economics. World Bank, Washington D.C., Apr. 28-30, 1999.

_____. Income Distribution and Development. In: ATKINSON, A., BOURGUIGNON, F. (Eds.) *Handbook of Income Distribution*. Amsterdam: North-Holland, 2000.

KAPSTEIN, E. B. Resolving the Regulator's Dilemma: International Coordination of Banking Regulations. *International Organization*, v.43, n.2, p.323-47, 1989.

KATES, R. W., HAARMANN, V. Where the Poor Live: Are the Assumptions Correct? *Environment (U.S.)*, n.34, p.4-11, 25-28, 1992.

KATO, K. Grow Now, Clean Up Later? The Case of Japa May, 1992. In: *Effective Financing of Environmentally Sustainable Development*. Environmentally Sustainable Development Proceedings Series n. 10. Proceedings of the Third Annual Conference on Environmentally Sustainable Development. Washington, D.C.: World Bank, 1996.

KAUFMANN, D. Challenges in the Next Stage of Anticorruption. In: *New Perspectives on Combating Corruption*. Washington, D.C.: Transparency International and the World Bank Institute, 1998.

KAUFMANN, D. et al. Aggregating Governance Indicators. Policy Research Working Paper n. 2195. World Bank, Policy Research Department, Washington, D.C., 1999a. Disponível em http://www.worldbank.org/wbi/governance/.

_____. Governance Matters. Policy Research Working Paper n. 2196. World Bank, Policy Research Department, Washington, D.C., 1999b.

_____. Governance Matters: From Measurement to Action. *Finance and Development*. International Monetary Fund, Washington, D.C., 2000. Disponível em http://www.imf.org/faudd/2000/06/kauf.htm.

_____. New Frontiers in Anti-corruption Empirical Diagnostics: From In-Depth Survey Analysis to Action Programs in Transition Economies. Poverty Reduction and Economic Management Note n. 7. World Bank, Washington, D.C., 1998.

KAUFMANN, D., WANG, Y. Macroeconomic Policies and Project Performance in the Social Sectors: A Model of Human Capital Production and Evidence from LDCs. *World Development*, v.23, n.5, p.751-65, 1995.

KAUFMANN, D., WEI, S.-J. Does "Grease Money" Speed up the Wheels of Commerce? World Bank Policy Research Working Paper n. 2254. World Bank, Washington, D.C., 1999.

KEEFER, P., KNACK, S. Why Don't Poor Countries Catch Up? A Cross-National Test of Institutional Explanation. *Economic Inquiry*, v.35, n.3, p.590-602, 1997.

KEELER. W. International R&D Spillovers and Intersectoral Trade Flows: Do They Match? New Haven, Connecticut: Yale University, 1995. (Processado).

_____. Are International R&D Spillovers Trade-Related? Analyzing Spillovers among Randomly Matched Trade Partners. *European Economic Review*, v.42, n.8, p.1469-81, 1998.

KELLEY, A. C. Economic Consequences of Population Change in the Third World. *Journal of Economic Literature*, v.26, n.4, p.1685-728, 1988.

_____. The Impacts of Rapid Population Growth on

Poverty, Food Provision, and the Environment. Working Paper. Chapel Hill, North Carolina: Duke University, 1998.

KELLEY, A. C., SCHMIDT, R. M. Economic and Demographic Change: A Synthesis of Models, Findings, and Perspectives. Working Paper n. 99-01. Chapel Hill, North Carolina: Duke University, forthcoming. In: BIRDSALL, N. (Ed.) *Population Change and Economic Development*, 1999.

KHAN, M. S. The Implications of International Capital Flows for Macroeconomic and Financial Policies. *International Journal of Finance and Economics (U.K.)*, n.1, p.155-60, Jul. 1996.

KIM, J. et al. Can Private School Subsidies Increase Schooling for the Poor? The Quetta Urban Fellowship Program. *World Bank Economic Review*, v.13, n.3, p.443-65, 1999.

KIM, J.-II, LAU, L. J. The Sources of Economic Growth of the East Asian Newly Industrialized Countries. *Journal of the Japanese and International Economies*, v.8, n.3, p.235-71, 1994.

KING, E. M. et al. Central Mandates and Local Incentives: The Colombia Education Voucher Program. *World Bank Economic Review*, v.13, n.3, p.467-91, 1999.

KING, E. M., HILL, M. A. (Eds.) *Women´s Education in Developing Countries: Barriers, Benefits, and Policy*. Baltimore, Maryland: The Johns Hopkins University Press, 1993.

KING, R. G., LEVINE, R. Financial Intermediation and Economic Development. In: MAYER, C., VIVER, X. (Eds.) *Capital Markets and Financial Intermediation*. Cambridge, U.K.: Cambridge University Press, 1993.

KING, R. G., REBELO, S. Public Policy and Economic Growth: Developing Neoclassical Implications. *Journal of Political Economy*, v.98, n.5, part 2, s126-50, 1990.

_____. Transitional Dynamics and Economic Growth in the Neoclassical Model. *American Economic Review*, v.83, n.4, p.908-31, 1993.

KISHOR, N. M., CONSTANTINO, L. Sustainable Forestry: Can it Compete? *Finance and Development*, v.31, n.4, p.36-9, 1994.

_____. Voting for Economic Policy Reform. Dissemination Note n. 15. World Bank, Latin America Technical Environment Department, Washington, D.C., 1996.

KLENOW, P., RODRÍGUEZ-CLARE, A. Economic Growth: A Review Essay. *Journal of Monetary Economics*, n.40, p.597-618, 1997a.

_____. The Neoclassical Revival in Growth Economics: Has It Gone Too Far? In: *NBER Macroeconomic Annual 1997*. Cambridge, Massachusetts: National Bureau of Economic Research, 1997b.

KLITGAARD, R. *Controlling Corruption*. Berkeley, California; London: University of California Press, 1988.

KLITGAARD, R. et al. *Corrupt Cities: A Practical Guide to Cure and Prevention*. Oakland, California; Washington, D.C.: ICS Press; World Bank Institute, 2000.

KNACK, S., KEEFER, P. Institutions and Economic Performance: Cross-Country Tests Using Alternative Institutional Measures. *Economics and Politics*, n.7, p.207-27, 1995.

_____. Does Social Capital Have An Economic Payoff? A Cross-Country Investigation.

Quarterly Journal of Economics, n.112, p.1251-88, 1997.

KNIGHT, J. B., SABOT, R. H. Educational Expansion and the Kuznets Effect. *American Economic Review*, v.73, n.5, p.1132-6, 1983.

KNIGHT, J. B., SHI, L. The Determinants of Educational Attainment in China. Oxford Applied Economics Discussion Paper n. 127. Oxford, U.K.: Oxford University Press, 1991.

KORNAI, J. *Ten Years After "The Road to a Free Economy"*. The Author's Self-Evaluation. Relatório apresentado na Annual Bank Conference on Development Economics. World Bank, Washington, D. C., Apr. 20, 2000.

KRONGKAEW, M. A Tale of an Economic Crisis: How the Economic Crisis Started, Developed, and Ended in Thailand. Relatório apresentado na International Conference on Economic Crisis and Impacts on Social Welfare. Taipei, China, Jun. 14-15, 1999.

KRUEGER, A. O. The Political Economy of the Rent-Seeking Society. *American Economic Review*, v.64, n.3, p.291-301, 1974.

KRUEGER, A. O. et al. (Eds.) *The Political Economy of Agricultural Pricing Policy*, v.1-5. Baltimore, Maryland: The Johns Hopkins University Press, 1991.

KRUGMAN, P. The Myth of Asia's Miracle. *Pop Internationalism*. Cambridge, Massachusetts: MIT Press, 1996 (reimpresso). *Foreign Affairs*, v.73, n.6, p.62-78, 1994 (original).

_____. Fire-Sale FDI. Relatório apresentado no National Bureau of Economic Research Conference on Capital Flows to Emerging Markets. Cambridge, Massachusetts, 1998.

(Processado). Também disponível em http://web.mit.edu/krugman/www/FIRESALE.htm.

KUZNETS, S. Economic Growth and Income and Income Inequality. *American Economic Review*, n.45, p.1-28, 1995.

_____. *Toward a Theory of Economic Growth*: With *Reflections on the Economic Growth of Modern Nations*. New York: Norton, 1968.

LA PORTA, R. et al. The Quality of Government. *Journal of Law, Economics, and Organization*, v.15, n.1, p.222-79, 1999.

LA PORTA, R., LOPEZ-DE-SILANES, F. The Benefits of Privatization: Evidence, From Mexico. *Quarterly Journal of Economics*, v.114, n.4, p.1193-242, 1999.

LAM, D., LEVISON, D. Declining Inequality in Schooling in Brazil and its Effects on Inequality in Earnings. *Journal of Development Economics*, v.37, n.1-2, p.199-225, 1991.

LANJOUW, P., STERN, N. Agricultural Change and Inequality in Palanpur 1957-84. Discussion Paper n. 24. London: London School of Economics and Political Science, Development Economics Research Programme, 1989.

_____. *Economic Development in Palanpur over Five Decades*. New York: Oxford University Press, 1998.

LEE, J. W. Government Interventions and Productivity Growth. *Journal of Economic Growth*, v.1, n.3, p.392-415, 1996.

LEE, J.-W., BARRO, R. J. Schooling Quality in a Cross-Section of Countries. Working Paper n. 6198. National Bureau of Economic Research, Cambridge, Massachusetts, 1997.

LEFF, N. H. Economic Development through Bureaucratic Corruption. *The American Behavior Scientist*, v.2, p.8-14, 1964.

LEIPZIGER, D. M. (Ed.) *Lessons from East Asia*. Ann Arbor. Michigan: University of Michigan Press, 1997.

LEIPZIGER, D. M. et al. *The Distribution of Income and Wealth in Korea*. Washington, D.C.: World Bank Institute, 1992.

LERNER, A. P. *Economics of Control*. New York: Macmillan, 1944.

LEVINE, R. Financial Development and Economic Growth: Views and Agenda. *Journal of Economic Literature*, v.35, n.2, p.688-726, 1997a.

_____. Napoleon, Bourse, and Growth in Latin America. Conference on the Development of Securities Markets in Emerging Economics: Obstacles and Preconditions for Success. Washington, D.C., Oct. 28-29, 1997b.

_____. Law, Finance, and Economic Growth. *Journal of Financial Intermediation*, v.8, n.1-2, p.8-35, 1999.

LEVINE, R., ZEVOS, S. Capital Control Liberalization and Stock Market Development. *World Development*, v.26, n.7, p.1169-83, 1998a.

_____. Stock Markets, Banks, and Economic Growth. *American Economic Review*, v.88, n.3, p.537-58, 1998b.

LEVINSOHN, J. et al. Impacts of the Indonesian Economic Crisis: Price Changes and the Poor. Working Paper n. 7194. National Bureau of Economic Research, Cambridge, Massachusetts, 1999.

LEWIS, W. A. *The Theory of Economic Growth*. New York: Harper Torchbooks, 1955.

LI, H. et al. Explaining International and Intertemporal Variations in Income Inequality. *Economic Journal*, n.108, p.26-43, 1998.

LIM, D. Capturing the Effects of Capital Subsidies. *Journal of Development Studies*, v.28, n.4, p.705-16, 1992.

LIN, J. Y. Rural Reforms and Agricultural Growth in China. *American Economic Review*, v.82, n.1, p.34-51, 1992.

LIU, F. An Equilibrium Queuing Model of Bribery. *Journal of Political Economy*, v.93, n.4, p.760-81, 1985.

LOCKHEED, E. M., VERSPOOR, A. M. *Improving Primary Education in Developing Countries*. New York: Oxford University Press, 1991.

LOH, J. et al. Living Planet Report 1998. World Wildlife Fund International, New Economics Foundation, and World Conservation Monitoring Center, Gland, Switzerland, 1998.

LONDOÑO, J. L. Kuznetsian Tales with Attention to Human Capital. Relatório apresentado na Third Inter-American Seminar in Economics, Rio de Janeiro, Brazil, 1990.

LÓPEZ, R. Protecting the "Green" Environment in a Context of Fast Economic Growth: The Case for Demand-Based Incentives. University of Maryland, College Park, Maryland, 1997. (Processado).

_____. Growth and Stagnation in Natural Resource-Rich Economies. University of Maryland, College Park, Maryland, 1998a. (Processado).

_____. Where Development Can or Cannot Go:

The Role of Poverty-Environment Linkages. Relatório apresentado na Annual Bank Conference on Development Economics. World Bank, Washington, D.C., Apr. 30-May 1, 1998b.

LÓPEZ, R. et al. Addressing the Education Puzzle: The Distribution of Education and Economic Reform. Policy Research Working Paper n. 2031. World Bank, Washington, D.C., 1998a.

_____. Economic Growth and the Sustainability of Natural Resources. University of Maryland, Department of Agricultural and Resource Economics, College Park, Maryland, 1998b.

LÓPEZ, R., VALDES, A. *Rural Poverty in Latin America: Analytics, New Empirical Evidence, and Policy.* London; New York: MacMillan Press; St. Martin' s Press, 2000.

LOPEZ-MEJIA, A. Large Capital Flows – A Survey of the Causes, Consequences, and Policy Responses. Working Paper n. WP/99/17. International Monetary Fund, Washington, D.C., 1999.

LOURY, G. C. Social Exclusion and Ethnic Groups: The Challenge to Economics. Relatório apresentado na Annual Bank Conference on Development Economics. World Bank, Washington D.C., Apr. 28-30, 1999.

LUCAS, R. On the Mechanics of Economic Growth. *Journal of Monetary Economics*, v.22, n.1, p.3-42, 1988.

LUCAS, R. E. Making a Miracle. *Econometrica*, v.61, n.2, p.251-72, 1993.

LUNDBERG, M., SQUIRE, L. Growth and Inequality: Extracting the Lessons for Policymakers. World Bank, Washington, D.C., 1999.

LUSTIG, N. Crises and the Poor: Socially Responsible Macroeconomics. Inter-American Development Bank, Sustainable Development Department, Poverty and Inequality Advisory Unit, Washington, D.C., 1999.

LVOVSKY, K. et al. Environmental Health. Background Paper for the Environment Strategy. Draft. World Bank, Environment Department, Washington, D.C., 1999.

LYNCH, O. J., TALBOTT, K. Balancing Acts: Community-Based Forest Management and National Law in Asia and the Pacific. World Resources Institute, Washington D.C., 1995.

MAAS, J. van L., CRIEL, G. Distribution of Primary School Enrollments in Eastern Africa. Working Paper n. 511. World Bank, Washington, D.C., 1982.

MAMINGI, N. et al. Spatial Patterns of Deforestation in Cameroon and Zaire. Working Paper n. 8. Research Project on Social Environmental Consequences of Growth-Oriented Policies. World Bank, Policy Research Department, Washington, D.C., 1996.

MANKIW, G. et al. A Contribution to the Empirics of Economic Growth. *Quarterly Journal of Economics*, v.105, n.2, p.407-37, 1992.

MAURO, P. Corruption and Growth. *Quarterly Journal of Economics*, v.110, n.3, p.681-712, 1995.

_____. The Effects of Corruption on Growth, Investment, and Government Expenditure: A Cross-Country Analysis. In: ELLIOT, K. A. (Ed.) *Corruption and the Global Economy.* Washington D.C.: Institute for International Economics, 1997.

_____. Corruption and the Composition of

Government Expenditure. *Journal of Public Economics*, v.69, n.2, p.263-79, 1998.

McGRANAHAN, D. *Contents and Measurement of Socioeconomic Development*. New York: Praeger, 1972.

McKINLEY, T. *The Distribution of Wealth in Rural China*. New York: M. E. Sharpe, 1996.

McKINNON, R. I., PILL, H. Credible Liberalizations and International Capital Flows: The Over-Borrowing Syndrome. *American Economic Review, Papers and Proceedings*, v.87, n.2, p.189-93, 1997.

MEGGINSON, W. J., NETTER, J. M. From State to Market: A Survey of Empirical Studies on Privatization. Working Paper. Norman, Oklahoma: The University of Oklahoma Press, 2000.

MEHREZ, G., KAUFMANN, D. Transparency, Liberalization, and Banking Crises. World Bank Policy Research Working Paper n. 2286. World Bank Institute, Washington, D.C., 2000.

MIDDLETON, J. et al. *Skills for Productivity*. New York: Oxford University Press, 1993.

MILANOVIC, B. *Income Inequality and Poverty during the Transition from Planned to Market Economy*. Washington, D.C.: World Bank, 1997.

MINCER, J. On the Job Training Costs: Returns and Some Implications. *Journal of Political Economy*, n.70 (supplement, part 2), p.50-79, Oct. 1962.

_____. *Schooling, Experience, and Earnings*. New York: Columbia University Press, 1974.

MINGAT, A., TAN, J.-P. *The Mechanics of Progress in Education, Evidence from Cross-Country Data*. Policy Research Working Paper n. 2015. World Bank, Washington, D.C., 1998.

MINK, S. D. Poverty, Population and the Environment. World Bank Discussion Paper n. 189. World Bank, Washington, D.C., 1993.

MISHKIN, F. S. Understanding Financial Crises: A Developing Country Perspective. In: *Proceedings of World Bank Annual Conference on Development Economics*. Washington, D.C.: World Bank, 1997.

MONTIEL, P. The Capital Inflow Problem. Working Paper. World Bank Institute, Washington, D.C., 1998.

MOORE, S. Corporate Subsidies in the Federal Budget. Testimony before the Budget Committee, the U.S. House of Representatives, Jun. 30, 1999. Disponível em http://www.cato.org/testimony/ct-sm063099.html.

MORRIS, M. D. *Measuring the Condition of the World's Poor*: The Physical Quality of Life Index. New York: Pergamon Press, 1979.

MUELLER D. C. Constitutional Constraints on Governments in a Global Economy. *Constitutional Political Economy*, v.9, n.3, p.171-86, 1998.

MUNASINGHE, M. Towards Sustainomics: A Trans-Disciplinary Metaframework for Making Development more Sustainable. In: MUNASINGHE, M. et al. (Eds.) *The Sustainability of Long-Term Growth*: Socioecomomic and Ecological Perspectives. London: Edward Elgar, 2000.

MURPHY, K. M., et al. Industrialization and the Big Push. *Journal of Political Economy*, v.97, n.5, p.1003-26, 1989.

_____. The Allocation of Talent: Implications for Growth. *Quarterly Journal of Economics*, v.106, n.2, p.503-30, 1991.

MURPHY, K. et al. Population and Economic Growth. *American Economic Review*, n.89, p.145-9, May 1999.

MURRAY, C. J. L., LÓPEZ, A. D. (Eds.) *The Global Burden of Disease and Injury Series*. Cambridge, Massachusetts: Harvard School of Public Health for the World Health Organization and Word Bank, 1996. v.1.

NARAYAN, D. et al. *Voices of the Poor: Can Anyone Hear Us?* New York: Oxford University Press, 2000.

NARAYAN, D., PRITCHETT, L. Cents and Sociability: Household Income and Social Capital in Rural Tanzania. *Economic Development and Cultural Change*, v.47, n.4, p.871-97, 1999.

NEHRU, V., DHARESHWAR, A. A New Database on Physical Capital Stock: Sources, Methodology, and Results. *Revista de Analysis Economico*, v.8, n.1, p.37-59, 1993.

NEHRU, V. et al. A New Database on Human Capital Stock in Developing and Industrial Countries: Sources, Methodology, and Results. *Journal of Development Economics*, v.46, n.2, p.379-401, 1995.

NELSON, R. R., PACK, H. The Asian Miracle and Modern Growth Theory. Policy Research Working Paper n. 1881. World Bank, Development Research Group, Washington, D.C., 1998. *New Steel*. Editorial comment 14, n.8, 1998.

NORDHAUS, W. D., TOBIN, J. *Is Economic Growth Obsolete?* Fiftieth Anniversary Colloquium V.

National Bureau of Economic Research. New York: Columbia University Press, 1972.

NORTH, D. C. Institutions and Economic Growth An Historical Introduction. *World Development*, n.17, n.9, p.1319-32, 1989.

_____. The Ultimate Sources of Economic Growth. In: SZIRMAI, A. et al. (Eds.) *Explaining Economic Growth: Essays in Honor of Angus Maddison*. Amsterdam: North-Holland, 1993.

NURKSE, R. *Problems of Capital Formation in Underdeveloped Countries*. New York: Oxford University Press, 1953.

O'NEIL, D. Education and Income Growth: Implications for Cross-Country Inequality. *Journal of Political Economy*, v.103, n.6, p.1289-301, 1995.

OBSTFELD, M. Models of Currency Crisis with Self-Fulfilling Features. *European Economic Review*, v.40, n.3-5, p.1037-47, 1996.

OECD (Organisation for Economic Co-operation and Development). *Liberalization of Capital Movements and Financial Services in the OECD Area*. Paris, 1990.

OMAN, C. P. Policy Competition for Foreign Direct Investment. OECD Development Centre, Paris, 2000. (Processado).

OSTROM, E. Governing the Commons: The Evolution of Institutions for Collective Action. Cambridge, U.K.: Cambridge University Press, 1990.

OWEN, A. L. International Trade and the Accumulation of Human Capital. Board of Governors of the Federal Reserve System, Finance and Economics Discussion Series 95/49. Washington, D.C., Nov. 1995.

PANAYOTOU, T. Demystifying the Environmental Kuznets Curve: Turning a Black Box into a Policy Tool. *Environment and Development Economics*, v.2, n.4, p.465-84, 1997.

PARK, J. H. Korea's Crisis Resolution and Future Policy Directions. Relatório apresentado no World Bank Institute Senior Policy Seminar on Managing Capital Flows in a Volatile Finacial Environment. Bangkok, Thailand, Febr. 21-24, 2000.

PAULY, L. W. Capital Mobility, State Autonomy, and Political Legitimacy. *Journal of International Affairs*, v.48, n.2, p.369-88, 1995.

_____. *Who Elected the Bankers?* Ithaca, New York; London: Cornell University Press, 1997.

PEARCE, D., WARFORD, J. J. *World without End*: *Economics, Environment, and Sustainable Development*. New York: Oxford University Press, 1993.

PERSSON, T., TABELLINI, G. (Eds.) Growth, Distribution, and Politics. In: *Monetary and Fiscal Policy*, v.2, *Politics*. Cambridge, Massachusetts: MTI Press, 1994.

PRITCHETT, L. Where Has all the Education Gone? Policy Research Working Paper n. 1581. World Bank, Policy Research Department, Poverty and Human Resources Division, Washington, D.C., 1996.

_____. Patterns of Economic Growth: Hills, Plateaus, Mountains, and Plains. Policy Research Working Paper WPS 1947. World Bank, Washington, D.C., 1998.

PSACHAROPOULOS, G., ARRIAGADA, A.-M. The Educational Attainment of the Labor Force: An International Comparison. Report n. EDT38. World Bank, Washington, D.C., 1986.

PUTNAM, R. D. et al. *Making Democracy Work*: Civic Traditions in Modern Italy. Princeton, New Jersey: Princeton University Press, 1993.

QIAN, Y. The Institutional Foundation of China's Market Transition. Relatório apresentado na Annual Bank Conference on Development Economics. World Bank, Washington D.C., Apr. 28-30, 1999.

QUINN, D. The Correlates of Change in International Financial Regulation. *American Political Science Review*, v.91, n.3, p.531-51, 1997.

QUINN, D., INCLAN, C. The Origins of Financial Openness: A Study of Current and Capital Account Liberalization. *American Journal of Political Science*, n.41, p.771-813, Jul. 1997.

QUINN, D., TOYODA, A. M. Measuring International Finacial Regulation. Georgetown University, Washington, D.C., 1997. (Processado).

RADELET, S., SACHS, J. The East Asian Financial Crisis: Diagnosis, Remedies, Prospects. In: BRAINARD, W. C., PERRY, G. L. (Eds.) *Brookings Papers on Economic Activity*, Washington, D.C.: The Brookings Institution, 1998. n.1.

RAM, R. Composite Indices of Physical Quality of Life, Basic Needs Fulfillment, and Income: A "Principal Component" Representation. *Journal of Development Economics*, n.11, p.227-47, Oct 1982a.

_____. International Inequality in the Basic Needs Indicators. *Journal of Development Economics*, v.10, n.1, p.113-7, 1982b.

_____. Educational Expansion and Schooling Ine-

quality: International Evidence and Some Implications. *Review of Economics and Statistics*, v.72, n.2, p.266-74, 1990.

RAMEY, G., RAMEY, V. A. Cross-Country Evidence on the Link between Volatility and Grpwth. *American Economic Review*, v.85, n.5, p.1138-51, 1995.

RANIS, G. et al. Economic Growth And Human Development. *World Development*, v.28, n.2, p.197-219, 2000.

RAVALLION, M. Can High-Inequality Developing Countries Escape Absolute Poverty? *Economics Letters*, n.56, p.51-7, 1997.

RAVALLION, M., CHEN, S. What Can New Survey Data Tell Us about Recent Changes in Distribution and Poverty? *World Bank Economic Review*, v.11, n.2, p.357-82, 1997.

RAVALLION, M., DATT, G. Why Have Some Indian States Done Better Than Others at Reducing Rural Poverty? *Economica*, n.65, p.17-38, 1998.

_____. When Is Growth Pro-Poor? Evidence from the Diverse Experiences of India's States. Policy Research Working Paper n. 2263. World Bank, Development Research Group, Washington, D.C., 1999.

RAVALLION, M. et al. A Less Poor World, but a Hotter One? Working Paper n. 13. Research Project on Social and Environmental Consequences of Growth-Oriented Policies. World Bank, Policy Research Department, Washington, D.C., 1997.

RAVALLION, M., SEN, B. Impacts on Rural Poverty of Land-Based Targeting: Further Results for Bangladesh. *World Development*, v.22, n.6, p.823-38, 1994.

RAWLS, J. A *Theory of Justice*. Cambridge, Massachusetts: Harvard University and Belknap Press, 1971.

RAZIN, A., ROSE, A. K. Business-Cycle Volatility and Openness: An Exploratory Cross-Sectional Analysis. In: LEIDERMAN, L., RAZIN, A. (Eds.) *Capital Mobility: The Impact of Consumption, Investment, and Growth*. Cambridge, U.K.: Cambridge University Press, 1994.

REBELO, S. Long-Run Policy Analysis and Long-Run Growth. *Journal of Political Economy*, v.99, n.3, p.500-21, 1991.

REINHART, C., KAMINSKY, G. On Crises, Contagion, and Confusion. 1999. (Processado).

ROBBOY, R. *Today*, Sept. 8, 1999, World Bank, Washington, D.C.

ROBERTS, J. T., GRIMES, P. E. Carbon Intensity and Economic Development 1962-91: A Brief Exploration of the Environmental Kuznets Curve. *World Development*, v.25, n.2, p.191-8, 1997.

RODRIGUEZ, A. G. The Division of Labor, Agglomeration Economics, and Economic Development. Palo Alto, California, 1993 (Ph. diss.) – Stanford University.

RODRIK, D. Getting Interventions Right: How South Korea and Taiwan Grew Rich. National Bureau of Economic Research Working Paper n. 4964. National Bureau of Economic Research, Cambridge, Massachusetts, 1994.

_____. TFPG Controversies, Institutions, and Economic Performance in East Asia. Working paper 5914. National Bureau of Economic Research, Cambridge, Massachusetts, 1997a.

_____. *Has Globalization Gone too Far?* Washington,

D.C.: Institute for International Economics, 1997b.

_____. Where Did All the Growth Go? External Shocks, Social Conflict, and Growth Collapses. Discussion Paper Series 1789. Centre for Economic Policy Research, London, 1998. Disponível em www.cepr.demon.co.uk/pubs/papers.htm.

_____. *The New Global Economy and Developing Countries*: Making Openness Work. Policy Essay n. 24. Washington, D.C.: Overseas Development Council, 1999. (Distribuído pela Johns Hopkins University Press).

ROEMER, J. E. A Pragmatic Theory of Responsability for the Egalitarian Planner. *Philosophy and Public Affairs*, n.22, p.146-66, 1993.

ROGERS, E. *Diffusion of Innovations*. New York: Free Press, 1983.

ROMER, P. Increasing Returns and Long Run Growth. *Journal of Political Economy*, v.90, n.6, p.1002-37, 1986.

_____. Endogenous Technological Change. *Journal of Political Economy*, v.98, n.5, s71-102, 1990.

_____. Two Strategies for Economic Development: Using Ideas and Producing Ideas. In: *Proceedings of the Annual World Bank Conference on Development Economics 1992 Supplement*. Washington, D.C.: World Bank, 1993.

ROSE-ACKERMAN, S. Corruption and the Preivate Sector. In: HEIDENHEIMER, A. J. et al. (Eds.) *Politial Corruption*: *A Handbook*. New Brunswick, New Jersey; Oxford, U.K.: Transaction Books, 1989.

_____. *Corruption and Government*: Causes, Conse-

quences, and Reform. Cambridge, U.K.; New York; Melbourne: Cambridge University Press, 1997a.

_____. The Political Economy of Corruption. In: ELLIOT, K. A. (Ed.) *Corruption and the Global Economy*. Washington D.C.: Institute for International Economics, 1997b.

RUGGIE, J. G. International Regimes, Transactions, and Change: Embedded Liberalism in the Postwar Economic Order. In: KRASNER, S. D. (Ed.) *International Regimes*. Ithaca, New York: Cornell University Press, 1983.

RUITENBEEK, H. J. Social Cost-Benefit Analysis of the Korup Project, Cameroon. World Wildlife Fund for *Nature*. London, 1989. (Processado).

RUZINDANA, A. The Importance of Leadership in Fighting Corruption in Uganda. In: ELLIOT, K. A. (Ed.) *Corruption and the Global Economy*. Washington D.C.: Institute for International Economics, 1997.

SACHS, J. et al. Financial Crises in Emerging Markets: The Lessons from 1995. Discussion Paper n. 1759. Harvard University, Harvard Institute of Economic Research, Cambridge, Massachusetts, 1996.

SALLY, R. Classical Liberalism and International Economic Order: Na Advance Sketch. *Constitutional Political Economy*, v.9, n.1, p.19-44, 1998.

SANDEL, M. J. *Democracy's Discontent*: *America in Search of a Public Philosophy*. Cambridge, Massachusetts: The Belknap Press of Harvard University, 1996.

SCHAFFER, M. E. Government Subsidies to Enterprises in Central and Eastern Europe: Budgetary Subsidies and Tax Arrears. In:

NEWBERRY, D. M. B. (Ed.) *Tax and Benefit Reform in Central and Eastern Europe*. London: Centre for Economic Policy Research, 1995.

SCHMIDHEINY, S., ZORRAQUIN, F. *Financing Change*. Cambridge, Massachusetts: MIT Press, 1996.

SCHULTZ, T. P. Inequality in the Distribution of Personal Income in the World: How It Is Changing and Why. *Journal of Population Economics*, v.11, n.3, p.307-44, 1998.

SCHULTZ, T. W. Investment in Human Capital. *American Economic Review*, v.51, n.1, p.1-17, 1961.

SELDEN, T. M., SONG, D. Environmental Quality and Development: Is There a Kuznets Curve for Air Pollution? *Journal of Environmental Economics and Management*, v.27, n.2, p.147-62, 1994.

SEN, A. L. Equality of What? In: McMURRIN, S. (Ed.) *Tanner Lectures on Human Values*, v.I. Cambridge, U.K.: Cambridge University Press, 1980.

_____. The Concept od Development. In: CHENERY, H., SRINIVASAN, T. N. (Eds.) *Handbook of Development Economics*. New York: Elsevier Science Publishers, 1988. v.I.

_____. Economic Regress: Concept and Features. In: *Proceedings of the World Bank Annual Conference on Development Economics*. Washington, D.C.: World Bank, 1994.

_____. Development Thinking at the Begining of the 21st Century. *Development Economics Research Programme*, n.2, London Scholl of Economics, Mar. 1997a.

_____. What Is the Point of a Development Stra-

tegy? *Development Economics Research Programme* n. 3, London School of Economics, Apr. 1997b.

SENGUPTA, J. K., FOX K. A. *Economic Analysis and Operations Research*: Optimization Techniques in Quantitative Economic Models. Amsterdam: North-Holland, 1969.

SHAFIK, N. Economic Development and Environmental Quality: An Econometric Analysis. *Oxford Economic Papers*, v.46, n.5, p.757-73, 1994.

SHAFIK, N., BANDYOPADHYAY, S. Economic Growth and Environmental Quality: Time Series and Cross-Country Evidence. Policy Research Working Paper WPS 904. World Bank, Washington, D.C., 1992.

SHLEIFER, A., VISHNY, R. W. The Politics of Market Socialism. *Journal of Economic Perspectives*, v.8, n.2, p.165-76, 1994.

_____. (Ed.) *The Grabbing Hand*: Government Pathologies and Their Cures. Cambridge, Massachusetts: Harvard University Press, 1998.

SIEH LEE, M. L. Competing for Foreign Direct Investment: The Case of Malaysia, 1998. (Processado).

SIMON, J. Population Growth May Be Good for LDCs in the Long Run: A Richer Simulation Model. *Economic Development and Cultural Change*, v.24, n.2, p.309-37, 1976.

SLOTJJE, D. J. Measuring the Quality of Life across Countries. *Review of Economics and Statistics*, v.73, n.4, p.684-93, 1991.

SMITH, J. H. Aggregation of Preferences with Variable Electorate. *Econometrica*, v.41, n.6, p.1027-41, 1973.

SOLOW, Robert M. Georgescu-Roegen Versus Solow/Stiglitz. *Ecological Economics*, v.22, n.3, p.267-8, 1997.

SRINIVASAN, T. N. Long-Run Growth Theories and Empirics: Anything New? In: ITO, T., KRUEGER, A. (Eds.) *Growth Theories in Light of the East Asian Experience*. Chicago: University of Chicago Press, 1995.

_____. As the Century Turns: Analytics, Empirics, and Politics of Development. Discussion Paper n. 783. New Haven, Connecticut: Yale University, 1997.

_____. Growth, Poverty, and Inequality. New Haven Connecticut: Yale University, 2000. (Processado).

STEINHERR, A. *Derivatives: The Wild Beast of Finance*. New York: John Wiley, 1998.

STERN, D. I. et al. Economic Growth and Environmental Degradation: The Environmental Kuznets Curve and Sustainable Development. *World Development*, v.24, n.7, p.1151-60, 1996.

STERN, N. The Future of the Economic Transition. Working Paper (International) n. 30. European Bank for Reconstruction and Development, London, 1998.

STIGLITZ, J. E. The Theory of "Screening", Education, and the Distribution of Income. *American Economic Review*, v.65, n.3, p.283-300, 1975.

_____. The Role of the State in Financial Markers. In: *Proceedings of the World Bank Conference on Development Economics, 1993*. Washington. D.C.: World Bank, 1993.

_____. Georgescu-Roegen Versus Solow/Stiglitz. *Ecological Economics*, v.22, n.3, p.269-70, 1997.

_____. More Instruments and Broader Goals: Moving toward the Post-Washington Consensus. Relatório apresentado na World Institute for Development Economics Research Annual Lecture.Helsink, Finland, Jan. 1998.

_____. Whither Reform? Tem Years of the Transition. Relatório apresentado na Annual Bank Conference on Development Economics. World Bank, Washington D.C., Apr. 28-30, 1999.

STIGLITZ, J. E., BHATTACHARYA, A. Underpinnings for a Stable and Equitable Global Financial System: From Old Debates to a New Paradigm. Relatório apresentado na Annual Bank Conference on Development Economics. World Bank, Washington D.C., Apr. 28-30, 1999.

SUMMERS, L. H. *A New Framework for Multilateral Development Policy*. Remarks To the Council On Foreign Relations. New York, Mar. 20, 2000.

SUMMERS, R., HESTON, A. The Penn World Table (Mark 5): An Expanded Set of International Comparisons. 1950-88. *Quarterly Journal of Economics*, v.106, n.2, p.327-68, 1991.

TAN, J.-P. et al. Student Outcomes in Philippine Elementary Schools: An Evaluation of Four Experiments. *World Bank Economic Review*, v.13, n.3. p.493-508, 1999.

TANZI, V. Corruption around the World: Causes, Consequences, Scope, and Crues. *International Monetary Fund Staff Papers*, v.45, n.4, p.559-94, 1998.

TANZI, V., DAVOODI, H. Corruption, Public Investment, and Growth. Working Paper n. WP/97/139. International Monetary Fund, Washington, D.C., 1997.

TEMPLE, J., JOHNSON, P. A. Social Capability and Economic Growth. *Quarterly Journal of Economics*, v.63, n.3, p.965-90, 1998.

THOMAS, V. Economic Globalization and Sustainable Development in Costa Rica. Relatório apresentado na conference on Stability and Economic Development in Costa Rica: The Pending Reforms. Academy of Central America, Costa Rica, Apr. 23-25, 1998.

THOMAS, V., BELT, T. Growth and Environment: Allies or Foes. *Finance and Development*, n.34. Jun, 1997. p.22-4.

THOMAS, V. et al. Embracing the Power of Knowledge and Partnerships for a Sustainable Environment. Background paper prepared for the *World Development Report* 1998/99. 1998. (Processado).

_____. Measuring Education Inequality: Gini Coefficients of Education. Working Paper. World Bank Institute, Washington, D.C., 2000.

THOMAS, V., WANG, Y. Distortions, Interventions, and Productivity Growth: Is East Asia Different? *Economic Development and Cultural Change*, v.44, n.2, p.265-88, 1996.

_____. Education, Trade, and Investment Returns. Working Paper. World Bank Institute, Washington, D.C., 1997.

TOWNSEND, R. Agricultural Incentives in Sub-Saharan Africa: Policy Challenges Technical Paper n. 444. World Bank, Washington, D.C., 1999.

UNCTAD (United Nations Conference on Trade and Development). *Directory of Import Regimes, Part I: Monitoring Import Regimes*. Geneva: United Nations, 1994.

_____. Income Inequality and Development. In: *Trade and Development Report 1997*. New York; Geneva: United Nations, 1997.

UNDP (United Nations Development Program). *Human Development Report 1998*. New York: Oxford University Press, 1998.

_____. *Human Development Report 2000*. New York: Oxford University Press, 2000.

UNESCO (United Nations Educational, Scientific, and Cultural Organization). *1998 World Education Report*. Paris, 2000.

UNRISD (United Nations Research Institute for Social Development). Studies in the Methodology of Social Planning. Geneva, 1970.

VAN RIJCKEGHEM, C., WEDER, B. Sources of Contagion: Finance or Trade? Working Paper n. WP/99/146. International Monetary Fund, Washington, D.C., 1999.

VERDIER, D. Domestic Responses to Capital Market Internationalization under the Gold Standard, 1870-1914. *International Organization*, v.52, n.1, p.1-34, 1998.

VISHWANATH, T., KAUFMANN, D. Toward Transparency in Finance and Government. World Bank, Washington, D.C., 1999. (Processado). Disponível em http:// www.worldbank. org/wbi/governance.

WANG, H., CHEN, M. Industrial Firm's Pollution Control Efforts under a Charge-Subsidy System: An Empirical Analysis of Chinese Top Polluters. World Bank, Policy Research Department, Washington, D.C., 1999.

WANG, H., WHEELER, D. Pricing Industrial Pollution in China: An Econometric Analysis of the Levy Sistem. Policy Research Working

Paper n. 1644. World Bank, Policy Research Department, Washington, D.C., 1996.

WARFORD, J. J. et al. The Evolution of Environmental Concerns in Adjustment Lending: A Review. Working Paper n. 65. World Bank, Environment Department, Washington, D.C., 1994.

WARFORD, J. J. et al. The Greening of Economic Policy Reform. World Bank, Environment Department and World Bank Institute, Washington, D.C., 1997. v.1-2.

WATSON R. et al. *Protecting Our Planet, Securing Our Future*: *Linkages among Global Environmental Issues and Human Needs*. Nairobi; Washington, D.C.: United Nations Environment Programme; United States National Aeronautics and Space Administration; World Bank, 1998.

WEBB, M. C. *The Political Economy of Policy Coordination*: International Adjustment Since 1945. Ithaca; New York; London: Comell University Press, 1994.

WEI, S.-J. How Taxing Is Corruption on International Investors. Working Paper n. 6030. National Bureau of Economic Research, Cambridge, Massachusetts, 1997.

_____. Corruption in Economic Development: Beneficial Grease, Minor Annoyance, or Major Obstacle? Policy Research Working Paper n. 2048. World Bank, Development Research Group, Public Economics, Washington, D.C., 1999.

WESSELS, J. H. Redistribution from a Constitutional Perspective. *Constitutional Political Economy*, v.4, n.3, p.425-48, 1993.

WHEELER, D., AFSAH, S. Going Public on Polluters in Indonesia: BAPEDAL's PROPER-PROKASIH

Program International Executive Reports. World Bank, Washington, D.C., 1996.

WHO (World Health Organization). *The World Health Report 2000*. Geneva, 2000.

WILLIAMSON, J., MAHAR, M. A Survey of Finacial Liberalisation. In: *Essays in International Finance Series*, n. 211. Princeton, New Jersey: Princeton University, Department of Economics, International Finance Section, 1998.

WOLFENSOHN, J. D. Address to the Board of Governors. World Bank, Washington, D.C., Oct. 1998. (Processado).

_____. A Proposal for a Comprehensive Development Framework. World Bank, Washington, D.C., 1999. (Processado).

WOOLCOCK, M. Social Capital and Economic Development. Toward a Theoretical Synthesis and Policy Framework. *Theory and Society*, n.27, p.151-208, 1998.

WORLD BANK. *World Development Report 1990*. New York: Oxford University Press, 1990.

_____. *World Development Report 1991*: *The Challenge of Development*. New York: Oxford University Press, 1991.

_____. *World Development Report 1992*: *Development and the Environment*. New York: Oxford University Press, 1992.

_____. *Averting the Old Age Crisis*: *Politics to Protect the Old and Promote Growth*. Washington, D.C.: World Bank, Oxford University Press, 1994.

_____. *Global Economic Prospects 1996*. Washington, D.C., 1996a.

BIBLIOGRAFIA E REFERÊNCIAS

_____. *World Development Report 1996: From Plan to Market*. New York: Oxford University Press, 1996b.

_____. *Can The Environment Wait in East Asia? Priorities for East Asia*. Washington, D.C., 1997a.

_____. Chile: Poverty Reduction and Income Distribution in a High-Growth Economy: 1987-95. Repport n. 16377-CH. World Bank, Latin America and the Caribbean Region, Washington, D.C., 1997b.

_____. *Clear Water Blue Skies. China's Environment in the New Century*. China 2020 series. Washington, D.C., 1997c.

_____. *Expanding the Measures of Wealth*: *Indicators of Environmentally Sustainable Development*. In Environmentally Sustainable Development Studies and Monograph Series n. 17. Washington, D.C., 1997d.

_____. *Five Years after Rio: Innovations in Environmental Policy*. In: Environmentally Sustainable Development Studies and Monograph *Series n. 18*. Washington, D.C., 1997e.

_____. *Private Capital Flows to Developing Countries*: *The Road to Financial Integration*. World, Bank Policy Research Report Series. Oxford, U.K.; New York: Oxford University Press 1997f.

_____. *Sharing Rising Incomes*: *Disparities in China*. China 2020 Series. Washington, D.C., 1997g.

_____. *Trends in Developing Economies*. Washington, D.C., 1997h.

_____. *World Development Indicators*. Washington, D.C., 1997i.

_____. *World Development Report 1997*. Oxford University Press: New York, 1997j.

_____. *Assessing Aid: What Works, What Doesn't, and Why? A World Bank Policy Research Report*. New York: Oxford University Press, 1998a.

_____. *East Asia: The Road to Recovery*. Washington, D.C., 1998b.

_____. The Business Environment and Corporate Governance. Discussion Draft. Private Sector Development Department, Business Environment Group, 1998c.

_____. *Education Sector Strategy*. Washington, D.C., 1999a.

_____. Environmental Implications of the Economic Crisis and Adjustment in East Asia. East Asia Environment and Social Development Unit Discussion Paper Series n. 1. Washington, D.C., 1999b.

_____. *Global Development Finance*. Washington, D.C., 1999c.

_____. Poverty Trends and Voices of the Poor. Poverty Reduction and Economic Management, Human Development, and Development Economics, Washington, D.C., 1999d. (Processado). Também disponível em http://www. worldbank.org/poverty/data.

_____. *World Development Indicators*. Washington, D.C., 1999e.

_____. *Transition toward a Healthier Environment*: *Environmental Issues and Challenge in the Newly Independent States*. Washington, D.C., 1999f.

_____. Towards Collective Action to Improve Governance and Control Corruption in Seven African Countries. Action programs prepared by African countries for the Ninth Annual International Conference Against Corruption. Durban, South Africa, Oct. 10-15, 1999g.

Disponível em http://www.worldbank.org/wbi/governance.

_____. New Empirical Tools for Anticorruption and Institutional Reform: A Step-by-Step Guide to their Implementation. Washington, D.C.: Europe and Central Asia Public Sector, 1999h.

_____. *Global Economic Prospects and the Developing Countries.* Washington, D.C., 2000a.

_____. *World Development Report 1999/2000: Entering the 21st Century.* Washington, D.C., 2000b.

_____. *World Development Indicators.* Washington, D.C., 2000c.

_____. *Greening industry: New Rules for Communities, Markets, and Governments.* New York: Oxford University Press, 2000d.

_____. *Bolivia, Ecuador, and Paraguay Governance and Anticorruption Empirical Diagnostic Studies.* Washington, D.C.: Wold Bank Institute, 2000e. Disponível em http://www.worldbank.org/wbi/governance.

_____. *East Asia: Recovery and Beyond.* Washington, D.C., 2000f.

_____. *Engendering Development.* New York: Oxford University Press, 2000g.

_____. *Anticorruption in Transition: Confronting the Challenge of State Capture.* Washington, D.C., forthcoming, 2000h.

_____. *World Development Report 2000/2001. Attacking Poverty.* Washington, D.C., 2000i.

_____. Reforming Public Institutions and Strengthening Governance: A World Bank Strategy. A Sectoral Strategy Paper. Public Sector, Poverty Reduction, and Economic Management Network, Washington, D.C., 2000j.

_____. *Commodities Quarterly.* Washington, D.C. (Várias edições).

_____. *Global Development Finance.* Washington, D.C. (Várias edições).

WORLD COMMISSION ON FORESTY AND SUSTAINABLE DEVELOPMENT. Our Forestes, Our Future. In: *Summary Report of the World Commission on Forestry and Sustainable Development.* Winnipeg, Manitoba, Canada, 1999.

WYPLOSZ, C. Ten Years of Transformation: Macroeconomic Lessons. Relatório apresentado na Annual Bank Conference on Development Economics. Washington, D.C., Apr. 28-30, 1999.

YOUNG, A. Learning by Doing and the Dynamic Effects of International Trade. *Quarterly Journal of Economics*, v.106, n.2, p.369-405, 1991.

_____. Tale of Two Cities: Factor Accumulation and Technical Change in Hong Kong and Singapore. *NBER Macroeconomics Annual 1992.* Cambridge, Massachusetts; London: MIT Press, 1992.

_____. Lessons from East Asian NICS: A Contrarian View. *European Economic Review*, v.38, n.3-4, p.964-73, 1994.

_____. The Tyranny of Numbers: Confronting the Statistical Realities of the East Asian Growth Experience. *Quarterly Journal of Economics*, v.110, n.3, p.641-80, 1995.

ZANOWITZ, V. Theoy and History behind Business Cycles: Are the 1990s the Onset of a Golden Age? *Journal of Economic Perspectives*, v.13, n.2, p. 69-90.

SOBRE O LIVRO

Formato: 19 x 23 cm
Mancha: 35 x 50 paicas
Tipologia: Iowan Old Style
Papel: Offset 75 g/m^2 (miolo)
Cartão Supremo 250 g/m^2 (capa)
1ª edição: 2002

EQUIPE DE REALIZAÇÃO

Coordenação Geral
Sidnei Simonelli

Produção Gráfica
Anderson Nobara

Edição de Texto e Diagramação
Milfolhas Produção Editorial
Eliana Sá (Coordenação)
Ada Santos Seles (Preparação de original)
Beatriz de Freitas Moreira (Revisão)
Lilian Queiroz (Diagramação)

Impressão e Acabamento
na Gráfica Imprensa da Fé

FUNDAÇÃO EDITORA DA UNESP

Presidente do Conselho Curador
José Carlos Souza Trindade
Diretor Presidente
José Castilho Marques Neto
Editor Executivo
Jézio Hernani Bomfim Gutierre
Conselho Editorial Acadêmico
Alberto Ikeda
Antonio Carlos Carrera de Souza
Antonio de Pádua Pithon Cyrino
Benedito Antunes
Isabel Maria F. R. Loureiro
Lígia M. Vettorato Trevisan
Lourdes A. M. dos Santos Pinto
Raul Borges Guimarães
Ruben Aldrovandi
Tania Regina de Luca

A QUALIDADE DO CRESCIMENTO